About Island Press

Island Press is the only nonprofit organization in the United States whose principal purpose in the publication of books on environmental issues and natural resource management. We provide solutions-oriented information to professionals, public officials, business and community leaders and concerned citizens who are shaping responses to environmental problems.

In 1994, Island Press celebrated its tenth anniversary as the leading provider of timely and practical books that take a multidisciplinary approach to critical environmental concerns. Our growing lists of titles reflects our commitment to bringing the best of an expanding body of literature to the environmental community throughout North America and the world.

Support for Island Press is provided by The Geraldine R. Dodge Foundation, The Energy Foundation, The Ford Foundation, The George Gund Foundation, William and Flora Hewlett Foundation, The James Irvine Foundation, The John D. and Catherine T. MacArthur Foundation, The Andrew W. Mellon Foundation, The Joyce Mertz-Gilmore Foundation, The New-Land Foundation, The Pew Charitable Trusts, The Rockefeller Brothers Fund, The Tides Foundation, Turner Foundation, Inc., The Rockefeller Philanthropic Collaborative, Inc., and individual donors.

A New Century for
Natural Resources Management

A New Century for
Natural Resources
Management

EDITED BY

Richard L. Knight and Sarah F. Bates

ISLAND PRESS

Washington, D.C.   Covelo, California

Library of Congress Cataloging-in-Publication Data

A new century for natural resources management / edited by Richard L.
    Knight & Sarah F. Bates.
        p.   cm.
    Includes bibliographical references and index.
    ISBN 1-55963-261-5 (cloth). — ISBN 1-55963-262-3
(paper)
    1. Natural resources—Management.   I. Knight, Richard L.
II. Bates, Sarah F.
HC21.N44   1995
333.7—dc20   94-28051
                                                    CIP

Printed on recycled, acid-free paper ∞ ♲

Manufactured in the United States of America

10   9   8   7   6   5   4   3   2   1

To Wallace Stegner, whose writings have inspired generations of land stewards working to ensure there is a new century for natural resources management

Contents

Part III. The Future

Preface

The natural resource disciplines originated in the 20th century. Forestry science was first in time (it actually preceded the century), and was followed by range science, then fisheries and wildlife management, watershed science, and recreation management. These disciplines developed and matured around managing for commodities and amenities primarily on vast areas of public lands. The preeminent rationale for their existence was the need to deliver natural resources for a better human society. Trees were viewed as timber, grass as forage, wildlife as meat and sport. Land-grant universities were the custodians of academic departments focusing on research and teaching that enhanced either sustained yield extraction of trees, forage, fisheries and wildlife, or visitor days.

Over time these specialties developed alliances with the users of these resources: wildlife science with sportsmen's organizations, forest science with the timber industry, range scientists with ranchers. On retirement from the Forest Service, silviculturists would go to work for a timber company; recreation scientists would find employment with National Park Service concessionaires. These close associations between resource agencies and resource user groups would eventually be a primary reason for public skepticism of agency commitment to land stewardship.

As the 20th century nears conclusion, each of these disciplines finds itself in upheaval. Increasingly, each is being critically examined internally by its own practitioners. The depth of discontent became apparent when a Forest Service employee began publishing an unauthorized newspaper called *The Inner Voice* and founded an organization called the Association of Forest Service Employees for Environmental Ethics. Today, as many as one-third of Forest Service personnel read *The Inner Voice*.

In addition to internal dissent, natural resource agencies are being assailed from without by disenchanted traditional user groups (e.g., logging industry) and newly invigorated groups (e.g., wildlife viewers). The economics of public lands and resources—which have long included substantial subsidies—have come under attack from fiscal conservatives and environmental advocacy organizations. And, in the rural communities traditionally dependent on extractive uses of public lands, the growing importance of tourism and recreation are causing resource managers to reconsider earlier priorities.

This skepticism of the historical approach to managing natural resources has permeated academic departments. Today's students are expressing nontraditional views and responding in heretofore unexpected ways. Student interest in conservation biology is growing in traditional natural resource departments in many universities. The Wildlife Society has a static student membership while students are flocking to join the nascent Society for Conservation Biology.

As if these changes were not enough, agencies are finding their ability to manage resources being usurped by the courts and litigation by nongovernmental organizations (NGOs). For example, lead shot from waterfowl hunters was poisoning millions of waterfowl and scores of bald eagles annually. For years, the U.S. Fish and Wildlife Service blocked attempts to substitute nonlethal steel shot for lead shot. Repeated litigation by the National Wildlife Federation eventually forced the federal government to require the use of steel shot by waterfowl hunters.

Additional pressures have come from the political sector, such as congressionally mandated timber harvest targets in the Pacific Northwest that placed the Forest Service squarely at odds with the Endangered Species Act and other environmental legislation. Again, the agency's discretion has been limited by environmental NGOs' litigation to enforce federal laws.

In short, the old tenets of natural resources management are in a crisis. These approaches were designed around the utilitarian conservation philosophy of the 19th century, which assumed needs and conditions different from those that exist today. Moreover, the American public is increasingly demanding that noneconomic values of resources be considered. For their part, resource managers have lost many of the guiding principles once viewed as "gospel"; they are seeking new guidelines for a new century of natural resources management.

In this book we have compiled a diverse array of essays by a variety of authors—educators, economists, philosophers—each of whom offers a unique perspective on the past, present, and future of natural resources management in the United States. The essays are grouped into three broad categories. The first part takes an historical viewpoint, tracing the emergence of natural resources management and the professional disciplines such as forestry, range, and wildlife. The second part describes the conflicts that arose as the U.S. population—and its demands for natural resources—grew in the middle of this century. Natural resource managers initially tried to respond from the historical, compartmentalized perspective of separate disciplines, but such an approach proved to be inadequate. The crisis of natural resources management is represented by the increasing influences of judges and courts on important resource decisions.

The final part looks toward the 21st century and suggests new approaches to more integrated resource management. Although we asked each of our authors to address their topic within these broad categories of past/present/future, we also encouraged them to include their own interpretations of how we got here and where we are heading. Thus, the collection of essays necessarily includes overlapping time frames, as well as considerable diversity of perspectives on historical and contemporary events.

We intend this book for anyone interested in reading and thinking about natural resources and their use. This includes practicing resource managers working for agencies or NGOs, and lay people with an interest in how our environment is treated. It is our desire that within these covers readers may tread familiar ground, be exposed to changes that are sweeping natural resource disciplines, and be introduced to thoughts that may become the "gospel" of the 21st century.

Acknowledgments

RLK wishes to thank the students and faculty of Colorado State University for their support and encouragement. In particular, he wishes to acknowledge his debt to Heather Knight for her unwavering belief that our land requires the best that we have to give. We both wish to acknowledge Amy D. Lauderdale, editorial assistant, who patiently and expertly shepherded the manuscripts through an editorial maze, and who emerged with much better chapters in hand than when she entered. Finally, both editors give their deepest appreciation to the authors who provided the thoughtful essays in this collection. Their work is leading us toward a future in which we will be able to live on this land responsibly.

PART I

The Beginning of Natural Resources Management

THE OPENING PART OF THE BOOK takes an historical approach. The time period varies, as the natural resource disciplines originated in different decades; however, the focus of the chapters is on the period of the 1890s to late 1950s. During this time the uses of natural resources were distinct and viewed primarily through the demands of specific commodity interests: trees were for logging, grass was for grazing, wildlife was for hunting.

This early view of natural resources as commodities should not be surprising. After all, America was a young nation with its eyes to the west, where a seemingly unlimited treasure trove of natural abundance awaited those with the courage and vision of building something that would reflect the greatness of the human dream. Even without this grandiose explanation for exploiting resources, there was a surplus of people hungry for a better life, a life where there was the hope of land ownership and the "big chance."

Looking back on this beginning of the natural resource fields, it is interesting to speculate on how it could have been different. For example, state wildlife management agencies took the approach of selling hunting and fishing licenses to raise monies for wildlife managers' salaries. By this particular quirk of fate, wildlife science was committed to pursue a path of focusing on a handful of economically important game species. Thus, the science largely ignored the vast majority of our nation's biological diversity. This was clearly not the intent of the discipline's originator. Aldo Leopold had more on his mind than meat on the hoof and its accompanying sport when he developed his land ethic. The ramifications of taking this fork in the trail are being fully appreciated today as state and federal wildlife agencies attempt to redefine themselves amid a shrinking hunting constituency and rapidly growing groups concerned with wildlife but who fail to relate to the traditional state fish and game agency.

Such morning-after prognostications are the grist of historians, and the book's first part begins with a chapter by Curt Meine, who examines the lineage of the natural resource disciplines. No account of these times could be written without ideas, dates, and accomplishments woven around the names of Gifford Pinchot, John Muir, and Aldo Leopold. Meine describes the commodity orientation of Pinchot, the transcendentalist philosophy of Muir, and introduces the synthetic viewpoint of Leopold and his "land ethic." Meine's careful, encompassing review describes how resources and agencies arose and merged, creating disciplines. His historical treatise is compelling evidence of how our natural resources have always been used by societies that were shaped by their times: historical events, such as World War II, which resulted in rampant logging of public lands; by breakthroughs in technology such as the automobile, which fueled an explosion in outdoor recreation; and also by people and their ideas such as the contributions of Leopold and his writings. Meine concludes with an examination of how the education of natural resource practitioners went awry in the classroom, where myopic attention to detail splintered any attempt at understanding the holism of ecosystems, and how increased specialization resulted in disciplines that, although outwardly sharing common goals, found themselves feuding over resources. Meine concludes his chapter with a look at the present where new ideas, concepts, and disciplines—such as biodiversity, ecosystem management, and restoration ecology—have emerged as our attempts to redress the question that Leopold once asked, how to live on a piece of land without spoiling it.

Robert Nelson, in the book's second chapter, provides an overview of the four federal agencies primarily responsible for managing our public natural resources: the United States Forest Service, the National Park Service, the Fish and Wildlife Service, and the Bureau of Land Management. This chapter adds flesh to topics briefly mentioned in the preceding chapter. Here we learn the details of each agency, from their early formative days to the amount of acres they manage. Pinchot and Muir are once again mentioned as principal players, Pinchot with the development of the Forest Service and Muir with the concept of national parks and wilderness. Nelson goes on to explore how our federal land management agencies matured under the "progressive gospel of efficiency," a concept that placed science at the heart of progressive thinking and allowed us the illusion of controlling nature. The application of scientific principles to resource development was viewed as the answer to economic progress that would, in turn, lead to a prosperous society. This philosophy soon enveloped the natural resource agencies. The importance of science in controlling and understanding how to use natural resources was accepted with all the fervor of a religion. Nelson concludes his chapter by exploring what he believes is a crisis brought on by the gospel of efficiency: "Created in the name of efficiency, public land agencies in practice gave little heed to efficiency." The emergence and popularity of today's environmental movement is openly hostile to the paradigm that has literally controlled how these government agencies operated. Nelson believes that today there is little logic to the division of lands and responsibilities of these four big agencies. He concludes by presenting a new model for public land management, one not based on the premise that science is value free. Instead, he argues, the pluralism of our society, in concert with what science can contribute, will shape how we view and manage our public lands.

The final four chapters in the book's first part deal with the traditional approaches of managing natural resources, and provide insights into the education, economics, and ethics of natural resource use. Collectively, they offer an historical overview of how the nation has viewed land and commodities. Stan Anderson begins this quartet of chapters with a look at the traditional approaches and tools in natural resource management. Focusing on the twin themes of "harvest" and "sustained yield," he covers forestry, range management, and wildlife. Forest management was preoccupied with the harvest of trees for use in wood products and, more often than not, focused on producing even-aged stands of rapidly growing trees through techniques such as clearcutting and thinning. Insecticides and herbicides were often used to increase the growth rate of desired trees. Range management involved the concept of rotating livestock between pastures to allow the grass to regenerate. Heavy use of riparian areas resulted in trampled vegetation, causing erosion and eventual drops in the water table. Wildlife management was single-species management and focused on game species, even if that meant eliminating or reducing other species such as predators. Harvest regulations were based on population estimates and the concept of a harvestable surplus that could be removed from a population without deleterious effects. This approach did not consider that these "harvestable surpluses" might be important to other species of wildlife in ecosystem processes such as predation or competition.

The Morrill Act of 1862 provided federal support to create land-grant colleges across America. In these public schools natural resource curricula rapidly spread, even though a private school, Yale, was instrumental in the development of forestry education. Beginning with the "Harvard influence," Dale Hein's chapter traces the beginning of natural resource education in America with its early emphasis on taxonomy and natural history.

Emphasizing identification, inventory, management, and wise use, colleges offered programs that fell within one of two categories. Schools might prescribe coursework with rigor and structure to prepare students for employment as managers of natural resources. These "ranger factories" were primarily found in the west and emphasized technical skills for entry-level jobs. The second category was less structured and had more of a liberal arts emphasis, with fewer required courses and more electives. Eastern and midwestern schools tended to offer the latter type of curricula. Hein also touches on the idea that an education in natural resource management allowed entry into an "exclusive fellowship of professionals," identified by unique clothing and language. Hein observes that, "In the past decade, videos replaced dissections, calculators replaced slide rules, geographic information systems replaced maps, and models replaced survey data from the field. And, teaching assistants replaced many professors in classes. We continue to proclaim the importance of teaching students how to think with little progress toward understanding what that means."

Economics allocates use of natural resources over time by recognizing that resources are assets with value. Helfand and Berick present an overview of traditional natural resource economics, beginning with a model of nonrenewable resources and moving on to the more complex case of renewable resources. They argue that traditional economics, with its emphasis on marketable resources from lands, has not been at fault for the unsustainable exploitation of resources. Instead, they blame public policies that have violated economic principles and contributed to these market failures affecting public land management. They illustrate this theme with a discussion of why forest management on public lands has not worked. Two critical factors have been ignored. First, the stock of a resource is an asset that must be managed as carefully as any other investment; and second, when the asset is marketed, its price must reflect all the costs involved in its development, including externalities. Using "sales below costs" as an example, they show what can go wrong when economic principles are ignored.

The first part of the book concludes with an examination of the ethics that dominated early natural resources management. Eric Katz discusses the ideas of John Locke and his thoughts on the role of property. In Locke's opinion, property was those parts of nature that were used and valued by human beings. Accordingly, nature was valuable only in that it was used by humans. An essential component to this thinking was that nature could be appropriated as private property. This property had to be removed from the commons if it was to have any significant use. The moral legitimacy of this approach was expressed in the observation that every ". . . individual is morally free to use his labor to act upon the common resources of nature." Locke was so committed to this anthropocentric perspective that he even defined the intrinsic values of nature as their uses by humans. Katz takes this utilitarian ethic and contrasts it with the thoughts and writings of Pinchot, Muir, and Leopold. Pinchot was quite content with a utilitarian ethic in that it mirrored his own thinking: "the use of the natural resources for the greatest good of the greatest number for the longest time." Muir, with his spiritual view of nature, was appalled by this ethic and was its leading critic. Aldo Leopold, a visionary, offered his ethic, a compromise emphasizing land stewardship and respect for nature.

Chapter 1

The Oldest Task in Human History

Curt D. Meine

The whole world is coming,
A nation is coming, a nation is coming,
The Eagle has brought the message to the tribe.
The father says so, the father says so.
Over the whole earth they are coming.
The buffalo are coming, the buffalo are coming,
The Crow has brought the message to the tribe,
The father says so, the father says so.

Sioux Ghost Dance Song (1890)(1)

We end, I think, at what might be called the standard paradox of the twentieth century: our tools are better than we are, and grow better faster than we do. They suffice to crack the atom, to command the tides. But they do not suffice for the oldest task in human history: to live on a piece of land without spoiling it.

Aldo Leopold (1938)(2)

One way to understand the roots of conservation in the United States is to examine the documentary evidence from official meetings, policy decisions, and legislative actions that took place a century ago. Another way is to examine the evidence outdoors, *in situ*, in the landscapes we inhabit, in the places we are.

Most of the tangible links to conservation's origins have disappeared. The bones of the myriad bison were long ago hauled off the plains to meet their ends in glue pots and gardens. The plumes of the egrets have gone the way of all fashion. The remains of the last passenger pigeons roost beneath bell jars, growing fustier with every passing decade. The topsoils of the midwestern prairies rest in downstream mucks; the plants that made them—and that they made—have lost their claim on the horizon, and do well to hold on in their graveyard and railway refugia.

Some objects, however, remain to bear witness. Walk among the aspen, balsam fir, paper birch, and bracken fern forests in the upper Great Lakes and you will find them: the old stumps of the fallen white pines. Some hunker down in the shade of sugar maples (to become, with a minor leap of imagination, bears). Others stand out, weathered gray, in grassy openings. Their insides have rotted away, moss, lichen, and insects doing the work of the ages. Only the outer annual rings of punky wood remain, disintegrating easily in the human hand. Many of the stumps are charred about their sides—reminders upon reminders, signs of the fire last time.

The epoch of white pine logging reached its climax in northern Wisconsin and adjacent Michigan in the late 1880s and early 1890s. The seeds from which those trees sprouted had sifted to earth two, three, even four centuries before that. Who knows how deep their roots went. White pine sometimes followed white pine on the same site, the roots reinhabiting tried-and-true pathways carved through glacial soil, boulder fields, and bedrock by their patient ancestors.

An early forester, writing in 1898, described the effects of one brief generation of lumbering on northern Wisconsin. "Nearly the entire territory has been logged over. The pine has disappeared from most of the mixed forests and the greater portion of pineries proper has been cut. . . . Nearly half of this territory has been burned over at least once, about three million acres are without any forest cover whatever, and several million more are but partly covered by the dead and dying remnants of the former forest. . . . Here are large tracts of bare wastes, 'stump prairies,' where the ground is sparsely covered with weeds and grass, sweet fern, and a few scattering, runty bushes of scrub oak, aspen, and white birch" (3). By the time those words were written, the smart lumbermen of the white pine states had already shifted their attention and capital to the pinelands of the south and the astonishing conifer forests of the Pacific Northwest.

From the standpoint of the culture whose three centuries of expansion brought them down, the extensive stands of *Pinus strobus*, from Maine to Minnesota, were in exactly the right place at exactly the right time, providing the raw material it desired most ardently and insatiably. From the white pine's perspective—if we may grant a perspective to another species—its distribution placed it in the worst possible place at the worst possible time, directly in the path of a gathering force that had little inclination to pause, even to consider the circumstances conducive to its self-perpetuation. As the "inexhaustible" pineries were, in due course, exhausted, pause came of necessity, at least for some people and some forests (4).

The old stumps will not last much longer. In a few more years, they will have melted back to the soil, reabsorbed by the medium, returned fully to the flow of time and nutrients. For a little while more, they will record the extreme to which a concept of social and economic development was taken, and the moment when a new commitment to "the oldest task in human history" germinated.

. . .

The delirious climax of white pine logging coincided with other indicators of changing times, landscapes, and social conditions. In 1889, weary remnants of the Indian nations across the west undertook the Ghost Dance in a desperate effort to revive their lost world. The dance and the dream came to an end on December 29, 1890, at the Battle of Wounded Knee (5). The report of the 1890 census, noting that the "unsettled" area of the United States had become broken into isolated fragments, declared that the "frontier of settlement" had closed. Three years later, at the Columbian Exposition in Chicago, historian Frederick Jackson Turner would build on this finding in his seminal discussion of "the significance of the frontier in American history" (6). In the fall of 1890, Congress acted to protect the lands now included within Yosemite and Sequoia National Parks (7). And on March 3, 1891, Congress passed the Forest Reserve Act; later that month President Harrison signed into existence the Yellowstone Park Timber Land Reserve, the nation's first forest reserve and the germ of the national forest system (8).

A century ago, some of these "current events" were widely reported; others were hardly noticed. A century later, they appear as transition points in a pattern of cultural change. The pattern is still emerging. There is no definitive agreement on its development in the past or its implications for the future, and it contains much room for debate, varied emphasis, and alternative visions. But the changes that began in the 1890s would be fundamental; the basic and tacit assumptions of the preceding era would no longer go unchallenged. Few contemporary citizens, for example, saw the lumber barons' "large tracts of bare wastes" as anything but evidence of the latest welcome advance of civilization. And while deforestation has continued to be visited upon other lands, and the attitudes behind deforestation persist, stumpfields at least are no longer what they were a century ago—a universal emblem of human progress.

The changes of the 1890s did not arrive unanticipated. Although belief in the creed that the stump symbolized had long dominated American society, undercurrents of reaction against it had welled up intermittently, emerging through various cultural channels. Early and mid-18th century poets, writers, and thinkers—most notably Ralph Waldo Emerson and Henry David Thoreau—articulated an alternative view of the natural world, as a source not simply of material goods, but also of aesthetic satisfaction, philosophical insight, and spiritual solace. Landscape artists of the period, including Thomas Cole, Asher Durand, Frederick Edwin Church, Albert Bierstadt, and Thomas Moran, conveyed a similar view in their light-suffused canvasses. Other adventuring artists—Karl Bodmer and George Catlin prominent among them—gave real faces and lives to the generic "savages" that existed beyond the ken of "civilization." At the same time, a diverse group of proto-conservationists, including George Perkins Marsh, Frederick Law Olmsted, John Wesley Powell, George Bird Grinnell, and Carl Schurz, insisted that the attitudes and policies that had until then guided European settlement and development of the North American land-scape required adjustment.

For most of the century, these remained the expressions of a responsive few. As of 1890, there was no coherent body of philosophy, science, history, literature, economics, policy, and law through which the American people could understand and govern their long-term relationship with the natural world, and little evidence that such was regarded as an important social goal. Although there were important antecedents to a coming transforma-tion—among them, the establishment of Yellowstone National Park (1872) and the Adirondack Forest Preserve (1885); the organization of the Amer-ican Forestry Association (1875); and the founding of the original Audubon Society and Boone and Crockett Club (in 1886 and 1887, respectively)—these were sporadic developments. In 1890, there was no U. S. Forest Ser-vice; there was, for that matter, no actual profession of forestry in the United States. Nor were there professions devoted to wildlife or range man-agement, or government agencies overseeing these concerns. There was little public discussion of the responsibility of private citizens and private in-dustry toward the natural objects, processes, and conditions on which their livelihoods, and the well-being of the society, depended. By 1890, however, the doctrine of conquest and the undercurrents of opposition to it had begun to precipitate out the social and political movement that would come to be called *conservation* (9).

No one person can be said to have ushered in the new movement. Two figures, however, stand out as exemplars of the impulses that drove it and the tensions that divided it: John Muir and Gifford Pinchot.

In 1889 and 1890, John Muir was primarily occupied with the effort to gain federal protection for the lands surrounding his beloved Yosemite Valley. His success in this endeavor led to the formation of the Sierra Club in 1892, and to Muir's ascendance as the country's leading voice for the pro-tection and preservation of wild nature—a role he would maintain until his death in 1914. Building on philosophical foundations laid by Emerson and Thoreau, but bringing to his arguments a lifetime of experience in wild country, Muir made the public case for preservation on several grounds. Like many who were agitating on behalf of forests, Muir could cite the benefits of forest cover in protecting soils and regulating water flows. However, the protection of forests, and wilderness in general, involved a broader spectrum of values. Muir strongly emphasized the restorative powers of "a little pure wilderness": exposure to original nature provided aesthetic, psychological, and spiritual benefits that could not be gained in urban or even pastoral landscapes. There was in Muir's outlook, too, an abiding sense of the intrinsic beauty and value of all things within "the one great unit of creation." The plunder and waste that went by the name of progress thus constituted nothing less than acts of desecration, attributable ultimately to the hubris of "Lord Man."

As the embodiment of the "romantic-transcendental preservation ethic" (as J. Baird Callicott has characterized it), Muir defined one wing of the nascent conservation movement (10). What guidance did this ethic offer in the effort to "live on a piece of land without spoiling it"? It said, in effect, that for those remnants of yet unspoiled land, one succeeds in the task by not living on them at all, but rather by setting them aside as places where, in the words of the later Wilderness Act, "man . . . is a visitor who does not remain."

At the end of 1890, Gifford Pinchot was returning to the United States, having spent the previous year studying forest management in France, Switzerland, and Germany. Although interest in forestry had been growing in the United States (primarily among scientists) through the 1870s and 1880s, Pinchot was the first American to receive formal training in the field. He returned determined to bring professional forestry to a country where, as he put it, "the most rapid and extensive forest destruction ever known was in full swing" (11). Within 15 years, Pinchot, riding the wave of the Progressive movement with his friend and political patron Theodore Roosevelt, would succeed. With the creation of the Forest Service in 1905, Pinchot established forestry as the locus of conservation within the government and within the public mind.

And what was forestry? "Forestry," he maintained until the end of his life, "is Tree Farming." Its purpose: ". . . to make the forest produce the largest possible amount of whatever crop or service will be most useful, and keep on producing it for generation after generation of men and trees." "The forest," he added, "rightly handled—given the chance—is, next to the earth itself, the most useful servant of man" (12). This utilitarian emphasis lay at the heart of the "resource conservation ethic" that defined the other wing of the conservation movement, and that Pinchot more than any other individual promulgated and operationalized. Where Muir saw "one great unit of creation," Pinchot found "just two things on this material earth—people and natural resources" (13). "The first great fact of conservation," it followed, "is that it stands for development" (14).

The guiding principle of utilitarian conservation was to manage resources so as to produce commodities and services "for the greatest good of the greatest number for the longest time." To this end, wild nature was not to be preserved, but actively manipulated by scientifically informed experts to improve and sustain yields. Those yields were to be harvested and processed efficiently, and the economic gains allocated equitably. How, then, to live on a piece of land without spoiling it? By strengthening the oversight role of government, enacting science-based regulations and resource management practices, developing the resources with a minimum of waste, and distributing the benefits of development fairly among all users.

During the 1890s and 1900s, Muir and Pinchot and their respective followers jostled for primacy, with the overarching figure of the day—Teddy Roosevelt—maintaining a precarious position between them. Although the sheer amount of energy and action invested in conservation during Roosevelt's presidential years served to divert attention from the movement's internal tensions, the two approaches to conservation could not and would not coexist for long. The tensions finally surfaced in the much-discussed battle over the damming of the Tuolomne River in Yosemite's Hetch Hetchy valley (15). The battle, waged over a 20-year period, reaching its denouement in 1913, drew the lines uncompromisingly: Hetch Hetchy could not be both preserved as natural parkland and used to store water. And so the controversy begged the ultimate question: what was it to *conserve* this place—or any place? Was there *a* conservation movement, or were there in fact two movements, born of related concerns but moving toward radically different ends?

The dam at Hetch Hetchy was built, but the underlying issue remained unresolved. Muir fought against the destruction of wild nature and the attitude that had allowed legitimate use to be perverted into rampant abuse. Pinchot fought against the inefficient use of natural resources, the political corruption that such use often entailed, and the inequitable distribution of wealth and power that had both allowed and followed rapid resource depletion. The preservationists and the utilitarians both opposed the destructive forces of the day, and their goals often overlapped. But their visions could not be accommodated (much less reconciled) until conservation itself was redefined, its scientific underpinnings reformulated, and its social implications reconsidered.

. . .

That process would not begin until the 1930s. In the meantime, activism metamorphosed into administration. The political movement for conservation reform was transformed into the more mundane execution of conservation policy. And as that transformation occurred, Pinchot's vision held sway. By the late 1930s, the principles of utilitarian resource conservation had been applied not only to forests, but to other "useful" components of the landscape: river systems, agricultural soils, rangelands, sport and commercial fisheries, game animals, scenic areas. As new laws, policies, and bureaucracies were created to promote sustained yields of and from these components, resource management became fully institutionalized and professionalized.

The late 1930s stand out as an especially dynamic period in conservation history, as new resource problems arose, new scientific concepts and information emerged, and new thoughts on the social and economic context of conservation took form. In retrospect, World War II and its aftermath altered profoundly the roles of and relationships among the different resource management professions. For these reasons it is worth reviewing the origins and development of the various professions, and their status on the eve of the war.

Forestry

Forestry continued to serve as the lead conservation profession in the three decades following Pinchot's early campaign. Its role expanded as the Weeks Law (1911) and Clarke–McNary Act (1924) extended the national forest system to the eastern states, strengthened forestry research, and supported increased forestry activity at the state level. Training opportunities also expanded. Led by the Pinchot-endowed Yale Forest School, colleges and universities throughout the country established forestry departments to stock the Forest Service and state agencies, as well as the timber industry. As the most solidly established and, in many ways, broadest of the resource management professions, forestry also tended to attract those whose primary interest lay in related fields (such as wildlife conservation, recreation, soil conservation, and range management) that as yet lacked formal training and employment opportunities.

One result of this breadth was that the Forest Service—still a young agency with diverse responsibilities (and, significantly, a relatively flexible structure of administrative authority)—became a proving ground for new ideas in conservation. Through the 1910s and 1920s, many of the founding principles in range and wildlife management, soil conservation, wildland recreation, and wilderness protection derived from work on the national forests. Similarly, many of the rising leaders in conservation—including Aldo Leopold and Robert Marshall—came from the ranks of the Forest Service.

Forestry's flexibility in these early years is best appreciated against the background of the nation's changing timber supply and demand. The goals of the Forest Service in managing the national forests (as rather modestly stated in the 1905 *Use Book*, the governing manual of the Forest Service) were to "[preserve] a perpetual supply of timber for home industries, [prevent] destruction of the forest cover which regulates the flow of streams, and [protect] local residents from unfair competition in the use of forest and range" (16). While the focus within the Forest Service gradually shifted over the next two decades toward timber harvesting and silviculture, there remained much room to consider alternative uses and diverse approaches to forest management. As Robert Nelson points out in this volume, timber interests actually pressured the Forest Service to limit production from the national forests as a means of propping up prices for timber taken off of private holdings. As a result, recreation remained a (if not *the*) leading use of the forests until World War II (17).

There was, however, a further consequence to this trend that would have long-term consequences for the forestry profession. As the cut of timber on privately held lands continued apace, the specter of their depletion began to loom. By the early 1930s, many foresters, foreseeing the inevitable pressures this would bring to bear on public forests, began to argue for much stronger federal control of private forestlands. (Pinchot himself would inveigh against the "forest butchery" on private lands, calling on the government to exercise its "right to prevent forest destruction by private owners") (18). The warnings, for a variety of reasons, went largely unheeded. The upshot was that, when the supply of private timber inevitably tightened, the Forest Service and the profession of forestry as a whole would have less room politically and philosophically in which to maneuver. Even as forestry would come to define itself ever more narrowly by its emphasis on timber production, the conditions under which the profession operated were constricting.

Agriculture

The depletion and erosion of agricultural soils had been a concern among conscientious landholders since the earliest days of the republic. Thomas Jefferson, to cite one notable example, conducted early experiments in crop rotation and contour plowing. However, as long as new farmland remained cheap and readily available, farmers had little incentive to follow Jefferson's lead. No concerted national movement to protect soil and other farm resources would emerge until expansion into new arable lands was economically prohibitive or geographically infeasible.

In the first three decades of the 20th century, however, agriculture confronted several overarching trends that would, by the late 1930s, place unprecedented emphasis on the conservation of soil, water, and wildlife on the farm. At the turn of the century, industrialization was rapidly altering the farm landscape through the mechanization and intensification of agricultural production. These transformations affected soils and wildlife habitat directly, not only by encouraging agricultural expansion (especially in the midwest and plains states), but by changing the nature of farm inputs, outputs, and cropping practices. At the same time, the draining of wetlands and the appropriation of surface waters for irrigation altered hydrological processes and aquatic systems over large portions of the midwest, high plains, intermountain west, and far west.

Agricultural expansion continued into the 1920s, as World War I gave increased impetus to preexisting pressures. New technologies and the complex agricultural economy of the 1920s allowed the number of farms to increase to a high of 6.8 million in the early 1930s, even as rural people moved into cities and towns and farm labor became more scarce (19). By the late 1920s, the changes in agriculture had begun to take their toll in the form of more widespread soil erosion (and associated problems with siltation and flooding), accelerated losses of wildlife habitat, and increasing economic instability and dislocation. These forces were felt to varying degrees in different regions of the country, but culminated in the mid-1930s with the disaster of the Dust Bowl in the southern high plains.

The U.S. Department of Agriculture issued its first advisory bulletin on soil erosion in 1928. Its coauthor, Hugh H. Bennett, would in the years that followed become the leading public advocate on the issue, proselytizing among farmers and politicians, pressing the federal government into a more active role. In 1935, with the problem literally looming in the air of Washington, Congress established the Soil Conservation Service. Significantly, the new SCS began to promote watershed-wide conservation measures that integrated soil conservation with other resource management practices.

As these broad changes overtook agriculture, science played a growing but dichotomous role. Operating through the land-grant colleges and their associated extension services, agricultural scientists increasingly found themselves drawn into two camps. On one side were those who, adopting industrial systems as their model, focused on increasing production through the development of new farm equipment, crop varieties, fertilizers, and other purchased inputs. On the other side were those who, adopting natural systems as their model, focused on maintaining fertility and productivity through traditional methods and materials, while selectively integrating new technologies into their operations. At the end of the 1930s, the schism between these two approaches was not yet wide; the disaster on the plains had given all involved a sober lesson in the pitfalls and promises of modern agriculture.

Range Management

Like forestry, range management in the United States arose in response to the depletion of a resource once regarded as inexhaustible. By the end of the 1890s, overstocking with cattle and sheep had degraded forage resources throughout the expansive arid and semi-arid grasslands of the trans-Mississippi west. The number of livestock on the western ranges had risen precipitously in the 30 years following the Civil War as the bison herds were exterminated and the plains Indians subdued, and as distant livestock markets became accessible via new railroad lines. But in the late 1880s, a combination of overproduction, hard winters, low rainfall, and financial jitters among distant speculators brought an end to the livestock boom—though not before damaging grasslands throughout the west.

Ranchers themselves were the first to draw attention to the situation. By the turn of the century, their observations of deteriorating range conditions had been confirmed in a series of official surveys and reports. Soon thereafter, the first range experiment programs were developed with the aim of improving grazing practices and increasing the forage resources available to domestic livestock. By 1910, the Forest Service and eight states had established agricultural experiment stations devoted to range research, while state universities throughout the west began to offer coursework in range management (20). More conservative use of range resources, however, was slow in coming. In many parts of the west (especially the southwest), ranges were once again overstocked (mainly with cattle) in anticipation of higher demands during World War I—demands that failed to materialize before the war ended. The result in many areas was further deterioration of the range and accelerated rates of soil erosion (21).

Federal land policies had for decades abetted the decline of rangeland both through ill-conceived programs for parcelling out the public domain and through poor administration of grazing on those lands that remained publicly owned. Beginning in the 1890s, the government initiated a series of land policy changes to improve conditions for settlers while exercising stronger control over public lands. These policy changes included, prominently, the establishment of grazing regulations on the newly created national forests. The Forest Service thus came to assume a key role in the development of range management.

Meanwhile, there remained the vast unreserved rangelands outside of the national parks and forests—lands that, after their appropriation from the native Indian inhabitants, had been used freely by both small ranchers and large livestock interests, and that had continually been the object of intense turf battles and heated political dispute. The battle for control of the public rangelands culminated in 1934 with the passage of the Taylor Grazing Act, which withdrew these lands from further disposition, established the Grazing Service to administer them (the Grazing Service was later combined with the General Land Office to form the Bureau of Land Management), and provided for a system of land leasing through organized grazing districts. Much as the creation of the Forest Service had stimulated the development of forestry as a profession, the establishment of the BLM would prompt the rise of range management as a discrete field.

Wildlife Management

Although concerns about the decline of wild plant and animal populations had long fueled the conservation movement, wildlife management did not emerge as a separate profession until the 1930s.

Through the 1800s, market hunting and habitat loss had resulted in the depletion, and in some cases extirpation, of many important wild game species—most visibly the bison and passenger pigeon, but also the black bear, white-tailed deer, elk, beaver, turkey, prairie chicken, and many waterfowl and wading birds. Efforts to reverse this trend were often initiated at the state level, since states retained jurisdiction over what was then termed "wild life." At the same time, sportsmen's organizations and other citizen groups had formed around the issue and pressed for reforms. By the end of the century, most states had established fish and game agencies, outlawed market hunting, and enacted strong fishing and hunting regulations. The new agencies, however, were often ineffective, and enforcement of regulations was uneven at best. Thus, in most regions, the movement for wildlife conservation focused initially on the protection of game species through stronger law enforcement, tighter restrictions on hunting, and the designation of refuges—as well as the persecution of large predators (which were by common consent regarded as "vermin" rather than legitimate "wild life").

While states often took the lead in protecting game, many of the most important reforms occurred at the federal level. The U.S. Bureau of Biological Survey was established in 1896 (having originated as the Division of Economic Ornithology and Mammalogy in the Department of Agriculture). Though lacking law enforcement powers, the Bureau provided a focus for the growing interest in wildlife protection. The Lacey Act (1900) strengthened the states' hands by prohibiting the interstate transportation of game killed in violation of state laws. Through the national forests and parks, the federal government assumed a larger role in protecting some of the most important and visible wildlife populations and habitats. (And in suppressing others: in 1914 Congress allocated the first funds for predator control on the nation's public lands.) Theodore Roosevelt had also created, by presidential proclamation, the earliest federal refuges and sanctuaries—the forerunners of the later system of national wildlife refuges. And in 1916, the United States and Canada signed the landmark Migratory Bird Treaty, granting both governments new authority to protect waterfowl and other migratory birds.

By the mid-1920s, game *protection* had begun to evolve into game *management*. The need was evident. The decline of many game species—including even species of small game whose populations had initially benefited from the expansion of agriculture—accelerated as a result of intensified habitat loss and hunting pressures following World War I. Responses to the situation within the conservation community varied. Some argued for outright bans on hunting. Others argued for the rebuilding of game populations through predator control, artificial propagation programs (especially for waterfowl and upland game birds), and the introduction of exotic species. A new school of thought, however, focused on the protection and restoration of habitat as a way of allowing populations of native species to reestablish and perpetuate themselves. Aldo Leopold, the leading proponent of this approach, summarized his views in *Game Management* (1933), the first text in the field. By applying concepts from the emerging science of ecology to the conservation of animal populations and their habitats, Leopold's work would revolutionize the field—with repercussions that extended far beyond the management of game.

The field evolved rapidly in the 1930s. Under the energetic leadership of Jay N. "Ding" Darling, the Bureau of Biological Survey broadened its mission and its budget. New funds for research, habitat protection, and other management activities became available with the passage of the Migratory Bird Hunting Stamp ("Duck Stamp") Act (1934) and the Pittman-Robertson Federal Aid in Wildlife Restoration Act (1937). Research and training programs opened up in universities throughout the country. During these years, too, the conceptual foundations of the field broadened.

Ingrained antipredator attitudes began to shift as the ecological functions of predators came to be more widely appreciated (and, in particular, as resurgent deer herds burgeoned beyond the carrying capacity of their habitats). The idea of management itself began to extend beyond game animals to include "nongame" animals and plants. Rare and endangered species began to receive increased attention. The clearest indication of these trends was the rapid adoption, beginning in 1936, of the one-word term "wildlife," which for at least some wildlife managers included all forms of wild plants and animals. By 1940, wildlife management was established as a distinct field with its own professional society and journal, and a strengthened federal agency—the Fish and Wildlife Service (22).

Fisheries Management

The early development of fisheries management in the United States paralleled that of wildlife management. By the late 19th century, populations of many economically important freshwater, anadromous, and marine fish were depleted as a result of overharvesting, habitat loss, dam construction and water diversion, and water pollution from industrial, urban, and agricultural sources. In response, states initiated efforts to place the exploitation of fisheries on a sustained yield basis. Most states enacted strict regulations or prohibitions on commercial fishing in inland waters. Fish hatcheries began to supplement natural reproduction as early as the 1870s; along with law enforcement, the development of hatcheries soon became the primary activity of state fishery departments. The rise of fish culturing led to the formation of the American Fish Culture Association (later renamed the American Fisheries Society) in 1870. A year later Congress established the U.S. Fisheries Commission, and directed it to promote the artificial propagation, distribution, and introduction of game and food fishes.

Fish culture came to dominate the field so completely that, by the early decades of the 20th century, "fishery management" was already essentially synonymous with "hatchery management." The well-established fisheries profession found a ready home in the new utility-minded and efficiency-driven conservation movement. Advances in the study of fish biology, behavior, and ecology were applied quickly in the operation of hatcheries to improve production. But while money and hopes were increasingly invested in hatcheries as the key to sustained fish yields, there was scant evidence of their effectiveness in actually increasing or maintaining catches. Meanwhile, relatively little attention was given to other aspects of fishery conservation: the size, methods, and timing of harvesting; the genetic and behavioral impacts of artificially propagated fish (especially nonnative species and strains) on native wild populations; the status of nongame fish and other organisms within the aquatic community; the effects of surrounding land uses on water and habitat quality; or the hydrological and biological impacts of large-scale irrigation systems, dams, and other engineering projects (especially on the large midwestern and western river systems).

From the beginning, a persistent minority of fisheries biologists had questioned the prevailing management approaches, especially the heavy emphasis on artificial fish stocking. This was attributable in part to the concurrent development of the science of limnology, which had an impact on fisheries management analogous to that of animal ecology on wildlife management (23). In addition, biologically informed anglers—of whom there were increasing numbers—began to question the authority of the fishery managers. By the 1930s, an alternative school had arisen that placed greater emphasis on the management of habitat (for both coldwater and warmwater species) (24). According to fisheries biologist J. T. Bowen, "During the 1930s . . . fish culture assumed a less important role in the [American Fisheries] Society, and by 1936 the membership reflected a completely new outlook" (25). Although fish culture would remain dominant, the "new outlook" would begin to address previously neglected aspects of fishery management, including systematic research on fish populations and their aquatic environment, the protection and restoration of habitat, and the development of effective fishing regulations.

Recreation

Camping, hiking, hunting, fishing, and other forms of outdoor recreation were important but nonetheless secondary conservation concerns during the Progressive era. And when recreational values were wedded to the preservation ethic, as in the case of Hetch Hetchy, they could be considered a positive impediment to development by commodity-oriented resource managers. The status of recreation began to change with the establishment of the National Park Service in 1916, and with the early manifestations of the automobile culture in the 1920s. The Park Service was created to bring some order to the management of the nation's 13 existing national parks (and, in part, to bind political wounds following the Hetch Hetchy dispute). Many of the parks, including Yellowstone, Yosemite, Grand Canyon, and Glacier, were conceived and developed with the support, if not the outright lobbying, of the railroad lines that served them. As the private automobile and new highways provided even greater mobility to the public, areas of important aesthetic and recreational value (at both the state and federal level) became subject to increasing use. Accordingly, conservation agencies and organizations began to devote greater attention to them.

The prosperity of the 1920s, the advent of two enthusiastic fishermen-presidents (Coolidge and Hoover), and the rise (beginning in 1922) of the Izaak Walton League as an important force in national conservation politics all fed the trend. Coolidge convened two National Conferences on Outdoor Recreation (in 1924 and 1926), firmly establishing recreation as a basic conservation concern. This momentum carried over into the New Deal years, especially as the Civilian Conservation Corps provided increased manpower for development of park facilities. At the same time, in part as a result of the heightened visibility of recreational values, regard for wilderness protection rose within the Forest Service, and the level of competition between the Forest Service and Park Service over potential park and recreation lands increased.

An important aspect of national park management in the early 1930s was the increasing interest in scientific research and management of wildlife in the parks. In 1931, a Wild Life Division was created within the Park Service and placed under the directorship of George Wright, a young biologist familiar with the contemporary advances in ecology and wildlife management. Over the next five years, Wright led a team of like-minded scientists who endeavored "to supplement protection with more constructive wildlife management" (26). Their efforts to promote an ecologically sound and scientifically informed approach to the management of parklands suffered a crucial setback, however, when Wright was killed in a car accident in 1936.

Wilderness

Wallace Stegner wrote that, "if the national park idea is, as Lord Bryce suggested, the best idea America ever had, wilderness preservation is the highest refinement of that idea" (27). The preservationist impulse had not dissipated after Hetch Hetchy. To a degree, its energies had been diverted into the work of the National Park Service, but a small minority of dedicated wilderness enthusiasts continued to struggle against the tide of development from within the federal agencies, while other nonprofessional activists pushed from outside the agencies.

After Hetch Hetchy, the first concrete moves to protect wilderness on public lands came from within the Forest Service. In 1919 and the early 1920s, landscape architect Arthur Carhart persuaded his Forest Service supervisors to limit resort development at Trappers Lake in Colorado and in the boundary waters of Superior National Forest in northern Minnesota. In 1924, Aldo Leopold and several of his colleagues in the Forest Service succeeded in reserving a large portion of New Mexico's Gila National Forest as the Gila Wilderness Area—the first such area to be so designated. Through the mid-1920s, Leopold led a faction of foresters who supported the "preservation of a system of wilderness remnants" in the national forests (28). In response, the Forest Service gave increasing support to wilderness protection, culminating in the issuance of the "L-20" regulations in 1929, which formally established wilderness protection as a Forest Service responsibility (29).

During the 1930s wilderness advocates, led by forester Robert Marshall, continued to press for the inventory and protection of roadless areas on public lands. Opposition to the wilderness idea had hardly subsided. Pressures to intensively manage and exploit the public lands mounted both within and beyond the federal agencies, often abetted by New Deal conservation programs that stressed intrusive development as a means of providing employment. These continuing threats led Marshall and other wilderness activists to form The Wilderness Society in 1935. Its goal, in part, was to secure stronger statutory support for the administratively vulnerable wilderness areas. Progress toward this goal would prove to be slow, but the wilderness idea continued to gain support in the federal agencies in the late 1930s. In 1939, for example, the Forest Service issued updated "U" regulations that gave greater protection to some 14 million acres of roadless land within the national forests.

· · ·

Where, then, was conservation *as a movement* in the late 1930s? It was broader and deeper than it had been three decades before. It was more urgent, more fully appreciated by the general public, and more thoroughly woven into the public discourse and public institutions. It had gained greater professional definition—and bureaucratic bulk—but it was also more actively promoted by dedicated nonprofessionals and citizen organizations.

Yet for all the strides taken, the recurring challenge of conservation that Aldo Leopold noted in 1938 had not been satisfactorily addressed. In the dust of the times, neither the utilitarian nor the preservationist philosophy seemed adequate for the "oldest task." For a small but growing cohort of conservationists, a new way of approaching the challenge was required. In formulating that approach, they would focus their attention on key elements of both. They embraced the preservationist critique of human arrogance and greed, while carrying forward the high regard for and aesthetic appreciation of wild nature. At the same time, they accepted and relied upon the authority of science—a legacy of their training as resource managers in the utilitarian mode. But it was a new and different kind of science upon which they drew.

. . .

At the conclusion of *Breaking New Ground*, his autobiographical account of the rise of forestry and conservation, Gifford Pinchot laid out his vision of a future in which injustice, inordinate profit, and concentrated wealth would cease to determine the social order of mankind. "When it comes," he wrote, "I hope and believe the new order will be based on cooperation instead of monopoly, on sharing instead of grasping, and that mutual helpfulness will replace the *law of the jungle*" [emphasis added] (30). Notwithstanding the legitimacy of the ideal that Pinchot hoped to communicate, his choice of metaphors (which he repeated several lines later) revealed much about the world view upon which he—and much of the conservation establishment—had built their policies and their professions. The implication? Nature unmanaged was ruled by unbridled red-in-tooth-and-claw competition. It was a world, in the end, of constant struggle for existence, a wild world that should and would be civilized through the application of human managerial skill.

Pinchot was writing in the mid-1940s, near the end of his life. The irony is that, by that time, the world view on which his metaphor was based was already outmoded—at least in the minds of a growing number of scientists and conservationists. Moreover, the new view was being formulated and promulgated in part by conservation scientists from the official ranks. In a critical passage from a 1939 address to a joint meeting of American foresters and ecologists, Aldo Leopold made the point:

> Ecology is a new fusion point for the sciences. . . . The emergence of ecology has placed the economic biologist [read "forester," "wildlife manager," "range manager," etc.] in a peculiar dilemma: with one hand he points out the accumulated findings of his search for utility, or lack of utility, in this or that species; with the other he lifts the veil from a biota so complex, so conditioned by interwoven cooperations and competitions, that no man can say where utility begins or ends. No species can be "rated" without the tongue in the cheek. The old categories of "useful" and "harmful" have validity only as conditioned by time, place, and circumstance. The only sure conclusion is that the biota as a whole

is useful, and biota includes not only plants and animals, but soils
and waters as well (31).

By the late 1930s, ecology had begun to revolutionize the scientific view
of "the jungle" and the environmental context within which human society
operates. As Baird Callicott writes, ecology was beginning to reveal the natural world as "more than a collection of . . . useful, useless, and noxious
species arrayed upon an elemental landscape of soils and waters. Rather, it
is a vast, intricately organized and tightly integrated *system* of complex
processes" [emphases in original] (32). The progress of human civilization,
it followed, could not be understood apart from its evolutionary backdrop
and its ecological foundations. Writing in 1933, Leopold suggested that
"civilization is not, as [the historians of its progress] often assume, the en-
slavement of a stable and constant earth. It is a state of *mutual and interdependent cooperation* between human animals, other animals, plants, and
soils, which may be disrupted at any moment by the failure of any of them"
[emphasis in original] (33).

Conservation, its scientific and historical context thus recast, could no
longer be defined in either pure utilitarian or preservationist terms. Utility
was a far more complicated matter than even the most ardent utilitarians realized. "Usefulness" was a property not simply *of* discrete commodities, but
derived *from* the entire biotic community. Moreover, a broad range of ecological factors determined the quality and quantity of any given service, resource, or commodity that the community might provide. "Yields" could be
sustained only if economic pressures and resource management practices
did not undermine what Leopold termed "land health"—the evolutionary
coadaptations and ecological interactions that allowed the community to
function properly. Wilderness, by the same token, had more than just aesthetic or recreational value. It stood at one end of a land use *continuum.* It
served as a "land laboratory"—a place against which to compare landscapes
altered by intensive human use. And the preservation of wildlands afforded
protection (at least to a degree) to their diverse parts and their ecological
processes, which had much to offer in the effort to understand "how healthy
land maintains itself " (34).

Seeking a more comprehensive ethic to guide conservation, Leopold and
a minority of like-minded individuals stressed the need to combine conservative use and preservation, based on an appreciation of ecological health
and the diversity, integrity, stability, and beauty of the biotic community.
Conservation could then strive for more than just the sustained yield of resources and commodities, or even the preservation of the nation's dwin-
dling and increasingly isolated remnants of wilderness. "The real end [of
conservation]," Leopold held, "is a *universal symbiosis with land,* economic

and esthetic, public and private" [emphasis in original] (34). Or, as he stated more succinctly, conservation is "a state of harmony" between people and land.

How then to live on a piece of land without spoiling it? The answers provided by the "evolutionary-ecological land ethic" (for which Leopold was only one, albeit particularly eloquent, spokesperson) turned out to be much more delicate and complex than either the utilitarian or preservationist schools of thought had suggested. Begin with a basic appreciation of the biotic community as a whole, its composition, its structure and processes, and the historical changes that have taken place within it. Protect at least samples of each different kind of community. Use the resources of the land and waters conservatively, with high regard for native diversity, and with the fullest possible awareness of the ecological functions that maintain the system's health. Develop and revise management strategies based on the best information that the *integrated* natural sciences can provide. Actively restore, wherever feasible, that which has been lost, degraded, or unwisely altered. Identify and work to change the social and economic forces that constrain such actions. Be active, since time is short; but be patient, since success is by definition incremental and long-term.

And something more. In "The Land Ethic," Leopold's final expression (drafted in 1947) of his long-evolving philosophy, he calmly nudged conservation forward with these words:

> The land ethic . . . enlarges the boundaries of the community to include soils, waters, plants, and animals, or collectively: the land. . . . A land ethic of course cannot prevent the alteration, management, and use of these "resources," but it does affirm their right to continued existence, and, at least in spots, their continued existence in a natural state. In short, a land ethic changes the role of *Homo sapiens* from conqueror of the land community to plain member and citizen of it (36).

Of the many messages embedded within this passage, the most important may be the most subtle: Leopold's deliberate placing of the term "resources" within quotation marks—perhaps the only time he ever did so. With that slightest of rhetorical gestures, Leopold simultaneously acknowledged the reality of human resource use and the limits of utilitarian conservation philosophy, even as he confirmed the inherent worth and dignity of "things natural, wild, and free." Conservation would not, and *could not* succeed as long as people regarded—and hence managed—nature merely as a disaggregated assortment of "natural resources." Success in the oldest task in human history could not be gained simply by developing more powerful and sophisticated tools to extract goods and services from the natural world.

Success required more comprehensive ways of perceiving, understanding, and appreciating the relationship between people and nature. Success, in other words, required that we not simply change the land, but that we change ourselves.

This redefinition of conservation had profound implications for the various resource management professions. For one thing, it raised fundamental questions about the validity and viability of separate professions, disciplines, and departments. Within his own area of expertise—wildlife management—Leopold tried to push those who "[saw] utility and beauty only in pheasants and trout" to see more fully the "utility and beauty of the biota as a whole." By the early 1940s, all the conservation fields had "dissenters" (to use Leopold's term) who had arrived at the same conclusions: in trying to understand natural systems and human activity within them, the assumptions and approaches of reductionist science (valid knowledge is gained by dividing reality up into ever-smaller parts), utilitarian philosophy (this knowledge achieves its highest end when used to meet strictly human needs), and conventional economics (human needs are always served through increases in raw productivity) were inadequate. In the view of the "dissenters," attention had to be given to the connections and relationships in nature over various scales of space and time. In other words, one could not simply manage trees, or soils, or game animals, or scenic vistas, or any other resource, as isolated entities; one had to consider the diverse components within the landscape as a whole and their ecological interactions over time. Professional labels notwithstanding, conservation implied—demanded—integration (37).

. . .

World War II changed everything. The promising synthesis that had begun to emerge within conservation was overwhelmed by the war, and inundated by social changes in the war's aftermath. Even before Leopold put the finishing touches on "The Land Ethic," the natural resource management professions had begun to move in other directions—indeed, each in its own direction. Instead of growing more flexible, the boundaries between scientific disciplines, departments, and agencies became more rigid. Instead of converging on a shared vision of ecological health and integrity, the conservation professions became increasingly specialized and focused on increasing the output of their particular commodities. Instead of narrowing, the gaps in understanding only widened—gaps separating the various natural sciences, the basic and applied sciences, the sciences and other areas of human knowledge, the academic departments and the conservation agencies, the different conservation professions, the professionals and the public.

Writing in 1945, Paul Sears traced much of the problem "back to college classrooms, where a type of fragmental teaching has been going on that breaks the world of human experience up into air-tight compartments." He insisted that "this sort of piecemeal teaching simply has to be stopped. It is getting to be too costly to our modern society" (38). For most, however, those costs (if they were admitted at all) were too far removed to be of much concern. The new generation of postwar resource managers slipped easily (and for the most part unknowingly) into a disciplinary framework to which there were few alternatives. The ramifications were, and remain, far-reaching. As Reed Noss and Allen Cooperrider have observed:

> Disciplinarianism . . . resulted in a pattern of natural resource management that is fragmented and inefficient. Individuals trained in one discipline work on problems in isolation from other specialists, even within the same agency. Agency land use plans are often written as if there are separate landscapes to provide for timber, wildlife, livestock forage, clean water, and recreation (39).

The forces of technological innovation, population growth, and economic expansion reinforced the trend. The demand for all natural resources increased dramatically during the postwar boom years. As the pressure to increase production—of crops, timber, livestock forage, fish stocks, game animals, visitor days—grew, so did the faith that all conservation problems could be solved through technical solutions. At a point in history when conservation problems were becoming more complex, clear communication more valuable, and unity of purpose more necessary, the counterforces seemed inexorable.

The development of forest management in the postwar years serves as a useful case study. While "dissenting" foresters had argued for a broader view of the composition, function, and management of forest ecosystems, the profession as a whole drifted in the other direction. Historian Samuel Hays notes:

> As early as the 1920s the dendrology textbooks and courses in forestry schools that described forest species and their distribution became restricted to commercial types. The texts explained that foresters need not know all forest species—foresters were not botanists—but only those that were useful for wood production. This narrowed their conception of a forest considerably (40).

As the profession's conception of the "resource" further narrowed in the postwar years, the demand for forest products rose rapidly, especially in response to the housing and construction boom. The effects were most apparent in, though not confined to, the national forests. The means to the all-but-universally accepted end of sustained timber yields began to shift. The selective cutting methods that prevailed in forestry through the 1930s began to give way after the war to even-aged management of larger-scale forest units. Productivity gains were sought through increased inputs in the form of fertilizers and genetically "improved" tree stocks. Pest management was sought through increased applications of synthetic pesticides and intensified control of competing vegetation. Clearcutting became the preferred method of harvest, replanting with trees of the same age and species the preferred method of reforestation. According to Hays, "by the 1960s the elements of this technical system had been worked out in great detail" (41).

Economies of scale and economic incentives reinforced the shifts in forest practices. At the same time, the *subculture* of the forestry profession had changed. Timber interests played an ever-growing role in setting the education, research, and policy agenda. The postwar cohort of foresters grew farther away from the vision of unified conservation that was in many ways their own professional inheritance. Even when, for example, the Multiple Use–Sustained Yield Act of 1960 directed the Forest Service to balance timber production with other uses, the underlying idea—wiser coordination of forest management's means and ends—remained essentially dormant. Timber production remained the primary use, within the subculture if not in the law. There was simply too little integration of thought or action among the managers—much less among the users—much less within society—to give "multiple use" meaningful expression, or meaningful criticism.

Variations on the same pattern played out in the other fields of resource management. Hence: to improve agricultural productivity, expand and intensify farm operations using artificial fertilizers and pesticides, a limited number of "modern" seed varieties, and an ever-growing array of "labor-saving" technologies; to improve range forage production, remove woody vegetation, apply herbicides, and seed with more "desirable" forage species; to build up stocks of fish and game, introduce exotic species and expand artificial propagation programs; to prevent floods and manage water resources, dam the headwaters, straighten the channels, channelize the streambeds, and raise the levees. The same generic forces could be perceived in agriculture, range management, wildlife management, fisheries management, recreational planning: increasingly sophisticated management techniques, with an emphasis on large-scale, input-intensive practices and systems; primary, often exclusive, focus on a few commercially valuable components of the ecosystem; increasing economies of scale; standardization in planning and production methods; simplification of natural systems and processes; the development of an insular professional priesthood; increasingly close ties between resource management agencies and politically (and financially) influential user groups and industries. The various fields also shared derelictions: a lack of attention to the particulars of place, to the complexity and diversity of ecosystems, to the inevitable harmful effects of fragmented thought on both the natural and human communities.

There was, however, a counter-counterforce. World War II had had other, more positive impacts on conservation. It tempered the near-religious faith in science as the font of all progress and technological innovation as the solution to all human problems. It gave a generation international experience and increased the availability of information, transforming conservation into a global concern. It spawned technologies that would revolutionize human understanding of natural systems and their evolution. It galvanized those who saw, not specialization, but synthesis of knowledge as the essential requirement in the modern age.

These factors coalesced around particular issues—including the loss of wilderness, the nuclear arms race, and pollution problems—with increasing regularity in the 1950s, then surfaced dramatically in 1962, when Rachel Carson published *Silent Spring*, giving rise to the modern environmental movement. The new environmentalists and the older resource managers were far from sympathetic in their motivations, their experience, or their approaches. There was, however, common ground. Starting from it, many within both the natural resource management professions and the environmental movement began a gradual return, still far from complete, toward the integrated understanding that Leopold and others had first tried to articulate 30 years before.

If the years 1945–1965 were characterized by increasing specialization, the remainder of the 1960s and 1970s saw the increasing acceptance of environmental values and goals within the conservation professions and within society at large. Translating these values into effective conservation action, however, would prove to be a slow and fitful process. The political and economic obstacles to reform (both within and beyond the professions) remained formidable. Specialization continued to exercise its drag; even in seeking to attain broader environmental goals, conservationists of all sorts still tended to focus on single species, single resources, single parts of the landscape—single aspects of any conservation dilemma. But as younger resource managers, agency officials, and scientists, trained in the post-Earth Day era, began to enter and rise through the ranks, they carried with them a stronger sense that, in order to conserve anything, the professions had to be brought together in the human mind and in the landscape.

By the mid-1980s, the consequences of *disintegrated* conservation could no longer be avoided or misinterpreted. The effects could be seen across the landscape, from the innermost city to the outermost wildland: in the decline and waste of urban neighborhoods; in the desperate spread of suburbia and the frenetic rise of "edge cities"; in the stresses placed on agricultural soils and waters, and on farm families, economies, and communities; in the clearing and fragmentation of forests under intensified logging pressures; in the continued loss and degradation of wetlands, deserts, and other wild-lands; in the inability to insulate national parks and other protected areas from air- and waterborne pollutants and other transboundary threats; in the decline of important fisheries as a result of overharvesting and the disrup-tion of the aquatic systems that support them; in the endangerment of life's genetic, species, and ecosystem variety to such a degree that a new term, "biodiversity," had to be coined to comprehend the situation; in the incur-ring of long-term social and environmental costs under so many different ecological circumstances that another new term, "sustainability," had to be coined to communicate the dilemma.

The systemic nature of these by-now familiar problems has become steadily more apparent, as have the limits of the traditional conservation professions acting separately to address them. Especially in the latter half of the 1980s, the need for interdisciplinary approaches became more formally recognized within the established professions. The problems themselves defined new foci for scientific research and application, including conserva-tion biology, restoration ecology, landscape ecology, and sustainable agricul-ture. Concepts that had hovered on the periphery of resource manage-ment—sustainability, ecological health, ecosystem management—moved toward the center of the discussion. The social sciences and humanities reentered the discussion as ecological economics, environmental history, and environmental philosophy became established subjects of study.

By the 1990s, a century after conservation first began to take form, it was again reinventing itself, evolving in response to both internal tensions and external challenges. Behind these recent adaptations is the tenacious idea that conservation is more than a simple matter of long-term human eco-nomic self-interest; that it entails moral choices and responsibilities in-volving the community of life in which we evolved and to which we belong. Like conservation itself, the evolutionary-ecological land ethic has emerged fitfully over the last century, and is only now growing into the role it must play in human affairs in the future. Muted by a generation of cornucopian dreams and Cold War fears, ignored by those "[for] whom education and culture have become almost synonymous with landlessness," dismissed by many as an impractical and ill-defined ideal—and often advanced by those disinclined to confront the dilemmas it suggests—the land ethic now rings with increasing definition and resonance as conservation enters its second century (42). But it remains, in Wallace Stegner's words, "not a fact, but a task" (43).

. . .

Conservation is, and has always been, a radical endeavor, "radical" in the first and literal sense of the word: pertaining to, and proceeding from, *roots*. Conservation pertains to and proceeds from the roots of experience; of knowledge, value, and wealth; of dreams and the divine. We who are about to confront the sobering realities of this brave new century can sense only with difficulty the historical roots of conservation. For now, we can still find them hidden deep in the shade of the recovering northwoods, where the stumps of fallen white pines mark the reckless and restless past. We can still hear them in the words of a Ghost Dance song chanted, in dire need, on the high plains a century ago. In the world that the Ghost Dancers tried to dance back into existence, wildness had free reign. That wild world cannot be fully regained, but its loss may be at least partially redeemed. Perhaps, after all, a nation is coming—a world is coming—to recognize that wildness, properly known, is not the antithesis of civilization, but its complement and its context, essential to its vitality, inherent in its definition. The revival of the white pine and the northwoods forest, the restoration of the bison and the prairie, the building of healthy human communities able to coexist with and within nature—these may yet signify the return of wildness, not as an enemy but as a guide, as another generation prepares to take on the newest, oldest task in human history.

Acknowledgments

For assistance in providing background materials for this essay, I would like to thank Baird Callicott, Allen Cooperrider, Tom Fleishner, Art Hasler, Rick Knight, Reed Noss, and Phil Pister. For their encouragement and support, I would especially like to thank my colleagues at the International Crane Foundation.

Notes

1. Armstrong, V.I., ed. 1989. I have spoken: American history through the voices of the Indians., 129. Athens, Ohio: Swallow Press/Ohio University Press. Original source: Mooney, J. 1893. The ghost dance religion and the Sioux outbreak of 1890. U.S. Bureau of American Ethnology, 14th Annual Report, 1892–1893, part 2, 178.
2. Flader, S.L., and J.B. Callicott, eds. 1991. The river of the mother of

god and other essays by Aldo Leopold, 254. Madison, Wisconsin: University of Wisconsin Press. This passage originally appeared in a lecture, "Engineering and Conservation," which Leopold delivered April 11, 1938, to the University of Wisconsin College of Engineering.

3. Roth, F. 1898. On the forestry conditions of northern Wisconsin. Wisconsin Geological and Natural History Survey Bulletin 1. Madison, Wisconsin. See Curtis, J.T. 1959. The vegetation of Wisconsin, 469. Madison, Wisconsin: University of Wisconsin Press.

4. Much has been written about the history of white pine exploitation and its role in the development of forestry in the United States. Two especially helpful, recent discussions can be found in Williams, M. 1989. Americans and their forests, 160–237. New York: Cambridge University Press; and Cronon, W. 1991. Nature's metropolis: Chicago and the Great West, 148–206. New York: Norton and Company.

5. A basic account of the Ghost Dances and the events at Wounded Knee can be found in Andrist, R.K. [1964] 1993. The long death: the last days of the plains Indian, 330–354. New York: Macmillan Publishing Company.

6. Turner's original essay has been widely reprinted and debated. See Turner, F.J. 1920. The frontier in American history. New York: Holt, Rinehart, and Winston. For helpful interpretations, see especially Cronon, W. 1987. Revisiting the vanishing frontier: the legacy of Frederick Jackson Turner. Western Historical Quarterly 18 (April):157–176; and Limerick, P.N. 1992. The forest reserves and the argument for a closing frontier. In Origins of the National Forests: a centennial symposium. H.K. Steen, ed., 10–18. Durham, North Carolina: Forest History Society.

7. Fox, S. 1981. John Muir and his legacy: the American conservation movement, 103–107. Boston, Massachusetts: Little, Brown, and Company. See also Cohen, M. 1988. The history of the Sierra Club, 1892–1970. San Francisco, California: Sierra Club Books.

8. Frome, M. Whose woods are these: the story of the National Forests, 48. Garden City, New Jersey: Doubleday and Company, Inc. Pinchot, G. 1987. Breaking new ground, 85. Washington, D.C.: Island Press.

9. Helpful summaries of this period include Stegner, W. 1992. A capsule history of conservation. In Where the bluebird sings to the lemonade springs: living and writing in the West, 117–132. New York: Random House; Mumford, L. 1955. The renewal of the landscape. In The brown decades: a study of the arts in America, 1865–1895, 57–106. New York: Dover Publications, Inc.; and Runte, A. 1991. Public lands, public heritage, and the National Forest idea. Niwot, Colorado: Roberts Rinehart Publishers.

1C Callicot, J.B. 1991. Whither conservation ethics. Conservation Biology 4:15–20.

11. Pinchot, 23 (8).

12. Pinchot, 31,32 (8).

13. Pinchot, 325 (8).

14. Pinchot, G. 1910. The fight for conservation, 42. New York: Doubleday, Page, and Company.

15. Fox, 139–147 (7); See Hott, L. and D. Garey. 1989. The wilderness idea: John Muir, Gifford Pinchot, and the first great battle for wilderness. Documentary film. Florentine Films.

16. Pinchot, 266 (8).

17. Nelson, R.H. The federal land management agencies. This volume.

18. Pinchot, 20–21 (8).

19. Harwood, R. 1990. A history of sustainable agriculture. In Sustainable agricultural systems. C.A. Edwards, R. Lal, P. Madden, R.H. Miller, and G. House, eds., 3–19. Ankeny, Iowa: Soil and Water Conservation Society.

20. Stoddart and Smith. In press. Development of range management. In Range management, 76–103.

21. Meine, C., Aldo Leopold: his life and work, 187–193. Madison, Wisconsin: The University of Wisconsin Press. E.A. Tucker, ed. 1991. The early days: a sourcebook of southwestern region history, book 2. Cultural resources management report no. 11. Albuquerque, New Mexico: USDA Forest Service, Southwestern Region.

22. Meine, C. 1994. Conservation biology and wildlife management in America: an historical perspective. In An introduction to conservation biology. G. Meffe and R. Carroll, eds., 310–312. Sunderland, Massachusetts: Sinauer Associates.

23. See Beckel, A. 1987. Breaking new waters: a century of limnology at the University of Wisconsin, and Egerton, F. The Wisconsin limnology community. In Transactions of the Wisconsin Academy of Sciences, Arts, and Letters. Madison, Wisconsin: Wisconsin Academy of Sciences, Arts, and Letters.

24. Stroud, R. 1966. Fisheries and aquatic resources: lake stream and inland waters. In Origins of American conservation. H. Clepper, ed., chapter 4, 57–73. New York: The Ronald Press Company.

25. Quoted in White, R.J. Why wild fish matter: balancing ecological and aquacultural fishery management. Trout 33 (4):16–33,44–48. See also: White, R.J. Why wild fish matter: a biologist's view. Trout 33 (3): 25–35; Bowen, J.T. 1970. A history of fish culture as related to the development of fishery programs. In A century of fisheries in North America. G. Benson, ed. 71–93. Washington, D.C.: American Fisheries Society.

26. Wright, G.M., J.S. Dixon, and B.H. Thompson. 1933. Fauna of the National Parks of the United States, 4. Fauna series number one. Washington, D.C.: Government Printing Office. See Chase, A. 1987. Playing god in Yellowstone: the destruction of America's first national park, 232–239. New York: Harcourt Brace Jovanovich Publishers.

27. Stegner, 128 (9).

28. Flader and Callicott, 131. For a discussion of Leopold's wilderness protection activities during this period, see Flader and Callicott, 24–27 (2).

29. See Nash, R. 1982. Wilderness and the American mind, 191. 3rd ed. New Haven, Connecticut: Yale University Press.

30. Pinchot, 509 (8).

31. Flader and Callicott, 266–67 (2). The original address, "A biotic view of land," was published in the September 1939 issue of the Journal of Forestry.

32. Callicott, J.B. Conservation ethics and fishery management. Fisheries 16(2):22–28.

33. Flader and Callicott, 188 (2).

34. Flader and Callicott, 288 (2). See Meine, C. 1992. The utility of preservation and the preservation of utility: Leopold's fine line. In The Wilderness condition: essays on environment and civilization. M. Oelschlaeger, ed., 131–172. San Francisco, California: Sierra Club Books. See also Norton, B.G. 1991. Toward unity among environmentalists. New York: Oxford University Press.

35. Flader and Callicott, 188 (2).

36. Leopold, A. 1949. A sand county almanac and sketches here and there, 204. New York: Oxford University Press.

37. Meine, 312 (22).

38. Sears, P.B. 1988. The fourth r: resources. In From *The Land*. N.P. Pittman, ed., 431–436. Washington, D.C.: Island Press.

39. Noss, R., and A. Cooperrider. 1994. Saving nature's legacy, 142. Washington, D.C.: Island Press.

40. Hays, S. 1987. Beauty, health, and permanence: environmental politics in the United States, 1955–1985, 396. Cambridge, Massachusetts: Cambridge University Press. The point is a fundamental one. In Breaking New Ground, for example, Pinchot admitted that the scientific study of plants was valuable ("trees," he allowed, "are unquestionably vegetable"), but nonetheless insisted that "forestry is not botany, but something vastly different." He distinguished between "forester's facts" and "mere botanical observations;" Pinchot, 3, 88, 97 (8). But see Miller, C. Old growth: a reconstruction of Gifford Pinchot's Training of a Forester, 1914–1937. Forest and Conservation History 38(1):7–15.

41. Hays, 395 (40).
42. Leopold, L. 1953. Round river: from the journals of Aldo Leopold, 155. New York: Oxford University Press.
43. Stegner, W. 1987. The legacy of Aldo Leopold. In Companion to a sand county almanac: interpretive and critical essays. J.B. Callicott, ed., 245. Madison, Wisconsin: University of Wisconsin Press.

Chapter 2

The Federal Land Management Agencies

Robert H. Nelson

> Conservationists envisaged, even though they did not realize their aims, a
> political system guided by the ideal of efficiency and dominated by the
> technicians who could best determine how to achieve it.
> —Samuel P. Hays
> *Conservation and the Gospel of Efficiency*

The lands owned by the federal government total 662 million acres, representing 29 percent of the land area of the United States (1). Many of the most important natural resource issues—including forestry, wilderness, grazing, endangered species, and others—involve the management of federal lands. In this chapter I will give a brief overview of the history and the responsibilities of the four federal agencies that are principally responsible for the management of federally owned lands (2). These agencies are the United States Forest Service (USFS), National Park Service (NPS), Fish and Wildlife Service (USF&WS), and Bureau of Land Management (BLM).

Other federal agencies such as the Corps of Engineers, Bureau of Reclamation, Tennessee Valley Authority, and Bonneville Power Administration are responsible for management of water resources of the nation. These agencies in many cases have origins in the same intellectual trends and political and economic developments as the federal land management agencies. They are not, however, as central to the natural resource issues addressed in this book.

The ownership of federal land is concentrated in the western United States. Federal lands include more than 60 percent of five western states (Alaska, California, Nevada, Idaho, and Utah); and of the 11 lower 48 states that are entirely located west of the 100th meridian, federal lands represent fully 48 percent of their total land area. These federal lands are mostly the less settled parts of the West, primarily forests and rangelands (3).

Two agencies, the Bureau of Land Management (Department of Interior) and the Forest Service (Department of Agriculture), manage the

Table 2.1

Area of Federal Lands by Management Agency in Millions of Acres

Agency	11 Western states[a]	Alaska	Other states	Total
Bureau of Land Management	177.0	90.4	1.6	269.0
Fish and Wildlife Service	7.2	76.5	7.2	90.9
Forest Service	140.9	22.2	28.4	191.5
National Park Service	16.8	52.9	6.8	76.5
Other federal agencies	21.9	5.8	6.6	34.3
Grand total	363.8	247.8	50.6	662.2

[a] Includes AZ, CA, CO, ID, MT, NV, NM, OR, UT, WA, and WY.

largest areas of federal land (Table 2.1). Large areas are also managed by the Fish and Wildlife Service and the National Park Service, both located in the Department of the Interior. The Alaska National Interest Lands Conservation Act of 1980 (ANILCA) transferred many millions of acres of land from the BLM to these agencies, more than doubling their holdings. At present, fully 34 percent of BLM land, 84 percent of Fish and Wildlife Service land, and 69 percent of National Park Service land are located in Alaska.

In terms of human resources, the Forest Service, with 36,172 employees in 1992, is the largest of the federal land management agencies (Table 2.2). The National Park Service ranks second in this regard with 22,427 employees, followed by the BLM with 12,105 employees and the Fish and Wildlife Service with 9,043 employees. The budgets for these agencies have similar relationships (see Table 2.2).

Table 2.2

1992 Employment and Budget by Land Management Agency

Agency	1992 Employment[a]	1992 Budget[b]
Bureau of Land Management	12,105	$ 815 million
Fish and Wildlife Service	9,043	802
Forest Service	36,137	2,902
National Park Service	22,427	1,412

Sources: Department of the Interior, *The Interior Budget in Brief Fiscal Year 1993;* and U.S. Forest Service, *Report of the Forest Service. Fiscal Year 1992.*

[a] Full-time employment equivalent.

[b] Fiscal year 1992 appropriation, excluding formula payments to states.

Natural Resources on Federal Lands

Federal lands are a significant source of oil, natural gas, coal, timber, and other resource outputs. The oil and gas resources of the Outer Continental Shelf are federally owned beyond 3 miles (with the exceptions of the Texas coastline and the west coast of Florida, where state management extends to about 9 miles). These oil and gas resources are managed by the Minerals Management Service, yet another of the agencies located within the Department of the Interior. The leasing of oil and gas located onshore is conducted by the BLM, although the royalties from these leases are collected by the Minerals Management Service. In 1992, federal leases located on the Outer Continental Shelf supplied almost 14 percent of the total oil production of the United States and 26 percent of U.S. natural gas production. Federal lands onshore, in 1991, supplied almost 5 percent of U.S. oil and almost 7 percent of natural gas.

Production of coal from federal leases has increased rapidly, from a mere 2 percent of total U.S. production as recently as 1972, to fully 26 percent in 1991. One western state, Wyoming, is now the leading coal-producing state. By itself, Wyoming supplies about 20 percent of U.S. production, the great majority of this coal coming from federal leases (5).

The Forest Service manages 47 percent of the United States inventory of softwood timber, which is about two-thirds of the total U.S. timber harvest. Harvests from Forest Service lands as recently as 1988 equaled 20 percent of the total U.S. softwood harvest. By 1995, Forest Service lands are expected to supply less than 10 percent of the U.S. softwood harvest. This reflects declining availability of "old growth" timber and new policies curtailing harvests in order to preserve the endangered northern spotted owl and to protect other environmental assets.

The BLM manages some of the prime forest lands in the United States, located mostly in western Oregon. These lands are known as the "O&C lands," reflecting the fact that they were recovered in 1917, after the Oregon and California Railroad Company (and its successors) were judged by the Supreme Court (in 1915) to have failed to meet the original terms of the railroad land grant (made in 1866). In 1988, timber sales on the O&C lands equaled about one billion board feet, representing 2 percent of the total U.S. harvest in that year. Timber harvests on BLM lands have since also declined sharply in response to owl preservation and other new environmental demands.

More than 300 million acres of federal lands are grazed by cattle and sheep, representing greater than 45 percent of the total federal land acreage and 13 percent of the total land area of the United States. The federal grazing lands are generally of low productivity; in many areas 20 or more acres are required to support the grazing of a single cow for a period of one month. Reflecting this low productivity, federal grazing lands provide only 7 percent of total forage and 2 percent of feed supplies (of all kinds) consumed by U.S. beef cattle. Federal grazing lands nevertheless contribute significantly to the economic viability of many individual ranch operations in the West. While it may be as little as a month or two, approximately 33 percent of all beef cattle in the 11 westernmost lower 48 states spend at least some portion of their lifetime grazing on federal lands.

The first wilderness area was created in 1924, on the Gila National Forest in New Mexico. This action was taken administratively by the Forest Service, inspired in part by the efforts of Aldo Leopold, then an agency employee. The first statutory designation of wilderness did not occur until 1964, when Congress established a national wilderness system and placed 9.1 million acres of Forest Service land in this system. The wilderness system represented a significant departure in federal land management in that units of this new system continued to be held by the same agencies that had previously managed them. Earlier, when a new national park or a new wildlife refuge was created from public lands, the redesignation also typically meant the transfer of the land to a new managing agency.

The national wilderness system has grown rapidly since 1964 and now equals 95 million acres. Fully 60 percent of this wilderness acreage is in Alaska. Excluding Alaska, there are 38 million acres of wilderness (about the size of the state of Michigan), 74 percent of which are managed by the Forest Service.

Origins of the Public Land Agencies

The organizational arrangements for managing the vast expanses of federal lands were largely set in place at the end of the 19th century and in the early part of the 20th century (5). The first National Park, Yellowstone, was established in 1872. The setting aside of lands in national forests (then called "forest reserves") was authorized by Congress in 1891. The first wildlife refuge was created in 1903. Most of the lands today managed by BLM were removed from availability for disposal and placed under active federal management in 1934.

The public land agencies in their current form were usually created somewhat later than the beginnings of the land systems themselves (6). The Forest Service was established in 1905 when Gifford Pinchot persuaded Theodore Roosevelt and the Congress to transfer the forest reserves from their management within the Interior Department to the Agriculture Department. The National Park Service was formed in 1916 by bringing together a number of individual national parks that previously had been administered separately. The Fish and Wildlife Service was created in the Interior Department in 1940 from two agencies that had been located for most of their existence in the departments of Commerce and Agriculture. Finally, the BLM was established in 1946 through a merger of the General Land Office and the Grazing Service.

The decision to retain the public lands in federal ownership represented a sharp departure from the public land policies of the 19th century. Throughout that century, the federal government sought actively to dispose of its landholdings in the west. Initially, the primary objective was to raise revenue. However, the disposal of federal lands gradually came to be seen more as a means of promoting the economic development of the West and of serving other social policy goals. The free grants of land to settlers under the Homestead Act of 1862 and the large grants of land to railroads in the 1860s represented the full triumph of this strategy.

Eventually, 288 million acres (almost three times the current size of California) would be transferred to homesteaders and 94 million acres to railroads. In addition, under statehood acts, swamplands drainage legislation, and various other enactments, the federal government transferred a vast domain of 328 million acres (about 15 percent of the current U.S. land area) to state governments. By 1991, the total disposition of federal lands under all the various land laws equaled 1.1 billion acres, almost half the lands found today in the United States.

By the end of the 19th century, the greater part of the most productive land was already in private hands. In addition, there was deep discontent with the workings of the existing federal laws. Relying on earlier experience, the laws for disposal of lands in the west had been designed by Congress with the geographic and climatic circumstances of midwestern states such as Iowa and Illinois in mind. In the West, however, rainfall was much lower, and in many places conventional farming was impossible without irrigation—certainly on a plot as small as the 160 acres allowed by the Homestead Act and much other disposal legislation. Westerners sought to adopt a variety of practical accommodations to form larger farm or ranch units and to otherwise circumvent flawed laws, but to many eastern eyes these steps all too often appeared as mere fraud and illegality.

Another critical factor was a general shift in the national mood to look to the federal government as a regulator and manager of the affairs of the nation. Working out the intellectual grounds for this shift occupied many of the best minds of the progressive era, typically said to date from 1890 to 1920. Applied to federal lands, the progressive philosophy meant that the government should itself manage the lands, rather than dispose of them.

The federal land management agencies were all significantly shaped by progressive thinking, which still influences their decisions and methods of operation in many ways.

The Progressive Gospel of Efficiency

Because progressivism, as applied to natural resources through its conservationist offshoot, was so central to the history of the federal land management agencies, it is worth reviewing briefly the historical significance of the progressive movement. In 1850, most Americans still lived a rural and agricultural existence, one not so much altered from previous centuries. By 1950, however, all this was changed. The automobile, airplane, radio and television, electric light, penicillin, and other products of science had created a mode of living virtually unknown in human experience. Indeed, the average person in 1950 possessed a standard of living that with respect to some important matters such as medicine, transportation, and communications far exceeded that of even the richest kings and queens of a mere few centuries earlier.

It was in the progressive era that Americans first sought to come to terms with these remarkable developments. One result was a new sense of the United States as one community. Railroads, highways, the telegraph and other inventions linked the nation much more closely together as a single economy. The Civil War had already focused Americans on Washington in a new way. In the progressive era, many Americans came to believe that the federal government should manage political and economic affairs, as it had already shown it could manage war.

If science was at the heart of the revolutionary changes occurring in American life, it seemed logical that science must remake American government as well. Indeed, the core of progressive thinking was the introduction of scientific management throughout government. A new era required that public decisions be made on an objective basis, replacing the ineffective and often corrupt patronage systems of the past. Government should rely on neutral experts to administer its affairs "in the public interest."

The progressives created new governing institutions to advance these purposes. Besides federal land management, they included the independent civil service, the independent regulatory commission, the Federal Reserve System, the Bureau of the Budget, and other instruments of the executive branch administration of the federal government. The new agencies drew heavily for staffing on recently created professional associations. The forestry, economics, public administration, and other new professions brought together a community of experts linked throughout the nation by a common aim to further the application of science to the affairs of the world. Harvard, Yale, Princeton, and other universities turned from religious and philosophical subjects to create new disciplinary boundaries within which specialized training in expert fields was offered.

The progressives were devout believers in the transforming powers of economic progress. The record of human history demonstrated, as many progressives believed, that the problems of the world lay in economic conditions—in poverty and material deprivation. Human beings fought, stole, lied, and otherwise often behaved badly because they were driven to it by material necessity. Eliminate economic scarcity, it seemed to follow, and a whole new era of happiness and harmony in human affairs would be at hand. This secular religion—a faith in which the progressive movement was grounded—in fact offered the promise of a future heaven on Earth, taking the place for many people of the earlier hope for heaven in the hereafter (7).

Economic progress required that labor, capital, and other inputs be used to maximal efficiency. The goal of efficiency was exalted to such a degree that some observers have labeled progressivism as the "gospel of efficiency." Historian Samuel Hays describes the implications of progressive thinking as it was applied to natural resources and public lands:

> The broader significance of the conservation movement stemmed from the role it played in the transformation of a decentralized, nontechnical, loosely organized society, where waste and inefficiency ran rampant, into a highly organized, technical, and centrally planned and directed social organization which could meet a complex world with efficiency and purpose. This spirit of efficiency appeared in many realms of American life, in the professional engineering societies, among forward-looking industrial management leaders, and in municipal government reform, as well as in the resource management concepts of Theodore Roosevelt. The possibilities of applying scientific and technical principles to resource development fired federal officials with enthusiasm for the future and imbued all in the conservation movement with a kindred spirit. These goals required public management, of the nation's streams because private enterprise could not afford to undertake it, of the Western lands to adjust one resource use to another. They also required new administrative methods, utilizing to the fullest extent the latest scientific knowledge and expert, disinterested personnel. This was the gospel of efficiency—efficiency which could be realized only through planning, foresight, and conscious purpose (8).

The Forest Service

In the late 19th century, as federal forests were being rapidly cut over, popular writers aroused the public with descriptions of the "looting" and the "plunder" of the Lake State pineries and other areas. Much of this overcutting was in fact due to the absence of property rights and the existence of a forest "commons." Other harvesting was occurring simply to remove the wood to make way for farms and other new uses. Yet, many Americans were convinced that the motive of private profit could only lead to further "forest devastation." Federal management and ownership seemed to them the only way out.

In 1891, Congress took the first step in establishing a system of federal forests. The General Reform Act included a provision, not much noticed at the time, allowing the President to set aside "forest reserves" from the ordinary application of the disposal laws. Within a few years, Presidents Benjamin Harrison and Grover Cleveland had placed 17 million acres within the federal forest system. The largest additions—equal to 148 million acres—were then made during the administration of Theodore Roosevelt. Responding to western protests that excessive lands were being locked away, Congress, in 1907, revoked the authority of the President to designate further forest areas within six western states. However, shortly before signing this legislation, Roosevelt added 16 million acres to the national forest system, creating a total system then equal to 195 million acres.

Following the 1891 legislation, many people expected at first that the new forest reserves would be managed as a type of park, supplying recreational and aesthetic enjoyments for the American public. However, a controversy soon erupted concerning the appropriate management philosophy for federal forests. Westerners sought to ensure that the lands would continue to be available for timber harvesting, livestock grazing, mining, and other traditional uses. Many progressive intellectuals agreed; they regarded public ownership as a way not of restricting use of the lands, but of maximizing their economic productivity. In their view this goal was best served through the comprehensive application of science, a task for which government was best suited in the case of the nation's forests. Gifford Pinchot first came to public visibility as an untiring and skilled advocate for such an approach (9).

Pinchot won one of his first major victories as a member of a National Academy of Sciences committee, formed in 1896, to decide the future management philosophy for the federal forests. The committee eventually recommended a management regime grounded in progressive concepts of maximal efficiency in the use of resources. Pinchot also came to believe that true scientific management could never be adequately realized with the forests remaining in the Department of the Interior. He therefore orchestrated their transfer, in 1905, to the Department of Agriculture, along with the creation of a new agency, the Forest Service, to manage the lands (named the "national forests" in 1907).

Pinchot also became the first chief of the Forest Service. In a letter signed by Secretary of Agriculture James Wilson in 1905, but actually written by Pinchot, the guiding philosophy of the Forest Service was set out for future generations:

> In the administration of the forest reserves it must be clearly borne in mind that all land is to be devoted to its most productive use for the permanent good of the whole people, and not for the temporary benefit of individuals or companies. All the resources of forest reserves are for use, and this use must be brought about in a thoroughly prompt and businesslike manner, under such restrictions only as will ensure the permanence of these resources. The vital importance of forest reserves to the great industries of the Western States will be largely increased in the near future by the continued steady advance in settlement and development. The performance of the resources of the reserves is therefore indispensable to continued prosperity, and the policy of this department for their protection and use will invariably be guided by this fact, always bearing in mind that the conservative use of these resources in no way conflicts with their permanent value. In the management of each reserve local questions will be decided upon local grounds; the dominant industry will be considered first, but with as little restriction to minor industries as may be possible; sudden changes in industrial conditions will be avoided by gradual adjustment after due notice; and where conflicting interests must be reconciled the question will always be decided from the standpoint of the greatest good of the greatest number in the long run (10).

In government, the undertaking of scientific management must, of course, ultimately take place in a political context. Indeed, in retrospect, Pinchot's skills appear greater as a political activist than as a scientific administrator. Pinchot repeatedly declared, for example, the scientific certainty of a disastrous "timber famine"; yet, none ever appeared (11). These claims nonetheless proved useful to Pinchot in justifying greater funding and authority for the Forest Service.

Pinchot himself acknowledged that the achievement of his goals depended on his mastery of skills in public relations. As he observed, "part of my job, in office and out, and the most essential part, has been to estimate public opinion, and to arouse, create, guide and apply it" (12). In the main, Pinchot did not accomplish this through technocratic appeals based on rational analysis. The appeal had to be to a stronger emotion; Pinchot thus sought—and often obtained—public support as a matter of the moral triumph of good over evil. Pinchot portrayed himself as the heroic fighter against the forces of private greed and venality. As one former chief said, the Forest Service was "born in controversy and baptized with the holy water of reform" (13).

Despite Pinchot's stated intent, the creation of a national forest at first actually served more to withdraw its lands from intensive uses and to place them in a custodial status. Timber harvesting, for example, was for many years limited on the national forests. Nationally, timber supplies were abundant and prices low; the timber industry pressured the Forest Service to withhold further public supplies from the market, aiming in this way to hold up prices (as, it might be noted, the Texas Railroad Commission and then the Organization of Petroleum Exporting Countries did for oil).

After World War II, however, private timber supplies began to run low; industry thus reversed its position, seeking greater access to Forest Service lands through public sales of timber. Much higher rates of timber sales and harvests resulted, which prevailed for several decades, until a number of factors caused timber harvests to be sharply reduced in the early 1990s. The management of the national forests today seems to be returning to the focus on park and recreational objectives that 100 years ago motivated many supporters of the original forest reserve legislation.

The legacy of Pinchot and other leaders of the early conservation movement is complex. The Forest Service preached science but practiced politics. In a democracy, political control is both necessary and appropriate, but it is difficult to reconcile with the dominant role for professional expertise prescribed in the progressive theory of government. The official goal of the Forest Service was to maximize efficiency in order to contribute to economic prosperity, but in practice the presence of a national forest for many years served to hold lands out of intensive productive use. Such tensions, especially those arising from the scientific claims versus the political motives and the moral preaching underlying many Forest Service actions, have bedeviled the agency throughout its history. The inability ever to achieve a satisfactory resolution has contributed significantly to the erosion of public confidence that faces the Forest Service today (14).

The National Park Service

In the creation of the National Park System, the closest counterpart to Pinchot in spreading the guiding ideas and arousing public support was John Muir. It was significantly due to the efforts of Muir that Yosemite National Park was established in 1890. A tireless writer and crusader for preservation of wild areas, Muir was also a skilled political activist and founder in 1892 of the Sierra Club.

In the late 19th century, Muir was reacting to the same rapid pace of social and economic change in American society, but in a way much different from Pinchot. Both could see that modern science and industry were everywhere transforming the world, but Muir found many of the results to be deeply offensive. If Pinchot sought new methods and institutions to better perfect progress, Muir sought to escape progress. He preferred instead to go into the wilderness, where signs of a human presence were few and it was still possible to encounter nature in an unaltered state (15).

For Muir, the wilderness was explicitly a place of spiritual inspiration. Employing religious terminology throughout his writings, he referred, for example, to wild areas as his "temples" and to the trees of the forests as "psalm-singing" (16). In an ever more secular world that was increasingly preoccupied with material concerns, it was still possible in the wilderness to encounter the work of God—to feel genuinely in the divine presence. Muir was a follower of Emerson for whom, as the intellectual historian Arthur Ekirch has said, "Nature was the connecting link between God and Man. . . . God spoke to man through nature and his conscience" (17).

Despite their basic differences, Muir was on good personal terms with Pinchot for many years. However, the two ended up fighting bitterly over the proposal to build Hetch Hetchy Dam in Yosemite National Park. Pinchot strongly supported the dam—which was approved in 1913 and is still today an important source of water for San Francisco—while Muir regarded it as the desecration of a sacred site. The loss of this epic battle led many preservationists to conclude that the Forest Service was an unreliable ally—if not an outright antagonist—in the battle to preserve wild areas. A new organization with a much clearer preservation mission would be needed.

A number of national parks had already been created, including Yellowstone, Yosemite, Glacier, Sequoia, Crater Lake, Mount Rainier, and Mesa

Verde. For many years they were operated separately under diverse arrangements. In 1916, however, the National Park Service was established to bring these units together under a single management. The first director of the Park Service was Stephen Mather, who proved an able and inspiring leader. Like Pinchot, public relations was one of his strong points. With the help of an equally talented deputy, Horace Albright, the National Park Service soon generated wide public support for its activities. It also expanded its domain, often at the expense of the Forest Service, which much resented the losses of its lands. A number of new major parks were created by the 1930s, including Grand Canyon, Everglades, Mount McKinley (now Denali), Olympic, Shenandoah, Bryce Canyon, Grant Teton, and Great Smoky.

The National Park Service is associated above all in the public mind with Yellowstone, Grand Canyon, Yosemite, and other "crown jewel" parks. However, over the years, the Park Service has worked energetically to expand its mission to other types of park units. It sought to establish eastern parks near large centers of population but with fewer distinguishing natural features. Following years of Park Service campaigning, President Franklin Roosevelt, in 1933, transferred the Civil War battlefields and the management of the Washington Monument, Lincoln Memorial, and other Washington, D.C. sites to the Park Service. The White House is today a unit of the National Park System.

Subsequently, still further types of park system units have been added, including national seashores, national rivers, national lakeshores, national recreation areas, and others. The National Park System has at present 711 units (or 365 units, excluding the 346 units within the National Capital Park System), divided among 19 administrative categories. Within the Park System, the expansion to cover such a wide range of areas and uses has significantly altered the original focus on preservation of large and majestic natural features. By 1992, the National Park System consisted of 76.5 million federal acres (80.7 million acres, including nonfederal lands within Park boundaries) and served 275 million visitors for a wide range of purposes.

The most difficult issue for the Park Service in its early years—and often still so today—is the tension between the use of the parks for tourism and other recreation, and the preservation of the parks. In the great majority of cases, timber harvesting, mining, grazing, and hunting are excluded. However, many roads, lodges, restaurants, and other facilities (e.g., golf courses) have been built in the national parks. The American public loves its parks at least in part because it can easily enter and enjoy them. Yet, the large volume of visitation also threatens and, in some cases, may undermine the natural conditions that the parks were created to protect.

As traditional sources of jobs and income grounded in natural resource development have declined, many rural areas have looked to tourism and other recreational activities to boost the local economy. They have discovered that a unit of the Park System can be a big help in this regard. It also generates local employment through construction of Park facilities and the subsequent operation and maintenance. The National Park Service has thus come to be seen by many in Congress as yet another object of patronage politics—leading some to declare that the old "pork barrel" has been replaced by a new "park barrel." The long-standing issue of the appropriate criteria and related quality standards for inclusion in the National Park System is today further than it has ever been from resolution.

Despite their much different histories, the National Park Service and the Forest Service share some challenges in common as the end of the 20th century approaches. Both agencies have declining employee morale and a confused sense of purpose; both have suffered a significant erosion of public support. These trends have been more visible with respect to the Forest Service but are also apparent to those who observe the operation of the National Park Service close at hand. On the occasion of its 75th anniversary, the Park Service initiated a review of its basic roles, responsibilities, and prospects. In conjunction with this effort, a 1991 symposium was held in Vail, Colorado, bringing together almost 700 experts and interested parties from inside and outside the Park Service. The resulting report stated that "throughout the symposium process, the steering committee has heard variations on a repetitive theme. The National Park Service has lost the ability to exercise leadership in determining the fate of the resources and programs it manages" (18).

The Vail report found that a core set of problems tends to undermine the Park Service's ability to accomplish its mission: "The National Park Service faces some severe challenges—budgetary constraints, eroding professionalism, a cadre of senior managers nearing retirement, inheritance and imposition of inappropriate new units, inadequate training and employment standards." A particularly important problem is that "the National Park Service is extraordinarily deficient in its capacities to generate, acquire, synthesize, act upon, and articulate to the public sound research and scientific information" (19).

There are, to be sure, great strengths as well. The Park Service "has a phenomenally dedicated work force"; it manages "some of the Nation's most treasured resources"; and it has "widespread support from the American public." Yet, overall, the Vail Report found that "in spite of the fact that the National Park Service is widely and deeply respected by the general public, which sees the service reflected through the national treasures in its charge, the agency is beset by controversy, concern, weakened morale, and declining effectiveness" (20).

The Fish and Wildlife Service

If predecessor agencies are considered, the Fish and Wildlife Service is older than both the Forest Service and the National Park Service. In 1871, Congress voted to establish the Bureau of Fisheries in the Department of Commerce. In 1886, the Biological Survey was created in the Department of Agriculture. The two agencies were transferred to the Interior Department in 1939, and then merged in 1940, to form the Fish and Wildlife Service. In 1970, the Bureau of Commercial Fisheries, which had been a part of the Fish and Wildlife Service, was transferred to the Department of Commerce to become the National Marine Fisheries Service.

The major land management responsibility of the Fish and Wildlife Service is the National Wildlife Refuge System, consisting of 485 refuge units and including 88.6 million acres. Among its further responsibilities, the Fish and Wildlife Service administers international treaties and laws relating to wildlife, the Migratory Bird Hunting Stamp Act of 1934, the Endangered Species Act of 1973, and the Convention of International Trade in Endangered Species (CITES).

Yet another product of the progressive era, the first federal wildlife refuge was established on Pelican Island in Florida in 1903 (21). The three-acre island was set aside as a reservation to protect the 2000 to 3000 pelicans that occupied it during the breeding season. This action was taken by executive order of President Theodore Roosevelt. Additional wildlife refuges were soon added, including the Wichita Mountains Refuge in 1905, in Oklahoma, the National Bison Range in 1908, in Montana, and the National Elk Refuge in 1912, at Jackson, Wyoming.

The Migratory Bird Treaty Act of 1918 set the stage for later actions establishing migratory bird refuges, including the creation of the Upper Mississippi River Wild Life and Fish Refuge in 1924. Congress, in 1929, enacted the Migratory Bird Conservation Act, establishing a statutory foundation for the systematic acquisition of lands for bird refuges. A large expansion of the refuge system followed during the New Deal years, funded in part through a tax of $1 per waterfowl hunter authorized under the Migratory Bird Hunting Stamp Act of 1934. It was not until 1966 that the National Wildlife Refuge System Administrative Act provided an official legislative blessing for and set policies for the management of a national system of wildlife refuges.

The Alaska National Interest Lands Conservation Act of 1980 added 54 million acres in Alaska to the National Wildlife Refuge System, nearly tripling its size. Alaska wildlife refuges typically involve very large areas with a mission to protect the overall ecology of the area. The largest refuge is the Yukon Delta National Wildlife Refuge, about equal in size to the state of Maine. In many ways the Fish and Wildlife Service management functions for Alaska lands are similar to the functions typically performed by the BLM and National Park Service—and less like the management of lower 48 refuges with their common focus on a particular type of wildlife.

Although hunting was prohibited on the early wildlife refuges, it was subsequently allowed on waterfowl refuges, beginning in 1924. Later, hunting of deer, moose, mountain goats, and other game animals was permitted on many refuges. To some extent, this hunting is today regarded as necessary to regulate animal populations. It is also an important source of national recreational opportunity that generates public support for the refuge system. In addition, other forms of recreation such as bird watching, hiking, swimming, and picnicking have also attracted many visitors with 4.4 million visitor-days spent on Fish and Wildlife Service lands in 1990.

Among the federal land management agencies, the Fish and Wildlife Service has had probably the least public visibility. Its lesser public profile partly reflects the diversity of its tasks. The agency also has not been the object of the fierce controversies that have so often taken place with respect to the management of Forest Service, National Park Service, and BLM lands. Even the recent disputes over the Endangered Species Act have tended to direct more attention to the affected land agencies than to the Fish and Wildlife Service, which administers the Act.

The precise mission of the Fish and Wildlife Service and the purposes of the National Wildlife Refuge System are still not clear to many people. Is the aim of the refuges to protect wildlife for their own sake; to protect game populations for hunting; or to provide hiking and other recreational opportunities? The Fish and Wildlife Service says that its first priority must be protecting wildlife, but in practice the answer is some of each of the above—and other political and policy goals as well. The migratory waterfowl refuges, for example, serve the needs of and are most actively supported by bird hunters. The National Bison Refuge in Montana enables tourists to see bison close at hand, and today perhaps resembles most closely an animal farm.

The Bureau of Land Management

The Bureau of Land Management (BLM) is in one respect the oldest and in another the youngest of the federal land management agencies. A predecessor organization, the General Land Office, was created in 1812. This office oversaw the disposal of federal lands and played an essential role in the history of western settlement during the 19th century.

Despite the creation of national systems of parks and forests, there were, in 1930, still large areas of public lands that went unsupervised and unmanaged. Livestock grazing was the principal use on what amounted to a grazing "commons"—although in practice, arrangements to allocate grazing access were often worked out informally among nearby ranchers. Open access to the lands was finally ended, however, with the passage, in 1934, of the Taylor Grazing Act. A new federal agency, the Grazing Service, was formed to administer the Act.

With the 1934 closing of the public domain to disposal, the General Land Office had little left to do. In 1946, it was merged with the Grazing Service to create a new agency, the Bureau of Land Management. The BLM assumed responsibility for the management of what was then a vast domain of over 450 million acres. Today, largely because of the transfer of 87 million acres to the state of Alaska under the Alaska Statehood Act of 1959, 37 million acres to Alaska Natives under the Alaska Native Claims Settlement Act of 1971, and many millions of additional acres to the National Park Service and Fish and Wildlife Service in Alaska, the domain over which BLM exercises management responsibility has shrunk to 270 million acres, about 12 percent of the U.S. land area.

The Grazing Service was created essentially to establish and police a system of controls over the grazing use of the public domain. As such, its greatest impacts were on the ranching community. Indeed, ranchers traditionally have exercised a large influence on BLM decisions. When the Grazing Service sought to raise the fees charged for livestock grazing in the early 1940s, Congressional spokesmen for western ranching interests, in 1946, slashed the Service budget by about 50 percent. Although ultimately unsuccessful, ranching groups threatened to obtain the transfer of grazing lands to state ownership or the sale of the lands to the ranchers themselves. In short, the BLM was born into weakness and barely survived its first few years.

For the longer run, however, employees of the BLM looked to the Forest Service as the model. The BLM view has been that the management of the public rangelands should be scientific management. Expert professionals should guide the agency independent of political interference and in the pursuit of the public interest. Reflecting the character of the land managed by BLM, the most relevant professional group should be rangeland scientists—although wildlife, forestry, and other professions should also be involved. True to the progressive gospel, a chief goal should be efficiency of management; as the second director of the Bureau of Land Management, Marion Clawson, wrote in his autobiography, "I think our greatest accomplishment was to make BLM operate reasonably efficiently." (22)

Over time, the BLM lands would prove increasingly attractive as recreational lands. The large areas of BLM desert lands, previously seen by many as hot, unattractive, and unproductive, today appear to more and more people as a sanctuary from the stresses of urban and industrial life. The total recreational use of BLM lands equaled 43 million visitor-days in 1990.

The emergence of new recreational and preservationist claims on BLM lands has generated fierce political conflicts with livestock, mining, and other traditional user groups. A related major development has been the emergence in the past two decades of the federal judiciary as a key decision maker in public rangeland (and forestry) management. In a 1974 case, *NRDC* v. *Morton,* a federal judge ordered the BLM to enter a 13-year process of redoing all its local land use plans in order to reexamine the traditional role of livestock grazing (23). Due in part to the tensions stirred up by this case, some long-time public land users in the late 1970s sought a transfer of the lands to state ownership and management—the so-called Sagebrush Rebellion (24). The greater willingness of federal judges to intervene in the administrative decisions of federal land management agencies is one sign of the loss of confidence in agency claims to independent professional expertise and authority. It is another indication of the fading of the progressive model of scientific management.

The Crisis of Progressive Faith

It often happens in science that a theory persists even as evidence of its many failings accumulates. The old paradigm simply lives on as long as no new theory arrives that is capable of replacing it. This is in fact the current circumstance of the public lands. The progressive model of scientific management is being challenged by hostile critics ranging all the way from deep ecologists to free-market economists. Yet, no other vision has emerged to guide agency behavior.

One of the tensions—if not outright contradictions—in progressive thinking was that its proponents believed in science with all the fervor of religion. In truth, progressivism was as much a religious movement—grounded in the "gospel of efficiency"—as a scientific movement. Ultimately, the theological foundations for this secular religion lay outside science; yet, it was a feature that progressive thinkers could not address explicitly, because it would have seemed to belie their claims to "value-free" science.

Progressivism was also a movement that sought to elevate scientific expertise to a controlling role and yet sought at the same time to introduce a new vitality into American democracy. The progressive era witnessed the introduction of the direct election of Senators, the establishment of procedures for voter referenda and recalls, the extension of the vote to women, and other democratic reforms. However, science is an elite enterprise that seeks objective truth—whatever popular opinion may say. Thus, at its very core the progressive governing scheme had two basic objectives in major conflict.

With hopes of resolving this tension, the progressives did proclaim a dichotomy in government between the domains of "administration" and of "politics." In concept, the former would be scientific and value-free, the latter democratic and the arena in which the overall goals of society would be set. Yet, in practice, American government seldom conformed to the progressive design. American political scientists would soon be making their careers by showing the major practical and theoretical inadequacies of the progressive prescription. In one of the most famous articles of post World War II social science, Charles Lindblom wrote of "The Science of 'Muddling Through'"—describing how government typically moved incrementally without any clear goals set in advance (25).

Created in the name of efficiency, public land agencies in practice gave little heed to efficiency. Part of the reason was that public land management proved in the event not to be scientific management but politicized management. The reality of a large role for democratic politics was finally recognized officially with the public participation and consultation requirements of the National Forest Management Act, FLPMA, and other legislation of the 1970s. It represented a formal victory for the actual practices of the previous decades—the formal triumph of "interest-group liberalism," as this approach to governing has been characterized by Theodore Lowi (26).

Just at this point, however, a new moral vision was asserting a growing power in American life. The environmental movement proclaimed new standards of proper management of the public lands. If interest-group liberalism (and scientific management before it) had emphasized the proce-

dures by which public land decisions were made, the environmental movement now was much more concerned with the actual substantive results
achieved on the land.

The moral vision of the environmental movement was often overtly hostile to the "gospel of efficiency." If Gifford Pinchot had advocated timber
harvesting and other intense commercial development of even national
park areas, such a prospect horrified environmentalists today. Indeed, in
wilderness areas the goal was to minimize the signs of human impact. The
American public increasingly looks to public lands as a place of educational
and spiritual uplift, not of the production of goods and services.

These changes have been nowhere more evident than in the public
forests of the Pacific Northwest. Driven by the requirement of the Endangered Species Act to preserve the northern spotted owl, timber harvesting
has been eliminated from large areas of these forests. Events are leading nationwide toward a much greater preservation mission for the future Forest
Service. The BLM is following in a similar direction, if less rapidly.

With the shift toward a preservation and ecological orientation, there is
today little logic or rationality to the division of lands and responsibilities
among federal land management agencies. Should the lands now being set
aside for spotted owl and other species preservation in the Pacific
Northwest be declared a wildlife refuge and placed under the management of the Fish and Wildlife Service? Administrative logic and consis-
tency of agency function would say yes, although history and politics at this
time say no.

All these developments raise an intriguing question: Although Congress
gave a strong formal blessing in the 1970s to the existing public land system,
could this mean that its days also are numbered? Congress has been slow in
the past to recognize new forces at work. Major shifts in public land policy
ironically have often followed formal Congressional ratifications of the
status quo—as when the Homestead Act of 1862 seemed to enshrine the
disposal philosophy of the 19th century, but actually inaugurated an era
ending with the abandonment of this philosophy.

The chances of large-scale changes in future public land policy are increased by the current budget woes of the federal government. In the face
of continuing strong pressures to find new revenues and/or to reduce
spending, it will be more difficult to justify the many subsidies of grazing,
recreation, timber harvesting, and other uses. The federal government may
well attempt to cover a larger share of its costs by charging higher fees from
users. Yet, if the flow of funds from the federal government declines significantly, user groups in western states may decide that the federal presence
is much less necessary. Federal money in the past has made up for the

annoyances of dealing with federal bureaucracy and oversight; this *quid pro quo* may no longer apply in the future.

Conclusion: Toward a New Paradigm for the Public Lands

The last period of fundamental change in the management of the public lands was the progressive era. A basic paradigm shift occurred, from the disposal philosophy of the 19th century to a new philosophy of government ownership and scientific management of the lands in the collective interest of all the people. The current era resembles the late 19th century in that the existing public land system is in a state of intellectual and political crisis. Perhaps one hundred years later, there will be yet another basic paradigm shift, offering a new vision to shape the public land system of the 21st century.

A new paradigm will probably have to include an abandonment of the idea that science is value-free. It will need to provide a better way to discuss issues of appropriate social values, because the choice of values today seems to lie at the heart of so many public land decisions. In the progressive model, the experts could simply assume that someone else provided the values—and implicitly there was an assumption that "good" values were not a big problem, that society would readily agree on some set of desirable goals.

The necessary mixing of expert and value considerations in public land management may further mean that the manner of application of the expertise of the forestry, economic, and other professions will have to be rethought. At present, they all tend to operate independently of one another, as if their knowledge and skills can be applied in a piecemeal fashion. In seeking to integrate knowledge from many areas, public land management in the future may have to devise new institutional mechanisms for blending disciplinary insights—to accomplish in its arena what, for example, the goal of "liberal arts" has been in the arena of college education.

If a new paradigm along these lines were to emerge, it would no doubt also involve new prescriptions for the organization of the federal lands. The centralized and bureaucratic structures of the current federal agencies have been shaped by the progressive concept of scientific management. Science establishes one truth, so the full application of science requires the dissemination of its truths from the center. Bureaucratic hierarchy reflects scientific hierarchy—the tendency for a limited number of elite individuals and institutions to dominate in establishing the one scientific truth. In another model of the world, where the critical decisions are more frequently value decisions, claims to authority will inevitably be more varied and dispersed. An explicit abandonment of the progressive paradigm of scientific management thus is likely to lead to a significantly greater decentralization in the management of public lands. It is even possible that for many of these lands the federal government will no longer have a large direct management role in the future.

All around the world, governments are at present privatizing poorly run state enterprises. The federal land management agencies have many of the same inefficiencies, suggesting that some of their lands as well might reasonably be examined for possible privatization. Decentralization of public land management could also mean a turn to management by existing state and local governments, or perhaps the creation of brand new institutional mechanisms at the local level. It might be appropriate to undertake a comprehensive classification of existing federal lands with the purpose to identify lands in several categories: (1) suitable for privatization, (2) suitable for state and local management, (3) suitable for continued federal management, and (4) suitable for management under other arrangements.

The sorting out of the various philosophical (if not theological), economic, administrative, and other forces for change will have to occur in the political process. And politics is, of course, never predictable. Yet, the need for a new public land paradigm and a new organizational structure for managing the federal lands is more widely recognized each year (27). A new paradigm might turn out to reflect something like the following: "the blending of inseparable moral and scientific elements in diverse ways to serve a world of growing value pluralism." Organizationally, a new structure to serve such a vision could well require a sharp decentralization of current federal authorities.

Notes

1. Data on federal land holdings are obtained from: Bureau of Land Management, U.S. Department of the Interior. 1992. Public land statistics. Washington, D.C., September.
2. See Clarke, J.N., and D. McCool. 1985. Staking out the terrain: power differentials among natural resource management agencies. Albany, New York: State University of New York Press.
3. Shands, W.E., and R.G. Healy. 1977. The lands nobody wanted. Washington, D.C.: Conservation Foundation.
4. See Bureau of Land Management, U.S. Department of the Interior. 1992. Fiscal year 1991 federal coal management report. Washington,

D.C.: October. See also Nelson, R.H. 1983. The making of federal coal policy. Durham, N.C.: Duke University Press.

5. The leading history of the public lands is Gates, P.W. 1968. History of public land law development. Washington, D.C.: Government Printing Office. See also Hibbard, B.H. 1964 [1924]. A history of the public land policies. Madison, Wisconsin: University of Wisconsin Press.; and Robbins, R.M. 1976 [1942]. Our landed heritage: the public domain, 1776–1970. Lincoln, Nebraska: University of Nebraska Press.

6. See Dana, S.T., and S.K. Fairfax. 1980. Forest and range policy: its development in the United States. New York: McGraw-Hill.

7. See Nelson, R.H. 1991. Reaching for heaven on earth: the theological meaning of economics. Lanham, Maryland: Rowman and Littlefield.

8. Hays, S.P. 1959. Conservation and the gospel of efficiency: the progressive conservation movement, 1890–1920, 265-266. Cambridge, Massachusetts: Harvard University Press.

9. Pinchot, G. 1947. Breaking new ground. New York: Harcourt Brace.

10. Cited in Pinchot, 261 (9).

11. Olson, S.H. 1971. The depletion myth: a history of railroad use of timber. Cambridge, Massachusetts: Harvard University Press.

12. Pinchot, 505 (9).

13. Schiff, A.L. 1962. Fire and water: scientific heresy in the forest service. Cambridge, Massachusetts: Harvard University Press.

14. Nelson, R.H. 1985. Mythology instead of analysis: the story of public forest management. In Forestlands: public and private. R.T. Deacon and M.B. Johnson, eds. San Francisco, California: Pacific Institute for Public Policy Research.

15. Fox, S. 1985. The American conservation movement: John Muir and his legacy. Madison, Wisconsin: University of Wisconsin Press.

16. Cited in Nash, R. 1973. Wilderness and the American mind, 125–126. New Haven, Connecticut: Yale University Press.

17. Ekirch, A.A. 1963. Man and nature in America, 52. New York: Columbia University Press.

18. National parks for the 21st century: the Vail agenda—report and recommendations to the director of the National Park Service. 1991. From the steering committee of the 75th anniversary symposium, 26. Vail, Colorado: October.

19. National parks, 26,31 (18).

20. National parks, 1,4 (18).

21. Gabrielson, I.N. 1943. Wildlife refuges, 8–9. New York: Macmillan Co.

22. Clawson, M. 1987. From sagebrush to sage: the making of a natural resource economist, 246. Washington, D.C.: Ana Publications.

23. Nelson, R.H. 1985. *NRDC v. Morton:* the role of judicial policy making in public rangeland management. Policy Studies Journal 14:2.

24. See Nelson, R.H. 1984. Why the sagebrush revolt burned out. Regulation May/June.

25. Lindblom, C.E. 1959. The science of "muddling through." Public Administration Review, Spring.

26. Lowi, T.J. 1969. The end of liberalism: ideology, policy, and the crisis of public authority. New York: Norton.

27. See comments of Frank Gregg and others. In Multiple use and sustained yield: changing philosophies for federal land management. Proceedings and Summary for a Workshop Convened on March 5 and 6, 1992, Washington, D.C., prepared by the Congressional Research Service—Committee Print No. 11 of the Committee of Interior and Insular Affairs, U.S. House of Representatives.

Chapter 3

Traditional Approaches and Tools in Natural Resources Management

Stanley H. Anderson

> . . . this scenery already rich, pleasing and beautiful was still further heightened by immense herds of buffalo, deer, elk, and antelope which we saw in every direction feeding on the hills and plains I do not think I exaggerate when I estimate the number of buffalo which could be comprehended at one view to amount to 3000. . . .
>
> —*Lewis and Clark Journal*
> Along the Missouri River, near the Nebraska, South Dakota border

In the late 1400s, John Cabot landed on Newfoundland's northern coast. At this time, about 500 years after Lief Erickson's settlement in the same area and five years following Columbus' first voyage, Cabot noted the mast-sized trees that came to the water's edge. He also marveled at the abundance of salmon, large sole, and codfish that could be caught in a basket over the side of his ship. Later, his son, Sebastian Cabot, was to report that fish were so abundant in this area that they slowed up the advance of ships (1).

Shortly after Cabot's return to Europe, word spread rapidly of the abundance of natural resources off the North American continental coast. Within a few years, 350 to 400 vessels were visiting these areas each year to catch and process fish. At the same time, settlers began to dot the coastline of eastern North America. They cleared forests, harvested wildlife, and planted crops. Wood products were used for virtually everything from boat and house building material to fuel.

In addition, early settlers found that they could obtain a variety of foods from the plants along the coastline. Fifty species of nut-bearing plants and more than 200 species of trees, bushes, vines, and small fruits were commonly used. Settlers soon learned from the Native Americans to grow corn, climbing beans, pumpkins, gourds, and melons (2).

In the 1700s, the middle and western parts of the continent were traversed by explorers such as Lewis and Clark, thus opening the way for settlers. As the United States continued to develop, the railroad cut across the nation's extensive grasslands. At the same time, the western part of the

United States, which had been sparsely inhabited, saw a large influx of people. The movement of European settlers into this area had a dramatic impact on both the vegetation and the wildlife. For example, Europeans introduced domesticated livestock. While Columbus reportedly left domestic stock, including horses and sheep, in the West Indies, it was not until 1515 that Cortez landed in Mexico, bringing horses and cattle to the continent of North America (3).

When the settlers from the East came to the Mississippi Valley, in about 1830, and merged with people moving up from the south, a range-livestock industry was developed. Apparently unlimited forage created a major boom during the Civil War years. Following the Civil War, miners, soldiers, trappers, and others pushed westward, and cattlemen increased in numbers. At the same time, farmers found this area to be productive for a variety of marketable crops. Thus, they came westward interested in tilling the ground, fencing the area, and developing communities. By the late 1800s, most of the Midwest was either under cultivation or in some form of livestock grazing.

Settlers found western mountains (including the Rocky Mountains) to be ideal sources of lumber and used this resource as if it were inexhaustible. Miners and railroad workers began extensive logging. Trappers moved westward. Beaver and other furbearers were eagerly taken for their pelts. Settlers hunted antelope, bison, elk, and deer in large numbers. Unlike European countries in which wildlife were used for sport and considered a luxury for the rich, wildlife in the New World became an integral part of daily life. This resulted in three major impacts on North American animal communities.

First, people used wildlife for commercial purposes. Fur- and feather-bearing animals became a source of revenue when it was discovered that Native Americans would trade for their pelts and plumes. Furs were also sent back East and to Europe to supply an ever increasing market.

Second, people began to exploit the resources on which the wildlife depended for survival. Increased soil erosion from improper farming practices contributed to sediment damage downstream in rivers and reservoirs, affecting the fish and other wildlife species associated with the river. People began to encroach on the ecologically valuable wetlands, destroying wildlife habitat, reducing the ability of land to retain rainfall, and contributing to flood damage in the process. Wind erosion increased as farmers plowed away much of the native grass. This effect culminated in the dust bowl of the 1930s.

Third, sport hunters and bird enthusiasts began to demand that natural resources be available for their use. At this time, major efforts to manage the resources began. The true environmental movement, however, did not become well established in the United States until the mid to later part of the 20th century. It was at that time, through a growing awareness of the decline of our natural resources and the pollution of air and water, that people began to press in earnest for better controls and management of our natural resources.

Exploitation of Natural Resources

Our natural resources are communities of living organisms interacting among themselves and with the physical components of their environment. As natural communities change over time, the types of resources (trees, grasses, wildlife) change in an area. Likewise different physical factors (moisture, sunlight, altitude) shape communities on a global basis (4). Natural resources are used by people for recreation, food, and lodging. People enjoy hunting, fishing, wildlife viewing, and hiking. Grasses and shrubs are consumed by livestock which are, in turn, eaten by people. Humans use timber as fuel for warmth and as material to build houses.

Harvest is probably the most profound impact people have on natural communities. For example, commercial forestry practices remove (arguably in an unsustainable fashion) large numbers of trees. "Modern" practices add to the loss of forests started by the early settlers.

In grasslands, grazing, as well as farming, has changed the natural composition of shrubs and grasses. Grazers only snip the top off vegetation, which causes minimal impact if managed properly. However, when the vegetation is cropped too short, fields are unable to recover and are ultimately destroyed.

People remove wildlife through hunting and fishing. Big game populations were, historically, managed for hunters. In this tradition, we have effectively removed many predators, like wolves, and controlled others, such as coyotes. We have altered our streams so that many of the native fishes are gone, and we now operate hatcheries to stock streams with a variety of exotic game species. These types of actions have altered natural communities to the point that some populations undergo catastrophic changes.

Resources may be classified as *renewable* or *nonrenewable*. Typically, renewable resources are those that can replace themselves. Trees, shrubs, grasses, wildlife, and fishes are all considered renewable resources if we remove only some of their annual production. There are, however, many nonrenewable resources. Soils and minerals are two that are not replaceable in ecological time. Constantly removing vegetation from even the most fertile areas of North America depletes the soil nutrients and changes the community structure which, in turn, affects biological diversity. Thus, it is important to evaluate any removal of renewable or nonrenewable resources.

It was assumed for many years that vegetation and wildlife were renewable natural resources simply because they were alive and capable of reproducing. Natural populations do indeed renew themselves, providing the conditions within the natural system remain stable for reproduction and growth (5). If conditions become unsuitable, through pollution, habitat conversion, or other human activities, then the ability of a population to renew itself may be lost.

Sustained Yield as Dominant Paradigm of Traditional Natural Resource Management

Sustained yield is an important concept that has formed the basis for traditional resource management. It is the concept that natural resources (forests, wildlife, grasslands) can produce continuously under a given intensity of management. In other words, renewable resources can provide continuous production. To accomplish sustained yield, managers must determine the balance between reproduction and removal. Sustained yield can be applied to a local population or on a broad scale. In wildlife and fisheries, it is necessary to look at the local populations. Range managers and foresters sometimes look at regional systems.

In reality, sustained yield means that population surplus is being harvested by humans. In the case of forests, regeneration of new trees must be initiated in the harvested area. This can be done naturally or by planting. In grasslands, sustained yield means identifying the threshold below which the grasses cannot retain enough nutrients to survive. In fisheries and wildlife, managers must look to find the number of animals of each sex necessary to allow an adequate breeding stock. The amount of biomass or the number of organisms harvested can vary based on the assessment of managers. They, in effect, can control the size of the population by increasing or reducing harvest.

Sustained yield can be examined using fishing as an example. To obtain the maximum number of fish from a population on a sustained basis, we need to know the number of fish we can remove. If we underfished a population, fish production would exceed resource availability; some would die, or all would be stunted in size. Natural mortality factors would take over. If we overfished the population, we would cause the breeding stock to decline and thus reduce the population. Overfishing can lead to behavioral changes so that schools of fish no longer exist. This alters the entire social structure and reproductive behavior. In wildlife, underharvesting may mean that there are more animals for predators to eat or animals for recreationists to view. When forests or grasslands are underharvested, it means that downed trees and decaying grass accumulate, creating conditions for wildfires.

The goal of the fishing industry, then, is to establish a sustained yield. Closed seasons, catch quotas, nets with large mesh size, and maximum fish size can help achieve a sustained yield. This concept of sustained yield also applies to hunting, removal of forest products, and the use of grasslands for grazing. Theoretically, once we determine what the optimal intensity of removal is for a stock, we can develop and continually use that particular resource. If we go to the point of overexploitation, however, we have a negative impact on the total natural system. The concept of sustained yield has been the foundation for most natural resource management in the 20th century.

Methods of Traditional Natural Resource Management

Disciplines have developed around management of forests, grasslands, and wildlife. Techniques involve manipulation of the resource to preserve or supply products on a sustained basis.

Forests

Foresters originally directed their thinking toward harvest of trees for use in wood products. Forestry management then took on the perspective of harvesting timber and regeneration of new trees to replace the ones removed. In an ideal situation, timber removal should mimic natural processes, in which succession and sustained yield are planned in a fashion that allows forests to regenerate the same amount of timber removed. This is not always possible in a society that relies on economics to spur the management of forests (6).

Management of forests for timber requires an understanding of such variables as temperature, rainfall, soil type, and tree species. These variables interact to dictate growing time and the methods and period during which forests may be cut. Foresters often classify even-aged stands by their stage of development. They arrange them in increasing size categories: seedlings, saplings, pole, mature, and overmature (7). Seedling stands are recently disturbed stands in which the new trees are usually less than three feet tall. On the other hand, sapling stands have trees up to four inches in diameter. Pole stands have trees between four and 10 inches in diameter. The size range of the mature stands varies according to species and location. Overmature are trees that exceeded their value for foresters. Often these have many dead or dying branches with broken trunks.

The most common methods of harvesting timber are even-aged and un-even-aged removal. In even-aged stands, large or small plots of similar sized trees are cut. If all the trees are about the same age, clearcutting (complete timber removal) can occur. This presumably allows the open plots to be re-generated through seed dispersed by wind, birds, and other means. It cre-ates edge, which alters existing wildlife habitat. To achieve sustained yield in even-aged timber management, consider a simple example. A land owner has 50 acres of forest that takes 50 years to mature to harvestable timber. He can then remove one acre of timber per year. In other words, he would have 50 stands of equal productivity. Foresters refer to this as rotational age—the time from the harvest of one plot to the next. In this case, the rotational age is 50 years.

In reality, the age of forest stands in natural forests is not uniform but has trees of different age class based on physical variables of that particular area. Ecological processes, such as forest-gap formation, further diversify a forest stand. There is probably a 20- to 30-year difference in even-aged stands simply because the forest is dynamic, in a state of continual growth and decay.

In uneven-aged stands, shrubs and tree seedlings are mixed in a stand with different size classes of trees. The understory development begins to accelerate, and the mature trees begin to die, resulting in a variety of gaps. To accomplish uneven-aged management, foresters selectively cut trees in a stand. They may cut all trees larger than a certain size class and leave a mixture of smaller trees. Sometimes large forests are cut at intervals. For ex-ample, every five years, foresters may cut all trees that have grown to a cer-tain size class. The time between major cuts is called a cutting cycle (8). Un-even-aged management can also be viewed on a landscape or watershed level. Small clearcuts may be done at different times throughout a forest. Thus, the forest is in different stages of regeneration at all times.

Under natural conditions, trees are a mix of age classes. The natural forest is a mixture of most seral stages of plant succession with gaps in each stage from blowdowns or fires. Some argue that this dynamic is better at keeping the diversity of the forest and reducing susceptibility to disease. Forestry practices have historically tried to minimize this natural state.

Whether the practices are of even-aged or uneven-aged management, once trees are removed, natural regeneration often occurs. Problems arise when topsoil erodes away, such as when steep slopes are clearcut, and topsoil washes down into the river systems. When conditions are right, natural regeneration can occur very quickly. In a matter of years, seeds are carried by wind or animals from forests into adjacent, cut areas. Soil, aspect, moisture, and temperature all contribute to successful regeneration. In the eastern deciduous forests, regeneration generally occurs quite rapidly. In the more arid areas, regeneration is slower and often requires some assistance.

Foresters have developed a number of methods of artificial regeneration. In some cases, they simply seed an area knowing this will assist forest regeneration. The seeds can be spread directly then covered with mulch to maintain the moisture while they are taking hold. In other cases, such as tree farms, foresters plant seedlings and till them in rows.

Fires have been a major tool used to manage forests. Early foresters burned forests to clear the understory along areas to be accessible for logging. Today, fires are more commonly used to clear debris following timber harvest. Generally, foresters want a hot, rapid burn to eliminate as much of the dead debris as possible. The forester needs the fire to move rapidly, burning off downed vegetation and debris and sparing the trees. When fire is used in the management process, it is called a prescribed burn. The most common objectives are reduction of logging debris or litter (fuel) accumulation, preparation of a seed bed, or control of the understory vegetation.

Wildfires were historically listed as having disastrous effects on forests because they often destroyed people's homes and were perceived to destroy forests. As a result, we went through a period where all fires were suppressed. Debris built up in many areas, and conditions developed in which fires were very difficult to control. An example was the Yellowstone fire of 1988. Debris that had accumulated for years burned for months. Today foresters see small prescribed burns as a means to manage forests and reduce chances of wildfire.

Forest managers use a number of methods to increase the growth rate of desired trees. Manipulating tree species composition is one option, but it can be difficult. Each forest usually has several species of trees dependent on a certain amount of shade, moisture, and soil. In some cases, succession allows undesirable species to dominate, and these species quickly regenerate when cut. The standard treatment of "release cutting" improves composition of the desirable species when trees are young and still capable of responding. Release cutting frees targeted seedlings and saplings from competition with more opportunistic, unwanted species (9). An example is the removal of hardwoods from conifer stands. Later cuts may be necessary to remove poorly formed trees to ensure the stands have the best quality trees.

When forests are so thick that large, mature trees are unable to grow, a form of prescribed *thinning* is initiated. Usually a local logging outfit confers with forest managers to cut a number of trees and use them for pulp or other products. This allows some of the trees to grow larger and be made available for other wood products in great demand.

Foresters often tried to improve the quality of soil by adding fertilizers or needed nutrients in order to enhance the growth of the trees. This was frequently done before seeding to help the young plants take hold. While not common in forestry practices, other chemicals have been used to accelerate tree growth as an intermediate management technique.

Forestry involves more than just growing trees. By law, the United States Forest Service must consider multiple uses: logging, recreation, wildlife, grazing, and other potential uses of the forest. To maintain a forest for multiple use, it is necessary at times to allow forests that would otherwise be cut to grow, or to cut forests of younger age classes that would normally be exempted. In some ways, the concept of multiple use is contrary to that of sustained yield. Given this, forests are deterred from their continual productivity of wood for consumption. Old growth must be left for wildlife. Recreation in forests requires removal of downed vegetation.

Grasslands

As ranchers began to graze cattle and sheep in the Great Plains of the United States, they initially enjoyed an unrestricted use of the area. Cattle were allowed to roam the plentiful grass. As settlers moved in, cattlemen fenced off regions to keep their cattle in check. They found that certain characteristics, such as the type and growth rate of grass, affected the number of cattle that could be put on an area. The growth rate was mainly dependent on climate and water.

During severe winters, it was necessary to bring cattle into feed yards and supply them with hay cut from rangelands. From the early procedure of simply letting cattle roam until round-up, the science of range management developed. One force that caused the development of range management was the realization that the grasslands did not provide an inexhaustible supply of forage. The concept of sustained yield was explored. Coupled with the influx of people, some seeking recreation or wanting to farm, grasslands became areas of multiple use.

Range management, therefore, was the manipulation of rangeland components to obtain an optimal combination of goods and service for society on a sustained basis (10). Range management generally was approached through the protection of the soil/vegetation complex and improvement and maintenance of consumable range products. Different methods were developed to provide a consistent supply of herbage for livestock. Under high moisture conditions, cattle and sheep selected different varieties of plants that varied by season. It was necessary to adjust the number of cattle to suit range growing conditions. In other areas it was found that continuous grazing reduced the total amount of available forage. Ranchers began to rotate their stock between pastures, developing several different types of rotation systems. Principle among these were *deferred rotation* and *rest rotation* (11).

Deferred rotation kept livestock from grazing in pastures until seeds of key forage plants matured. Rest rotation is distinguished from deferred rotation in that the range goes unused for a period of time (usually a full year) rather than just during the growth period of some plants. This gives plants a longer period of time to recover from grazing. Both systems require an understanding of the carrying capacity or number of livestock that the system (all pastures combined) can support. Overgrazing in one or all pastures results in preventing use of the pastures for extended periods.

In the United States, a variety of deferred and rest rotation systems are used (12). These systems all require some form of division of the rangelands into different pastures. Depending on the system or the need, cattle can be moved from one pasture to another, thereby reducing impact on one area. Each area with its particular climatic conditions and moisture will benefit from different forms of grazing systems. Therefore, there is no single system that can be classified as ideal. If ranchers are to benefit the most from this system, they will look for the best rotation plan in relation to the whole concept of sustained yield as it applies to their operation.

Fencing is used by ranchers to manage and distribute their animals in order to maintain an adequate supply of grass. In winter, or years of poor moisture, supplemental feeding may be necessary, particularly in the arid plains of the north central part of the country. In these areas fields are set aside to grow hay. The hay must be cut and stacked so it is available when needed.

Range fertilization is common when soils lack some essential minerals. Minerals may be naturally low or below optimum because of natural conditions, erosion, or heavy grazing. In addition, some forms of fertilizers, such as nitrogen, make some plant species attractive to grazing animals by increasing the plant's protein content.

Prescribed burning is sometimes used in rangeland to improve grazing or to remove plant growth from previous years. If litter builds up on top of the soil, some plant growth may be retarded, or new plant species may become dominant. The decomposition process changes as litter piles up, changing the characteristics of the vegetation. At times the variety of vegetation that occurs with litter accumulation is desirable. In such cases, ranchers use strip burns, which promote different forms of vegetation.

Vegetation along riparian communities and wetlands often attracts livestock because of water, shade, and lush foliage. These areas are critical for wildlife and assist in retaining the water quality of an area. Heavy livestock use of riparian areas results in trampled vegetation, causing erosion and an eventual drop in the water table. Riparian zones have been rehabilitated in a number of areas of high livestock concentration. Different grazing systems have been used, such as rest or short-term rotation, to prevent livestock from overusing riparian systems. In other cases, fencing was used to allow access only at selected points along a waterway.

Generally, ranchers evaluate each rangeland, look at the potential for cattle, and determine the number of cattle that can use the area. Ranchers may adjust the number of head of cattle that can use rangeland, year to year, based on moisture. When moisture is high, vegetation grows more rapidly, enabling heavier use. On the other hand, during drought years, the number of cattle should be reduced. In evaluating land use, ranchers should consider the amount of forage available, the amount needed for the grazing animal to allow the pasture to remain in good condition, and impacts of the wildlife that can consume large quantities of the forage.

Wildlife

Wildlife are often impacted by many forms of natural resource management that alter habitat. In addition, wildlife are affected by urbanization and other human activities such as oil and gas development. There are two main types of management: *single-species* and *community* management. Traditionally, managers have focused on single-species management; however, community management with the concept of biodiversity has become more popular in recent years (13).

Single-species management evolved because early forms of wildlife management consisted of encouraging desirable species to multiply or undesirable species to decline. When it was perceived that desirable species were declining, managers began to examine methods to enhance populations. Early efforts were mostly preservation of the natural community and enforcement of hunting regulations. Thus, wetlands and forests were retained to supply game species. Regulations were put into effect to provide legal protection for wildlife in decline. Early wildlife regulations were almost exclusively related to a single species. The federal government was given the responsibility to regulate migratory birds and developed partnerships with the states to set migratory game bird regulations. States assumed the responsibility to regulate nonmigratory species such as game birds and big game. Eventually states assumed responsibility for managing and regulating all wildlife except migratory birds and endangered species.

Regulations were based on population estimates. If population numbers were low, regulations prevented the removal of any animals. If the managers wanted a constant breeding stock, they allowed for the removal of surplus animals. In cases where trophy animals were desired, specific requirements were imposed such as the size of antlers. In waterfowl, managers developed an elaborate point system allowing hunters to accumulate only so many points, corresponding with set categories of waterfowl, during a season. More points were given to the sex or species that the managers wanted to preserve, so that the hunters removed fewer of these individuals (13). When managers wanted to reduce numbers of animals (such as deer causing damage), they allowed hunting of females and young.

Fishing is also a form of single-species management. Seasons are set that allow the removal of fish that reach a certain size. The number of fish that a fisherman may take is based on what the manager feels the system can produce and still have a breeding stock. Unfortunately, fishing pressure in many areas has reduced the breeding stock so it can no longer provide a sustained yield. In addition, fishermen also like to fish in some areas where fish cannot survive the winter. Lakes may freeze causing winter kill. As a result, a very expensive form of management—the fish hatchery—has evolved. Hatcheries raise fish and release them into water for recreation. Fish managers have found that many exotic species survive better than native species, so most fish placed in our waterways are nonnative.

Another form of early single-species management that continues today is predator control. As people began to move into an area, demands to control predators increased. Wolves were shot and extirpated from most of their historic range. In some areas they were replaced by coyotes, which adapt easily to living around people. Extensive predator control programs were organized by the federal government beginning in the 1800s, and continue to the present time. These removal programs, including shooting and poisoning, have reduced many predators. In some cases, misinformed individuals will shoot predators that actually provide a great benefit. Raptors, in particular, tend to keep small mammal populations down. Small mammals, if uncontrolled, will grow to large numbers and consume much of the grass foliage. This means less food for livestock and other wildlife species.

Endangered species management is also a form of single-species management. In cases where a species has declined to such a level that it is in danger of extinction, it can receive special protection from the federal government. Biologists tended to look at habitat enhancement as a key method of managing endangered species. For example, the grizzly bear was a species threatened with extinction due to habitat alterations and one that habitat enhancement could potentially assist and protect. Some species lend themselves to captive breeding programs. The black-footed ferret has benefited from this program to the extent that groups of individuals are now being reintroduced in the wild. In other cases, special types of techniques need to be developed. For example, power lines are a major cause of mortality in whooping cranes. In certain key areas, power lines are now marked with aviation marker balls, thereby reducing the collision rate.

Managers may encourage desired species by providing nesting sites, such as for waterfowl. Refuges often plant preferred foods in fields. Where desired species cannot maintain their breeding stock, agencies may breed animals for release. Thus, bird farms raise quail, pheasant, and other game birds for the hunters.

Single-species management involves maintaining individual species. If one looks at traditional wildlife management, this is the type of effort that managers have undertaken for many years. In the case of some game species, the entire species is maintained as a hunting resource. If the animals were not hunted, they would expand and destroy the range. This is primarily true because the predators that normally keep the animals in check are no longer found.

While some people want to define the activity as "good" or "bad" for wildlife, it is really a question of desirable species. If we want particular species of wildlife, we must ensure usable habitat. If we want a diversity of wildlife, a diversity of habitat must be available.

By the late 1900s, people began to change how wildlife was managed as they realized how interconnected the entire community was. As a result, it became more common to look at community management for wildlife, within which a number of concepts were developed. Community structure was maintained along with a diversity of communities themselves, in order to maintain the greatest number of wildlife species. The edge between two different communities offers increased diversity by including animals from both communities.

Threats

Major threats to our natural resource management today stem principally from a lack of understanding of natural community dynamics, an ignorance of sustained yield concepts, and finally, the continuous loss of nonrenewable resources. Each biome requires a different management approach. We are learning that forestry practices initiated in the eastern deciduous forest may not apply in the intermountain West where soil nutrients differ. Wetlands are important not only for fish and waterbird productivity, but essential during the migration of many birds.

If a diversity of reasonably sized habitats is maintained, other natural activities in the community, such as succession, competition, and predator–prey interactions, will likely occur. These areas must have controlled access to prevent people from being disruptive. While plants normally can sustain themselves, animals become acclimated to people and so form a different type of wildlife community.

The sustained yield concept has perhaps been the key to natural resource management as we have understood it in this century. But, as people push the system to its limits and increasingly ignore the concept of sustained yield, populations of trees, grass, and wildlife will continue to decline. This opens the way for an increase in some less desirable species that can adapt well to humans.

. . .

Natural resource management is an elaborate science that requires knowledge of how our natural systems operate. We must plan and set goals to function within the natural system, or suffer the consequences. If we practice sound resource management, we can provide a sustainable supply of natural resources and a place for people to live in union with the natural system.

Notes

1. Morison, S.E. 1971. The European discovery of America. In The European northern voyages, A.D. 500–1600. New York: Oxford University Press. 712 pp.
2. Kimball, T.L., and R.E. Johnson. 1978. The richness of American wildlife. In Wildlife in America. H.P. Brokaw, ed. 3–17. Washington, D.C.: Council on Environmental Quality. 532 pp.
3. Stoddart, L.A., and A.D. Smith. 1955. Range management. New York: McGraw-Hill. 433 pp.
4. Anderson, S.H., R.E. Beiswenger, and P.W. Purdom. 1993. Environmental science. New York: MacMillan. 488 pp.
5. Dasmann, R.E. 1975. Wildlife and ecosystems. In Wildlife in America. H.P. Brokaw, ed. 18–27. Washington, D.C.: American Council on Environmental Quality. 532 pp.
6. Leuschner, W.A., H. Wisdon, and W.D. Klemperer. 1990. Timber

management. In Introduction to forest sciences. R.A. Young and R.L. Giese, eds. 326–339. New York: John Wiley and Sons.

7. Lorimir, C.G. 1990. Silviculture. In Introduction to forest sciences. R.A. Young and R.L. Giese, eds. 300–325. New York: John Wiley and Sons.

8. Leushner et al. 1990 (6).

9. Lorimir 1990 (7).

10. Holechek, J.L., R.D. Pieper, and C.H. Herbel. 1989. Range management. Englewood Cliffs, New Jersey: Prentice Hall. 501 pp.

11. Heimlich, R.E., and A.B. Daugherty. 1991. America's cropland: where does it come from? In Agriculture and the environment, 3–9. The 1991 Yearbook of Agriculture. Washington, D.C.: Superintendent of Documents. 532 pp.

12. Holechek et al. 1989 (10).

13. Anderson, S.H. 1991. Managing our wildlife resource. Englewood Cliffs, New Jersey: Prentice Hall. 492 pp.

Chapter 4

Traditional Education in Natural Resources

Dale Hein

> Half of what you are taught as students will in ten years have been shown
> to be wrong, and the trouble is, none of your teachers know which half.
> —C. Sidney Burwell

America's intellectual declaration of independence was proclaimed in 1837 by Ralph Waldo Emerson in his renowned address, *The American Scholar*, given to the Phi Beta Kappa Society of Harvard College. Emerson argued that American scholarship should reflect the spirit of a new, self-confident democracy, rather than imitate old-world academies.

This call to innovate fostered fresh models of higher education and invited new fields of study that were especially relevant in a new land. Both public and private colleges proliferated. Anyone could aspire to college, and access became a tenet of higher education in America.

The Morrill Act of 1862 provided federal land grants to endow academic institutions offering instruction in "such branches of learning as are related to agriculture and mechanic arts" and promoting "liberal and practical education of the industrial classes in the pursuits and professions of life." These public land grant colleges subsequently produced many of the leading programs of study in natural resources, although private universities such as Yale and Duke were also early leaders in forestry education.

How did natural resources education emerge and grow in this climate of freedom, innovation, open doors, and applied studies in American colleges? The "Harvard influence" was preeminent. Louis Agassiz (1807–1873) dominated biology in 19th century America. In 1848, this Swiss-American naturalist was named professor of zoology and geology at Harvard, a vantage point that he used to exert enormous influence on academic appointments and on what paradigms would rule biology. Agassiz staunchly opposed evolution, and he inculcated biology with the importance of comparative descriptions of an immutable living world. However, he also gained legitimacy, even primacy, for natural history among the sciences in America.

Asa Gray (1810–1888) was a physician turned naturalist, who left the University of Michigan for Harvard in 1842. There he became Agassiz's colleague, protégé, rival, and counterpoint, vigorously defending Darwinism. Gray dominated systematic botany and defined the main task of biologists as describing, classifying, and preserving the biota.

Agassiz and Gray left two legacies for traditional curricula that would soon emerge for natural resources. The first was a preoccupation with taxonomy and identification. Study skins, pressed plants, and pickled fish filled our laboratory courses. The second was license to pursue our passion for natural history. Guide books, binoculars, notebooks, vasculum, and boots were scientific tools! Furthermore, the spirited, public debate between Agassiz and Gray over Darwinism must have helped scholars see the value of criticism and dissent, that biology was unfinished, and that more scientific inquiry was needed.

Establishment of Natural Resources Curricula

Education in natural resources arose from an expanding interest in nature and from efforts to develop and exploit nature's riches. College courses, first in fisheries, then in forestry, appeared around 1900, followed by range science in the 1920s and wildlife management in the 1930s. Courses in management of other natural resources followed.

Use preceded education in fisheries. Leif Erickson was seeking fishing grounds when he landed on the northeast coast a thousand years ago. Soon after John Cabot reported abundant cod off Newfoundland in 1497, enormous catches from the Grand Banks began feeding Europe's appetite for fish. Immigrants brought fish culture to America, and by 1865 Ohio and Connecticut had state fish hatcheries.

Fisheries education is rooted most strongly in ichthyology of the 18th and 19th centuries, first by Europeans, then in studies of taxonomy, life histories, and distributions of fishes by Americans, such as Agassiz, his student Charles F. Girard, and coauthor Spencer Baird, who later started the U.S. Fish Commission. The "golden age" of ichthyology culminated with the work of David Starr Jordan during 1880–1920. This "father of fisheries" authored 600 publications, won the Nobel Peace Prize, and was president of Stanford University for 24 years. The new science flourished.

The emphasis on science and research in fisheries education was strongly influenced by early limnology. Stephen Forbes established an ecosystem emphasis with his 1887 essay, *The Lake as a Microcosm,* and he founded a freshwater biological station for the Illinois Natural History Survey in 1894.

From 1895 to 1940, the limnological studies of E.A. Birge and Chancey Juday at the University of Wisconsin strongly reinforced the research emphasis in fisheries in American universities. The early limnological work provided the ecological knowledge of nutrient cycling, energy transfers, and environmental influences that were needed to teach management of fish for harvestable yields.

The first curriculum to train professional fisheries biologists was under John Cobb at the School of Fisheries of the University of Washington in 1919. The field grew under research professors, such as Carl Hubbs at University of Michigan, H.S. Swingle and E.V. Smith at Auburn, and K.D. Carlander at Iowa State. In the 1950s, new books on fisheries management included Kenneth Carlander's *Handbook of Freshwater Fishery Biology* (1950), Karl Lagler's *Freshwater Fishery Biology* (1952), W.E. Ricker's *Handbook of Computations for Biological Statistics of Fish Populations* (1958), and the first text book, *Fishery Science, Its Methods and Applications* (1953) by G.A. Rounsfel and W.E. Everhart. Throughout, the main goal was to teach how to manage fish for maximum sustained yield of harvest, later modified to include optimum yields, with innovative measurements, such as recreational days by anglers.

Forestry education had the greatest impact among natural resources disciplines. Gifford Pinchot was truly the "father" of this field in America, founding the Yale School of Forestry in 1900. Pinchot had studied silviculture in Europe and later established the first forest management system on the private Biltmore Forest in North Carolina. He served on the Forest Commission of the National Academy of Science that recommended the preserves that became our national forests. From these experiences, Pinchot's forestry stressed inventory, management, national forests, and wise use. Consequently, from the start, the curricula emphasized mensuration, protection against fire, economics, silviculture, and timber harvesting.

Yale provided the model for most of the forestry curricula in America. Soon, a dozen more universities had established programs, often as separate schools. This autonomy within universities and one dominant model (Pinchot's) were important in establishing a traditional forestry curriculum as the most influential paradigm for natural resource education in America.

Wildlife education developed later and was most diverse. Aldo Leopold was clearly the "father" of wildlife education. Modern wildlife management began in 1933 with Leopold's text *Game Management* and with professorships and fellowships that Leopold persuaded private industry to establish at four universities—Wisconsin, Michigan, Iowa State, and Minnesota. Unlike forestry, no single model prevailed. Wildlife programs emerged within agriculture, biology, forestry, and zoology.

Cooperative Wildlife Research Units were established at 15 universities in the 1930s and subsequently increased to more than 30 units by 1990, often with companion Cooperative Fisheries Research Units. These units featured research and graduate education. They were funded mainly by the U.S. Fish and Wildlife Service with state wildlife agencies, universities, and private sources contributing. Surprisingly, this federal presence in universities did little to unify wildlife education. The administration of units by committees, zealous independence of many unit leaders, concentration on research, and negligible involvement with undergraduate programs, all limited the influence of units in colleges.

More than 85 percent of all natural resources students have majored in wildlife, forestry, or fisheries. Other majors in natural resources frequently were adjuncts to these. Range science/management often arose as an option in agriculture. At the University of California at Davis, Arthur W. Sampson's 1923 text, *Range Management*, was seminal. Curricula in outdoor recreation often developed in the 1950s and 1960s as options in wildlife majors or from physical education programs. Occasionally such programs as watersheds, marine biology, conservation education, landscape architecture, geology, and agriculture are grouped with wildlife, forestry, or fisheries in academic units.

Strategies of Natural Resources Education

First, a caveat: I believe the following views are largely applicable in 1995. However, by 1987, many educators and students perceived some of the changes that were needed in the traditional education in natural resources. The status and need for educational reform is not the same everywhere, and changes are occurring now.

Perhaps every natural resources college or major could claim a unique philosophy. However, one of two broad ideologies usually predominates. One approach prepares students for employment as managers of a natural resource with *prescribed* coursework that emphasizes extracting, providing, or creating products and/or experiences from the Earth in accordance with the demands of the perceived owners, often the general public. Such a prescribed curriculum may require courses in many fields, particularly as prerequisites for specialized management courses in the major discipline. Rigor and structure characterize the program.

The other strategy adopts a different means to achieve similar goals for a professional career. A curriculum with this second approach is often less structured, mainly because the school sees a greater responsibility for employers to provide specific training for whatever natural resources job the student obtains. Consequently, the coursework appears more liberal, often with more electives and fewer courses required within the major. Actually, these *general* curricula seldom require a truly liberal education with arts, humanities, social sciences, languages, and natural sciences equally important. Students in general curricula in natural resources are often encouraged to use their abundant electives to complete minors related to their major or to pursue additional specialized coursework.

Western universities are "ranger factories" graduating managers for national forests, parks, wildlife refuges, and BLM districts, and for state fish and game departments. Rates of professional employment of graduates measure the success of curricula. Technical skills for entry-level jobs dominate course work. Most students have one or more summer jobs with agencies, often as a major requirement. Courses at field camps often emphasize species identification, mapping, inventory methods, and measurements of physical environment, such as climate and weather, stream flows, site factors, and soil features.

Eastern and midwestern universities offer less structured and more general coursework, especially in wildlife and fisheries. In the East and Midwest, basic sciences outweigh management. Field courses at biological stations are as common as forestry summer camps.

Forestry education is more uniform nationwide and is highly driven by job requirements. Professional employment is a goal in all natural resources disciplines, but it controls curricula most in western schools and in forestry. Range management belongs almost exclusively to western schools with a philosophy similar to forestry.

While one or the other competing strategies of prescribed versus general education somewhat characterized regions or particular disciplines, by the 1970s two other priorities competed in virtually every natural resource curriculum. Should a baccalaureate or a graduate degree culminate a natural resources education? Many of the schools with applied, technical, undergraduate programs also developed successful graduate programs featuring both applied and basic research. Other schools with graduate programs offered undergraduate studies largely as preparation for graduate school. Efforts to channel individuals into an early choice between a management or a research curriculum leading to graduate school often failed, because goals and performance of many undergraduates changed later in their college years.

Two-year curricula for technicians and correspondence courses in wildlife flourished from the 1950s into the 1970s and then withered. There were too many graduates from 4-year accredited colleges winning the jobs in highly competitive natural resources fields. A few 2-year programs survived, mainly in the northeast. In that region, many of the 4-year programs of study in natural resources were small but highly selective in admissions, at prestigious universities such as Yale, Cornell, Syracuse, Pennsylvania State, and Massachusetts. Therefore, 2-year, technical programs at smaller colleges with easier admissions standards remained a noncompeting alternative for different students.

Themes in Traditional Natural Resources Education

What themes dominate natural resources education in the mid-1990s? The same themes persist a half century after natural resources education claimed to have entered a modern era.

We teach intervention management to benefit humans. We teach how to identify and manipulate proximate factors to achieve human goals, which predominantly (not exclusively) feature the consumptive use of products from the Earth. We use empirical examples to verify the management practices that we teach. For example, we instruct how to increase distribution and abundance of wood ducks by citing successes with artificial nest boxes. We instruct how to increase carrying capacity of ranges for cattle by citing the success of chaining to remove shrubs that compete with grass.

Teddy Roosevelt's Conservation Doctrine permeates natural resources education: *Science offers the tools with which we fulfill a public duty to manage multiple natural resources for optimum values to humans.* According to our textbooks, conservation as wise *use*, more than preservation of options, should determine management. I believe that this Conservation Doctrine captures the dominant philosophy of traditional education in natural resources.

Increasingly, we also teach a Conservation Ethic, based largely on Aldo Leopold's (1948) *A Sand County Almanac* and a few other safe writers within the natural resources professions (e.g., Paul Errington, Jack Ward Thomas, et al.). These may emphasize a love of nature, more than a moral responsibility for nature comparable to human needs. Our students overflow the emerging courses in environmental ethics—courses that we do not teach, nor yet require.

We teach identification, inventory, harvest, applied ecology, applied sciences, communications skills, and a guiding principle that natural resources are renewable. We emphasize populations—runs of salmon, stands of firs, herds of deer—more than ecosystems. We convey that individual organisms are mainly the concern of horticulturists, veterinarians, and animal rightists, not of our students.

There is another great theme, a strong subtext in many natural resources courses. It is that a natural resources education admits one to an exclusive fellowship of professionals. This powerful precept boosts retention of students. I remember forestry students at Oregon State all wearing Filson cruiser jackets and caulked ("cork") boots at every opportunity. The fisheries students at Iowa State wore their thin cotton shirts from summer jobs with Iowa Conservation Commission to classes all winter; the prominent ICC and fish shoulder patches kept them warm. Student chapters of the professional societies are central to campus life for many in natural resources majors and further the bonding among students. These clubs and activities are promoted by professors. Students see pickups with agency decals, smokey bear hats, uniforms, and sidearms not just as the accouterment of government employment but as emblems of an exclusive profession.

The Traditional Curriculum Today

The large majority of today's natural resources managers and biologists completed their BA/BS degrees since 1960. Their undergraduate education shares these common features:

> Science: 1 year of general biology or general botany and zoology; 2 advanced botany courses (except fisheries) or 2–3 advanced zoology courses (fisheries and wildlife); 1 year of chemistry; 1 basic and 1 advanced ecology course; physics in about half of the curricula.

> Mathematics: 1 year of math, with calculus in two-thirds of the curricula; 1 or 2 statistics courses; 1 computer science course.

> Communications: 1 year of composition; 1 course in speech; 1 specialized communications course (e.g., public relations).

> Arts, humanities, and social sciences: 2–4 courses, often with economics required (recreation majors take more social sciences).

> Natural resources: 1 introductory/orientation, 1 principles of management course, 1 techniques, and 2–3 advanced courses within a discipline; 1 course in a related discipline; 1 course in law/policy/administration; 1 course in integrated or multiple-use management of natural resources. Additional, specialized requirements in natural resources vary greatly.

> Free electives: 10–20 percent of course work, but varies greatly.

Numerous articles in professional publications and many panels and papers at professional meetings have examined coursework in various natural resources disciplines. Invariably, these reviews deplore insufficiency of something—economics, writing, speaking, planning, business, calculus, practical skills, problem solving, biodiversity, research design, multiculturalism, political science, free electives—depending on the prejudice or perspective of the critic. I find little optimism, constructive evaluation, or scientific merit in these. The keys to improvement of curriculum may not be found in the details, but in the goals and philosophies of education.

Comparisons, Contrasts, and Characteristics of Curricula

Natural resources curricula can be ranked from most to least structured. All the disciplines prescribe some mix of sciences, humanities, social sciences, communications, and specialized courses. Forestry is most prescribed, approaching engineering in a dearth of electives. Students commonly take 50 percent of their courses from foresters. Range management also specifies many courses as it attempts to cover both animal husbandry and natural resources management.

Wildlife and fisheries are more diverse. These majors often require courses in 12 to 15 different academic departments. Majors often take 25 percent of their courses from fisheries or wildlife professors. Requirements in recreation are also diverse; less natural science but more social science is often specified than for the other disciplines.

Revisions of curricula in the last 15 to 20 years have added computer technology, integrated resources management, biopolitics, planning, and human dimensions in natural resources management. More students are taking supplementary minors and interdisciplinary studies. However, integration of the various natural resources disciplines is usually presented as cooperation among specialists, instead of each student learning fundamentals and responsibilities for managing all resources. A few natural resources colleges (e.g., universities of Idaho and Michigan) have attempted more integration by eliminating departments within colleges; however, specific majors remain.

Traditional methods of teaching and learning dominate. Pedagogy pervades natural resources education. Few professors have taken an education course or explore cognition and learning theory. We teach as we were taught in a didactic manner. Innovation, which once meant using colored chalk, now means overheads from computer graphics—are neater visual aids the key to more effective teaching? Labs serve mainly to verify lectures. Class discussion allows professors to answer questions from students who missed lecture. Amazingly, many students remain captivated to hear the number of needles in a fascicle of pine or the number of eggs in a mallard's nest, even when the professor reads from curling, yellowing notes.

In the past decade, videos replaced dissections, calculators replaced slide rules, geographic information systems replaced maps, and models replaced survey data from the field. And, teaching assistants replaced many professors in classes. We continue to proclaim the importance of "teaching students how to think" with little progress toward understanding what that means.

Fortunately, traditional curricula have included many fundamental principles that will be necessary in the foundation of a new era of natural resources management. For example, the "old" holococnotic principle of ecology is the scientific basis for the "new" ecosystem management. Sustainable resource management will require understanding the dynamics of populations and ecosystems, taught in traditional courses. Management for biodiversity or species richness requires the same knowledge of life histories and limiting factors as was necessary in management of featured species. Human dimensions in natural resources is an emerging expansion of principles in D.L. Gilbert's (1971) *Natural Resources and Public Relations*, the widely adopted first textbook for this subject. R.T. King's (1966) *Wildlife and Man* outlined the multiple values of wildlife that beget a realization that wildlife management goals must include more than harvest, economics, and sport.

Faculty and the students who graduate in all natural resources disciplines share some convictions. They believe that their curricula are basically sound, despite imperfections. They believe that the graduates are better prepared for their futures than is true for most fields. They believe that they are joined in a worthwhile, even noble, endeavor to prepare as best they can to assume responsibilities as stewards of natural resources.

Influences on Natural Resources Education

How did we build the current model of traditional natural resources education? External influences were as strong as internal beliefs in science, wise use, multiple-use management, optimum yields, and human dominion over the Earth and its biota.

Government employment standards exert major control. Especially in forestry and range, the specific requirements for a rating on a federal job register demand substantial numbers of specific courses. The colleges have encouraged these in order to exclude "unqualified" students in general programs of study from competing with "our" students for natural resources jobs. These civil service (now, U.S. Office of Personnel Management) stipulations appear somewhat arbitrary. One wonders why four times as many specialized courses are required for a forester rating as are needed for a rating in fisheries, when management of the two resources appears to be equally challenging.

Professional certification and accreditation help shape natural resources majors. The Society of American Foresters has a strong accreditation program that tends to standardize forestry education. Graduates of SAF-accredited colleges get bonus points on their ratings on federal job registers.

The Wildlife Society and the American Fisheries Society offer certification to qualified individuals. Many educational requirements are specified, although only 6 semester credits in wildlife or fisheries courses must be included.

Special interest groups, such as employers, hunters/anglers, and citizens' advocacy organizations, also exert pressures on natural resources education. Timber companies, commercial fisheries, and others often hire graduates with specific job skills for initial employment, rather than hire well-educated persons with the most potential for leadership a decade later. Schools feel pressure and sometimes succumb to teaching chain saw operation, horse packing, boat operation, telemetry, and word processing in their management courses.

Various alliances and groupings of natural resources programs within academia greatly affect curricula. Certain college requirements are often specified for all students in whatever majors are in that college. Thus, an integrated management course could be required for a fisheries major in a forestry college, but genetics would more likely be required where fisheries is in a college of natural sciences.

Transitions in Natural Resources Education

As we approach a new century, the changes needed in natural resources education are as obvious as they are essential. However, the current education is really a continuum of past changes in the students, their backgrounds, enrollment patterns, curricula, and the educators who are the trustees for the future.

Who are the students? Complex factors determine the choice of a field of study. Students in natural resources appear to be strongly influenced by their perceptions of career opportunities, by childhood experiences in the outdoors, particularly with adults, and by a strong love of or fascination with nature. Factors with little influence include family preferences in careers, academic ability, and future salary expectations.

Although education in natural resources in America is only 50 to 100 years old, varying among the disciplines, some significant changes have occurred in its scope and emphasis. Earth Day 1970 and the concomitant environmental revolution demonstrated new idealism and an environmental conscience in our students. Their demands broadened not only curricula but also the content of individual courses. Stewardship was as important as technocracy to students in natural resources, but their courses had lagged behind their evolving interests. Perhaps the professors were too complacent and comfortable in a traditional philosophy of conservation.

Backgrounds of our students changed. By the 1960s, urban students outnumbered rural students in natural resources. These urban students had less outdoor experiences, but they often expressed different values for the natural world than did earlier generations of farm and ranch kids. By the 1980s, students were choosing Semester at Sea, study abroad, or perhaps a minor in political science or English, instead of management electives. They read Edward Abbey and revered Rachel Carson. However, they still wanted a job with the Forest Service or with the state wildlife agency; so, they accepted much of the traditional education necessary to get a job in their field. Their teachers and mentors generally urged them to work for progress within the system, and the students still saw few alternative role models. By 1990, Jeff DeBonis, editor of *The Inner Voice*, the underground newspaper for environmental ethics in the U.S. Forest Service, was known and respected by more students than was the chief of the USFS.

Greater diversity of students included a gender breakthrough, mainly during the 1970s. From an occasional oddity in the 1960s, women increased to a third of all natural resources students by 1990. However, no increase in racial minorities occurred, and they remain significantly underrepresented into the 1990s.

An enrollment roller coaster has also influenced natural resources education. Students on the GI Bill after World War II were the first huge wave. Another surge more than doubled enrollments during the 1960s to about 1977. Enrollments then declined sharply until the mid-1980s and stabilized in the late 1980s. Enrollments in natural resources were increasing 5–10 percent per year in the early 1990s. Each enrollment climb impacted education. Larger classes meant fewer laboratories, fewer field courses and field trips, and more graduate students taught courses.

What is the number of natural resources students? In recent years, approximately 4000 degrees in natural resources are awarded annually in the United States, 80 percent BS/BA, 17 percent MS/MA, and 3 percent Ph.D. Fewer than half of the students who enter natural resources majors complete a degree in that major within six years. In my own college of natural resources, two-thirds of the students change majors at least once. Retention of students depends on many factors (e.g., trends in numbers of jobs, rigor of curricula, finances, and satisfaction of students as consumers of education). I believe that substantial and increasing numbers of students who enter these majors leave because of their dissatisfaction with a traditional education in natural resources. Many new students soon foresee their education as too prescribed, management/production focused, too narrow, and impersonal. We don't know if they are attracted to specific alternatives or are mainly just rejecting unsatisfactory programs when they leave.

I estimate 150,000 persons will have earned a baccalaureate degree in a natural resources discipline in the United States in the 20th century. This would include roughly one-third in forestry, one-third in wildlife, and one-third in all other natural resources majors. Perhaps one-fifth will have earned a postgraduate degree. Unlike many college majors, a large majority of natural resources graduates pursue careers in their fields.

Who are the educators? During the era of establishment of natural resources education—up to mid-20th century—practitioners often became professors. Researchers then began to fill more faculty positions, partly due to post-Sputnik increases in external funding for research in academia. Perhaps a watershed was reached in the early 1990s when a publish-or-perish philosophy for professors was increasingly criticized within academia and by external publics. Since then, greater emphasis on teaching has been gaining favor in higher education.

What Grade for Natural Resources Education?

For originality, natural resources education merits a grade of A. New disciplines were invented and then developed in American colleges in the 20th century. Fisheries emerged from ichthyology and limnology, forestry from European timber production, and wildlife from husbandry of game for sport hunting. These and related disciplines, such as range and recreation, converged toward education designed to produce commodities and experiences desired and demanded by the large majority of citizens.

For achieving its given goals, natural resources education earns an A. Educators have taught the techniques to achieve objectives based on definitions, such as maximum sustained yield and multiple use, that are widely accepted by interested publics. The goals for resource management in America were determined in social and political processes, not in academia. Educators taught the applications of science to solve management problems in working toward those goals. Students have learned, and applied these lessons well to management of the nation's natural resources.

For attracting excellent students and motivating them toward high goals, natural resources educators deserve a grade of B. The large majority of students strive toward high standards of scholarship and professionalism. The graduates are good citizens and good persons, loyal to their employers and to their responsibilities for the resources that they manage. The natural resources schools could have done more in exposing students to ethics and diverse values and to models for continued learning and personal growth after graduation.

For innovation in education, integration of disciplines, and preparation of students for leadership in developing natural resources policies, traditional education receives a C. Technical training for entry-level jobs usually has priority over a broader education, which is needed in political, social, and scientific arenas that confront natural resources managers later in their careers.

I am loath to grade courses not selected, to criticize paths not taken, or to assign blame for failures to solve problems not identified nor understood. Looking through a retrospectascope now reveals that our futuresighters were broken. Most disciplines, including natural resources, would get D or F for the inadequacy of yesterday's education for tomorrow's needs.

The traditional education has served the nation well in many respects, but it will not suffice to meet the new challenges of the next century. Whether or not natural resources education will evolve rapidly enough will depend largely on how the students in natural resources perceive their futures and on how aggressively they demand the most relevant education possible.

Overall, traditional education in natural resources merits a B.

Chapter 5

The Traditional Economics of Natural Resources Management

Gloria E. Helfand and Peter Berck

> Only that shall happen which has happened
> Only that shall occur which has occurred
> There is nothing new beneath the sun!
>
> —Ecclesiastes, Chapter 1, verse 9

The economics of resource extraction is sometimes blamed for mismanagement on the public lands of the United States (1). This argument says that the profit motive leads people to treat the land only for its immediate, extractable market values, and to ignore the nonmarket, "land ethic" values, such as natural heritage or intrinsic value of species or ecosystems. According to this thesis, although forests have value in their undisturbed condition, economic forces compel people to view the forest only for the lumber it can provide.

This perception, that economics argues for emphasis only on the marketable resources from lands, is based on a misunderstanding of the lessons of economics. To the extent that economics is a descriptive science, it cannot be blamed for these policies; it can explain them, but not cause them. Economics can be prescriptive, though; it can argue that certain policies are more efficient than others, in the sense that they achieve social objectives at lower cost than other policies, or that social welfare is improved more by some policies than others. Nevertheless, even prescriptive (or normative) economics does not support rapid exploitation of timber, minerals, grazing lands, or other public resources, without regard to the scientific or recreational value of these lands.

Instead, public policies have violated economic principles and contributed to needless environmental degradation. Federal land management programs have often encouraged immediate use of lands, rather than allocating resource use over time. Pricing of federally owned resources frequently does not reflect all the costs of their development. More incorporation of economic principles into public lands management could reduce much environmental damage caused by these inefficient policies.

The following discussion will first review the traditional economic theories of resource extraction, starting from the basic case of a nonrenewable resource and moving to more complex renewable resources. It will then examine "market failures" affecting public lands management, due to externalities. Finally, it will use the example of "sales below cost" in the national forests to show how violation of economic principles can lead to environmentally harmful management practices.

The Theory of Resource Management

The theory of resource management requires recognition of three parts to the value of a resource: (1) resources in their undeveloped state are capital assets in which people can invest by purchasing them; (2) developers of solely owned resources pay, and therefore must recover, the tangible costs of development; (3) resource development usually involves costs that are not borne by extractors but are nevertheless true costs they should pay. Private resource developers must recognize the first two parts of this value, or they will not compete successfully in the marketplace; the third part will be treated further in the next section of this chapter. The following discussion will analyze first the economic rules for development of nonrenewable resources. It will then extend those principles to reflect rules for management of renewable resources.

Nonrenewable Resources

With a nonrenewable resource, such as oil, the use of one unit today means that unit will not be available in the future. Resource owners, then, must decide on a continual basis whether to make the resource available for extraction now or save it until the future. If they make the resource available now, they can take the earnings from selling the deposit and invest them, for instance, in a bond or in the stock market. A resource owner who wants to maximize profits will compare the returns from selling the deposit to the returns from holding it for future sale. If the value of the deposit does not change, the resource owner will sell all the resource now and earn interest from investments into the future. If, on the other hand, the deposit is increasing in value more rapidly than alternative investments, the resource owner will hold the deposit into the future and sell none of it now. Only if the deposit is increasing in value at the same rate as the alternative investment opportunities will the resource owner be willing both to sell some now and to save some for later. This increasing "asset value" implies an increasing price for the deposit over time.

The value of an unmined deposit is the quantity of the deposit times the price per unit. For the value of the deposit to increase, the price must increase. If investing $1 in a bond over one year yields $(1 + r)$ (where r is the interest rate), the resource deposit must give an equivalent return. If the current resource price is P_1 per unit, then $1 buys $1/P_1$ units of the resource. If P_2 is the price for the resource next year, then the $1/P_1$ units purchased are worth P_2/P_1 next year. P_2/P_1 must equal $(1 + r)$, or $P_2 = (1 + r)P_1$. This is the Hotelling rule: a resource must earn the same return as any other asset (2).

The developer of a deposit, when pricing the extracted resource for sale, plans to recover both the costs of extraction and the cost of purchasing (the asset value). Because the asset value increases over time, the market price must also increase (unless extraction costs decrease). Consumers decide how much of it to buy based partly on the resource's price. A higher price will induce consumers to use less of the resource, or to use substitutes for it. Over time, then, as the asset value increases, consumption will decrease. As long as consumers are willing to pay a high enough price, extractors will save some for the future. When the resource runs out (that is, all deposits that are economically feasible to develop have been exhausted), the price will be high enough that consumers will no longer want to use the resource.

In sum, the asset value must increase over time to provide investors with a rate of return high enough that they will not deplete the resource all at once. As long as costs of extraction do not fall, the market price of the resource must rise to provide the increasing value. As the market price rises, consumers will not want to buy as much of the resource. Thus, over time, the price will increase, and the quantity extracted per period will decrease. Eventually, the price may get high enough that consumers will not be willing to purchase the resource. At that point, either it will be entirely depleted, or it will be too expensive to extract. The resource will have effectively been used up, but only when consumers do not want it anyway.

In reality, of course, most patterns of resource extraction do not follow this simple model (3). Several factors complicate reality. First, improved extraction technologies, recycling possibilities, and exploration for new deposits make more of the resource available. When more of the resource is economically recoverable, it is possible to have more now and later; the expected price increases are muted. Second, substitutes for the resource (such as alternative fuels for gasoline in vehicles) reduce the demand; because people want less of the resource, it will take longer for supplies to run out. Even with these alterations to the basic model, if markets for nonrenewable resources are functioning properly, resource extraction will take place gradually, especially because increasing prices encourage consumers to conserve and suppliers to find more of the resource.

This analysis shows that a private owner of a nonrenewable resource is unlikely to deplete the resource as long as people are willing to pay a fair rate of return on it. In contrast, federal land management policies have often encouraged immediate use of lands, rather than allocating resource use over time. Many federal actions, such as the Homestead Act, the General Mining Act, and railroad land grants, offered free or inexpensive land only if the owners developed it rapidly (4). Economic theory would not oppose the granting of property rights. Conditioning the rights on development of resources, however, violated economic principles. If the land were economically feasible to develop, the requirement would not be necessary. These conditions instead forced resource use faster than market forces might induce, and they led to the development of inappropriate land.

Renewable Resources

The theory of renewable resources builds on the theory of nonrenewable resources (5). With nonrenewable resources, the asset does not change size except through its depletion. In contrast, renewable resources, by their nature, can reproduce. If a stock of fish, timber, wildlife, or other renewable resource is left undisturbed, it will reproduce until it reaches the carrying capacity of its environment; at that point growth ceases. Usually, ecologists assume that how rapidly a species grows depends on population size. The growth starts slowly when there are very few members of the population; as the population increases, growth does as well, until it reaches a maximum. After this point, the species continues to grow, but reproduction yields fewer new members, until growth ceases at the carrying capacity. The *change in growth* indicates how reproduction changes with an increase in the population level. The change in growth is initially positive (increasing the population increases growth) but declining; when growth is maximized, the change in growth is zero (increasing the population cannot increase growth, since growth at that point is at its peak); and the change in growth is negative as growth declines to zero.

If the growth of the species is harvested, the original stock will be unaffected, just as taking interest earnings out of a bank account leaves the principal untouched. Thus, a sustained yield harvest can occur for any population level, if the harvest is limited to the growth. The maximum sustained yield (MSY) of a species occurs when growth is maximized (the change in growth is zero). Which population level to maintain and which related growth level to harvest are the key questions for renewable resource management.

With nonrenewable resources, the price for the deposit in the basic model had to increase over time; because the investor could always sell the deposit and put the profits into an interest-bearing asset, the resource had to increase in value if it were to provide a competitive return. In contrast, because a renewable resource can provide a return by growing, the price per unit can be constant. Alternatively, if the stock has reached its carrying capacity and is no longer growing, the resource must appreciate in value for its owner to maintain it at that level. A combination of value per unit increase and resource growth must provide a return comparable to that of an alternative investment.

If the value per unit of the resource is constant, an investor must decide whether to invest more heavily in the resource by letting it grow; to harvest just the growth, which would just maintain the stock; or to deplete the stock, by harvesting faster than growth. Let the price of a renewable resource be P. A \$1 investment in the resource can purchase $1/P$ units of stock. Those units of stock grow: if 1 unit of stock produces a growth of g (the percent change in growth), next year the population will grow to $(1 + g)/P$, the original stock plus the growth provided by that stock. If the price is constant, the value of the new population from the \$1 investment is $\$P(1 + g)/P = \$(1 + g)$. As with a nonrenewable resource, that return must equal the return from the alternative investment yielding $(1 + r)$ dollars; $\$(1 + g) = \$(1 + r)$, or $g = r$. If g is greater than r, an investor will increase the resource stock; if g is less than r, the investor will harvest the stock.

As discussed above, the percent change in growth, g, is positive for small stock levels, reaches 0 at MSY, and becomes negative at higher populations. The rule $g = r$ determines the level of stock at which the investor does not want either to increase or to decrease the stock; there is a steady state. Because r is positive, the percent change in growth must be positive, which only occurs at a population level below the stock corresponding to MSY. In other words, the optimal harvest is not MSY, but some level below it (6).

This result seems counter-intuitive; why sustain a harvest that is smaller than it could be? A resource manager, however, has to consider not only the size of the harvest, but also the size of the stock being managed. By reducing the stock below the level corresponding to MSY and selling the asset, the resource owner is able to get a large initial sum of money. That money can be invested and will earn interest. The owner gets a sustained yield harvest of the resource forever, at a slightly lower level than MSY, plus the initial money for investment.

This result is reflected in the history of forest management in the United States. When settlers first arrived in North America, forests dominated the eastern landscape. They were harvested at an unsustainable rate (the stock was reduced) to clear land for farming. As forest resources became more scarce, they were managed more closely. The National Forest System was established "to furnish a continuous supply of timber for the use and necessities of citizens of the United States" (7). Once the stock was reduced, sustainable harvest was a goal on the remaining forest lands.

As with nonrenewable resources, the price of the resource to the consumer must reflect both the asset value of the resource and the costs of harvesting it. Otherwise, a private resource manager will not be able to stay in business, and a public resource manager will be wasting public money on subeconomic harvesting.

Rotation Length for Renewable Resources

Renewable resource management involves decisions on stock size and the harvest level as well as, for timber especially, the age of the species at harvest. The advantages of harvesting earlier are: (1) that the owner of the timber gets revenues early, which can be invested; and (2) that the next stand of timber can be planted more quickly, providing returns sooner. The disadvantage of harvesting earlier is that the trees are still growing; the longer they are left to grow the greater the volume of timber that each tree will produce. The Faustmann equation (8) expresses the tradeoff between letting trees increase in volume versus getting revenues sooner and replanting sooner. If $X(L)$ is the volume of a tree at age L, $X'(L)$ is the growth of the tree at age L, r is the interest rate, and L is the rotation length, the Faustmann equation can be written as

$$\frac{X'(L)}{X(L)} = \frac{r}{1 - e^{-rL}}$$

$X'(L)/X(L)$ is the percent change in growth at age L. The Faustmann formula suggests that the optimal rotation length involves a positive percent change in growth rather than maximum growth. As with determining optimal stock, there is a tradeoff in rotation length between maximizing biological growth and maximizing economic returns. The economic rule suggests trading off some volume to increase total economic value; by sacrificing a small amount of growth, a resource manager gains earlier returns from both current and future harvests.

Industrial timber growers generally pursue much shorter rotations than do public land managers, in explicit recognition of these tradeoffs. While some might argue that longer rotations on public lands reflect subeconomic management, Hartman (9) has also shown that rotation lengths should perhaps be longer when trees have value *in situ* as well as for timber. As the next section of this chapter will discuss, these *in situ* values, which would otherwise not be provided by private lands, are in fact a major rationale for holding lands in public ownership.

Summary of the Traditional Economics of Resource Management

Natural resource economics allocates resource use over time by recognizing that resources are assets with value, just as a stock or a bond is a valuable asset. Because it is possible to invest in assets that provide a return on an investment, resources must provide a return. For nonrenewable resources, that return comes through an increase in value while in the ground; for renewable resources, it comes primarily from the reproduction of the species. As long as resource owners can manage their resources in accord with these principles, resources should not be depleted as long as they are valuable enough to people to develop.

The prerequisite for these markets to function well is a well-defined system of property rights, for the resources themselves and for related goods. The owners need to be able to control the extraction of the resources, and the prices of related goods (especially the costs of extraction and substitutes for the resources) should be neither subsidized nor taxed. If these conditions fail, as they frequently do, the resulting "market failure" can lead to undesirable patterns of resource use.

Market Failure in Resource Management

After a resource is extracted, it is purchased by those who plan to convert it into goods for human consumption. Those purchasers, in deciding the price at which to sell, take into account the asset value of the resource plus the costs of developing it; otherwise, they will lose money. If consumers are not willing to pay a price reflecting the asset value and the costs of extraction, the resource will not be developed.

Because of limitations on ownership of resources or related goods, market prices may not be "full" prices—that is, prices that reflect the total value of a good. For instance, because nobody explicitly owns air, both those who want to keep it clean for breathing and those who want to pollute it can claim the right to use it. If ownership were established, users would have to compensate owners for reducing the amount of air available to the owner (10); without a system of rights, though, groups battle over access, and air resources are subject to abuse.

It can be argued that the land management systems of the federal government were originally established due to market failures (primarily externalities), and that many of the continuing conflicts over land management can also be attributed to these problems.

An externality occurs when someone undertakes an action for which they do not face the full consequences, either positive or negative. For instance, a positive externality occurs when a landowner maintains a beautiful landscape that others enjoy without paying for it; pollution from a factory that harms people who are not compensated constitutes a negative externality. Public ownership and management of land is best justified as a means to recognize and correct some market failures that would occur from private land ownership, although the public lands have not always served this role successfully.

Many services provided by public lands would not be provided by private lands, because the owners would not be able to receive full compensation for those services; without public provision of the services, not enough of these goods would be provided. Habitat for plants and animals, scientific research opportunities, aesthetic landscapes, and low-density recreation all provide benefits, but it could be difficult for a landowner to receive compensation from all who benefit from them. For instance, most private landowners have few incentives to preserve endangered species: some benefits from preserving the species (such as its contribution to genetic diversity) are unlikely to provide any financial remuneration; other benefits (such as the potential for a species to provide remuneration, perhaps as a medicine) may be very speculative; and the benefits may be hard to keep to oneself (because the species could be found elsewhere). Public provision of these goods, which would not be supplied adequately by private landowners, provides a strong rationale for government land ownership.

Government regulation of private land management practices is also justified, especially by negative externalities that these practices can create. Both logging and mining can cause water pollution and habitat disturbances, for instance. Although it is often difficult to determine the monetary costs of these externalities, they are real and significant, just as are the costs of the machinery and workers who perform logging and mining. These costs should be reflected in the market price of the extracted resources to indicate the true costs to society of these activities (11). If they are incorporated, the extractors have incentives to minimize costs by reducing environmental damages; and purchasers of the goods, facing higher prices, will buy less, leading to less extraction and environmental damage. If costs are not incorporated, both resource extraction and environmental damage are being subsidized.

Economics has long recognized the effects of externalities (12) and has argued for recognition of the total benefits and costs of an activity in the market price of that activity. Because of public desire for these services, resulting in public pressure to get them, governments, especially in their role as land managers, have provided many services unavailable on private markets. Additionally, governments have regulated negative externalities from private sources, though not always as efficiently as economists might like. Economic analysis can contribute to determining whether government policies are sound, and whether the correct level of services is being provided.

Economic Principles and National Forest Management: An Example

As stated above, the theory of resource management argues that the value of a developed resource should consist of its asset value, its tangible costs of extraction, and the external costs of development. In practice on public lands, two principles are frequently ignored: (1) that the stock of a resource is an asset that must be managed as carefully as any other investment; and (2) that when the asset is marketed, its price must reflect all the costs involved in its development, including explicit extraction costs, value as an asset, and any external costs or benefits of its extraction. Violation of these principles often leads to excessive resource extraction, negative externalities, and unnecessary conflicts over use of resources.

The "sales below cost" issue in national forest management reflects what can go wrong when economic principles are ignored (13). The U.S. Forest Service (USFS), which manages the National Forest System, sells timber to private harvesters, who cut the timber and turn it into wood products for sale. When the USFS calculates a minimum bid for its timber, it determines a price based on returns to the private harvesters, not the costs that are incurred in making the timber available to them. These costs, which include road building, sale administration, and replanting, often exceed the value of the timber being harvested. Because the USFS historically has not considered the costs of timber management in determining how much timber to sell, it loses money managing for and selling timber in most of this country's national forests.

Clearly this practice violates the principles for resource management outlined above. The USFS is not taking into account even the most obvious costs (the expenditures that it makes to sell timber) much less the asset value of the standing timber or the externality costs of harvesting. To the extent that the market price it charges for its timber does not reflect those costs, timber management on the national forests is subsidized, and too much timber is being produced. If timber management conflicts with other forest services, such as wildlife habitat or clean water, these other services are not being produced at a sufficient level. Additionally, private timber managers, who have to recognize at least their management expenditures and the asset value of the timber, face competition from a low-cost supplier; their incentive to grow and maintain timber is lessened, contributing to greater demand for national forest timber. Revision of USFS policy to reduce below-cost timber sales could lower costs of timber management in the national forests, encourage timber production from private lands, and smooth conflicts between timber management and other forest services that provide a major justification for public ownership of forests.

Conclusion

Economics is the study of the allocation of scarce resources, where "scarce" means anything of which there is limited availability even when there is also no cost. In the early years of European settlement of North America, forests and land were not scarce. The population was low enough, and the resources plentiful enough, that they could be exploited freely. Indeed, the federal government had trouble selling land because it was too easy for settlers to claim land without paying for it (14). By the late 1800s, though, forest land was perceived to be scarce, and the federal government started reserving public lands to ensure flows of forest products and services into the future.

In this chapter, we have reviewed the traditional economic rules for managing nonrenewable and renewable resources. When resources are scarce, they have value as assets and must be managed with their asset value in mind. Thus, nonrenewable resources must provide a return to their owners through price increases; renewable resources provide the return through a combination of price increases and reproduction. These returns give resource owners incentive to provide some of the resource now and to preserve some for future users as well.

When the resource is marketed, the seller must expect, at the least, to recover the costs of resource extraction through the resource price. That price should include not only the asset value of the resource and the extraction costs, but also the costs of any negative externalities generated, such as increased water pollution or destruction of wildlife habitat. Although negative externalities are all too frequently left unpriced, they reflect real costs that are imposed by resource extraction and should be incorporated into the market price of the goods.

Public ownership of lands is best justified by the positive externalities that these lands generate. Many of the services provided by public lands would not be available if left to private land managers, since they would not be able to receive the full benefits from doing so. As long as management of public lands for traditionally marketed goods such as timber or grazing complement, or at least do not interfere with, provision of other services (habitat protection and beautiful landscapes), the public lands can provide for all. To the extent that these uses conflict, resource development on public lands, as on private lands, must consider the costs imposed on those other services when deciding how much of the marketed goods to provide.

Despite some popular perceptions, economics does not focus only on resources for which there are market prices, and it does not promote profligate use of those resources in the present at the expense of future generations. Economics, instead, tries to reflect societal preferences for all goods and services in its calculation of resource allocation. Economics can be used to explain and predict human behavior by considering the incentives that resource managers face. Its normative role, of advocating certain resource management approaches over others, is more controversial, because there is greater disagreement over what society wants. Still, the lessons of economics are useful tools for determining the allocation of scarce resources and can prevent much unnecessary and wasteful environmental destruction.

Notes

1. Leopold, Aldo. 1966. The land ethic. In A sand county almanac. New York: Oxford University Press.
2. Hotelling, Harold. 1931. The economics of exhaustible resources. Journal of Political Economy 39:137–175.
3. Fisher, A.C. 1981. Resource and environmental economics. New York: Cambridge University Press.
4. Dana, S.T., and S.K. Fairfax. 1980. Forest and range policy. New York: McGraw-Hill Book Company.
5. Clark, Colin. 1976. Mathematical bioeconomics. New York: John Wiley & Sons.
6. This result does not hold if the costs of harvest depend on the stock—

for instance, greater fish stocks in a fishery make catching fish easier. In this case, the optimal stock is greater than the point where $g = r$.

7. Organic Administration Act of 1897, 16 U.S.C. 473–475, 477–482, 551.
8. Clark 1976 (5).
9. Hartman, Richard. 1976. The harvesting decision when the standing forest has value. Economic Inquiry 14:52–58.
10. In fact, the Coase Theorem (Coase, R. 1960. The problem of social cost. Journal of Law and Economics 3:1–44.) notes that, under some circumstances, it does not matter to whom the property rights are allocated; the same allocation of air between polluters and those who want clean air will result regardless of which group gets the rights.
11. Baumol, W.J., and W.E. Oates. 1988. The theory of environmental policy, 2nd ed. New York: Cambridge University Press.
12. Samuelson, Paul. 1954. The pure theory of public expenditure. Review of Economics and Statistics 36:387–389.
13. Clawson, Marion. 1976. The economics of national forest management. Washington, D.C.: Resources for the Future.

    Barlow, T.J., G.E. Helfand, T.W. Orr, and T.B. Stoel, Jr. 1980. Giving away the national forests. Washington, D.C.: Natural Resources Defense Council.

    Helfand, G.E. 1981. An analysis of the costs and receipts of national forest timber sales. Unpublished master's thesis, Department of Technology and Human Affairs. St. Louis, Missouri: Washington University.
14. Dana and Fairfax 1980 (4).

Chapter 6

The Traditional Ethics of Natural Resources Management

Eric Katz

> God, who hath given the World to Men in common, hath also given them
> reason to make use of it to the best advantage of Life, and convenience.
> The Earth, and all that is therein, is given to Men for the Support and
> Comfort of their being.
>
> —John Locke
> *The Second Treatise of Government*

The human use of natural resources is a practice as old as humanity itself. As the species *Homo sapiens* evolved, it necessarily made use of the material in its environment, as did every other species and living entity on Earth. The use of the natural environment by itself is not an ethical issue; it is a biological fact. Human life—indeed, all life—depends on the proper exploitation of the environment.

Ethics enters the picture when we begin to think about the meaning and value of the use of the environment, when humans examine the nature of their relationship with nature. Within ethics, judgments are made concerning the good or evil of specific actions, policies, and practices. This type of judgment, this type of self-conscious examination of the relationship with the natural environment, is also as old as humanity itself. Even the humans of prehistory reflected on their relationship with the natural world, as the famous Paleolithic cave paintings of animals and the hunt demonstrate.

Since both the use of nature and the reflective examination of this use are as old as the human species, we can very well ask what is meant by the "traditional" ethics of the use of natural resources. Within the duration of the human species there have been countless traditions, countless institutional practices and belief systems regarding the human relationship with the natural world. Most of these traditions are lost in prehistory. But even in the last 10 thousand years, the era of a recorded culture and history, there are a multitude of traditional world views. Where then do we begin to understand the ethical history of the human relationship with nature?

Older Western Traditions

In the Western cultural tradition, it is perhaps appropriate to begin with the first Greek philosophers (Thales, Anaximander, Anaximenes, Heraclitus) who, beginning in the 6th century B.C., began to ask fundamental questions about the physical relationship between humans and the natural world. The birth of the discipline of physics is really the birth of an environmental philosophy and an ethic of nature, for the essential questions the pre-Socratic Greek philosophers asked were "what is the nature of the physical universe?" and "what is the human place or role in this system?" These metaphysical questions provide the basis of the ethics of the use of natural resources. They establish a framework for any serious investigation into the meaning and value of human activity in the natural world. For unless we humans know what the universe is like, we cannot judge our actions concerning the natural system as either good or evil.

Yet the early Greek philosophers had no explicit conception of what we 20th-century humans would call an environmental policy; they made no conscious effort to develop a set of principles governing human action in the environment. Perhaps the first such set of principles appeared in the Old Testament, in the book of Genesis, where God commanded Adam and Eve to subdue the Earth:

> And God blessed them; and God said unto them: "Be fruitful and multiply, and replenish the Earth, and subdue it; and have dominion over the fish of the sea, and over the fowl of the air, and over every living thing that moves upon the Earth." (Genesis 1:28)

This passage is invoked in almost every discussion of the Biblical foundations of environmental philosophy, and it has aroused much controversy among scholars of the Judeo–Christian religious tradition. Much of the controversy originated with Lynn White Jr.'s argument in "The Historical Roots of Our Ecologic Crisis" that this passage has served to justify the domination of all natural resources on Earth—all nonhuman entities—for the sole benefit of humanity (1). According to White, the passage suggests that humanity rules over all nonhuman beings, that it is proper to "subdue" the Earth and all natural entities for the growth and maintenance ("be fruitful and multiply") of human life. If so, the Bible explicitly states what we will call an *anthropocentric* perspective on the value of nature and natural resources: the value of nature centers on humanity. Nature's effect on humanity and the use of nature by humanity are the major if not the sole determinants of the value of natural resources.

Obviously, this is not the proper place for a full discussion of the meaning of Genesis for the development of an ethics of environmental policy. Its importance for us, in this chapter, is to see that an anthropocentric attitude toward the use of natural resources is embedded so deeply into the Western philosophical and religious tradition that it is rarely articulated, examined, or criticized. The anthropocentric world view is the basic vision of Western civilization: nature and all its components are only evaluated—only seen—through the category of usefulness for humanity.

The Early Modern Tradition: John Locke and Nature as Property

The basic Western tradition of anthropocentrism was fully articulated when we entered the age of modern thought, after the Renaissance, at the beginning of the ages of exploration, the Enlightenment, and the Industrial Revolution. One convenient place to begin an investigation of the modern tradition would be with the thinker Francis Bacon. Bacon expressed the basic motivations and methodologies of modern empirical science. The goal of the new empirical science was not mere contemplation, but the active manipulation and understanding of Nature, to unlock the secrets of Nature, to bend her to the will of humanity, to better the lives of human beings and human society. This view of science and the human relationship to nature is summed up in Bacon's famous aphorism, "Knowledge is power." It has been the dominant view of the meaning of science and technology in the world today, an unquestioned and noncontroversial credo of modern humanity and the contemporary scientist. But Bacon, of course, wrote with little regard for the adverse impact of human power on the natural environment—although a true visionary, he was a creature of his times, almost completely ignorant of ecological relationships and natural systems. In that way too, he exemplified the modern age.

Although Bacon explained the presuppositions, methods, and purposes of modern science, it was the 17th century philosopher John Locke who more explicitly established the traditional modern world view of the human relationship with the natural environment. Bacon argued for the use of science to aid human life. Locke argued for the human evaluation of the natural world. Thus, Locke was the great modern theorist of anthropocentrism. For Locke, nature was valuable solely as it was used as property by human beings. Natural entities were valuable only insofar as they were actually removed from the natural system and became part of human culture.

It is important that we examine Locke's views in detail, for Locke, more than any other modern philosopher, truly formulated the foundation of the modern tradition of the use of natural resources. It is ironic, however, that Locke formulated this radically anthropocentric view of nature as a minor theme in the development of his political philosophy. His chief concern in the *Second Treatise of Government* was to establish the legitimacy of a popularly elected democratic government, and thereby to oppose the prevalent view of the divine right of the monarchy. He based the argument on a theoretical model of a "state of Nature" that supposedly preceded the establishment of the first government or civil society. It was from this state of nature that humans established a social order. Thus, it became important to understand the conditions of human life prior to the development of civil society.

> To understand Political Power right . . . we must consider what State all Men are naturally in, and that is, a *State of perfect Freedom* to order their Actions, and dispose of their Possessions, and Persons as they think fit, within the bounds of the Law of Nature, without asking leave, or depending on the Will of any other Man. II. 4 (2)

From this state of perfect individual freedom, humans agree to form a social order, by means of a social contract.

Governments, or civil societies, however, exert power over free and independent individuals and create an inherent political inequality. The existence of this unequal power can only be morally justified if it is the result of the rational consent of free individuals. The central idea of the social contract is the consent of free individuals, joining together to limit their freedom, each expecting to benefit in this contract.

> Men being . . . by Nature, all free, equal and independent, no one can be put out of his Estate, and subjected to the Political Power of another, without his own *Consent*. The only way whereby any one divests himself of his Natural Liberty, and *puts on the bonds of Civil Society* is by agreeing with other Men to joyn and unite into a Community, for their comfortable, safe, and peaceable living one amongst another. . . . (VIII. 95)

The source of legitimate political power, then, is the rational freedom of individual human subjects that exists as a condition of the state of nature. Political legitimacy lies in the consent of the governed, not in the absolute power of the king.

Within the context of this argument for a democratic political philosophy, Locke also examined and defended a specific notion of property. The right to property must be seen as an essential (or natural) right if meaningful political power is to reside in the consent of free people. Without property, political power would be empty, for individuals would have no possessions necessary for the maintenance of life. The right to property thus exists within the state of nature, prior to the establishment of the social contract.

According to Locke, property is just those parts of nature that are used and valued by human individuals. In this philosophy, it must be emphasized that Nature is deemed valuable solely because it is used by humans, solely as it becomes property, a possession of a human individual. Nature—the Earth, the natural environment, land and water—begins as a common resource that exists for the maintenance of human life. The natural world and all natural entities and resources exist to be useful for human beings. The quotation at the beginning of this chapter expresses the foundation of Locke's anthropocentric view of nature.

The usefulness of any natural resource depends on its private appropriation as property. Parts of the natural environment must be removed from the "commons" and used privately if they are to have any significant effect on the comfort and well-being of individual humans. The "fruits" and "beasts" of the commons are given to all, "yet being given for the use of Men, there must of necessity be a means to appropriate them some way or other before they can be of any use, or at all beneficial to any particular Man" (V. 26). Locke appears to have employed a model of eating as the basic method of using a natural resource. That is why the fruits and beasts must be individually appropriated before they can be used. After a natural resource is eaten it is no longer a part of the commons, but in the most literal way imaginable a private part of the individual. Locke completed the argument: "The Fruit, or Venison, which nourishes the wild *Indian* . . . must be his, and so his, *i.e.*, a part of him, that another can no longer have any right to it, before it can do him any good for the support of his Life" (V. 26). A person may eat something that is common property, but once it is eaten it is clearly private property, a part of the individual. The consumption of natural resources therefore requires the establishment of private property. For Locke, consumption was the primary, if not the only, model of the use of natural resources.

Although the appropriation of a natural resource from the commons is physically necessary to sustain life, Locke needed to determine its moral legitimacy, if he was to justify a right to property as an element of the natural freedom that precedes the social contract in the state of nature. He began with the physical body of the individual human being, since this was clearly the property of the individual. "Though the Earth and all inferior Creatures be common to all Men, yet every Man has a *Property* in his own *Person*. This no Body has any Right to but himself" (V. 27). If the physical body is the property of the individual, so is the labor of the body; a person owns the actions or physical motions of its body. Locke continued: "The Labour of his Body, and the Work of his Hands, we may say, are properly his" (V. 27). Thus the individual is morally free to use his labor to act on the common resources of nature. In Locke's metaphor, he "mixes" his labor with the natural entity. The mixing of the private property of individual labor with the unowned commons creates that act of appropriation. Locke used the example of harvesting acorns or apples:

> He that is nourished by the Acorns he pickt up under an Oak, or the Apples he gathered from the Trees in the Wood, has certainly appropriated them to himself. No Body can deny the nourishment is his. I ask then, When did they begin to be his? When he digested? Or when he eat? Or when he boiled? Or when he brought them home? Or when he pickt them up? And 'tis plain, if the first gathering made them not his, nothing else could. That *labour* put a distinction between them and common. (V. 28)

The moral basis of the existence of private property is thus the labor used by the individual to remove natural resources from the commonly owned natural world for the purpose of physical sustenance. "Whatsoever then he removes out of the State of Nature hath provided . . . he hath mixed his *Labour* with, and joyned to it something that is his own, and thereby makes it his *Property*" (V. 27).

To complete the argument for the moral legitimacy of privately owned natural resources, Locke imposed two limitations on the extent of the act of appropriation. The limitations appeared to protect people from the acquisition of private property by others. The first limitation was that no one could take more than could be used before spoilage. "Nothing was made by God for Man to spoil or destroy," and thus:

> But how far has [God] given it [i.e., the commons] us? To enjoy. As much as any one can make use of to any advantage of life before it spoils; so much he may by his labour fix a Property in. Whatever is beyond this, is more than his share, and belongs to others. (V. 31)

This restriction even applies to the appropriation of real property (land). A person cannot enclose, and thus acquire by labor, more land than he can cultivate.

The second limitation required that one leave enough common natural resources for others to use. As with the first limitation, this requirement seems imposed to ensure that no individuals are harmed by the general acquisition of private property. An individual only makes a justifiable appropriation of a natural resource if others can appropriate a similar amount. "Nor was this *appropriation* . . . any prejudice to any other Man, since there was still enough, and as good left; and more than the yet unprovided could use" (V. 33). Locke illustrated this point with one of his finest metaphors: "No Body could think himself injur'd by the drinking of another Man, though he took a good Draught, who had a whole River of the same Water left him to quench his thirst" (V. 33). As long as there are natural resources left in the state of nature, the commons, for the use of other individuals, then the creation of private property through labor for the purpose of consumptive use is not immoral or illegitimate.

The two limitations helped reinforce the moral foundation of the acquisition of private property, since they protected against two potential abuses: the waste of natural resources and harm to other human beings. From the perspective of an ethic of the use of the natural environment, these limitations may also have helped to demonstrate the roots of an awareness of environmental responsibility. Yet the existence of the limitations was clearly a minor theme in Locke's philosophy of the use of nature. The primary significance of Locke's notion of private property was that it established the anthropocentric use-value of nature, explicitly endorsing a model of the natural world as a reservoir of resources for the use of humanity.

An anthropocentric conception of value pervaded Locke's language and argument. He was so tied to an anthropocentric perspective of the natural world that he even defined the "intrinsic" value of natural entities as their use. "The intrinsick value of things . . . depends only on their usefulness to the Life of Man" (V. 37). This is a total reversal of the current meaning of the terms, for a value based on usefulness is what philosophers call an "instrumental" value, the exact opposite of intrinsic value. An intrinsic value of an entity would be the value in itself without regard to its use by anyone or anything. For Locke however, natural entities were resources, only valuable as they were used by human beings, having little or no value in themselves.

The key to Locke's argument was an empirical claim that cultivated land was almost a hundred times more valuable than uncultivated land lying fallow, in common:

> 'tis *Labour* indeed that *puts the difference of value* on every
> thing. . . . I think it will be but a very modest Computation to say,
> that of the *Products* of the Earth useful to the Life of Man 9/10
> are the *effects of labour*; nay, if we will rightly estimate things as
> they come to our use . . . what in them is purely owing to *Nature*,

and what to *labour*, we shall find, that in most of them 99/100 are wholly to be put on the account of *labour*. (V. 40)

Locke illustrated the point by a comparison of the productivity of the land in England with the vast amount of common land in America. Despite the richness of American soil, it lacked the value and productivity of the land of the advanced nations, because the land lay unused, fallow, uncultivated, as *waste*.

For Locke, then, the value of natural resources, the value of the natural world, depended on the labor of human beings to bring the natural world within the realm of human culture. Humans domesticated, cultivated, and used wild nature for the furtherance of human purposes. In discussing the value of a harvested corn crop, Locke concluded that "Nature and the Earth furnished only the almost worthless Materials" (V. 43). The value of natural entities in themselves was virtually worthless, since Locke perceived value only in the productive use of natural resources for human life.

Nature, for Locke, was merely the raw material for the development of human property. It was only human property—nature converted to a human resource through productive labor—that was useful for humanity. Locke's vision of the natural world was thoroughly anthropocentric. Nature, and all the living and nonliving entities therein, were evaluated almost entirely on their contributions to human well-being. Nature and natural entities had no intrinsic value; their value was determined by their instrumental use by humanity. The maintenance of human life and comfort was the primary focus of all policies of action, all determinations of value.

Locke's philosophy of nature thus expressed the dominant tradition of the modern age. In many ways, Locke represented the entire movement of modernism, the intellectual milieu of Western civilization since the Renaissance. According to one recent commentator, modernism was that historical movement that considered "science, technology, and liberal democracy" as the agents of change, "to transform a base and worthless wilderness into industrialized, democratic civilization" (3). We find in Locke a fusion of political philosophy (the source of the moral legitimacy of the state) with a philosophy of nature and the environment—a fusion based on the value of human progress. Human interests, the maintenance and improvement of human life, lie at the center of all value determinations. Human progress is the end of all policy, the purpose of all human activity. Nature and natural resources are worthless, mere objects for exploitation by the dominant human species, until they are transformed, through human labor, into instruments for human betterment. The entire nonhuman world becomes an instrument for the fulfillment of human needs and desires, for human life and comfort.

John Locke was no ordinary philosopher, for his ideas exerted enormous influence across the entire domain of Western civilization. His theory of political society, based on the fundamental natural rights of individual human beings, established the framework for political discussion throughout the period of modern liberalism, a period in which we still reside. In addition, his ideas concerning the value and meaning of nature and property established the primacy of the anthropocentric use-values of natural resources. This view of nature and property still sets the framework for the debate in environmental policy, as we will see in the ideas of Gifford Pinchot, John Muir, and Aldo Leopold. In the analysis of natural value, we are heirs to the Lockean tradition.

Recent Traditions: Utilitarianism and Beyond

The dominant tradition of the value of natural resources has focused on the use of these resources for humanity. The concept of use enframes the philosophical discussion of environmental policy: one is either an advocate or a critic of use and development, but the concept of use is inescapable. All environmental policies that affect the protection and/or development of natural resources are analyzed, evaluated, and criticized with some regard to their usefulness for humanity. The dominant tradition in the history of the ethics of environmental policy could not be clearer. In the modern world, we accept, at least as the starting point for discussion, the Lockean paradigm for the analysis of nature's value.

But it was only after Locke's lifetime that the philosophy of use-value was given a technical name by moral philosophers: *utilitarianism*. Utilitarianism is the ethical theory that claims that the morally correct action is the one, among several alternatives, that maximizes the good, pleasure, or happiness of those human beings affected by the action. It is an ethical doctrine based on the *consequences* of actions (or policies), for it is the *result* of an action that determines the amount of good or evil that it produces. Utilitarianism is, in the field of academic philosophy, a complicated, subtle, and controversial doctrine—and it is beyond the scope of this chapter to give it a full hearing and analysis. But the basic idea of utilitarianism appeals to common sense, since it encapsulates the idea that ethical judgments should, in the long run at least, promote good consequences and happiness. Its central idea can be summarized by the familiar maxim, "the greatest happiness for the greatest number."

In the late 19th and early 20th centuries, natural resource policy was debated along utilitarian lines. Gifford Pinchot was the leading proponent of the utilitarian analysis of natural resource policy. John Muir was the leading critic of that view (4). Aldo Leopold was the visionary who offered a compromise ethic of environmental respect (5). In the remainder of this chapter, I will briefly survey the basic philosophical and ethical ideas of these three thinkers.

Gifford Pinchot, who ultimately rose to the position of head of the new United States Forest Service, was trained, as a young man, in the science of forest management in Europe. The philosophical and ethical foundation of forest management was clearly the use-value of forests for human beings. The entire concept of "management" implies that the forests be directed, controlled, or designed for a particular purpose. The forests, or any other natural resource, must be used in such a way as to create benefits for humanity, and at the same time preserve the resource base for the future. Pinchot, in his autobiography, described the new policy with language that was an exact replication of the utilitarian maxim: "the use of the natural resources for the greatest good of the greatest number for the longest time" (6). All the aspects of policy that fell under the purview of the Forest Service—public lands, mining, agriculture, erosion, game management—could be understood as part of a utilitarian objective: "the one great problem of the use of Earth for the good of man" (7).

As Roderick Nash's history of wilderness preservation in the United States recounts, this utilitarian outlook was central to the arguments that help to establish the first national and state parks and wilderness preserves (8). Land was to be set aside, protected from the normal economic development of forestry, grazing, and farming because better results for humanity could be produced by preservation. The best possible use of the land was, paradoxically, not to use it in the manner of traditional development. New empirical evidence demonstrated that the overcutting of forests in sensitive watershed areas caused drought, flood, and erosion. Alternatively, the preservation of wilderness in these areas could prevent catastrophic results. Wilderness preservation was thus seen as compatible with economic progress, development, and the use-value of natural resources (9).

The arguments for the establishment of Yellowstone National Park and New York State's "Forest Preserve" of the Adirondacks were essentially utilitarian: the preserves would be more useful if they were not developed. Yellowstone was to be protected from the "private acquisition and exploitation of geysers, hot springs, waterfalls, and similar curiosities" (10). The key idea was that the public—not private individuals—should maintain ownership and access to these natural wonders because this would be of the greatest benefit for the greatest number. Most important, Nash recounts that the supporters of Yellowstone had to show that the area of the park was useless for development because of its altitude and temperature (its preservation would not harm material progress) (11). In New York, the preservation of the Adirondacks was urged because of the effects on water supply, not because of recreation or other noneconomic amenities. Preservation had to be seen as a matter of economic self-interest, entirely compatible with industry and development (12).

There were those who urged the preservation of natural wilderness on other than the utilitarian grounds of economic development—for reasons of aesthetics, recreation, and religious awe. John Muir, who founded the Sierra Club, was the leading advocate of this nonutilitarian position. But at the beginning of the movement for wilderness preservation, both kinds of "preservationists" were united in their fight against the so-called despoilers of nature—those developers who saw no reason not to use natural resources to the maximum degree, those who perceived natural resources to be limitless. To prevent the ever-increasing, rapid deterioration of nature and its resources, all kinds of environmentalists united, despite differing motivations and values, to fight a common enemy. Eventually, however, the differing bases of the environmentalist position would lead to divergent policy choices, and the division of the movement into warring factions. This historical result is not surprising, since it appears to validate the logic of the connection between ethical values and policy. The values that lie at the foundation of a policy are the ultimate justification of the policy; if one introduces a different set of values, then in the long run, policies will emerge that conflict with the original set of values.

John Muir's relationship with Gifford Pinchot is a perfect example of this clash of values (13). Muir's ideas of the value of wilderness were not based on the utilitarian use-value of natural resources. Although there is much scholarly debate about the precise meaning of Muir's thought, it seems clear that he had a nearly mystical, almost religious sense of the value of nature. In perhaps his most famous statement in the debate over wilderness preservation, when he fought to prevent the construction of a dam at Hetch Hetchy that would supply water for San Francisco, he clearly alluded to the sacredness of the undisturbed wilderness: "Dam Hetch Hetchy! As well dam for water-tanks the people's cathedrals and churches, for no holier temple has ever been consecrated by the heart of man" (14). For Muir, the wilderness was an expression of God's harmony, of the spiritual power of the universe—it was the place in which people could come closest to God.

It is easy to characterize Muir as a critic of utilitarian thought regarding natural resources; but it is also important to understand the source of his criticism, his own view of the value of wild nature. Muir rejected anthropocentrism and adopted what is now called a "biocentric" perspective, centering value on all living entities, rather than humans alone. He viewed nature as an organism in constant flux, not a fixed and determinate mechanism. This view of nature and the value of life was based on pantheism—a view that holds all of Nature sacred—that was itself informed by the new evolutionary insights of Darwin and other scientists of the late 19th century. He was also a critic of modernism, the relentless push for materialistic progress (15).

Muir's pantheistic view of nature was, of course, a religious view of the value of nature, but it yielded important philosophical and ethical conclusions. These conclusions helped to establish a rival tradition of the ethics of the use of natural resources. In a pantheistic perspective, God is in the world in its entirety: all the parts of the world are part of God. This view thus implies a radical equality among all the beings of nature as well as a universal harmony and kinship, a web of life in which humans do not dominate, use, or destroy. "The universe would be incomplete without man; but it would also be incomplete without the smallest transmicroscopic creature that dwells beyond our conceitful eyes and knowledge." We are, Muir wrote, "part of Wild nature, kin to everything." This implies a deep and equal respect among humans and all of wild nature (16). It is a view that is the exact opposite of the anthropocentric utilitarianism espoused by Pinchot (and explicitly formulated in the modern age by Locke). Nature is not the material for the development of human happiness. Nature is valuable in itself—intrinsically—as a manifestation of the Divine.

Originally allies in the fight for wilderness preservation, Muir and Pinchot clashed, and ended their relationship permanently, over the proposal to dam Hetch Hetchy. Pinchot argued on simple utilitarian grounds: which policy alternative created the most benefits for the affected human population? In his testimony before Congress on June 25, 1913, Pinchot claimed that the central issue was whether there was more advantage in leaving the valley natural and wild, or in using the water resources for the benefit of San Francisco. Preserving wilderness should not prevent the citizens of San Francisco from obtaining an adequate water supply. Pinchot defended his view by expressing his basic belief in conservation policy: "the fundamental principle of the whole conservation policy is that of use, to take every part of the land and its resources and put it to that use in which it will serve the most people" (17). The greatest good for the greatest number—utilitarianism pure and simple.

Muir, on the other hand, saw Hetch Hetchy as the first great test of the nation's new commitment to the preservation of wilderness. Although San Francisco clearly had a need for an adequate water supply, there was no reason to obtain this water from a beautiful, pristine wilderness park. Muir argued on aesthetic and spiritual grounds that the need for beautiful areas

of wilderness was important for the human soul and the minds of human beings. Moreover, the wilderness valley was a sacred or divine place that
needed to be protected from the materialistic and commercial interests of
the age (18).

Hetch Hetchy represented a classic case of the conflict between utilitarian and nonutilitarian values. These are different kinds of values, since
one is based on the amount of benefit or happiness to be produced as a result of a particular policy of action, and the other is based on nonquantifi-
able and intangible spiritual values, such as beauty and divinity. The early
American environmentalist movement was inspired by both traditions. It
was inevitable that a case like Hetch Hetchy would expose the inherent contradiction within a movement governed by two distinct ethical traditions.

As Nash comments, the most surprising aspect of the battle over the proposal to dam Hetch Hetchy was that it even happened (19). For the first
time in American history, serious consideration was given to a position
other than the direct material use of a natural resource. It was not surprising, however, that the dominant tradition of utilitarian use-values carried the day, but at least a minority tradition concerning natural resources
and the preservation of wilderness was beginning to take hold in American
consciousness.

With the thoughts of Aldo Leopold, the minority tradition would be
combined with a scientific theory of ecological land-use. Leopold invoked
both the use-value tradition of natural resources and the spiritual or ethical
tradition of respect for nature in itself. His ideas played a central part in the
history of the ethics of environmental policy. Leopold's classic essay "The
Land Ethic" in A Sand County Almanac is probably the most widely cited
source in the literature of environmental philosophy. His view of the moral
consideration of the land-community is the starting point for almost all discussions of environmental ethics. Although his views are not accepted
among all professionals in the field of environmental policy, Leopold's ethic
of land use is clearly the dominant tradition in the philosophy of nature and
the environment today—and his influence continues to grow.

Leopold was trained as a forester at the Yale School of Forestry, and so
was an early follower of the wise-use tradition of natural resource policy. But
his ideas matured over the years into a deep-seated respect for the harmonious dynamics of ecological processes. It was the biotic community, the interrelated system of living and nonliving natural entities, that was the source
of value. He recounted his conversion in an essay, "Thinking Like a Mountain," about the overhunting of wolves. Once the wolves are killed, the deer
population explodes, the vegetation on the mountainside is eaten until it too
is dead, and then the deer die also. "Only the mountain has lived long

enough to listen objectively to the howl of a wolf." We must think of the entire ecological system, and not try to manage one isolated part. If we try to overmanage parts of the natural system, without an appreciation of the interconnections, then we have "not learned to think like a mountain. Hence we have dustbowls, and rivers washing the future into the sea" (20).

In "The Land Ethic," Leopold presented the first ecologically based statement of an ethic based on the direct moral consideration of natural nonhuman entities. His guiding ethical maxim was simple: "A thing is right when it tends to preserve the integrity, stability, and beauty of the biotic community. It is wrong when it tends otherwise" (21). This statement is a remarkably clear alternative to the dominant tradition of anthropocentric use-value of the natural environment.

A detailed look at Leopold's land ethic reveals two major strands of thought: (1) the extension of ethical consideration to nonhumans, and (2) the recognition of an ecosystemic community. For Leopold, the extension of moral consideration to an ever increasing range of individuals and kinds of entities so as to include the natural environment was not only an "evolutionary possibility" but also "an ecological necessity." He called this extension of ethical consideration the "ethical sequence," and he saw it as an empirical and historical fact of human social development: as human society progresses, it increases the range of moral significance. Leopold begins "The Land Ethic" with a striking image from the *Odyssey* of Homer, where human female slaves are treated as property—they are considered mere things, outside of moral categories, subject only to the decisions of the owner regarding expediency and economics (22). Nonhuman nature, "the land," is treated similarly, as mere property. But Leopold thought that ethics was continually advancing, becoming more complex as a mode of cooperation and control. It enlarges its focus from the individual to the family to the society, and ultimately to nature itself.

The extension of ethical vision rests on the idea of community, and it is here that Leopold was able to combine his ecological insights with the foundation of ethics. Community, for Leopold, was the foundation of all moral activity. "All ethics so far evolved rest upon a single premise: that the individual is a member of a community of interdependent parts" (23). It is within communities that we perceive and acknowledge moral relationships and obligations. But from the perspective of ecological science, Leopold saw that biological systems, ecosystems, natural environments—in short, the land—are communities in the sense relevant for ethical obligation. Natural systems establish mutually interdependent relationships among the members of the systems; the members of natural systems also work toward common goals in a kind of natural cooperation, which we term symbiosis. Thus Leopold argues for the existence of a broader sense of community.

"The land ethic simply enlarges the boundaries of the community to include soils, waters, plants, and animals, or collectively: the land" (24). Membership in this land community is the source of moral respect and obligation. Since membership is not limited to human beings, the land ethic expresses a *nonanthropocentric* tradition of the ethics of the use of natural resources.

Leopold's vision of an ethic directed toward the land, and not merely toward the human use of the land, does contain utilitarian elements. Even Leopold could not escape the dominant tradition of the modern age. The surprise was that Leopold could be interpreted as proposing a *nonanthropocentric utilitarianism,* an ethical theory that seeks to maximize the good, not for humans, but for the natural world as a whole. Since he includes in his calculations of ethical behavior the good for the nonhuman world (its "integrity, stability, and beauty"), he can acknowledge the kinds of goods that Muir sought to maximize (the beauty, harmony, and divinity of the wilderness) with the kinds of goods that Pinchot sought (the overall maintenance of the natural system as a reserve for resources for the future). Preserving all of these goods tends to preserve the ecological system as a whole. An ethic of respect for natural processes and communities will result in benefits for both nature and humanity.

Leopold's contribution to the traditions of ethics regarding the use of natural resources can be defined by his rejection of an anthropocentric perspective and his focus on whole systems and natural communities. Although he celebrates many of the values of nature proposed by John Muir and other advocates of wilderness preservation, he does so from the perspective of a trained forester and game manager with a secure grounding in ecological science and ecosystemic relationships. Like Gifford Pinchot, he sought to use land wisely and conservatively, but this use must also imply a direct respect for the entities and processes of the natural world. His land ethic offers the best hope of developing an ethic for the use of natural resources while simultaneously respecting the integrity of the natural world.

Notes

1. White, L., Jr. 1967. The historical roots of our ecologic crisis. Science 155:1203–1207. For a fuller discussion of this philosophical tradition, see Passmore, J. 1974. Man's responsibility for nature: ecological problems and western traditions, 3–40. New York: Scribner; and Attfield, R. 1983. The ethics of environmental concern, 20-87. New York: Columbia University Press.
2. All references to Locke are to chapter and paragraph of the Second Treatise of Government.

3. Oelschlaeger, M. 1991. The idea of wilderness, 68. New Haven, Connecticut: Yale University Press.
4. My discussion of Pinchot and Muir owes much to three secondary sources that focus on the philosophical examination of the Pinchot/Muir split: Nash, R. 1982. Wilderness and the American mind, 3rd ed. New Haven, Connecticut: Yale University Press; Norton, B.G. 1991. Toward unity among environmentalists. New York: Oxford University Press; and Oelschlaeger 1991 (3).
5. Norton has a similar view of Leopold, though we may differ in the details of how Leopold effected a compromise. See Norton 1991 (4).
6. Pinchot, G. [1947]1987. Breaking new ground, 325–326. Washington, D.C.: Island Press. Cited in Norton 1991, 23 (4).
7. Pinchot [1947]1987, 322 (6); Norton 1991, 22 (4).
8. Nash 1982, 108–121 (4).
9. Nash 1982, 105 (4). The crucial argument was presented in Marsh, G.P. 1864. Man and nature: or, physical geography as modified by human action.
10. Nash 1982, 108 (4).
11. Nash 1982, 112 (4).
12. Nash 1982, 117–118 (4).
13. Note that Norton offers a revisionist interpretation of this clash, stressing the similarities between Pinchot and Muir. See Norton 1991, 31–38 (4).
14. Muir, J. 1912. The Yosemite. Cited in Nash 1982, 168 (4).
15. My view of Muir is based primarily on the interpretation of Oelschlaeger 1991, 172–204 (3). Nash sees Muir primarily as a Transcendentalist, a follower of Thoreau and the Romantic traditions of the 19th century. See Nash 1982, 125–129 (4); and Oelschlaeger 1991, 173, 178–182 (3).
16. Muir quotations cited in Nash 1982, 128–129 (4).
17. Pinchot's testimony before the House Committee on Public Lands is summarized in Nash 1982, 170–171 (4).
18. Nash 1982, 163–168 (4).
19. Nash 1982, 181 (4).
20. Leopold, Aldo. [1949] 1970. A sand county almanac: with essays on conservation from round river, 137–140. New York: Ballantine Books (originally published New York: Oxford University Press).
21. Leopold [1949] 1970, 262 (20).
22. Leopold [1949] 1970, 238–239 (20).
23. Leopold [1949] 1970, 239 (20).
24. Leopold [1949] 1970, 239 (20).

Tension: The Beginning of the Shift

EARTH DAY, PASSAGE OF THE WILDERNESS ACT and the Endangered Species Act, and other accompanying activities began a shift in how we view our environment, a shift that we are still witnessing today. Authors in Part II focus on the time period around the 1960s into the early 1980s, the beginning of the most recent "environmental movement." Once again, we see great turbulence in American society spilling over and affecting natural resources. While Americans were challenging their government's involvement in the Vietnam War, and an American president was being threatened with impeachment, things were equally volatile in the conservation arena. This was an era when the "new users" of natural resources gained a voice and insisted on being heard. Nongovernmental organizations emerged as powerful entities, influencing natural resource policy through lobbying and litigation. People within and without the natural resource agencies began questioning the overarching view of resources as commodities. Resource managers working for government agencies found themselves being asked to make decisions on more than just what the traditional users wanted from the land. Now, managers had to accommodate a whole new set of constituents. And these constituents were reinvigorated with increasing clout; they could no longer be ignored.

In this part's introductory essay, David Orr offers a personal perspective for the need of developing a sense of place if humans are ever to have a mutually respectful relationship with their world. Beginning with a description of his hometown, Orr illustrates how earlier American communities were "repair and reuse economies" which were predominantly locally owned and operated. "My mother bought groceries from the store in town. She bought vegetables from local farmers, including the Amish who went door to door selling everything from farm-fresh eggs to maple syrup. Milk was delivered daily in returnable glass bottles by a locally owned dairy company." As global economics and international conglomerates have undermined these previously reliant communities, people increasingly find themselves in towns and cities where they live but do not comprehend. They do not know the source of their water, where their waste goes, the origin of the food they eat, or who their county commissioners are. In short, Orr maintains we have lost a sense of place. A world that takes its environment seriously, the title of Orr's essay, will be one where its populace is firmly rooted in communities which believe that "problems that occur all over the world are not necessarily global problems, and some truly global problems may be solvable only by lots of local solutions."

Brunson and Kennedy follow Orr's essay by examining natural resource agency responses to changing social values. Using the concept of "multiple use" as a metaphor, they examine the relationship between four natural resource agencies and society. Their thesis is that managers have viewed themselves as responsible land stewards with exclusive expertise and responsibility for resources and their wise use; the public had none. By examining the demographic and societal transitions of the 1960s and 1970s, Brunson and Kennedy describe an American population that began to place more value on amenity attributes of nature and less on its commodity uses. Not that the demand for commodities ever wavered, it was just that the public wanted the agencies to "manage for *more* values, but to do so in a way that entailed *less* of what the commodity agencies traditionally called "management."

As the public cry for real multiple use rather than lip service to other than commodity use increased, Congress was drawn into the fray. The result was a flurry of environmental legislation that tended to restrict the federal agencies' decision-making latitude. Brunson and Kennedy illustrate this point with passage of the Wilderness Act. "The bill itself was no more restrictive than the Forest Service's 1939 primitive-area regulations, but authority to approve exemptions was transferred from the agency to Congress." The upshot was that resource agencies found themselves in a crossfire between urban constituents wanting amenity uses of public lands and rural communities dependent on these lands for grazing, logging, and mining. Returning to a theme presented in earlier chapters by Robert Nelson and Dale Hein, Brunson and Kennedy explore the idea that resource managers were not prepared for these changes, due largely to an educational system that focused on scientific solutions rather than "people skills." Looking ahead, the authors suggest that natural resource agencies will either have to change from within, or change will be imposed from without. They believe change is inevitable until the agencies truly are able to "reflect the relationship that society now demands between itself and the natural environment."

As though to illustrate Brunson's and Kennedy's point, the next two chapters offer point-counterpoint to the charge that agencies must redefine themselves. Jeff DeBonis has prepared a chapter that documents his personal story of working for a federal land management agency. Just back from the Peace Corps, he went to work for the Forest Service. There, instead of an organization that placed stewardship first, he found himself in an agency culture that focused on "getting the cut out." Disillusioned, he looked around to find that there were other like-minded employees. Not yet ready to quit the Forest Service, they instead tried to work within the system to effect change. DeBonis was transferred to another forest with an enlightened forest supervisor. There, for a time, he felt that the agency could find a way out of the vicious circle it had wormed its way into. From this forest, however, he moved to the Blue River District of the Willamette National Forest in western Oregon. At the time, the Willamette was cutting more timber than any other national forest. Shocked at the environmental destruction that was accompanying this level of logging, he wrote a letter expressing his concerns to the chief of the Forest Service, F. Dale Robertson. Receiving no response, he founded the Association of Forest Service Employees for Environmental Ethics (AFSEEE). AFSEEE's goal was "to foster an environmental ethic among employees that would change the culture of the Forest Service to one that was more environmentally oriented, would meet its regulatory laws, and would err on the side of resource protection." AFSEEE quickly gained more than a thousand members from within the agency. Soon, overwhelmed with the responsibilities of managing AFSEEE, DeBonis left the Forest Service to devote himself full time to AFSEEE. Realizing that other federal and state natural resource agencies had similar "commodity cultures," he formed an organization named Public Employees for Environmental Responsibility. DeBonis concludes with the wish that his example will inspire others to work for change so that resource agencies will be viewed as organizations that place primacy on land stewardship.

Almost in the form of a rebuttal, the next chapter by Kessler and Salwasser explains how one agency performed an internal analysis of its culture. Salwasser and Kessler, then Forest Service employees, were assigned to develop the initiative "New Perspectives," aimed at changing the direction of this agency from one preoccupied with commodity extraction to one with a focus on ecosystem management. Tracing the history of the Forest Service, the authors show how the agency attempted to address the perceived needs of the public, how it became indentured to the whims and wills of Congress, and how finally it floundered in a quagmire of litigation and

dropping employee morale. With the Forest Service in trouble, and this belief both within and without the agency, it took the bold step of performing
a public internal examination. What emerged were four principles and the
realization that top-down management was strangling the organization. The
principles are based on the twin concepts of ecosystem management and
empowering agency personnel to take charge and take chances, and they
embrace the belief that the diverse publics interested in national forests and
grasslands are essential components in any new way of doing business. Citizens' groups are to become full partners in decision making and resource
management, a concept alien to an agency model based on scientific expertise held only by those working for the organization. Kessler and Salwasser
conclude with the conviction that it is no longer a question whether the
Forest Service will change; rather they wonder at what speed it will adapt to
a different world.

Up to the present, nongovernmental organizations (NGOs) concerned
with nature conservation have had an adversarial role with government natural resource agencies. Perhaps someday this posture will change, but for
the present NGOs play this part in the unfolding natural resource drama.
Rupert Cutler describes the NGOs and their roles in shaping resource management. "Less constrained than government and corporate employees by
statutes, regulations, and job descriptions, considerations that tend to discourage creativity, innovation, and risk-taking, representatives of NGOs are
free to note what they consider agency and industry failures and shortcomings and propose changes in public policy." This, according to Cutler, is the
principal reason for the success of environmental NGOs and, he adds, a
reason why many government agency professionals have their jobs today.
This initially confusing statement is based on Cutler's belief that NGOs have
played key roles in environmental legislation which today provides job security for natural resource managers. Is this tension healthy or will the future see NGOs and agencies working together on common agendas? Cutler
believes the trend is in the direction of working for broadly acceptable
middle-ground solutions, though he is quick to note that "There has been
no reward, historically, for NGO leaders' public participation in any process
leading to compromise."

NGOs and resource agencies possess different levels of technical knowledge and emotional commitment, with the latter historically rich in science-
educated personnel and the former made up of people largely untrained in
natural resources. He notes, however, that this dichotomy is rapidly
changing with many of the nation's best graduates now preferring to work
for NGOs. The diversity of NGOs reflects the breadth of the environmental
movement today, and Cutler places them into one of three categories: con-

servationist, preservationist, and environmentalist. Conservation NGOs are principally concerned with the sustained use of natural resources, preservationist groups work to protect natural systems, and environmentalist NGOs are involved with issues such as clean air and water. Cutler suggests other ways that NGOs can be classified, including by geographical scope of their activities, which segment of policy they are involved with, and by their organizational structure. The role of environmental NGOs will continue to increase, perhaps in proportion to the decline of government agencies in natural resources management. Cutler concludes his chapter with several predictions: NGOs will have to seek compromise more and division less; be more willing to work with other groups and not always insist on going alone; and they will have to be more sensitive to human needs, particularly the economic well-being of people.

As alluded to in the previous chapter, NGOs have played a pivotal role in shaping environmental policy. In Chapter 12, Vawter Parker examines how NGOs have used litigation to force agencies to follow statutory mandates. Parker argues that "Courts are not managing our public lands. Increasingly, however, they are requiring federal agencies to comply with the law, and in doing that they are changing forever the way the agencies manage our lands." Parker sees environmental litigation as being important principally as a delaying action, allowing time for "the public to work its will through the political process." But certainly, litigation can also be directly instrumental in protecting nature. Parker concludes his chapter by illustrating how environmental NGOs successfully sued federal agencies to protect large amounts of land for red-cockaded woodpeckers and northern spotted owls, two species protected by the Endangered Species Act. It may seem surprising that citizen groups have to sue federal agencies to enforce federal laws. However, until the day that agencies comply with the laws that govern them, litigation appears a necessary safeguard for agency accountability.

Can natural resource economics, rooted in the concept of resource scarcity, make the transition to a discipline that "accords preservation of natural environments equal importance to development"? John Loomis addresses this question in Chapter 13, "Shifting and Broadening the Economic Paradigm toward Natural Resources." And, by and large, his answer is yes. Historically, our public land natural resources have suffered from overuse largely because they are common pool resources. Because no single person owned them, costs of using a resource did not fall on the principal user; instead these "externalities" were borne by others. For example, the logger who cut trees on a National Forest imposed costs on downstream users of the watershed, such as recreationists who paid the cost of reduced enjoyment due to more turbid water. The recognition of such "externalities" has played a significant role in altering how federal agencies compute benefit-cost analyses. In addition, acknowledging people's willingness to pay, and a survey-based method for valuing nonmarketed natural resources, have changed forever the way natural resource economics are conducted. Furthermore, the incorporation of "option," "existence," and "bequest" values into resource economic models has signaled recognition that human values are not strictly consumption oriented. Loomis concludes by asserting that economic models will continue to change, reflecting the shift in our society's concerns with ecosystem health.

The concluding chapter of Part II is by Thomas Power, who examines the conventional wisdom that natural resource economies are strictly commodity-based. As Power states, "The extraction and processing in our timber, mining, and agricultural industries are seen as the dominant source of income flowing into the local economy and, therefore, as the primary economic engine. Because these industries are seen as dominating the local economy, public land managers tend to take as one of their primary responsibilities the 'stabilization' of the local economy through the provision of 'necessary' raw material supplies." Power believes that this is a view through the rear-view mirror, and fails to reflect the present economic conditions in many western communities.

To illustrate his point, Power examines the economies of western areas where the traditional extractive-based economy has faltered. What he finds is that, in most cases, the economies of these areas have not flattened, but have either held steady or grown. For example, in the Bitterroot Valley of "timber-dependent" western Montana, almost 80 percent of the timber harvest has been lost in recent times. Instead of finding a depressed community, he reported brisk expansion of real personal income during this same period. This pattern is repeated in example after example, and Power concludes that contracting extractive employment is usually compensated for by rapidly expanding nonextractive economies, and that there are apparently unappreciated stabilizing forces operating that are not dealt with adequately in the extractive economic model.

Power goes on to examine what he believes are the new and more important aspects of local commodities, those within the rubric of "amenities." By focusing on the assumptions that (1) people do care where they live, and (2) firms do care about labor supply, he proposes a new "environmental" economic model that embraces the importance of living environments, areas that still offer healthy, intact landscapes. At this point, Power's take-home message is clear: "The natural resource of primary economic importance to the long-run economic well-being of the community may be environmental quality, not extractive resources."

Chapter 7

A World That Takes
Its Environment Seriously

David W. Orr

Find your place on the planet, dig in, and take responsibility from there
—Gary Snyder
Turtle Island (p. 101)

Recollections

I grew up in a small town amid the rolling hills and farms of western Pennsylvania. As towns go it wasn't much different from hundreds of others throughout the United States. There was a main street with shops and stores, a funeral parlor or two, four churches, a small liberal arts college, and perhaps two thousand residents give or take. It was a "dry" town filled with serious and hardworking Protestants and a disconcertingly large number of retired preachers and missionaries. It was not a place that quickly welcomed Elvis and rock 'n roll. The prevailing political sensibilities were sober and overwhelmingly Republican of the Eisenhower sort. The town would have seemed stuffy and parochial to a Sherwood Anderson or Theodore Dreiser. And it probably was. By the standards of the 1990s, the town, the college, and its residents would have failed even the most lax certification for political correctness. It was a man's world, neither multicultural nor multiracial. The sexual revolution lay ahead. And almost everyone who was anyone in town bought without question the assumptions of mid-century America about our inherent virtue, economic progress, communism, and technology. J. Edgar Hoover was a hero. Boys were measured for manhood on the baseball diamond or basketball court. It was also a place, like most others, in transition from one kind of economy to another.

Typical of most small towns, the main street of New Wilmington, Pennsylvania still reflected bits of the 19th century agrarian economy. There was, for example, a dilapidated and unused livery stable behind the main street where a funeral parlor parked a hearse. On the main street Mr. Meeks operated his watch repair shop and Mr. Fusco had his shoe repair shop. There were locally owned and operated businesses including two groceries, a hardware and plumbing store, a good bakery, an electronics/appliance store, a dairy store, a bank, a dry goods store, a magazine and tobacco shop, a movie theater, a building supply store, a butcher shop. The train station was located two blocks from the main street. A half mile to the south a local entrepreneur operated a tool-making plant. A quarter mile beyond lay the town dump on the banks of Neshannock Creek.

The small-town, repair and reuse economy of my childhood was predominantly locally owned and operated. My mother bought groceries from the store in town. She bought vegetables from local farmers, including the Amish who went door to door selling everything from farm-fresh eggs to maple syrup. Milk was delivered daily in returnable glass bottles by a locally owned dairy company. Soda pop also came in returnable glass bottles from a bottling plant 8 miles distant. Broken machinery could be repaired in town. Dull saws could still be sharpened for a dime. And some of the best Christmas presents I ever had were made by hand.

The forces that would undermine that sheltered world of small town, midcentury America were on the march. But I knew nothing of these as I joined the great exodus of self-assured and expectant young people leaving their home towns for some other place thought to offer greater opportunity and more excitement. Few of us could say with certainty why we were going, or where we were headed as long as it was somewhere else. Nor could we have said what we were leaving behind.

Looking back I can see that even then things were changing as the larger industrial economy began to undermine local economies nearly everywhere. We bought our first television set in the same year that Congress passed the Interstate Highway Act. I recall the lights on the big shovel at the strip mine across the valley burning into the night. The contractor for whom I worked in the summer went out of business shortly after I graduated from college. The farmer who gave me part-time employment, and thought to be the most progressive in the county, went bankrupt in 1975. He was not alone. People in New Wilmington now buy their milk in plastic jugs from interstate dairy cooperatives. The local bottling plant disappeared and with it the practice of returning glass bottles to the store. The nearby industrial cities of New Castle and Youngstown, Ohio, that I knew as busy and thriving places, are now mostly derelict and abandoned as are other cities in what was once a blue collar, industrial corridor stretching from Pittsburgh to Cleveland. Interstate highways to the north and east of town now slash across what was once farm country. Tourism is the main economic hope. Crime, I hear, is a growing problem.

Large Numbers

In the 30 years since the class of 1961 set out to find its way, world population grew from 3.2 billion to 5.5 billion; approximately 120 billion tons of carbon dioxide were emitted to the atmosphere, mostly from the combustion of fossil fuels; perhaps a tenth of the life forms on the earth disappeared in that time; a quarter of the world's rainforests were cut down; half or more of the forests in Europe were damaged by acid rain; careless farming and development caused the erosion of some 600 billion tons of topsoil worldwide; the ozone shield was severely damaged. Before the class of 1961 is just a faint memory, the earth may be 2–3 degrees centigrade hotter, with consequences we can barely imagine; world population will be 8–9 billion; perhaps 25 percent of the earth's species will have disappeared, and humans will have turned an area roughly equivalent to the size of the United States into desert. Something of earth-shattering importance went wrong in our lifetime, and we were prepared neither to see it nor to avoid complicity in it.

Hindsight

Looking back with more or less 20/20 hindsight, I believe that amid all of the many good things in my town, there were three things missing that bear on the issues implied in the title of this chapter. First, and most obvious, we were taught virtually nothing of ecology, systems, and interrelatedness. But neither were many others. This was a blind spot for a country determined to grow and armed with the philosophy of economic improvement. As a consequence we knew little of our ecological dependencies or, for that matter, our own vulnerabilities. The orchard beside our house was drenched with pesticides every spring and summer, and we never objected. The blight of nearby strip mines grew year by year, and we saw little wrong with that either.

We grew up in a bountiful region that was virtually opaque to us. In school I learned about lots of other places, but I did not learn much about my own. We were not taught to think about how we lived in relation to where we lived. The Amish farms nearby, arguably the best example we have of a culture that fits its locale, were regarded as a quaint relic of a bygone world that had nothing to offer modern people. There was no course in high school or the local college on the natural history of the area. To this day, little has been written about the area as a bioregion. So we grew up mostly ignorant of the biological and ecological conditions in which we lived and what these required of us.

I finished high school the year before publication of Rachel Carson's *Silent Spring*, but not before the projections of U.S. oil production by M. King Hubbert, and some of the best writings of Lewis Mumford, Paul Sears, Fairfield Osborn, William Vogt, and earlier writings of John Muir, John Burroughs, George Perkins Marsh, and Henry David Thoreau. Our teachers and mentors had been through both the Dust Bowl and the depression, but it was the latter that affected them most, and that fact could not help but affect us. Almost by osmosis we absorbed the purported lessons of economic hardship, but not those of ecological collapse that can also lead to privation and economic failure. When it came time to rebel, we did so over such things as "life-style" and music. But we in the class of 1961, had no concept of enough or any reason to think that limits of any sort were important. Inadequate though it was, we did have an economic philosophy, but we had no articulate or ecologically solvent view of nature. We were sent out into the world armed with a creed of progress, but had scarcely a clue about our starting point or how to "find our place and dig in." And none of us in 1961 would have had any idea of what those words meant.

Looking back I can see a second missing element. On one hand I recall no skepticism or even serious discussion about technology. On the other, the college-bound students were steered into academic courses and away from vocational courses. As a result the upwardly mobile became both technologically illiterate and technologically incompetent. All the while there was a "what will they think of next" kind of naiveté reinforced by advertisers hawking messages about "living better electrically" and "progress as our most important product" that we accepted without much thought. We were good at detecting the benefits of technology in parts per billion but did not see the fine print. Nor could we see the web of dependencies that was beginning to entrap us. The same "they" who would somehow figure it all out were taking the things that Americans once did for themselves as competent people, citizens, and neighbors and selling them back at a good markup. We were turned out in the world with the intellectual equivalent of a malfunctioning immune system, unable to think critically about technology. If we read Faust at all, we read it as a fable, not as a prophecy.

Third, had we known our place better, and had we been ecologically literate and technologically savvy, we still would have lacked the political wherewithal to be better stewards of our land and heritage. Our version of small town flag-waving patriotism was disconnected from the tangible things of livelihood and location, soils and stewardship. We mistook the large abstractions of nationalism, flag, and Presidential authority for patriotism. Accordingly, we were vulnerable to the chicanery of Joe McCarthy and J. Edgar Hoover, and to Lyndon Johnson's lies about Vietnam, Richard

Nixon's lies about nearly everything, and Ronald Reagan's fantasies about "morning in America," for which we are now paying dearly.

My classmates and I are, I think, typical of most Americans born and raised in the middle decades of the 20th century. Ours has been a time of cheap energy, economic and technological optimism, lots of patriotic huffing and puffing, and auto-mobility. We are movers and we move on average 8–10 times in a lifetime. We were educated to be competent in an industrial world and incompetent in any other. We did not much question the values and assumptions of the industrial "paradigm," or those underlying notions of progress. Those beliefs were givens. We were turned out in the world vulnerable to whatever economic, technological, or even political changes were thrust upon us as long as they were said to be economically necessary or simply inevitable. We were not taught to question the physical, biological, and psychological reordering of the world taking place all around us. Nor were we enabled to see it for what it was.

New Wilmington, Pennsylvania is still a nice town. Having little industry, it has not suffered the rustbelt fate of the nearby industrial cities. It has also been spared some of the uncontrolled growth that has desecrated many other regions. Housing developments outside town, though, are now filling up what was once good farmland. Aside from the Amish, the local farm economy is a shadow of what it once was. The effects of acid rain are beginning to show on trees. The region is increasingly dependent on tourism to make ends meet. New Wilmington, like most small towns, is an island at the mercy of decisions made elsewhere. It has been spared mostly because no one noticed it, or thought it a place likely to be profitable enough for an interstate mall, mine, regional airport, a Disneyworld, or new industrial "park." Not yet anyway. In the meantime, it too has become a full fledged member of the throw-away economy, and its young people still depart in large numbers for careers elsewhere.

If New Wilmington has so far gotten off lightly, other towns and regions have not. Within a few miles, New Castle and Youngstown are industrial disaster areas. The landfill on the outskirts of my present hometown sells space for garbage from as far away as New York City. In southern Ohio, the Fernald nuclear processing plant has spread radioactive waste over several hundred square miles. The same is true of Maxey Flats, Kentucky; Rocky Flats, Colorado; and Hanford, Washington—all sacrificed in the name of "national security." Urban sprawl and decaying downtowns afflict hundreds of other towns and cities throughout the United States. Large chunks of footloose capital ravage other places. In northern Alberta, the Mitsubishi Corporation has invested over one billion dollars to build a pulp mill that will impair or destroy an ecosystem along with the indigenous culture. One hundred thousand square kilometers of rainforest will be destroyed to supply Europe with cheap pig iron from the Carajas mine in Brazil (1). The resulting devastation will not show up in the price of steel in Europe. Nor will the devastation from the other mines, wells, clearcuts, and feedlots around the world that supply the insatiable appetite of the industrial economy be subtracted from calculations of wealth. The annual gross world economy now exceeds $20 trillion, and we are told that this must increase fivefold by the middle of the next century. That same global economy now uses, directly or indirectly 25 percent of the earth's net primary productivity. Can that increase fivefold as well?

A World That Takes Its Places Seriously

Custodians of the conventional wisdom believe that economic growth is a good and necessary thing. Growth, in turn, requires capital mobility, free trade, and the willingness to take risks and make sacrifices, including those that inflict damage on particular places. For the sake of growth, whole regions and entire industries may have to be sacrificed as production and employment go elsewhere in search of cheaper labor and easier access to materials and markets. Such sacrifices are necessary, they say, so that "we" can remain competitive in the global economy, and so that the things we buy can be as cheap as profit-maximizing corporations can make them. Conventional wisdom also holds that "transnational problems cannot be managed by one country acting alone" (2). Proponents of the global point of view often cite the Montreal Accord and subsequent agreements that phase out chlorofluorocarbons as proof positive.

The first bit of conventional wisdom denies the importance of place and environment in favor of global vandalism masquerading as progress. Its more progressive adherents believe that environmental improvement itself requires further expansion of the very activities that wreck environments. Devotees of the second piece of conventional wisdom ignore the political and ecological creativity of place-centered people, wishing us to believe that the same organizations who have ruined places around the world can be trusted to save the global environment.

On the contrary, a world that takes both its environment and prosperity seriously over the long-term must pay careful attention to the patterns that connect the local and regional with the global. I do not believe that global action is unnecessary or unimportant. It is, however, insufficient and inadequate. Taking places seriously would change what we think needs to happen at the global level. It does not imply parochialism or narrowness. It does not mean crawling into a hole and pulling the ground over our heads, or what economists call autarky. While we have heard for years that we should "think globally and act locally," these words are still more a slogan than a clear program. The national and international are still accorded a disproportionate share of our attention, and the local not nearly enough. I would like to offer five reasons why places, the local, and what William Blake once called "minute particulars" are globally important.

First, we are inescapably place-centric creatures shaped in important ways by the localities of our birth and upbringing (3). We learn first those things in our immediate surroundings, and these we soak in consciously and subconsciously through sight, smell, feel, sound, taste, and perhaps through other senses we do not yet understand. Our preferences, phobias, and behaviors begin in the experience of a place. If those places are ugly and violent, the behavior of many raised in them will also be ugly and violent. Children raised in ecologically barren settings, however affluent, are deprived of the sensory stimulus and the kind of imaginative experience that can only come from biological richness. Our preferences for landscapes are often shaped by what was familiar to us early on. There is, in other words, an inescapable correspondence between landscape and mindscape, and between the quality of our places and the quality of the lives lived in them. In short, we need stable, safe, interesting settings, both rural and urban, in which to flourish as fully human creatures.

Second, the environmental movement has grown out of the efforts of courageous people to preserve and protect particular places: John Muir and Hetch Hetchy, Marjorie Stoneman Douglas and the Everglades, Horace Kephart and the establishment of the Great Smokies National Park. Virtually all environmental activists, even those whose work is focused on global issues, were shaped early on by a relation to a specific place. What Rachel Carson once called the "sense of wonder" begins in the childhood response to a place that exerts a magical effect on the ecological imagination. And without such experiences, few become ardent defenders of nature.

Third, as Garrett Hardin argues, problems that occur all over the world are not necessarily global problems, and some truly global problems may be solvable only by lots of local solutions. Potholes in roads, according to Hardin, are a big worldwide problem, but they are not a "global" problem that has a uniform cause and a single solution applicable everywhere (4). Any community with the will to do so can solve its pothole problem by itself. This is not true of climate change, which can be averted or minimized only by enforceable international agreements. No community or nation acting alone can avoid climate change. Even so, a great deal of the work necessary to make the transition to a solar powered world that does

not emit heat-trapping gases must be done at the level of households, neighborhoods, and communities.

Fourth, a purely global focus tends to reduce the earth to a set of abstractions that blur over what happens to real people in specific settings. An exclusively global focus risks what Alfred North Whitehead once called the
"fallacy of misplaced concreteness" in which we mistake our models of reality for reality itself, equivalent, as someone put it, to eating the menu and
not the meal. It is a short step from there to ideas of planetary management
that appeal to the industrial urge to control. Indeed, it is aimed mostly at the
preservation of industrial economies, albeit with greater efficiency. Planetary managers seek homogenized solutions that work against cultural and
ecological diversity. They talk about efficiency but not about sufficiency
and the idea of self-limitation (5). When the world and its problems are taken
to be abstractions, it becomes easier to overlook the fine-grain of social and
ecological details for the "big picture"; and it becomes easier for ecology to
become just another science in service to planet managers and corporations.

A final reason why the preservation of places is essential to the preservation of the world has to do with the fact that we've not succeeded in making
a global economy ecologically sustainable, and I doubt that we will ever be
smart enough or wise enough to do it on a global scale. All of the fashionable
talk about sustainable development is mostly about how to do more of the
same, but with greater efficiency. The most prosperous economies still depend a great deal on the ruination of distant places, peoples, and ecologies.
The imbalances of power between large wealthy economies and poor
economies virtually assures that the extraction, processing, and trade in primary products and disposal of industrial wastes rarely will be done sustainably. Having entered the global cash economy, the poor need cash at any
ecological cost, and the buyers will deny responsibility for the long-term results, which are mostly out of sight. As a result, consumers have little or no
idea of the full costs of their consumption. Even if the sale of timber, minerals, and food were not ruinous to their places of origin, moving them long
distances is. The fossil fuels burned to move goods around the world adds to
pollution and global warming. The extraction, processing, and transport of
fossil fuels is inevitably polluting. And the human results of the global
trading economy include the effects of making people dependent on the
global cash economy with all that it portends for those formerly operating as
self-reliant, subsistence economies. Often it means leaving villages for over-
crowded shantytowns on the outskirts of cities. It means growing for export
markets while people nearby go hungry. It means undermining economic
and ecological arrangements that worked well enough over long periods of
time to join the world economy. It means Coca-Cola, automobiles, ciga-

rettes, television, and the decay of old and venerable ways. The rush to join the industrial economy in the late years of the 20th century is a little like coming on board the Titanic just after icebergs are spotted dead ahead. In both instances, celebrations should be somewhat muted.

Implications

The idea that place is important to our larger prospects comes as good news and bad news. On the positive side, it means that some problems that appear to be unsolvable in a global context, may be solvable at a local scale if we are prepared to do so. The bad news is that much of western history has conspired to make our places invisible and therefore inaccessible to us. In contrast to "dis-placed" people who are physically removed from their homes, but who retain the idea of place and home, we have become "de-placed" people, mental refugees, homeless wherever we are. We no longer have a deep concept of place as a repository of meaning, history, livelihood, healing, re-creation, sacred memory, and as a source of materials, energy, food, and collective action.

For our economics, history, politics, and sciences, places have become just the intersection of two lines on a map, suitable for speculation, profiteering, another mall, another factory. So many of the abstract concepts that have shaped the modern world such as economies of scale, invisible hands, the commodification of land and labor, the conquest of nature, quantification of virtually everything, and the search for general laws have rendered the idea of place impotent and the idea of people being competent in their places an anachronism. This, in turn, is reinforced by our experience of the world. The velocity of modern travel has damaged our ability to be at home anywhere. We are increasingly indoor people whose sense of place is indoor space and whose minds are increasingly shaped by electronic stimuli. But what would it mean to take our places seriously?

The Idea of Place

First, it means restoring the idea of place in our minds by reordering educational priorities. The disorder of ecosystems and of the biosphere reflects a prior disorder of mind, values, and thought that in one way or another put humanity outside its ecological context. Looking ahead to the 21st century, the young must do what we have been unable or unwilling to do. If they are to succeed in building a sustainable world they will have to: stabilize world

population now growing at the rate of a quarter of a million each day; reduce the emission of greenhouse gases that threaten to change the climate—perhaps disastrously; protect biological diversity now declining at an
estimated 100–200 species per day; reverse the destruction of rainforests
(both tropical and temperate) now being lost at the rate of 116 square miles
or more each day; learn how to grow their food without poisoning themselves and ruining the land; convert civilization to run on sunlight; rebuild
the repair, reuse, recycle economy in order to eliminate waste and pollution;
learn how to conserve resources for the long-term; and they must begin the
great work of repairing, as much as possible, the damage done in the past
200 years of industrialization. And they must do all of this while reducing
poverty and egregious social inequities. No generation has ever faced a
more daunting agenda.

It is commonly believed, however, that the role of education is only to
equip young people for work in the new global economy in which trillions of
dollars of capital roam the earth in search of the highest rate of return.
Those equipped to serve this economy—Robert Reich calls them "symbolic
analysts"—earn their keep by "simplify(ing) reality into abstract images that
can be rearranged, juggled, experimented with, communicated to other
specialists, and then, eventually, transformed back into reality" (6). Symbolic analysts "rarely come into direct contact with the ultimate beneficiaries of their work," rather they mostly:

> sit before computer terminals—examining words and numbers,
> moving them, altering them, trying out new words and numbers,
> formulating and testing hypotheses, designing or strategizing. They
> also spend long hours in meetings or on the telephone, and even
> longer hours in jet planes and hotels—advising, making presenta-
> tions, giving briefings, doing deals (7).

They seem to be a morally anemic bunch whose services "do not necessarily improve society," a fact that does not seem to matter to them, perhaps
because they are too busy "mov(ing) from project to project . . . from one
software problem to another, to another movie script, another advertising
campaign, another financial restructuring" (8). They are, in Reich's words,
"America's fortunate citizens," perhaps 20 percent of the total population,
but they are increasingly disconnected from any interaction with or sense of
responsibility for the other four-fifths (9). People educated to be symbolic
analysts have neither loyalty to the long-term human prospect nor are they
prepared by intellect or affection to improve any place. They are, in
Wendell Berry's words, "itinerant professional vandals" (10). And they are
sure signs of the failure of the schools and colleges that presumed to edu-

cate them but failed to tell them what an education is for on a planet with a biosphere.

The world does not need more rootless symbolic analysts. It needs instead hundreds of thousands of young people equipped with the analytical skills, practical competencies, and moral stamina necessary to rebuild neighborhoods, towns, and communities around the planet. The kind of education necessary to industrialize the earth will not help them much. They will need to be students of their places and competent to become, in Wes Jackson's words, "native to their places." They will need to know a great deal about new fields of knowledge such as restoration ecology, conservation biology, ecological engineering, and sustainable forestry and agriculture. They will need a more honest economics that enables them to account for all of the costs of economic-ecological transactions. They will need to master the skills necessary to make the transition to a solar powered economy. Who will teach them these things?

Economies of Place

Taking places seriously means learning how to build local prosperity without ruining some other place. It will require a revolution in economic thinking that challenges long-held dogmas about growth, capital mobility, the global economy, the nature of wealth, and the wealth of nature. My views about capital mobility and related subjects were influenced, no doubt, by growing up near a now derelict industrial city, a monument to failed ideas. Even the prosperous city of my memory, however, was an ecological disaster. On both counts, could it have been otherwise? What would "place-focused economies" (11) look like?

Historian Calvin Martin argues that the root of the problem dates back to the dawn of the Neolithic age and the "gnawing fear that the Earth does not truly take care of us, of our kind . . . that the world is not truly congenial to sapient Homo" (12). Perhaps this is why most indigenous cultures had no word for scarcity and why we on the other hand are so haunted by it. Long ago, out of fear and faithlessness, we broke our ancient covenant with Earth. I believe that this is profoundly true. But we need not go so far back in time for workable ideas. Political scientist John Friedmann argues that in more recent times:

> We have been seduced into becoming secret accomplices in our own evisceration as active citizens. Two centuries after the battle cries of Liberty, Fraternity, and Justice, we remain as obedient as

ever to a corporate state that is largely deaf to the genuine needs
of people. And we have forfeited our identity as "producers" who
are collectively responsible for our lives (13).

What can be done? While believing that "the general movement of the
last six hundred years toward greater global interdependency is not likely to
be reversed," Friedmann argues for "the selective de-linking of territorial
communities from the market economy" and "the recovery of political community" (14). This work can only be done, as he puts it, "within local
communities, neighborhoods, and the household."

But communities everywhere are now vulnerable to the migration of
capital in search of higher rates of return. In the case of Youngstown, after
the "keystone" manufacturer was purchased by a multinational conglom-
erate, its profits were used to support real estate investments, among other
things. This money should have been used for maintenance and reinvest-
ment in plant and equipment. Predictably, the business failed, taking with it
many other businesses. The decision to divert profits out of the community
was made by people who did not live in Youngstown and had no stake or interest in it. Their decision had nothing to do with the productivity of the
business, and everything to do with shortsightedness and greed.

From this and all too many other cases like it we can conclude that one
requisite of resilient local economies is, in Daniel Kemmis' words:

> The capacity and the will to keep some locally generated capital
> from leaving the region and to invest that capital creatively and ef-
> fectively in the regional economy (15).

This in turn means selectively challenging the "supremacy of the national
market" where that restricts the capacity to build strong regional
economies. It also means confronting what economist Thomas Michael
Power calls a "narrow, market-oriented, quantitative definition of economics" in favor of one that gives priority to cultural, aesthetic, and ecological quality (16). Economic quality, according to Power, is not synonymous
with economic growth. The choice of growth or stagnation is, in Power's
view, a false one that "leaves communities to choose between a disruptive
explosion of commercial activity, which primarily benefits outsiders while
degrading values very important to residents, and being left in the dust and
decay of economic decline" (17). There are alternative ways to develop that
do not sell off the qualities that make particular communities desirable in
the first place. Among these, Power proposes "import substitution"
whereby local needs are increasingly met by local resources, not by imported goods and services. Energy efficiency, for example, can displace ex-

pensive imports of petroleum, fuel oil, electricity, and natural gas. Dollars not exported out of the community, then, circulate within the local economy creating a "multiplier effect" by stimulating local jobs and investment.

Power, like Jane Jacobs in her 1984 book *Cities and the Wealth of Nations*, argues for development:

> built around enterprising individuals and groups seeing a local opportunity and improvising, adapting, and substituting. Initially, these efforts start on a small scale and usually aim to serve a local market (18).

This approach stands in clear contrast to the standard model of economic development whereby communities attempt to lure outside industry and capital by lowering local taxes and regulations, and providing free services all of which lower the quality of the community.

The development of place-focused economies requires questioning old economic dogmas. The theory of free trade, for example, originated in an agrarian world in which state boundaries were relatively impermeable to capital flows (19). These conditions no longer hold. Goods, services, and capital now wash around the world, dissolving national boundaries and sovereignty. Labor (i.e., people) and communities, however, are not so mobile. Workers in the developed world are forced to compete with cheap labor elsewhere with the result of a sharp decline in earnings (20). For previously prosperous communities, free trade means economic decline and the accompanying social decay now evident throughout much of the United States.

In place of free trade, World Bank economist Herman Daly and theologian John Cobb recommend "balanced trade" that limits capital mobility and restricts the amount that a nation can borrow by importing more than it exports (21). To restore competitiveness where it has been lost, they recommend enforcing laws designed to prevent economic concentration (22). To build resilient regional economies, they recommend enabling communities to bid for the purchase of local industries against outside buyers. To the argument that international capital is necessary for the development of Third and Fourth World economies, they respond that:

> we have come, as have many others, to the painful conclusion that very little of First World development effort in the Third World, and even less of business investment, has been actually beneficial to the majority of the Third World's people . . . for the most part the Third World would have been better off without international investment and aid [which] destroyed the self-sufficiency of

nations and rendered masses of their formerly self-reliant people
unable to care for themselves (23).

They believe that economies should serve communities rather than the
elusive and mythical goals of economic growth.

Why does the idea that economics ought to support communities sound
so utopian? The answer, I think, has to do with how fully we have accepted
the radical inversion of purposes by which society is shaped to fit the
economy instead of the economy tailored to fit the society. Human needs
are increasingly secondary to those of the abstractions of markets. Among
other things, people need healthy food, shelter, clothing, good work to do,
friends, music, poetry, good books, a vital civic culture, animals, and wildness. But we are increasingly offered fantasy for reality, junk for quality,
convenience for self-reliance, consumption for community, and stuff rather
than spirit. Business spends $120 billion each year to convince us that this is
good, while virtually nothing is spent telling us what other alternatives we
have or what we have lost in the process. Our economy has not, on the
whole, fostered largeness of heart or spirit. It has not satisfied the human
need for meaning. And it is not ecologically sustainable.

The Politics of Place

Taking the environment seriously means rethinking how our politics and
civic life fit the places we inhabit. It makes sense, in Daniel Kemmis' words,
"to begin with the place, with a sense of what it is, and then try to imagine a
way of being public which would fit the place" (24). I do not think it is a co-
incidence that voter apathy has reached near epidemic proportions at the
same time that our sense of place has withered and community-scaled
economies have disintegrated. As with the economy, we have surrendered
control of large parts of our lives to distant powers.

Rebuilding place-focused politics will require revitalizing the idea of citizenship rooted in the local community. Democracy, as John Dewey once
observed, "must begin at home, and its home is the neighborly community"
(25). But neighborly communities have been eviscerated by the physical imposition of freeways, shopping malls, the commercial strip, and mind-
numbing sprawl. The idea of the neighborly community has receded from
our minds as the centralization of power and wealth advanced. But neither
vital communities nor democracy are compatible with economic and political centralization, from either the right or the left.

We need an ecological concept of citizenship rooted in the understanding that activities that erode soils, waste resources, pollute, destroy biological diversity, and degrade the beauty and integrity of landscapes are forms of theft from the commonwealth as surely as bank robbery. Ecological vandalism undermines future prosperity and democracy alike. For too long we've tried to deal with resource abuse from the top down and with pitifully little to show for our efforts and money. The problem, as Aldo Leopold once noted, is that for conservation to become "real and important" it must "grow from the bottom up" (26). It must, in other words, become fundamental to the day-to-day lives of millions of people, not just to those few professional resource managers working in public agencies.

An ecologically literate people, engaged in and by its place, will discover ways to conserve resources. Like citizens in Osage, Iowa, they will learn how to implement energy efficiency programs that save thousands of dollars per household. They will discover ways to save farms through "community supported agriculture" where people pay farmers directly for a portion of their produce. They will limit absentee ownership of farmland and enable young farmers to buy farms. They will find the means to save historic and ecologically important landscapes. They will develop procedures to accommodate environmentalists and loggers as did the residents of Missoula, Montana. They may even discover, as did residents of the Mondragon area of Spain or the state of Kerala in India, how to successfully address larger issues of equitable development (27).

We are not without models and ideas, but we lack the vision of politics as something other than a game of winners and losers fought out by factions with irreconcilable private interests. The idea that politics is little more than the pursuit of self-interest is embedded in American political tradition at least from the time James Madison wrote Federalist Paper 10. It is an idea, however, that tends to breed the very behavior it purports only to describe. In the words of political scientist Steven Kelman:

> Design your institutions to assume self-interest then, and you may get more self-interest. And the more self-interest you get, the more draconian the institutions must become to prevent the generation of bad policies (28).

Kelman proposes that institutions be designed not merely to restrain the unbridled pursuit of self-interest but to promote "public spirited behavior" in which "people see government as an appropriate forum for the display of the concern for others." The norm of public spiritedness also changes how people define their self-interest. This is, I believe, what Vaclav Havel meant when he described "genuine politics" as "a matter of serving those around us: serving the community, and serving those who will come after us" (29).

The roots of genuine politics are moral, originating in the belief that what we do matters deeply and is recorded "somewhere above us."

Is it utopian to believe that our politics can rise to public spiritedness and genuine service? I think not. Evidence shows that we are in fact considerably more public spirited than we have been led to believe—not always and everywhere to be sure, but more often than a cynical reading of human behavior would show (30). On the other hand, it is utopian to believe that the politics of narrow self-interest will enable us to avert the catastrophes on the horizon.

Conclusion

Western civilization irrupted on the earth like a fever, causing, in historian Frederick Turner's words, "a crucial, profound estrangement of the inhabitants from their habitat." We have become, he continues, "a rootless, restless people with a culture of superhighways precluding rest and a furious penchant for tearing up last year's improvements in a ceaseless search for some gaudy ultimate" (31). European explorers arrived in the "new world" spiritually unprepared for the encounter with the place, its animals, and its peoples. Our discontent spread to native peoples caught in the way. None were able to resist either the firepower or the seduction of technology.

More than just a symbol of a diseased spiritual state, that fever is now palpably evident in the rising temperature of the Earth itself. A world that takes its environment seriously must come to terms with the roots of its problems beginning with the place called home. This is not a simpleminded return to a mythical past, but a patient and disciplined effort to learn, and in some ways re-learn, the arts of inhabitation. These will differ from place to place reflecting various cultures, values, and ecologies. They will, however, share a common sense of rootedness in a particular locality, aiming in Jacquetta Hawkes' words to reestablish "immemorial ties, personal and universal, relating men to their surroundings in time and space" that were once expressed as a "creative, a patient and increasingly skillful love-making that had persuaded the land to flourish" (32).

We are caught in the paradox that we cannot save the world without saving particular places. But neither can we save our places without national and global policies that limit predatory capital and that allow people to build resilient economies, to conserve cultural and biological diversity, and to preserve ecological integrities. Without waiting for national governments to act, there is a lot that can be done to equip people to find their place and dig in.

Afterword

Schools, colleges, and universities can use their considerable buying power to support local farms and businesses, particularly those operating "sustainably" (33). Campuses can be used as laboratories for the study of ecological design and resource efficiency (34). Institutional endowments can be invested in local projects that promote energy and resource efficiency, and sustainable resource use. And every educational institution should set standards for ecological literacy so that no student graduates without a thorough understanding of systems, ecological economics, ecological engineering, sustainable resource management, the literature of place, a knowledge of the local watershed, and basic analytical skills in least-cost, end-use analysis (35).

Towns and cities can carry out energy and resource audits to locate opportunities to reduce consumption, save money, lower pollution, and create local employment. Audits should lead to the development and implementation of energy efficiency goals and building standards such as those in communities as different as Osage, Iowa and Sacramento, California. Long-term goals to save energy by replacing windows, for example, are opportunities to create businesses in manufacturing and construction while reducing the amount of money that leaves the community to buy energy. Communities should encourage economic diversification, including the reemergence of the repair, recycle, and reuse economy. The goal, as Thomas Michael Power argues, is total quality, not just economic growth.

None of these changes will occur unless we restore democracy at the local level. Local governments should foster careful land-use planning to preserve open spaces, critical habitats, greenbelts, and bike trails (36). Local governments should be taking steps now to foster the emergence of a post-petroleum economy. They should encourage local investment in the local economy. They should establish building codes and incentives that promote energy and resource efficiency.

Notes

1. Carley, M., and I. Christie. 1993. Managing sustainable development, 24. Minneapolis, Minnesota: University of Minnesota Press.
2. Haas, P., et al., eds. 1993. Institutions for the Earth, ix. Cambridge, Massachusetts: MIT Press.
3. Gallagher, W. 1993. The power of the place. New York: Poseidon Press; Tuan, Yi-Fu. 1977. Space and place: the perspective of experience. Minneapolis, Minnesota: University of Minnesota Press.

4. Hardin, G. 1986. Filters against folly, 145–163. New York: Viking Press; Hardin, G. 1993. Living within limits: ecology, economics, and population taboos, 278. New York: Oxford University Press.

5. Sachs, W. 1992. One world. In The development dictionary. W. Sachs, ed. 111. London: Zed Books.

6. Reich, R. 1991. The work of nations, 177–179. New York: Knopf.

7. Reich, 179 (6).

8. Reich, 185–237 (6).

9. Reich, 250 (6).

10. Berry, W. 1987. Home economics, 50. San Francisco, California: North Point Press.

11. Kemmis, D. 1990. Community and the politics of place, 107. Norman, Oklahoma: University of Oklahoma Press.

12. Martin, C. 1992. In the spirit of the earth, 123. Baltimore, Maryland: Johns Hopkins University Press.

13. Friedman, J. 1987. Planning in the public domain, 347. Princeton, New Jersey: Princeton University Press.

14. Friedman, 385–387 (13).

15. Kemmis, 103 (11).

16. Power, T.M. 1988. The economic pursuit of quality, 3. Armonk: M.E. Sharpe.

17. Power, 174 (16).

18. Power, 186 (16).

19. Daly, H., and J. Cobb. 1989. For the common good, 209–235. Boston, Massachusetts: Beacon Press; Morris, D. Free trade. The Ecologist.

20. Batra, R. 1993. The myth of free trade. New York, New York: Scribners.

21. Daly and Cobb, 231 (19).

22. Daly and Cobb, 291 (19).

23. Daly and Cobb, 289, 290 (19).

24. Kemmis, 41 (11).

25. Dewey, J. 1954. The public and its problems, 213. Chicago, Illinois: Swallow Press.

26. Leopold, A. 1991. The river of the mother of god and other essays, 300. Madison, Wisconsin: University of Wisconsin Press.

27. Whyte, W., and K. Whyte. 1988. Making mondragon. Ithaca, New York: Cornell University Press; Franke, R. and Chasin, B. 1991. Kerala: radical reform as development in an Indian state. San Francisco, California: Institute for Food and Development Policy.

28. Kelman, S. 1988. Why public ideas matter. In The power of public ideas. R. Reich, ed. 51. Cambridge, Massachusetts: Harvard University Press.

29. Havel, V. 1992. Summer meditations, 6. New York: Knopf.
30. Kelman, 43, notes 38–41 (28).
31. Turner, F. 1980. Beyond geography: the western spirit against the wilderness, 5. New York: Viking Press.
32. Hawkes, J. 1951. A land, 200–202. New York: Random House.
33. Eagan, D., and D. Orr, eds. 1992. The campus and environmental responsibility. San Francisco, California: Jossey Bass.
34. Orr, D. 1990. Ecological literacy. Albany, New York: SUNY Press.
35. Orr (34).
36. Hiss, T. 1990. The experience of place. New York: Random House.

Chapter 8

Redefining "Multiple Use": Agency Responses to Changing Social Values

Mark W. Brunson and James J. Kennedy

> People love to do hard work together and to feel that the work is real; that
> is to say primary, productive, needed. . . . It is a tragic dilemma that much
> of the best work men do together is no longer quite right.
> —Gary Snyder (discussing logging)
> *The Practice of the Wild* (1990)

Public land managers have typically seen themselves as stewards who safeguard resources and maintain their production. In truth, they are charged
with maintaining a *relationship* between resources and society. This relationship changes as society changes, and natural resource agencies must adjust their attitudes, management styles, and institutional structures accordingly. The 1960s and 1970s brought dramatic changes to all American
institutions, including the federal land management agencies. Four societal
trends of that era greatly affected the society–nature relationship: economic
expansion; technological innovation; migration to cities and suburbia; and
increased public perception of resource scarcity.

In this chapter we will discuss how four public lands agencies—the
Bureau of Land Management (BLM), National Park Service (NPS),
United States Fish and Wildlife Service (USF&WS), and especially
the United States Department of Agriculture Forest Service (USDAFS)—
have responded to these changes.

Changing Society–Resource Relationships

Unprecedented growth and prosperity may have been the single most
defining characteristic of the Cold War years, when American society entered what Inglehardt (1) called the era of "post-materialism." Inglehardt
argued that when the United States and other western nations achieved a
level of societal well-being where the basic material needs of most citizens

were assured, it then became possible to place greater value on less tangible concerns such as environmental conservation. People in an affluent society had more personal resources (i.e., time and money) to devote to political causes such as the environment. Equally important, they had more personal resources to devote to gaining access to that environment. That meant a meteoric rise in visits to U.S. national parks, forests, and other wild areas.

Economic expansion was accompanied by a revolution in technology. Some of the most profound technological effects came, somewhat paradoxically, in remote and wild places. Americans' ability to enjoy the outdoors was directly linked to technology: civilian adaptations of wartime inventions such as diving gear or inflatable rafts; synthetic materials and fabrics that made boating, camping, and winter sports more affordable and comfortable; and specialized off-highway vehicles that took millions into remote lands, waters, and skies.

A less direct but more pervasive technological influence was communications. The popular media informed and transported Americans to places they had previously not heard nor cared about, but which suddenly became real and valued resources. Television fostered symbolic and romantic interpretations of nature. Its treatment of animals produced a generation that saw wildlife and wild places much differently than had their utilitarian forebears. Communications advances also greatly enhanced the ability of environmental advocacy groups to reach the public and thereby to influence policy.

Even more important was the effect technology had on traditional resource-based economies. Industrial automation and improved transportation meant fewer people were needed to cut timber, extract minerals, grow and harvest food, or process those materials in the small manufacturing centers of rural America. The children of loggers, miners, ranchers, and millworkers were forced to seek jobs in the cities and rapidly expanding suburbs rather than their hometowns. A nation that was 56 percent urban in 1950, was 69 percent urban by 1970 (2). States like Arizona, Colorado, Nevada, Oregon, and Utah, with their strong rural traditions and huge expanses of uninhabited federal land, soon had more than half of their populations living in one or two large metropolitan areas. But as quickly as urban America was spreading, the environment accessible to urbanites was increasing faster. That, too, meant rural change. Urbanites not only visited rural places, they also purchased second homes there or even took up permanent residence. These newcomers held urban values and sought urban amenities in their adopted communities. To some long-time rural residents, the new values posed the greatest urban threat of all.

Finally, the 1960s and 1970s offered increasing evidence that America's superabundant resource base had limits in peacetime as well as wartime. Scarcity was a frightening thing to a society whose most cherished myths were based on limitless expansion, on taming the frontier and making the desert bloom, on "rags to riches" and the "American Dream." Nowhere were people more alarmed than in the cities, where overpopulation pressures were most evident and people were least familiar with natural resources. Not only were urban publics most receptive to warnings, they were insulated from direct negative economic impacts of changing resource priorities.

As more urbanites gained appreciation for nature and a passing familiarity with wild places, and as the threats to nature gained currency, the value society placed on traditional commodity resources decreased relative to the value placed on amenity resources such as wildlife, scenery, and non-consumptive recreation. Yet growth in U.S. commodity demand never faltered. Instead, the public wanted agencies to manage for *more* values, but to do so in a way that entailed *less* of what the commodity agencies traditionally called "management." They began to see wild nature not simply as a bottomless cupboard holding their material needs, but as a trust fund, buffering society against environmental disaster and the excesses of the free enterprise system. Agencies had to learn how to adjust their management to fit this new image, and the learning curve was steep.

Evolution of "Multiple-Use" Policies

To understand how agencies responded to changes in society and its ideas about resources, we should first review the situation at the time the changes began. In the middle years of this century, federal land managers typically followed a *dominant use* approach that emphasized timber, recreation, forage, or game animals, depending on the agency. Initial attempts to meet the new demands for multiple resources often reflected the growth-is-everything optimism of the era, emphasizing commercially relevant resources and quantity over quality.

For example, the Forest Service in the 1950s and 1960s was preoccupied with meeting the national demand for lumber, which had exploded in the wake of programs that subsidized home purchases by returning veterans. Agency budgets and payrolls expanded to meet the need. The timber industry, which had harvested only 1.5 billion board feet (BBF) of timber from national forest land in 1941, cut 11.5 BBF in 1971 (3). National forest resources in that era were often dichotomized into timber and "resources other than timber;" the latter were sometimes abbreviated as ROTT, reflecting the value many foresters ascribed to them. Yet "multiple use" had been part of the Forest Service lexicon since the agency's earliest years (4). As demands for those "other" resources intensified, the agency responded by seeking congressional affirmation of long-standing policy. The Multiple Use–Sustained Yield Act (MUSYA) of 1960—the last in a long line of laws written by and for the Forest Service—canonized Gifford Pinchot's ideal of managing for the greatest good of the greatest number. While purporting to favor none of the main forest uses (forage, recreation, timber, water, wildlife, and fish), the act attempted in many ways to solidify the status quo.

The Bureau of Land Management (BLM) focused on commodities its lands had historically supplied: grazing, minerals, and (in Oregon and northern California) timber. Congressional supporters of the livestock industry ensured that the BLM's professional range staff was neither large nor powerful enough to resist ranchers' demands. Multiple-use was not BLM policy; indeed, the agency had no defined mission in its first 30 years of existence before the Federal Land Policy and Management Act passed in 1976. This was due largely to the public's comparative disinterest in grassland, desert, and tundra. The BLM attracted so little attention that when the Wilderness Act became law in 1964, its lands were left out—not by design, but by simple oversight (5).

The National Park Service bore the largest share of the growing demand for recreation. Under Interior Secretary Douglas McKay, whose pro-development policies foreshadowed those of James Watt a generation later, the agency had begun a 10-year program of tourist facility development called Mission '66. The effort reflected concerns about overcrowding in parks equipped to handle only half as many people as were visiting. While never intended to be a multiple-use agency, the Park Service was supposed to balance its often-paradoxical dual mandate to provide for public enjoyment and environmental preservation. It was accused of sacrificing the latter goal as early as the 1950s as critics such as naturalist Joseph Wood Krutch argued that easy access and modern facilities were the problem, not the solution. The parks, Krutch lamented, were "doomed . . . to become mere resorts" (6).

The Fish and Wildlife Service was established for the dominant use of preserving game habitat, but had long faced pressure to allow "compatible" uses such as "varmint" hunting and cattle grazing. After a 1949 Duck Stamp Act amendment allowed hunting on some refuges, the agency's "doctrine of compatibility" became a matter of policy. The McKay administration not only allowed such consumptive forms of recreation as fishing derbies and field trials, but opened refuges to oil and gas leasing and increased grazing. The 1962 Refuge Recreation Act placed the burden on the Secretary of the Interior to prove that any approved use would not harm the preservation purposes of a refuge, but enforcement of the Act varied in strictness depending on the views of the party in power (7).

Congress Changes the Rules

By the 1960s, the public had begun demanding uses that were more "multiple" than the agencies were prepared to offer. As the outcry grew louder, the Congress was drawn into the fray. That in itself was not unusual, but this was a Congress in transition—one that reflected the growing political strength of metropolitan communities, and was just as likely to consider a law proposed and authored by an interest group as one written by an agency. Lawmakers from sparsely populated, resource-rich states were no longer able to set the legislative direction of natural resource policy, though they could still influence details of those policies and (even more important) influence the amount and allocation of agency budgets. Thus the 1964 Wilderness Act was promoted not by the Forest Service but by an environmental group (the Wilderness Society) Moreover, it was shepherded through Congress by Senator Hubert Humphrey of Minnesota and Representative John Saylor of Pennsylvania, who represented states with large urban populations and little federal land. Powerful western legislators who fought against the act ultimately could not defeat it, though they did manage to restrict its size and create exemptions for special interests (e.g., mining claimants and certain motorized recreation users) (8).

The new laws, more so than before, tended to restrict managers' decision-making latitude. The Wilderness Act was an early example. The bill itself was no more restrictive than the Forest Service's 1939 primitive-area regulations, but authority to approve exemptions was transferred from the agency to Congress. The National Park Service had claimed it did not need to be covered by the act because it managed all its lands as wilderness, but Congress insisted that national park lands be studied for potential wilderness designation. Wildlife refuges and, ultimately, BLM lands were also added to the wilderness preservation system.

Thus began a 16-year period when Congress regularly passed laws setting boundaries on the use and management of federal lands. The National Trail System and National Wild and Scenic Rivers acts restricted commodity uses and mandated protective measures on portions of all four agencies' lands. The Highway Beautification Act broadened the requirement to protect scenery on public lands. The National Environmental Policy Act (NEPA), originally intended as a "gesture of congressional concern" more than a substantive change in natural resource policy (9), grew through court interpretation and agency usage to become the primary weapon of those who sought to slow the engine of bureaucratic progress.

Public land managers' discretion was further limited in the 1970s by a series of laws aimed at specific environmental threats: the Clean Air and Clean Water acts; an amended Federal Insecticide, Fungicide, and Rodenticide Act (FIFRA); the Wild Free-Roaming Horse and Burro Act; and the Endangered Species Act. Special land use designations continued to be imposed via the Eastern Wilderness Act, Endangered American Wilderness Act, and Alaska Lands Act. The 1970s also saw enactment of laws mandating systematic planning on public lands: the Forest and Range Renewable Resources Planning Act (RPA), the National Forest Management Act (NFMA), and the Federal Land Policy and Management Act (FLPMA). It was this last set of laws that would preoccupy the Forest Service and BLM for more than a decade thereafter, ultimately setting the stage for proposed substantive changes such as the adoption of "ecosystem management" policies and creation of a National Biological Survey.

Among the most difficult aspects of the new legislation for natural resource managers was that Congress increased its oversight of the agencies and imposed new tasks on them without increasing budgets accordingly. For example, Forest Service budgets were allocated partly on the basis of the agency's ability to earn revenues through user fees and commodity sales, and partly on the basis of output "targets." The latter theoretically reflected professional judgments of what the land could produce, but were set by Congress. Rural lawmakers, although no longer able to set legislative policy directly on the floor of Congress, learned to do so indirectly from their seats on the powerful appropriations committees, where they could adjust resource targets to protect rural commodity-based employment.

As a result, agencies sometimes found it difficult to obey the laws imposed upon them. The Forest Service in the 1970s greatly expanded its staffs in hydrology, wildlife biology, landscape architecture, and other noncommodity specialties (10), yet its budgets still were mostly allocated to timber, grazing, and other revenue-producing activities. If funds were diverted to noncommodity resources such as water, wildlife, or scenery, it meant forgoing those aspects of the commodity programs that were not directly related to meeting the targets or maintaining congressional delegation support. The most obvious budget casualty was monitoring the land and resources; as a result, the agencies became less and less sure of what the land actually could produce, and the targets consequently became harder and harder to meet. The problem was intensified when the agency badly underestimated the cost of developing its land management plans.

Similarly, agencies often were forced to try to protect trail corridors, wild rivers, and other settings without the funds needed to do so—especially if protection required acquiring title or easements to adjacent private lands. The problem began with a legal fiction in the 1964 Wilderness Act: "No appropriation shall be available for the payment of expenses or salaries for the administration of the National Wilderness Preservation System as a separate unit *nor shall any appropriations be available for additional personnel stated as being required solely for the purpose of managing or administering areas solely because they are included within the National Wilderness Preservation System*" (emphasis added) (11). While this clause was intended to offset criticism that the bill would create an entire new bureaucracy, its effect was to prevent the agencies from hiring staff necessary to meet conditions of the Act.

Multiple Use Means Multiplied Pressures

Even under the best of conditions, it would have been difficult for the agencies to shift along with the society resource relationship. First of all, the shifting process required managers to modify or reject deeply held and cherished beliefs about the nature of resources. Second, rural publics counterreacted as soon as the agencies made any move toward a significant change in policies or priorities. As often as not, rural ire was directed against the agencies rather than against the larger, urbanized society that was imposing its new values on traditional resource-based communities.

The relationship between rural America and the federal government has never been easy. Westward expansion was largely underwritten by the government, but such assistance came with restrictions attached. Once the frontier was settled, its citizens tended to embrace the fiction that their grit and independence alone had tamed the land and made America prosper. Federal employees were often viewed in the West the way carpetbaggers had been in the South—as interlopers whose mission in life was to frustrate or impede honest, hard-working citizens (12).

As a result, the agencies rarely maintained better than an uneasy truce with their rural neighbors. The history of national parks is replete with examples of cross-boundary disputes, from the Everglades to the Olympic Peninsula. Stock growers have feuded with the Forest Service ever since Pinchot announced the first grazing fees at the turn of the century. A recent sociological study of timber workers found that "negative evaluation of the Forest Service serves as an important unifying theme for loggers. . . . One logger candidly stated, 'I'm a logger, so I'm supposed to hate the Forest Service'" (13). Even though agencies like the Forest Service worked to sustain rural communities, and their employees often grew up in similar places, the social organization of small resource-based towns tended to prevent interactions between "locals" and federal workers and their families. Work patterns, gender roles, and lifestyles all differed between the two groups, fostering a "we–they" dichotomy and rural hostility toward the bureaucracy (14). The sense of separation was reinforced by an agency policy that called for regular employee transfers to ensure that professional decisions would not be swayed by personal loyalties to local publics (15).

The case of wilderness livestock grazing illustrates how rural constituencies were able to counteract agency attempts to change the balance of resource uses. Grazing is the most widespread "nonconforming use" in wilderness, occurring in more than half of all Forest Service and BLM wilderness areas. Although its backers originally wanted to phase out livestock, the Wilderness Act failed to gain sufficient congressional support until grazing was protected as an allowable use. When the Forest Service interpreted the law as allowing grazing itself but not any associated structures, water developments, or vehicle use, outraged stockgrowers responded through their congressional allies by blocking attempts to designate more wilderness. A compromise was finally reached in the 1980 Colorado Wilderness Act, which formally adopted guidelines allowing maintenance of existing facilities and even construction of new ones (16).

Besieged on both sides, agencies often took solace in the myth that "if both sides are mad at us, we must be doing a balanced job." Yet one side's "balance" was another's "bias," and even the agencies themselves began to experience interdepartmental friction that reached temperatures higher than any since the Depression. Newly elected presidents, eager to "do something" about the ongoing crisis in resource management, proposed reorganizations that made agency employees uneasy about their futures. Richard Nixon attempted to combine the Forest Service and several Interior agencies into a Department of Environment and Natural Resources, an idea revived in slightly different form by Jimmy Carter. Ronald Reagan took a different tack, proposing to swap vast tracts of land between the Forest Service and BLM. While none of these proposals succeeded, they did help make natural resource bureaucracies more sensitive to interagency differences and power balances.

Two other issues heightened tension between extractive and preservationist agencies. One was a 1980 Park Service report to Congress which warned that Yellowstone, Yosemite, the Everglades, and other parks were "experiencing significant and widespread adverse effects associated with external encroachment" (17). Often the "encroachment" was by another agency: clearcutting on adjacent national forest land, oil exploration approved by the BLM, or water projects of the Army Corps of Engineers. Though the Park Service has been criticized for not pursuing its case diligently enough (18), other agencies resented even the relatively low-key expressions of disapproval it was willing to voice publicly. The second, even more divisive issue arose when the Endangered Species Act gave oversight authority to the U.S. Fish and Wildlife Service. The agency's biologists were to review all federal actions to determine if they might compromise efforts to protect threatened and endangered species, and if necessary to issue a "jeopardy opinion" that would require revision of the proposed action. Because agencies such as the Forest Service and BLM employ their own biologists, they and commodity interests tended to view jeopardy opinions as unwarranted interference.

The Forest Service Struggles to Adapt

Obviously the agencies least able to accommodate demands for amenity values were those that had commodity traditions and clients (i.e., the BLM and Forest Service). The latter agency, being far more visible nationally than the BLM, took the most criticism. Conversely, the National Park Service and Fish and Wildlife Service were already positioned to accommodate the shift in values because of their historical focus on recreation and wildlife. The Park Service especially benefitted from a vast reservoir of good feeling from urban visitors. When a scientific review panel (19) concluded, in 1963, that practices such as strict fire suppression had contributed to the damage of park ecosystems, there was no great outcry against the Park Service. Yet, as we shall discuss shortly, the situation was quite different when Forest Service practices came under attack in West Virginia just a few years later.

There were several reasons, aside from its programmatic and budgetary focus on commodities, why the Forest Service had difficulty adapting to the new social order. One reason was that it had adapted so well to the old order. Midcentury analyses marveled at the agency's cohesiveness, pride, and commitment to its mission and to the organization itself (20). That success in an era of high public trust, when the goals of the conservation movement were more narrowly focused on human-dominant values, made it difficult for the Forest Service to quickly retrofit its organizational culture to succeed in a vastly different post-Earth Day milieu. The organization's culture reinforced in its employees a self-image of stewardship, of objective and scientific professionals assigned to guard the public forests. To such a proud professional monoculture, the interdisciplinary and public power-sharing imposed by NEPA represented a direct rebuke. Agency employees had to learn to adopt a public servant mode to succeed in the new multivalue, public-involvement setting (21).

A more subtle problem was that, unlike other agencies, the Forest Service had seen itself as managing for multiple use all along. Thus, when critics accused it of adhering to a single-use policy, forest managers often felt unfairly attacked. The difficulty lay in discrepancies between the agency's definition of multiple use and the emerging public definition. The public began to see timber as merely one element in an array of values that included not only other commodities, but an increasing array of non-commodity resources, some of which were diminished by timber management. While the official Forest Service definition put several products on an equal footing (wood, water, wildlife, recreation, forage), practical application gave greater value to timber. This was partly because every "major" forest product except wood also occurs on nonforested lands, and because timber harvests subsidize nonpriced forest uses. The Forest Service also tended to embrace the traditional notion that "proper" timber management is generally compatible with other forest uses. Foresters consequently were trained to understand tree-growing and tree-harvesting thoroughly, but had only minimal interest and technical competence in the production of other products.

As the public became increasingly restless with the timber-primacy version of multiple-use, critics scrutinized not only the mix of resources being provided, but also the means used to provide those resources. The focal point of controversy for the Forest Service was the practice of clearcutting, which scientific forestry research had established as the most efficient way to remove a mature, slow-growing forest and regenerate a new, fast-growing timber crop. What scientific forestry didn't tell foresters was that the public would not believe that a practice so ugly could possibly be good for forests or for society.

Ironically, the clearcutting controversy began not in an urban area but in the mountains of West Virginia, where the Forest Service accelerated timber harvests in parts of the Monongahela National Forest. Unhappy citizens turned for help to the West Virginia legislature, which registered repeated protests with the federal government. The Forest Service, however, did not respond as critics had hoped. At first the agency's leadership reacted defensively, arguing that the scientific training and professional expertise of its foresters made them the only credible judges of forestry practice. After repeated complaint, the agency adjusted its practices, but rejected an outright ban on clearcutting and agreed only to restrict the size of harvest units and to consider aesthetics when designing timber sales.

The agency had fallen victim to a malady endemic among natural resource professions. Most foresters, like their counterparts in range and wildlife management, were trained in the nation's land grant universities. The land grant schools were established in the mid-19th century to provide scientific solutions to rural agricultural and natural resource problems, and they were highly successful in doing so. A land-grant education instilled in future resource professionals a deep-rooted belief in the rational-scientific paradigm—the notion that for every problem there is a single best solution, that science is the only way to find it, and that competent professionals are the only people who can implement it. If the public failed to appreciate a scientific solution, its failure was blamed on uninformed emotionalism. The obvious scientific solution to *that* problem was to "educate the public."

Unfortunately for the forestry professionals, many members of the public did not believe emotional or value-based reactions were inherently wrong. Nor did they feel any need to be "educated" by professionals. Besides, these professionals were employed by the government. While agency employees saw themselves as experts sharing the fruits of their expertise, to many critics they were merely out-of-control bureaucrats who refused to obey their ultimate "bosses," the American people.

By the time the Forest Service made what it believed to be reasonable concessions in West Virginia, the debate had spread to other regions and to Congress. Dissatisfied West Virginia conservationists sued the agency, alleging that clearcutting violated provisions of the Organic Act of 1897, which had specified the purposes of the national forests. The court agreed. Its decision banned not only clearcutting but all commercial harvesting on the Monongahela forest. Lawsuits followed quickly in other states, and Congress was forced to act. But once again lawmakers declined to fix the problem in the manner prescribed by the Forest Service—a simple law legalizing clearcutting. Instead they passed the National Forest Management Act (NFMA).

National Forest Planning: A Case Study

The Forest Service approached NFMA in typical rational-scientific fashion. The law empaneled a Committee of Scientists to make recommendations on forest planning; rather than deciding which of the ideas had merit, the agency processed them all into a complex web of regulations. The result, as political scientist Bruce Shepard wrote, was "a nightmare. Billions of dollars were spent on planning; an agency that rightly prided itself on 'getting the cut out' missed its initial planning deadlines by a decade; and, as the plans finally hit the street, the street turned out to run straight to the courthouse" (22).

NFMA had been a simple political warning from Congress: Do a better job of listening to the public, or else. But, as had been the case a decade earlier in the Monongahela controversy, the enculturated belief in expert omniscience left foresters unprepared to listen. They believed in the ignorance of "the public," and saw it as unprofessional to choose societal preference over science. Moreover, they misjudged the scope and scale of publics to whom they needed to listen. Several factors reinforced the Forest Service's tendency to stress local rural concerns at the expense of more distant urban ones—even while knowing that pressure for change came largely from the latter. First, urban Americans were seen as out-of-touch with resource realities, often depicted in conversation as not knowing that two-by-fours and toilet paper come from trees. Second, the Forest Service is unusually decentralized in its decision-making. Managers found it hard to decide against the wishes of those with whom they lived and worked. Finally the agency had, by law and inclination, an abiding commitment to rural community stability. Forest Service staff officers, like rural politicians, often equated economic stability with the fortunes of absentee-owned corporations that offered jobs to rural residents as long as profits held out.

Along with its difficulty in truly "involving" the public in its decisions, the agency's planning process was susceptible to internal malfunction. One source of difficulty was its use of interdisciplinary teams of resource specialists. A typical team might consist of a timber sale planner, silviculturist, engineer, wildlife or fisheries biologist, landscape architect or recreation planner, maybe a hydrologist or soil scientist. In ideal circumstances, members of the "ID teams" complemented each others' skills; for example, a forester, engineer, and landscape architect could together design a timber sale that would be relatively easy to harvest and regenerate, yet address concerns about visual quality. But cooperation too often gave way to competition. Members became advocates for their special interests, with all of the polarization and power-jostling that characterized the larger struggle outside the office. This sort of dynamic had been foreseen, even intended as a way to foster exchange of diverse values and management responses. What was not foreseen was that advocates for amenity resources would see themselves as perpetually losing battles with the commodity specialists. Some resorted to whistle-blowing, taking their case to outside entities and circumventing an agency they considered biased. Eventually they founded the Association of Forest Service Employees for Environmental Ethics (AFSEEE). As the internal arguments gained external attention, it reinforced public perceptions that the Forest Service was not interested in protecting all resources.

The belief in rational solutions also led the Forest Service to rely too strongly on a computer model called FORPLAN to drive the planning process. Conceived and developed by economists, FORPLAN compared alternatives through a linear programming process in search of a solution that would optimize present net value. This approach, while scientifically elegant, perpetuated and disguised much of the commodity orientation that had gotten the agency into trouble in the first place. Resources that didn't fit neatly into the model—those that weren't traded in markets and therefore weren't easily converted into dollars—were treated as "constraints" on timber production, or else ignored altogether. There were other shortcomings, as well. The model showed little sensitivity to local ecological and social conditions. Because solutions weren't linked to specific places, they didn't consider the juxtaposition of activities, nor many cumulative effects. The "black box" approach, wherein large amounts of data were fed into one end of a computer that coughed out a single answer at the other end, gave the public little idea how their involvement influenced the plans. Perhaps most damaging of all, after two decades of shifting funds away from monitoring and inventory, the data that were fed into the model often bore only a cursory resemblance to actual conditions in the national forests. The land's ability to produce timber was routinely overestimated. All too often, the plans were not only unresponsive, but unrealistic.

It is unfair to characterize the national forest planning process as an abject failure. The public involvement process, while not as closely linked to ultimate decisions as it should have been, nonetheless greatly increased public awareness of forests and agency awareness of public demands. Similarly, data gathered for the plans advanced the agency's knowledge of forest conditions, even if it was often still inadequate. Monitoring procedures recommended in the plans will be invaluable if and when sufficient funds are available to implement them. Hundreds of thousands of acres have received administrative protection as research natural areas, scenic areas, and so on, thanks to the attention given to nontimber resources in the planning process. Still, few of the plans escaped administrative appeals or legal challenges, and many veterans of the planning battles emerged much less sure of the agency's mission, its image, or its ability to meet the challenges ahead.

The Stage Is Set for a New Paradigm

The national forest planning process offers the most prominent example, but by no means the only example, of an agency struggling to adapt to fundamental changes in social values and demands. The BLM, once insulated from intense scrutiny by its remote and austere land base, has emerged into the public eye. The long-simmering dispute over grazing fees now makes front-page headlines in Philadelphia and Miami as well as in Denver and Salt Lake City. A grazing-ban movement, with its battle cry of "Cattle Free in '93," has so frightened range conservationists that some warn of the impending demise of their profession (23). The National Park Service is regularly assailed by critics who charge that the agency's budget is heavily imbalanced in favor of tourist services. And debate rages in the wildlife profession over whether game management, as practiced in state agencies and the Fish and Wildlife Service, is unscientific, obsolete, and perhaps even immoral (24).

Organizations such as AFSEEE have drawn attention to the shortcomings of extractive agencies, but the price has been a kind of internal Balkanization. AFSEEE members disproportionately come from amenity resource specialties and entry-level ranks (25). Older practitioners of traditional specialties face a crisis in confidence as younger colleagues call for change and the agencies institute programs with names like "New Perspectives" or "Change on the Range," implying that the old perspective (and perhaps they personally) badly needed changing. Meanwhile, affirmative action programs have fostered resentment of women and minorities; some in the white male establishment assume that any nonwhite or female colleague was hired not on merit but to fill a quota, further souring intra-agency relations.

As scientists learn more about the complexity of natural systems, they discover new, unsuspected ways that the traditional mode of resource management went awry. The resulting loss of confidence from outside, coupled with the crisis of confidence within, increasingly leads critics to circumvent the agencies, seeking satisfaction instead from Congress and the courts.

Meanwhile, public confidence is higher in the National Park Service and U.S. Fish and Wildlife Service than in the extraction agencies, but not overwhelmingly so (26). The Yellowstone fires of 1988 convinced many in the public that the Park Service is not infallible. Pressure is mounting in all agencies to test holistic management strategies and new administrative structures.

It seems clear that natural resource management in the next century will not resemble the version described in this chapter. While conditions in the early 1990s have been painful for those involved, they also made it possible for a new "ecosystem management" approach to get an honest trial in the Forest Service and BLM. Respected upper-echelon agency employees have joined in the call for a "new resource management paradigm." They know that if change does not develop from within, it will be imposed from without. Federal land management agencies are poised on the brink of fundamental change—change that may finally reflect the relationship that society now demands between itself and the natural environment.

Acknowledgments

This research was supported by the Utah Agricultural Experiment Station, Utah State University, Logan, Utah 84322-4810 (MacIntire–Stennis Project No. 712), and by cooperative grants from the USDA Forest Service. Approved as journal paper no. 4512.

Notes

1. Inglehardt, R. 1977. The silent revolution: changing values and political styles among western publics. Princeton, New Jersey: Princeton University Press.
2. U.S. Census Bureau. 1991. Metropolitan areas and cities. 1990 Census Profile 3.
3. Steen, H.K. 1976. The U.S. Forest Service: a history. Seattle, Washington: University of Washington Press.
4. See, for example, Gifford Pinchot's 1907 book of Forest Service regulations, appropiately called "The Use Book."
5. Dana, S.T., and S.K. Fairfax. 1980. Forest and range policy, 229. New York: McGraw-Hill.
6. Krutch, J.W. 1957. Which men? What needs? American Forests, 63(April):23.
7. Curtin, C.G. 1993. The evolution of the U.S. national wildlife refuge system and the doctrine of compatibility. Conservation Biology 7:29–38.
8. Nash, R. 1982. Wilderness and the American mind. New Haven, Connecticut: Yale University Press.
9. Liroff, R. 1976. National policy for the environment: NEPA and its aftermath, 5. Bloomington, Indiana: Indiana University Press.
10. Kennedy, J.J. 1991. Integrating gender diverse and interdisciplinary professionals into traditional U.S. Department of Agriculture-Forest Service culture. Society and Natural Resources 4:165-176.
11. Title 16, Chapter 23, Section 1131(b), U.S. Code.
12. An insightful analysis of the federal government's role in developing the West is offered in White, R. 1989. It's your misfortune and none of my own. Norman, Oklahoma: University of Oklahoma Press.
13. Carroll, M.S. 1989. Taming the lumberjack revisited. Society and Natural Resources 2:91–106.

14. Colfer, C.J.P., and A.M. Colfer. 1978. Inside Bushler Bay: lifeways in counterpoint. Rural Sociology 43:204–220.

15. Kaufman, H. 1960. The forest ranger. Baltimore, Maryland: Johns Hopkins Press.

16. McClaran, M.P. 1990. Livestock in wilderness: a review and forecast. Environmental Law 20:857–889.

17. National Park Service. 1981. State of the parks—1980: a report to Congress, viii.

18. For example, Sax, J.L. and R.B. Keiter. 1987. Glacier National Park and its neighbors: a study of federal interagency relations. Ecology Law Quarterly 14:207-263.

19. Leopold, A.S. 1963. Wildlife management in the national parks. Washington, D.C.: U.S. Department of Interior.

20. Kaufman 1960 (see 15). Also Gulick, L.H. 1951. American forest policy. New York: Duell, Sloan, and Pearce.

21. Magill, A.W. 1983. The reluctant public servant. Journal of Forestry 81:82.

22. Shepard, W.B. 1990. Seeing the forest for the trees: "new perspectives" in the Forest Service. Renewable Resources Journal 8:8–11.

23. For example, Tueller, P.T., and W. Burkhardt. 1993. Range management: an obituary. Born 1930, died 1998. Rangelands 15:5–8.

24. The flavor of this debate is captured in a series of "In my opinion . . ." articles in Wildlife Society Bulletin 17:335–365.

25. Brown, G., and C.C. Harris. 1992. The U.S. Forest Service: Toward the new resource management paradigm? Society and Natural Resources 5:231–245.

26. A nationwide telephone survey by the first author in Spring 1993 found that 74 percent of Americans had "some" or "a great deal of" confidence in the Fish and Wildlife Service, compared to 66 percent for the Forest Service and 56 percent for the Bureau of Land Management.

Chapter 9

Natural Resource Agencies: Questioning the Paradigm

Jeff DeBonis

> If there is any duty which more than another we owe to our children and our children's children to perform at once, it is to save the forests of this country, for they constitute the first and most important element in the conservation of natural resources of the country.
>
> —Theodore Roosevelt

I vividly remember the first few days of my new "dream job" as a professional Forester Trainee with the United States Department of Agriculture Forest Service. Having recently completed a two-year tour with the Peace Corps in El Salvador, as a soils conservation and reforestation specialist, the frustration of watching that country's ecological health unravel was fresh in my mind. Now, though, I was in the most ecologically advanced country in the world, or so I thought. I was ready to learn how to do forestry the "right" way, working on the Kootenai National Forest, a large timber forest in northwestern Montana. I had received a degree in Forest Management from Colorado State University only four years prior. I still believed, as did many of my peers, that if one wanted to work for the good of the public trust, to practice true multiple-use management where wildlife, fisheries, soils, and long-term ecological health were considered more valuable than the industrial foresters' short-term profit motive, then one would work for a public land management agency. The good agencies were within the federal government, and the best was the USDA Forest Service. This was an agency untarnished by political scandals; an agency with the reputation of being the most high-minded in the history of U.S. public service. It boasted nearly 100 years of true public trust management, with visionaries like Gifford Pinchot and Aldo Leopold having been part of its ranks. This image left me unprepared for the paradoxical and narrowly focused culture that was the reality.

I had spent two agonizing years in El Salvador, trying to persuade small farmers to use soil conservation strategies and replant eroded hillsides that were denuded of vegetation and soon to be depleted of soil. These conditions were due more to social circumstances than to lack of technical expertise. A few rich families held most of the country's agricultural land, while the rest of the 3.5 million people had to manage with less fertile, steep, easily erodible lands for growing the crops they needed to feed themselves and their families. As a result, farmers practiced slash and burn agriculture on steep slopes. They would clear away the vegetation, burn off the organic matter, and plant crops in the exposed soil of hillsides typically 45 percent slopes or higher. This, combined with heavy rainfall during the warm, rainy season, resulted in massive erosion problems, leaving vast areas unfertile and often stripped to bedrock. Downstream, siltation was filling in reservoirs, shortening the life expectancies of hydroelectric projects, and destroying riverine and estuarine fisheries.

Most industrial forestry, as practiced in the United States, involves clearcutting; this entails removing all vegetation from a site and burning the cleared area, thus exposing the soil for planting. It is done in steep, mountainous terrain receiving heavy rainfall (the Kootenai National Forest has areas with 80 inches of annual precipitation). Weren't these the same policies I spent two years, at the request of a foreign government, trying to stop? The agency replied with a rote answer explaining that this was industrial forestry at its finest. Though there may be some soil erosion, it was always within "tolerable" limits.

The expected reaction was to accept the Forest Service's explanations at face value as the truth. After all, intuition was the only thing telling me the current practices were wrong, not seasoned experience. Initially, I suppressed my intuition, suspended my questioning, and believed the agency.

This immersion into USFS culture, which continued for nearly two years, entailed arresting my concerns over apparently significant environmental damage and participating in an agency willing to allow destruction in an attempt to meet quotas. The realization that this mindset was wrong came from a seasoned "combat" biologist, Ernie Garcia. Ernie moved to my district from the Gifford Pinchot National Forest on the western side of Washington. It had a huge timber cut, along with a reputation for ruthlessly getting the cut out. Ernie was the first wildlife biologist on the Troy Ranger District of the Kootenai NF. He soon became a thorn in the side of our timber program by doing the environmental analysis and documentation required by the National Environmental Policy Act (NEPA). It was obvious that our timber program was not meeting the spirit and intent of NEPA, and Ernie began to say so. At one particular interdisciplinary (ID) team meeting, Ernie was being pressured to back down on his analysis of grizzly bear habitat needs that conflicted with timber cutting units proposed. Ernie was correct in his assessment—ecologically, morally, and professionally. I, on the other hand, was part of an effort to discredit and intimidate him into joining the "team," in order to proceed with the timber cutting at any cost. At that point, I realized I had become part of the agency's institutionalized culture without even knowing it. I had capitulated in an attempt to be part of the Forest Service family. In the process, I had also surrendered my environmental ethic, my professional ethic, and my soul. My initial intuition about the timber sale program causing unacceptable environmental damage was true. The Forest Service's true mission became clear: get the cut out regardless of the law, the extensive environmental damage, and the advice of its own biologists.

My newly expanded outlook facilitated the discovery of other like-minded employees. There were soil scientists, hydrologists, wildlife biologists, and fisheries biologists who also felt that the agency was not adhering to environmental laws, was overcutting the forests, and had become the timber industry's lackey. We remained fairly quiet and discreet, believing that working quietly within the system and being team players would be the most effective approach. The Forest Service directors only needed to hear the truth in a nonconfrontational way, and they would change.

My next appointment was the Nez Perce National Forest in Idaho, where the idea of internal change was close to becoming reality. The Forest Supervisor at the time was Tom Kovalicky, known internally as a maverick. In fact, he dubbed the forest the "Nez Perce Anadromous National Forest," emphasizing the importance of anadromous fisheries alongside timber. This was a very unusual attitude.

The timber shop, planning, preparing, and administering timber sales were again my duties. I still believed the system could work. My apprehensions were escalating concerning the overcutting of our forests, timber primacy as a driving force, and the ensuing environmental damage. The same problems existed on the Nez Perce NF as on the Kootenai NF. For example, the Clearwater River Basin was an important anadromous fishery. There was abundant evidence of inappropriate cutting: soil slides, washed out roads, and erosion. The agency was obviously planning to remove too much timber; and, there were no plans to correct damage done from past timber cutting and road building. In response, I formed an interdisciplinary team and started working with the 'ologists: the wildlife biologists, fisheries biologists, and hydrologists. These were, in fact, the steps required by NEPA.

Most timber sales also went through the ID team process, resulting in either an Environmental Assessment or an Environmental Impact Statement. This time, however, the timber planner no longer had a timber bias, or at least he questioned this bias constantly. Working in conjunction with the scientists, I attempted to reduce or eliminate inappropriate cutting where possible. My behavior was unusual for a forester, especially a timber planner, whose primary duty was maximizing the cut at any cost and who typically assumed that his duty as ID team leader was to pressure the unbelievers into submission, if not conversion. This meant getting them to alter reports to allow higher cutting than they deemed appropriate. When the scientists wouldn't succumb to the pressure, the reports were usually ignored.

One planned timber sale in the John's Creek area of the Clearwater River Basin was reduced, with the help of the hydrologists and biologists, from an estimated 14 million board feet (MBF) to a salvage opportunity of less than 3 MBF. This was significant, because under Tom Kovalicky, no pressure was made to alter the report. The system was actually working. Good documentation and science could triumph over the agency's timber primacy mandate. My internal dissent became noticeably bolder because of the open atmosphere encouraging change on the forest. Problems did exist, and timber primacy still ruled the day; but internal dissent was not only tolerated, it was actually promoted by Tom Kovalicky.

In a private discussion once, Tom said that the difference between me and him was that he was a politician and would live to fight another day. I was a revolutionary and would die in the fight no matter which side won. We both knew that change needed to happen quickly. Tom had designed his career to achieve the status of Forest Supervisor, a position he believed to be the first "rung" in the ladder that could truly accomplish significant change. Once he achieved it, he did indeed push the envelope of change, and took risks many other supervisors avoided. I followed suit by sending internal messages challenging the agency's policies. An atmosphere of acceptance lulled me into believing something was about to change.

It soon became apparent that the Nez Perce NF and its supervisor were actually aberrations within the agency, not the hoped-for sign of widespread reform. That Kovalicky was not tolerated well within the agency hierarchy also came to light. His forest planning process and environmental position were under fire from the timber industry and from a hostile congressional delegation, dedicated to serving the traditional timber interests of the Forest Service. Jim Overbay, Regional Forester of Region One at the time and Kovalicky's boss, ordered him back to Missoula, Montana, to address the industry's concerns. Tom refused to compromise his position to the degree they wanted, and soon was asked to return to Washington, D.C., to talk directly with the Chief of the Forest Service and former Senator McClure from Idaho, one of the timber industry's greatest supporters. Tom Kovalicky never compromised sufficiently to meet the demands of the timber industry and their allies, and eventually retired early from the agency.

In 1988, I moved to the Blue River District of the Willamette National Forest in western Oregon. At the time, this forest was cutting more timber than any other national forest in the system, and Forest Supervisor Mike Kerrick and his staff were proud of it. Shock was my initial reaction to this forest's timber management; shock at the rate and ferocity of cutting, at the steepness of the cutting units, the resulting erosion and slope failures, and at the environmental damage so nonchalantly dismissed by my superiors. When the lack of data and models to estimate hydrological tolerance limits was questioned, I was told, "we cut until we hit puke level, and we haven't hit that yet." The Willamette NF was an accelerated look at the future of almost the entire National Forest System. The forests of western Oregon and Washington were an indicator of what was befalling most of our national forests as a result of the Forest Service's ingrained, timber-dominated mindset. There were no attempts here to meet the spirit and intent of NEPA or of other environmental laws.

My first timber sale assignment had a completed NEPA document. I was told to, "look it over; dot the i's, cross the t's, and get the decision notice signed." A field review of the proposed timber sale yielded appalling facts. An unnecessary road was being proposed for the sole purpose of lowering the costs of logging by a few dollars per thousand board feet. This road, according to the agency's own hydrologists and geotechnical engineers, had a high likelihood of failure. If this happened, it would dump tons of sediment into a tributary of the McKenzie River that contained salmon and steelhead and also served as a municipal water supply for the cities of Eugene and Springfield, Oregon. The sale included cutting units in Spotted Owl Habitat Areas, which were supposed to be left intact. There were several large areas of washouts, landslides, and erosion caused by previous cutting and road building in the drainage.

The Cumulative Effects Analysis (required by NEPA) based on reports from engineers and hydrologists, and my own investigations, clearly documented the fact that this timber sale would have significant, adverse environmental impacts and, therefore, should be dropped. I submitted this analysis and was later instructed to rewrite the report. My supervisor was conveying the District Ranger's command for a new report since "the original report might as well have written the appeal for the environmentalists." I did as instructed and wrote a new report minus the obvious references in question. A copy of my draft report, with the original cumulative effects analysis, then found its way to a local environmental group who appealed the timber sale. They won the appeal.

Despite that victory, I felt that I could no longer, in good conscience, be a part of this conspiracy of silence. I decided to start speaking out, and expected to be fired.

My first action was to send an internal memo to some scientist friends in the supervisor's office. The memo documented information I had obtained after attending an Ancient Forest Seminar held at the University of Oregon. The memo was extremely critical of both the timber industry and the Forest Service. I knew the reaction from management on the Willamette NF would not be the same as on the Nez Perce NF. However, the extent of what happened was unexpected. Some members of the timber industry had apparently received a copy of the memo as quickly as I had sent it. A typical timber industry response came from Troy Reinhart, director of a local timber industry support group called Douglas Timber Operators, asking for my resignation.

I alerted the local environmental constituency and the media. The controversy was commented on in the local paper and *The New York Times*.

In the meantime, I had written a letter to the chief of the Forest Service, F. Dale Robertson. My words were from the heart and extremely candid. The reality of what we were doing to our forests, and the role the Forest Service played in addressing this reality, had to be dealt with more honestly and openly. Since the media seemed so interested in the issue, *High Country News* received a copy of this letter for publication. I hoped to promote additional media coverage and get the word out to other Forest Service employees, many of whom read this particular paper.

I felt that the time had come for change, and that I had a unique perspective with which to bring it about. My international experience with deforestation and reforestation and soil conservation projects broadened my outlook, and perhaps gave me an advantage to see through the rhetoric and dogma to which so many had become obligate. I understood the necessity for beginning a transformation.

The agency's historically strong ties to resource-extraction industries, timber in particular, were now the focus of serious scrutiny as to its ramifications for the environment and future generations. In the letter to Robertson, I explained this assertion more fully, supported it with examples, and gave my input on what top management needed to do to move us into the 21st century as leaders of a new resource ethic instead of as unwilling participants being dragged along by a chain of court decisions.

I suggested we were overcutting our National Forests at the expense of other resource values. We were incurring negative, cumulative impacts to our watersheds, fisheries, wildlife, and other noncommodity resources in our quest to meet timber targets. I provided examples, including moving Spotted Owl Habitat Area (SOHA) boundaries and allowing fragmentation of those areas to accommodate timber sales; exceeding recommended cover/forage ratios on big game winter range; ignoring nongame wildlife prescriptions, such as snag and green replacement tree guidelines; exceeding watershed/sediment "threshold values of concern" in areas with obvious, cumulative damage, and so on.

At the planning level, I pointed out that Forest Plans had been built from the "top down" instead of the from the "ground up." In other words, we have taken the politically driven timber harvest level and manipulated the Forest Plan to support that amount, rather than letting the harvest level be determined by sound biological and ecological considerations mandated by our resource protection laws. I cited numerous examples of actual Forest Plans exhibiting these characteristics.

To put the issue in perspective, I posed a series of questions that the Forest Service and its employees should consider: Are we, as an agency, going to continue to support the current global epidemic of destruction of our biosphere's ecological diversity and survival, for short-sighted, short-term, economic "security"? Are we going to continue to ascribe to the timber industry's assertion that cutting our National Forests is imperative to maintain jobs, when the same industry exported three to five billion board feet of raw logs per year for the last 10 years from Oregon and Washington alone? Shall we sacrifice the public's lands because the economic view of standing timber deems it "under-valued" (and a leveraged buy-out opportunity)? In essence, why are we so biased in favor of the timber industry?

I believed this last question could be partially explained by the traditional mindset within the Forest Service that has been perpetuated over the years. A combination of partial truths and an unwillingness to look too deeply into a system that was "working," led the men and women of the agency to adopt a superficial attitude toward resource management. A common belief was that good intentions and aspirations to responsible land stewardship somehow negated any detrimental effects resulting from our accelerated rates of timber harvest. Another was the acceptance that current practices were just a continuation of an historically proven, successful method of timber management. A third tenet was the idea that money could solve any problems the agency might have, that any conflict could be mitigated financially with a win–win outcome.

As the negative impacts of agency actions became more and more obvious, employees tried to pretend it was not happening. And yet at some subconscious level, we knew that we were overcutting. When I talked to co-workers about this subject, it was almost universally agreed that there was, in fact, overcutting. Most of these people, though, failed to make the

connection between themselves and the agency and the direct contribution to the global, environmental onslaught. Most stopped short of
admitting that the resource and their credibility with the public were being
compromised.

Another contributing factor to this alliance between the Forest Service
and extractive commodity-based industry involved the agency's perception
of who environmental groups were and what they did. They were dismissed
as "special interests" by the agency. They should not, however, have been
equally weighted with the timber industry as just another special interest.
The timber industry's motives were short-term, quick profits, and tended
toward present-focused, economic gain. The environmental community, on
the other hand, had a long-range perspective. They promoted a vision of a
sustainable future, both economically and ecologically. Their motives were
altruistic, not exploitative.

Environmental groups wanted change. They threatened the agency's
long-held conception that it was acting in a responsible manner. That the
Forest Service had traditionally allied itself with the timber industry and
against the "environmentalists" only proved that it had followed a mis-
guided purpose for some time. Again, I included a variety of specific cases
to illustrate my point. The U.S. Forest Service did have the legal authority,
the personnel, the research facilities, the facts and data to promote and
make the needed changes to its internal value system and management
practices. It was my opinion that the Forest Service must associate itself
with the long-range, holistic, and altruistic motives of the environmental
community, which were more in line with its mission as a public resource
management agency. Granted, this would involve a major confrontation
with resource extraction industries, but it was something that had to be
done. The time was right for this type of realignment.

I then listed specific courses of action to initiate change: The Forest Service should encourage ideological diversity and support the existing "agents
for change" currently within the organization, like many wildlife biologists
and other specialists. Support should be given to those within the system
who try to promote the new vision. All members of the agency must insist
on absolute commitment to the spirit and letter of our resource protection
laws with as much energy as has been devoted to cultural diversity in the
workforce. They must further promote the substantial lowering of existing
and planned timber harvest levels throughout the National Forest System.
By doing this, the agency could start erring on the side of resource protection instead of extraction.

The "bottom up" approach to Forest Planning must take precedence over the current "top-down" strategy. We must demand realistic, specific, and meaningful Forest Plan standards and guidelines that truly protect other resource values and accurately display all effects of timber harvesting.

A new resource ethic should be encouraged by publicly endorsing an alignment with the environmental community and participating in the search for a sustainable future. It is time for everyone to accept the fact that change is imperative. The unfortunate truth is that future generations will look back at these last few decades of our history with a mixture of amazement, incredulity, and disgust that we allowed such an unprecedented slaughter of our natural ecosystems during this era of massive exploitation for so little real long-term value.

I wrote this letter hoping that it would have a maximum impact for change. Because of the import of its contents, F. Dale Robertson was unable to respond. If he had, he would have had to either concede to making changes or deny that any of the problems existed. Apparently, neither option was acceptable because I did not receive a response until eight months later (and at the request of a congressional committee), and it was only four lines acknowledging receipt of the letter and thanking me for my input.

This lack of any significant advancement left me frustrated and primed for the next opportunity to effect change. That chance came in March of 1989, when I attended an Old Growth Symposium, sponsored by the Forest Service, in Portland, Oregon. After listening to a speech by the Regional Forester on how well the Forest Service was protecting wildlife, ecosystems, and the public trust, I was stunned at the degree to which this individual was out of touch with current events. On impulse, I found a computer, made 200 flyers, handed them out, and created the Association of Forest Service Employees for Environmental Ethics (AFSEEE).

Over the next few weeks, the response was incredible, with membership requests and letters of support pouring in. I was asked to speak to agency employees, citizens, and environmental activist groups across the country. Media coverage grew, and I began traveling around the country organizing AFSEEE chapters and giving public speeches. I soon had two jobs: my usual timber planning job for the agency, and now director of a new organization of Forest Service employee dissidents. By the end of the first year, membership was more than 1000 employees, approaching 5 percent of the total agency workforce.

The goal of AFSEEE was to foster an environmental ethic among employees that would change the culture of the Forest Service to one that was more environmentally oriented, would meet its regulatory laws, and would err on the side of resource protection.

It was a pleasant surprise that I was not fired immediately. I believe this was due to my "kamikaze" approach. I was forceful, outspoken, and not afraid of the consequences. I also had an untarnished reputation as a good forester. The element of surprise and my air of unpredictability gave me an edge.

Even so, at first, the agency response was somewhat hostile. I was told that I could not talk about old-growth issues on or off the job. Though the agency had the prerogative to control my on-the-job contact with the public, news media, and others, my off-the-job activities were protected by First Amendment, free speech rights and not subject to agency or supervisory control. I informed my District Ranger and the Forest Supervisor of this, and they retreated from their initial stance. My circumstances were the impetus for a set of legal guidelines on the Willamette NF concerning free speech within and outside the workplace. Though my methods may seem to have been a little impulsive, in retrospect, I would not have changed my tactics. The time was right for my message, and the message had to be loud and clear.

I continued to work for the agency as a timber sale planner and to organize AFSEEE with no interference from management. When I resigned a year later, it was a personal decision to manage the rapidly growing AFSEEE, which needed a full-time director to realize its potential as a major force of change within the Forest Service.

Perhaps the most important achievement of AFSEEE to date is the enormous amount of media attention it has drawn to the issue of needed change in government agencies. We were able to speak out on topics that before had been taboo.

In fact, the results of a study on values and change in the Forest Service showed that a considerable number of employees went about their jobs differently (by speaking out, writing more responsible plans, and not ignoring pertinent data when arranging timber sales) as a direct result of the presence of AFSEEE (1). Local chapters became very active, commenting on their Forest's Plan and serving as liaisons with the public. Meetings were held to provide information on what was going on in the National Forests and what citizens could do to participate in effecting change.

Because many of the AFSEEE members had a high degree of technical expertise in the workings of timber and other resource management, they provided testimony for several congressional hearings that further encouraged change within the Forest Service. One example was a decision made by Federal Judge Dwyer, in 1991, enjoining the agency's timber sales program in the Western Cascades and northwest California because the Forest

Service still did not have a credible management plan for the Northern Spotted Owl. He was quoted as saying that

> More is involved here than a simple failure by an agency to comply with its governing statute. The most recent violation of NFMA [National Forest Management Act] exemplifies a deliberate and systematic refusal by the Forest Service and the FWS [Fish and Wildlife Service] to comply with laws protecting wildlife. This is not the doing of scientists, foresters, rangers, and others at the working levels of these agencies. It reflects decisions made by higher authorities in the executive branch of government (2).

It is too early to tell if AFSEEE will have a direct, tangible effect on the practices of the Forest Service, but we have determined that it is possible to organize concerned employees from within and put considerable pressure on higher echelons of the agency. Programs implemented by the Forest Service such as New Perspectives and Ecosystem Management are evidence that at least a shift in rhetoric is occurring. Perhaps the next century will be the arena in which these words will translate into action.

As soon as AFSEEE became a reality, it was obvious that the Forest Service was not the only agency that could benefit from such an organization. So, in January of 1993, I left as director of AFSEEE to start PEER, Public Employees for Environmental Responsibility. It was my intent to expand the AFSEEE model into other federal and state land management and environmental protection agencies. Again, there was a tremendous response, in particular from the employees of the Bureau of Land Management with regard to grazing reforms.

As we are on the cusp of the 21st century, there is a desperate need for governmental agencies to restructure in a way that will allow them to respond to the public's increasing concern over the future of our natural resources. Employee ethics groups will be instrumental in this transformation. As the current administration mandates new policy, the working levels of the agency can monitor the degree to which this policy is absorbed and implemented. They can then channel their findings outside of the agency, through AFSEEE or PEER, back to the administration. Adjustments can then be made and areas of more focused attention determined. In this manner, two-way communication and feedback can turn rhetoric into reality.

AFSEEE and PEER will hopefully inspire even more employee ethics groups in the years to come. By constantly applying pressure, adapting strategies to whatever political climate exists, and adhering to a strong commitment to resource stewardship and environmental protection, the paradigm shift will continue.

Notes

1. Brown, G., and C. Harris. 1990. Summary sheet: preliminary results of a study of values and change in the USDA Forest Service. Department of Resource Recreation and Tourism, College of Forestry, Wildlife, and Range Science. Moscow, Idaho: University of Idaho.
2. Quote is from an article in Forest Watch in May 1991, titled "Judge Dwyer does it again. Opinion rebukes forest service for 'remarkable series of violations.'"

Chapter 10

Natural Resource Agencies: Transforming from Within

Winifred B. Kessler and Hal Salwasser

> We aren't where we want to be. And we're not where we're going to be.
> But thank God Almighty, we're not where we used to be.
> —Martin Luther King, Jr.

Change is not just a fact of life. It is the very essence of life. We accept this reality for organisms and ecosystems; either they evolve in the face of environmental change, or they go the route of extinction. The same is true, however, for the "living" systems of human origin—for example, corporations, governments, and agencies that manage lands and natural resources. To remain relevant and viable, institutions must adapt to the changing environment that is the context of their existence.

In today's changing environment of natural resources management, the United States Department of Agriculture Forest Service (USDAFS) is a prime example of the need for institutional change and of the challenges of trying to do so from within. A major force in natural resources management and research throughout the 20th century, the Forest Service is caught in the maelstrom of the cultural, ecological, and economic changes that are the subject of this book. The context for natural resources management has changed significantly in recent years, and the "fitness" of the Forest Service in this new environment has been affected.

That is why, in 1990, the Forest Service embraced the need for change and launched an initiative to bring it about. Labeled "New Perspectives," the effort began with a critical look at how the national forests and grasslands were managed, for whose benefit, for what uses and values, and why. A new set of principles about land and resources management was developed—some would say it was the original, "old" set of principles—and field managers and scientists were encouraged to try innovative new approaches for solving problems on the national forests and grasslands. Based on these experiences, Forest Service leaders concluded that an ecosystem approach to management was needed to meet the cultural, ecological, and economic realities of the 1990s and beyond. Of course, many voices both within and outside the Service had been espousing this theme for years (1).

Earlier chapters in this book relate the shifts in thinking, values, economics, and scientific understanding that created the current environment of natural resources management. Our chapter relates how these forces came to bear on the Forest Service, and examines the important changes that have been set in motion.

Three Eras of Multiple-Use Management

The Forest Service Centennial in 1991 was a celebration of the National Forest System. This diverse and valuable resource, totaling 191 million acres, is managed by the Forest Service for multiple uses to benefit all Americans. Just how the Forest Service has gone about multiple-use management, however, has not remained constant during the agency's century of existence.

The First 50 Years

The origins of the National Forest System go back to the Forest Reserve Act of 1891, and the Organic Administration Act of 1897, whereby Congress authorized the setting aside of forest lands and directed that they be managed for purposes of "securing favorable conditions of water flows" and "furnishing a continuous supply of timber." Originally administered by the General Land Office in the Department of the Interior, in 1905 these lands were transferred to the Division of Forestry (soon to be renamed the Forest Service) within the Department of Agriculture. The original forest reserves were designated national forests in 1907 (2).

The Forest Service's approach during the first 50 years was largely a custodial one, reflecting the origins of the national forests as watershed protection areas and reserves against future timber shortages. Major accomplishments included forest restoration, watershed protection, wilderness, wildlife habitat protection, regulation of livestock grazing, and reduction in wildfires. Since demand for timber was largely met from private lands during this era, conflicts among the users of national forests and grasslands were few. This all changed around midcentury, however.

The Second 50 Years

During and after World War II, the custodial view of national forest management was supplanted by surging demand for timber to support housing construction and a rapidly growing economy. The time had come to "call in the chips" on that vast reserve of timber and other raw materials. This meant a new dominant theme for Forest Service management: the efficient, cost-effective production of timber as a crop from national forest lands. The Forest Service rose to the occasion, turning its organizational structure, workforce, management models, management philosophy, and monetary resources to the task of maximizing timber production.

Before long, the heavy emphasis on timber production came into conflict with other emerging uses and values that Americans desired from national forest lands such as recreation and wildlife viewing. One result was passage of the Multiple-Use Sustained Yield Act (1960), seeking a more equitable balance in national forest management (3). Another result was that national parks were carved out of national forests to forestall timber harvesting in areas perceived to be national icons. During this period, the Forest Service began to make extensive use of the practice of clearcutting. Public revulsion against clearcutting grew until lawsuits were filed against the agency in the late 1960s and early 1970s. Both the government and the timber industry thought the Forest Service would win the suits. They didn't. Rather than modify the timber sale provisions to allow clearcutting, the Congress decided to address the whole balance of resource programs on the national forests.

Perceiving that even the 1960 Act did not fully correct imbalances in Forest Service programs, Congress passed additional legislation specific to the agency: the Resources Planning Act of 1974 and the National Forest Management Act of 1976. These Acts launched the Forest Service on a massive planning effort to develop comprehensive land and resource management plans for all units of the National Forest System. Public involvement was integral to these planning efforts, as required by the National Environmental Policy Act of 1969.

Unfortunately during the 1980s, what Congress had designed to be a bottom-up process, emphasizing capabilities of the land and desires of the people, became instead a top-down process directed by political appointees and appropriations committees from Washington, D.C. The emphasis of the Reagan administration and powerful legislators in the Congress on supplying public resources for the U.S. economy created pressures to increase timber harvest levels provided for in the draft forest plans. Decision-making models were modified to meet "timber targets"; and resource relationships were handled as constraints on timber yield or as tradeoffs between timber yield and the other multiple uses. The projections and solutions churned out by these models, however, failed to address many of the conditions, values, and uses of national forests that really mattered to people (4).

The Forest Service may have misperceived the intent of public sentiment and new legislative mandates as calling for fine-tuning the scientific basis of forestry when what was needed and called for was fundamental reform in how the concept of multiple use is applied. Thus the massive forest planning effort of the 1980s, rather than dissipating the cloud of contention surrounding national forest management, instead revealed just how dissatisfied many Americans were with the agency's way of doing business. Having spent more than a decade and vast amounts of money, the Forest Service saw many of its plans flounder in a quagmire of appeals and litigation.

What went wrong? A great many issues were raised in plan appeals, but throughout them ran a common thread. Americans were not only concerned with the products and services to be provided from the national forests; they also cared very much about the *condition* of these special lands and resources. Their appeals talked about things that the plans, in their opinions, had neglected—such things as the health, beauty, and ecological integrity of forests and rangelands; the cumulative effects of management actions on air and water quality; the diversity and viability of plant and animal species; the special "sense of place" afforded by wildland settings; and questions of responsibility to future generations.

Many Americans were expressing quite different values and expectations for national forest management than could be properly addressed by the mechanistic, science-based, output-driven approach that characterized traditional Forest Service planning and management. The Forest Service needed to take a fresh new look at management of these lands and their relationships to the American people. The key question addressed in the planning process (how should we manage these lands?) would remain moot until a more basic question was answered first: for whom, and for what values and purposes, should we manage these lands (5)?

The fundamental premises that public lands should support a variety of values and uses, and that resources should be managed sustainably, were not (with a few exceptions) being debated. Instead, the problem was the particular "brand" of multiple-use management practiced by the Forest Service for several decades, namely a focus on outputs and yields of resources (6). This approach was growing increasingly discordant with society and with developments in the scientific community. It was time for a fresh look at how multiple-use management needed to change.

A New Era?

In 1990, Forest Service Chief F. Dale Robertson launched "New Perspectives for Managing the National Forest System" (New Perspectives for short) to try "a different way of thinking about managing the national forests and national grasslands, emphasizing ecological principles, to sustain their many values and uses" (7). The purpose was to point a new path for multiple-use management; a path better suited for society's evolving needs.

New Perspectives: An Experiment in Change

Unlike most Forest Service initiatives, New Perspectives was not a specific program of work, nor a prescribed set of management practices. It was an internal examination of the need for institutional change and how that might be brought about: seeking an appropriate evolutionary path for the agency within the changing national and global environment. New Perspectives did see a need for new guiding principles, appropriate for society's needs today and adaptive for future needs. These principles may turn out to be the most important legacy of New Perspectives: principles for sustaining healthy ecosystems, involving people as partners, broadening the scientific basis for management, and collaborative problem-solving.

Why and how these principles emerged, and their vital importance in the agency's transition to ecosystem management, are detailed in Part III. For now, it is important to understand that New Perspectives was an internal, grassroots process for change. Why? As has been painfully learned in the corporate world, organizational change does not result from even the most elaborate of top-down directives. Institutions transform themselves through the accumulation of individual actions, incremental changes, and the collective behaviors of everyone within the organizational structure. The best that leadership can do is articulate a vision and create the environment for change to happen (8)

Taking Charge and Taking Risks

One essential strategy of New Perspectives was creating an environment where creative juices could freely flow; where people were enabled and encouraged to be innovative; and where they felt empowered to take charge and take risks. That is why Forest Service leadership limited its direction concerning New Perspectives to a set of guiding principles and incentives for innovation in management and research.

The lack of specific direction made many people uncomfortable, however. Not all employees wanted the freedom granted by New Perspectives. Within the Forest Service workforce, a common response was: "tell us what New Perspectives is supposed to look like so we can go put it on the ground." Some outsiders, desiring to know how clearcutting and other specific practices would change, dismissed the whole thing as so much "smoke and mirrors." But the lack of direction from the top was both deliberate and necessary to bring about the type and magnitude of change required. Issues surrounding national forest management are so varied and complex that simple "fixes" issued from the top cannot possibly solve them. Each national forest and grassland fills a special niche within the unique ecological, cultural, and economic landscape of which it is an integral part. Therefore, solutions must be worked out case-by-case by the people who are closest to the lands and resources. This means Forest Service field personnel, both managers and scientists, working with whomever has a stake in the outcome of management involving a particular national forest or grassland.

Despite the initial skepticism, many Forest Service personnel and interested citizens saw New Perspectives as a green light to try new and creative approaches to reach shared objectives. In response, some 260 individual projects were initiated during the two-year life of New Perspectives (9). These represented tremendous variety in size, scope, and objectives. They included:

- Major regional programs of research and development engaging scientists, managers, government, educators, businesses, and citizen groups in sustainable ecosystem management. Examples include the Blue Mountains Natural Resources Institute, a partnership addressing the forest health crisis and other concerns in forest and rangeland ecosystems of northeast Oregon and southeast Washington; and the Great Lakes Biodiversity Program, a partnership facilitating landscape-level research and management in temperate forest ecosystems of the North Central states.

- Workshops, symposia, and shortcourses focusing on the New Perspectives principles and their application in land and resources management. Typically these addressed a particular landscape, ecosystem, or Forest Service administrative unit, and sought participation by diverse disciplines, affiliations, and points of view.

- A series of inter-university colloquia engaging students, faculty, and interested publics in dialog about the changing environment of natural resources management. These occurred as workshops, seminars, and semester-long courses, with topics representing the full gamut of social, scientific, and policy concerns.

- Projects applying innovative approaches to land and resources management on National Forest System lands. These varied from on-the-ground activities such as the "Living Barn/Living Snow Fence" project on the Arapaho and Roosevelt National Forest in Colorado (affecting 25 acres) to an entire forestwide plan developed for the Bridger-Teton National Forest in Wyoming.

What qualified these diverse efforts for the New Perspectives label is that they put into practice the four guiding principles of sustaining healthy ecosystems, involving people as partners, strengthening the scientific basis for management, and collaborative problem-solving.

What Was Accomplished?

Did New Perspectives succeed as an instrument of change? Did it improve the management of national forests and grasslands? Did it point a new or better path for multiple-use management?

Final answers to these questions must await the passage of time. The answer to the first question is an unequivocal yes. New Perspectives directly led to the policy change in multiple-use management made in June 1992, known as ecosystem management. The principles and aims of ecosystem management as an agencywide policy reflect the ideas and partnerships forged during New Perspectives. Some early answers to the other questions were obtained through an assessment done by the Pinchot Institute for Conservation (10). Developing a complete picture would require investigation of each of the 260 projects—a prohibitive task. Thus, phase one of the Institute's assessment examined three national forests where major New Perspectives efforts were initiated: the Ouachita, the Klamath, and the Shawnee National Forests (see box). The Institute also gathered information through formal seminars, informal interviews, and examination of New Perspectives documents.

Some interesting observations emerged during the assessment:

- Restoration and management of native ecosystems was a key theme in many New Perspectives projects, and especially in the three case forests examined.

- Unfettered creativity seemed a common element; forest personnel felt "more freedom to act from the gut than from directives from on high."

- Some efforts attributed to New Perspectives would likely have happened anyway, as something just had to "give" in view of the turmoil surrounding national forest management. This finding supports the

A Tale of Three Forests

The Ouachita is a 1.6 million acre national forest located within the short-leaf pine-hardwood ecosystem in western Arkansas and eastern Oklahoma. For many years, clearcutting to regenerate pine had been the subject of controversy and contention. By 1990, public dissatisfaction had reached the boiling point on this issue. Thus, New Perspectives focused on restoration and sustainable management of the native shortleaf pine-hardwood forest through silvicultural options other than clearcutting. Because little was known about alternative silviculture in this ecosystem, New Perspectives took on a strong research emphasis. The goal—development of the scientific basis for managing the Ouachita in a silviculturally sound and socially acceptable manner—is being pursued through integrated research and management with extensive collaboration of outside interests.

The Klamath is a 1.68 million acre forest in northern California. Ecosystems on the Klamath are diverse, ranging from coastal forest to high desert. Traditionally one of the major "timber" forests, harvesting has plummeted in recent years in connection with the spotted owl issue. Mill closings have put local communities in economic and social turmoil, and the shrinking timber program has triggered declines in the Klamath's operating budget and staffing. On top of all this, huge wildfires burned about 40 percent of the forest in 1987, forcing the forest "back to the drawing board" in its efforts to complete a comprehensive land management plan. The Klamath welcomed New Perspectives as an opportunity to develop a plan that would be more responsive to the dynamic mix of social, ecological, and economic problems playing out in the Northwest. The principles of ecosystem sustainability, public participation, integrated science and management, and collaboration became central to the Klamath's planning process.

The 256,000 acres of the Shawnee National Forest are extensively co-mingled with private lands in southern Illinois. Purchased as worn-out farmland in the 1930s, the Shawnee was reforested with both native hardwoods and nonnative pines. Because public land is relatively scarce here, the Shawnee is highly valued by local people for ecological, recreational, and aesthetic reasons. Even modest timber harvest is vigorously opposed unless justified by ecological or other nontimber objectives. Even before New Perspectives was initiated by Forest Service leaders, management of the Shawnee had already changed to an emphasis on restoring native ecosystems to the southern Illinois landscape. For the Shawnee, New Perspectives was an opportunity to promote and champion developments that were already underway.

view of New Perspectives as a catalyst for grassroots change already underway, rather than as the origin of change.

- More important than individual projects, New Perspectives was a symbol for changes in attitude and behavior. It gave forests flexibility and guiding principles for dealing with powerful social, economic, and political forces.

- A major contribution of New Perspectives was in empowering managers to take risks and be innovative. Although the end results remain to be seen, it is clear that "indeed something is going on out there."

New Principles for Land and Resources Management

In many respects New Perspectives was a testing of the waters of change. Given a set of guiding principles and a green light to be creative, many Forest Service managers and their partners set out to solve the "messy" problems that threatened to hold national forest management in limbo. Concurrently, the principles advocated in New Perspectives were being affirmed and promoted in a number of national and international arenas, strengthening the case for the chosen direction (11). It is important now to examine those principles to understand why and how they emerged, and to appreciate them as the foundation for ecosystem management.

.   .   .

Principle 1: Sustain healthy, diverse, and productive ecosystems in the long term. A key lesson of the 1980s was that a national forest or grassland is much greater than the sum of its multiple uses. People demanded that management goals and objectives go beyond the yields of board-feet of timber, user-days of recreation, animal-unit-months of grazing, and other "multiple-use outputs" projected in the endless tables and graphs within forest plans. For too long, federal land managers had been treating natural resources "as discrete entities, focusing on their economic value and paying little attention to underlying natural systems or processes" (12).

A narrow focus on uses obscures what these lands and resources really are: living, dynamic, complex systems of plants, animals, water, soil, climate, topography, and people. In a word, they are ecosystems. And it was the failure to recognize ecosystems as the context for multiple-use management that lay at the heart of many of the Forest Service's difficulties. In systems parlance, management had concerned itself with manipulating stocks and flows of resources, neglecting the state or condition of the ecosystems from which these resources were derived (13). This was a significant oversight, given the priority that contemporary society places on environmental quality and ecological matters (14).

This first principle suggests an important corollary for multiple-use management: the key to sustaining all benefits is in managing for ecosystem health. Earlier, it was simply assumed that land would be taken care of as long as management succeeded in sustaining the yields of the various multiple uses. It is now recognized that ecosystem health must be a conscious and deliberate goal as well as the overall context for multiple-use management. Achieving this goal means: (1) maintaining environmental quality by protecting soils, water, air, biological diversity, and ecological processes; (2) providing equitable and sustainable access to resources for people who depend on the land for subsistence, livelihood, commerce, recreation, and spiritual growth; and (3) producing natural resource products for sustainable economic development and resilience of human societies (15).

. . .

Principle 2: Involve people as full partners in land and resources management. The many conflicts surrounding national forest management—and the flurry of appeals and litigation by various citizen's groups—were vivid testimony that people had not been adequately involved in the decisions that affected them. Although public involvement was integral to the planning process of the 1980s, many people felt denied of a truly meaningful role in shaping land-use decisions. Perhaps the process was too stilted, or too restrictive; or simply that the mechanistic planning model could not handle the kinds of concerns and desires that people felt for the national forests and grasslands.

The lessons were painful but instructive. It is unwise to filter people's desires through our own scientific lenses, or to judge what is good for society from a scientific/technical perspective only. Those mistakes can be avoided in the future only if managers, citizens, and scientists hear each other's views. The Forest Service, to remain in tune with the society it serves, must constantly and meaningfully involve people in the planning and decision-making processes. Allowing people access only at specified "windows" in the planning process is not enough; they must help set direction from the outset, and then share responsibility for both successes and failures.

Significant roles for the public go well beyond the legal requirements for public involvement. Through cost-share and other programs, the Forest Service is increasing the opportunities for involvement. Today, interested people are serving active stewardship roles in on-the-ground projects, science advisory boards, monitoring and research, environmental education, and much more.

. . . .

Principle 3: Strengthen the scientific basis for management by integrating research and management. The Forest Service has a long history of research spanning a wide range of disciplines. The agency's programs include applied research, having immediate utility in land and resources management, as well as basic research to achieve advances in the relevant physical, biological, and social sciences. If success is measured only in terms of studies completed and papers published, Forest Service research has been a shining star indeed. But how effective has the research branch been in anticipating and helping solve complex problems of lands, resources, and people? Here the track record has been considerably less than stellar. These shortcomings are not unique to the Forest Service; they characterize the natural resources and ecological sciences generally (16). Important drawbacks include: research approaches dominated by disciplinary functionalism and reductionism; traditional isolation of research from management and policy arenas; and funding and incentive structures that foster competition and independence over collaborative, interdisciplinary problem-solving.

The scientific basis for national forest management concerns a great deal more than how to balance production of the multiple uses. It involves understanding how ecosystem structure, function, and related attributes (such as ecological health and sustainability) respond to the collective, cumulative, and long-term effects of management. It includes knowledge about people's value systems, and relationships of land management to livelihoods and quality of life. It includes information for predicting how management programs and actions relate to economics, landscape patterns, biodiversity, and other features at regional and greater scales. The scientific basis for management cannot be developed if Forest Service scientists and managers continue to operate in separate spheres (17).

Ecosystem management also implies a full recognition of the uncertainty that surrounds any land management program or activity. Uncertainty is unavoidable; only part of it reflects the quality and quantity of scientific information used in a management plan or decision. The rest stems from the inescapable fact that ecosystems, inherently complex and always responding to stochastic forces and events, are only partly predictable, and only in the short run.

From an ecosystem perspective, to implement a land management plan is to embark on a complex, landscape-scale experiment. Existing research may provide a reasonable basis for predicting responses of individual resources, at least at the stand or site level. But only crude predictions can be made of how ecosystems and associated values and attributes (such as biological diversity and resilience) will respond to the collective effects of numerous management actions superimposed on an already dynamic landscape.

Thus, it is vitally important to capture and apply new knowledge gained through the management experience—a process called adaptive management (18). The strength of adaptive management is its ability to "simultaneously test alternative landscape patterns and forestry options as rigorous management experiments," thereby positioning managers to "incrementally predicate forest policy upon an experimental basis" (19).

Adaptive management requires a coordinated effort by Forest Service researchers and managers. Researchers provide necessary scientific rigor to the process, and managers carry out the "treatments" (i.e., land management operations) and apply what is learned back into the cycle of planning and management. The partnership makes possible an adaptive approach as well as the interdisciplinary, big-picture perspective necessary to accurately define complex problems and to test solutions that encompass the full range of ecological, cultural, and economic concerns.

·   ·   ·

Principle 4: Integrate all aspects of natural resources conservation through collaboration within the community of interests. Ecosystem management requires a collaborative process that reaches well beyond the physical boundaries of national forest lands and that focuses problem-solving within the diverse community of interests. Collaboration is necessary to achieve convergence, if not consensus, among diverse interests and viewpoints. It is also necessary, for both ecological and social reasons, to achieve effective integration of all aspects of natural resources conservation. Managing national forests and grasslands to sustain diverse, healthy ecosystems—while meeting society's diverse needs—is both conceptually and practically a more difficult charge than management simply for sustainable use. Ecosystems occur at all spatial scales and levels of complexity, from a drop of pond water to the entire biosphere. Ecosystems do not exhibit clear boundaries, although humans commonly delineate lines that may reflect political, management, or research needs more than ecological relationships. An example is the national forest boundary: while having political significance, it really is just an arbitrary line imposed on a hierarchical complex of ecological systems.

With ecosystem health and sustainability as a goal, the purview of national forest management cannot be confined to what goes on within national forest boundaries. Processes and events outside these lines affect the condition of ecosystems and resources within. Conversely, what happens within a national forest or grassland affects the larger-scale ecosystems and landscapes of which it is an integral part. To make decisions consistent with ecosystem health, the community of interests must have knowledge about the larger ecological picture. Collaboration with other management jurisdictions, ownerships, and with diverse research institutions will be critical for ecosystem-based management (20).

Collaborative problem-solving is also necessitated by the diversity of views, values, and expectations of the American public. Some people live near to and derive their livelihoods from national forest lands, while others may never see a national forest in their lifetime. The values that individuals place on these lands run from the most practical and utilitarian to the spiritual and the sublime. People's understanding of forests and rangelands as complex ecological systems varies from none to extremely sophisticated. Their reactions to proposed management may reflect ethical beliefs, aesthetic values, ecological understanding, or simply a tendency to join popular causes. This mix of views, values, and understandings defines a community of interests for national forest management (21). There are important roles for scientists, resource managers, educators, planners, communication specialists, and citizens from all walks of life. It is only through close collaboration that common goals can be articulated, problems defined, and solutions sought.

The Transition to Ecosystem Management

Having tested these principles through the New Perspectives experience, the next logical step was to institutionalize them in Forest Service structure, function, and philosophy. This process began with an announcement on 4 June 1992, by Chief F. Dale Robertson, that, henceforth, the Forest Service would use "an ecological approach to achieve the multiple-use management of the national forests and grasslands" (22). He explained the new approach, termed "ecosystem management" to mean that "we must blend the needs of people and environmental values in such a way that the national forests and grasslands represent diverse, healthy, productive, and sustainable ecosystems." In principle and policy at least, the agency is headed into a third era of multiple-use management. Just how that translates into practice, however, remains to be seen. Change is never easy, and in this case it must extend to everything the Forest Service is and does as a land management agency.

The Pain of Institutional Change

Large organizations are notoriously resistant to change. The reasons are many and complex, reflecting basic human tendencies to preserve the comfort, security, and convenience of the status quo. Organizational change is extremely difficult to bring about, even when it is called for by top management, and the stakes are competitiveness and survival in a changing environment. The more hierarchical and bureaucratic the organizational structure is, the greater the struggle to bring about needed change (23).

All this is true of the Forest Service, even though the change to ecosystem management is a stated priority of the agency's leaders and is a move that most of the rank-and-file stand firmly behind. A main reason for the difficulty is that the basic architecture of the Forest Service—including its organizational structure and behavior, its budget system, its institutional culture, and its traditions—was forged in a distinctly different environment from that which exists today. The architecture remains basically intact from the second era of national forest management (roughly 1950 to 1990), when the identities of programs, budgets, and professional staff reflected the various "product lines" of multiple-use management. How well can this structure adapt to achieve more comprehensive but nebulous goals such as ecosystem health and "socially acceptable management"?

Some argue that the existing structure imposes no real barriers in the transition process. The history of the automobile may provide a useful analogy. The earliest automobiles, while modeled after carriages of the day, nonetheless made possible the quantum leap from horse-powered to gasoline-powered transportation. Progress after that tended to occur in steady, incremental steps leading to the comparatively efficient automobiles of today. Perhaps the Forest Service, having made the philosophical/conceptual "quantum leap" to ecosystem management, will be able to complete the evolution through incremental changes in its organizational structure, budgeting processes, staffing, incentive and reward systems, and other mechanical features.

Others argue that the agency's transition to ecosystem management is severely impeded by an organizational structure that, while well suited to the previous era of multiple-use management, is obsolete relative to today's needs and realities. In this view, Forest Service managers are ready and willing to step forward but find their feet firmly nailed down by output targets, accountability criteria, reward systems, and a culture that reflects the old way of doing business rather than the new. Indeed, significant evidence can be cited to support this view. For example, in the current organizational structure, Ecosystem Management is a small, specialized substaff, combined with land management planning at the headquarters level, a small room in the basic multiple-use architecture. Whether intended or not, this sends a message that the "niche" is less than the blueprint for institutional reformation. In reality, of course, transforming the Forest Service must be a shared responsibility of every individual, staff, and organizational niche within the Forest Service structure. Everyone, from top management to people on the Districts, must ask how *they* can help in the transition to ecosystem management.

Looking Ahead . . .

The Forest Service now toils to evolve from a manager of land uses to a manager of ecosystems. Whether speaking in relief or regret, most people today don't question *whether* the Forest Service is changing. Rather, they ask about the speed of change and how their particular interests in national forest and grassland management will be affected. Clearly, there is no going back.

The top ranks of Forest Service management have experienced some important changes within the past year. The appointment of Dr. Jack Ward Thomas to the position of chief is, in the minds of many, a milestone in the agency's history. A scientist and wildlife ecologist, Dr. Thomas brings new views and expertise to a leadership position that has traditionally been held by career foresters.

While vision and support from the top are important, the most important force affecting change in the agency is, and always has been, the people in the field. This includes dedicated and conscientious "field" professionals who desire to do right by the resources and the people who value them. It also includes those diverse individuals who form a community of interests around a national forest or grassland. While these people may differ greatly in their views, values, and relationships to the land, they all care enough about national forest management to voice their concerns and become some part of the problem-solving process. This is the real arena where ecosystem management takes place: within a given ecological/cultural/economic landscape, where people work together and find ways to meet their needs in a manner that sustains healthy, productive ecosystems for everyone's long-term benefit.

As learned in the corporate world, top-down direction can be a hindrance rather than a help in bringing about desired change. Thus the real challenge for Forest Service management is to facilitate a "nondirective" change process, whereby successful problem-solving from the bottom up becomes the driving force for agencywide revitalization.

Notes

1. See the chapters by DeBonis (Chapter 9), Brunson and Kennedy (Chapter 8), and others in this book.

2. The following were major sources for the historical overview: Wilkinson, C.F., and H.M. Anderson. 1987. Land and resource planning in the national forests. Washington, D.C.: Island Press; and Clary, D.A. 1986. Timber and the Forest Service. Lawrence: University of Kansas Press.

3. Section 1 of the Multiple-Use Sustained-Yield Act of 1960 (P.L. 86–517, 16 U.S.C. 528) defines the uses of the national forests to include "outdoor recreation, range, timber, watershed, and wildlife and fish purposes."

4. A thorough critique of the Forest Service planning process is provided in Shands, W.E., V.A. Sample, and D.C. Le Master. 1990. National forest planning: searching for a common vision. Washington D.C.: USDA Forest Service.

5. These ideas are developed in Clawson, M. 1975. Forests for whom and for what? Baltimore: Johns Hopkins University Press.

6. For a detailed review of multiple use and sustained yield as practiced by federal land management agencies, see Congressional Research Service. 1993. Proceedings of the workshop on multiple use and sustained yield: changing philosophies for federal land management? House Interior and Insular Affairs Committee Print.

7. USDA Forest Service. 1991. Charter for New Perspectives for Managing the National Forest System.

8. Beer, M., R.A. Eisenstat, and B. Spector. 1990. Why change programs don't produce change. Harvard Business Review, November–December:158–166.

9. USDA Forest Service, New Perspectives Project Notebook, 1992.

10. Shands, W.E., J. Giltmier, and G. Parker. 1992. From new perspectives to ecosystem management: a report of phase 1 of an assessment on new perspectives. Milford, Pennsylvania: Pinchot Institute for Conservation.

11. For example, see World Commission on Environment and Development. 1987. Our common future. New York: Oxford Press; and Canadian Council of Forest Ministers. 1992. Sustainable forests, a Canadian commitment.

12. Keiter, R.B. 1990. NEPA and the emerging concept of ecosystem management on the public lands. Land and Water Law Review 25, 1:43–60.

13. Brooks, D.J., and G.E. Grant. 1992. New approaches to forest management, parts 1 and 2. Journal of Forestry 90 (1):25–28, (2):21–24.

14. For example, see Times Mirror Magazines Conservation Council. 1992. National environmental forum survey.

15. Salwasser, H. 1991. New perspectives for sustaining diversity in U.S. national forest ecosystems. Conservation Biology 5:569–571.

16. For example, see National Research Council. 1990. Forestry research: a mandate for change. Washington, D.C.: National Academy Press; and Lubchenko, J., et al. 1991. The sustainable biosphere initiative. Ecology 72:371–412.

17. Forest Service Research and the National Forest System exist as separate branches at the highest level in the Forest Service organizational structure.

18. Holling, C.S., ed. 1978. Adaptive environmental assessment and management. London: John Wiley & Sons.

19. Irwin, L.L., and T.B. Wigley. 1993. Toward an experimental basis for protecting forest wildlife. Ecological Applications 3:213–217.

20. Society of American Foresters. 1993. Task force report on sustaining long-term forest health and productivity.

21. Reich, R.B., ed. 1990. The power of public ideas. Cambridge: Harvard University Press.

22. USDA Forest Service, June 4, 1992, letter from Chief to Regional Foresters and Station Directors.

23. See note 8.

Chapter 11

Old Players with New Power: The Nongovernmental Organizations

M. Rupert Cutler

> It is by taking a share in legislation that the American learns to know the law; it is by governing that he becomes educated about the formalities of government. The great work of society is daily performed before his eyes, and so to say, under his hands.
>
> —Alexis de Tocqueville
> *Democracy in America*

The plot of a best-selling work of fiction, John Grisham's *The Pelican Brief* (1992) is focused on the importance of environmentalist support for the President's choice to the Supreme Court (1). A Vice-Presidential candidate, Al Gore, is nominated and elected in part because of his appeal to environmentalists. Clearly, the day of recognition of the large number and political clout of those concerned about the fate of the Earth has arrived.

Whether or not the many nongovernmental organizations (NGOs) that represent this segment of society use their leverage on the political system to best advantage in the 21st century remains to be seen, but never has this community had so many legal tools at its disposal or so many friends in high places as it does today. Assuming a modicum of interorganizational coordination and mutual support, United States environmental NGOs are poised to continue their string of legislative and courthouse victories begun in the 1960s by the followers of Rachel Carson, who advocated pollution prevention including pesticide regulation, Howard Zahniser, who fought for ecosystem protection including wilderness-designation, and David Sive, who won the right of standing to sue in federal court for environmentalists in the *Scenic Hudson* case.

The NGOs can be expected to continue to help translate academic research findings into real-world policy directives for natural resource managers on the ground. They will do this through campaigns to effect the needed refinement of existing statutes, such as the Endangered Species Act (to emphasize protection of endangered *habitats* and to provide incentives for private landowner cooperation), and administrative rules, such as the Forest Service Manual (to require coordinated, transjurisdictional planning for *entire bioregions* to protect biological diversity).

The unique role of the nongovernmental organization is to observe that "the emperor has no clothes." If the news media in effect have become a fourth branch of government (after the executive, legislative, and judicial branches), then the NGOs are the fifth branch. Their rapid growth has been encouraged by federal tax code provisions that allow part of the dues paid to an NGO to be treated as a tax-deductible contribution—a tax status crucial to their financial well-being—and allow these nonprofit charitable organizations to spend a certain proportion of their income (up to $1 million) on lobbying.

Less constrained than government and corporate employees by statutes, regulations, and job descriptions, considerations that tend to discourage creativity, innovation, and risk-taking, representatives of NGOs are free to note what they consider agency and industry failures and shortcomings and propose changes in public policy. NGOs' public criticisms of what they regard as unsatisfactory aspects of the status quo provide welcome grist for the mills of the news media, legislative bodies, the court system, and candidates for elective political office. NGO oversight stimulates healthy scrutiny of government and industry programs, reminds public employees that they are trustees and not dictators, encourages private industry to fulfill its obligations to society at large, and creates a sociopolitical environment conducive to demonstrating environmental concern.

In the natural resources management field, government agency professionals—some of whom still regard any spokesperson for a private environmental group as an unwelcome gadfly—by and large have those NGOs, whose policies are set by enthusiastic amateurs, to thank for creating their jobs. For that matter, so do those employed in the private sector whose livelihoods are based on seeing that their employers meet government-imposed environmental-protection standards. Earlier generations of environmental activists—direct forebears of those who today complicate the lives of public servants and industrialists by filing appeals and lawsuits challenging their decisions—in fact conceived, fought for, and won passage of the laws that authorized creation of the very land management and environmental-protection agencies they work for and the policies they enforce that affect both the public and private sectors (2).

The relationship between the environmental NGOs, with boards made up of persons largely untrained in natural resources management, and the public conservation agencies, with staffs consisting of graduates of the professional natural resources schools of the nation's finest universities, is comparable to that between parent and child: The child/agency strives for independence—employing advanced technology, it develops a disdain for its parents'/NGO's imagined old-fashioned or simplistic view of the world—while the parent/NGO reminds the child/agency of the agency's roots in NGO lobbying, of its annual need for budgetary sustenance that only NGOs, with the help of allies on legislative appropriations committees, can provide, and that only the public can determine which course of action is in the public interest.

Evident in this long-running family feud are the weaknesses and strengths of both traditional NGO amateurism (possessing less detailed technical knowledge but emotionally committed and reflecting current societal values) and agency/industry professionalism (possessing highly refined technical skills but resistant to change). Thus the stage is set for what to some observers must seem inexplicable internecine warfare over the management of the Nation's natural resources: People who have in common a love of the out-of-doors, with its wildlife, wildness, beauty, and sense of freedom, fighting tooth and toenail in legislative chambers, courtrooms, and newspaper editorial pages across the country.

Healthy Tension or Unseemly Spectacle?

To many this condition represents a microcosm of healthy, or at least inevitable, political tension in a democratic society. To others it is an unseemly spectacle. A public fed up with the bickering could wish "a plague on both your houses" and reduce the financial support available for *all* conservation endeavors, private and public, creating a vacuum in which natural resource exploitation is allowed to proceed without necessary oversight.

While environmental true believers are needed to define ideal outcomes and will always be present, there is growing support for thoughtful accommodation ("politics is the art of the possible") as a way to avoid policy gridlock. Examples of government-sponsored dialogues involving representatives of diverse interest groups are the 1991 Keystone Policy Dialogue on Biological Diversity on Federal Lands (3), and President Clinton's April 1993 Forest Conference in Portland, Oregon, over the impasse in logging the endangered northern spotted owl's old-growth forest habitat (4). The popularity of such efforts suggests an impatience with intransigent posturing and locked-in polarization on natural resources issues and a strong interest in discovering broadly acceptable middle-ground solutions.

NGO–Agency Power Parity

It would appear to be going against the grain for environmental NGOs to move from the role of uncompromising advocate for the "best" solution (from their constituents' standpoint) to that of full participant in the search for a win–win consensus outcome. There has been no reward, historically, for NGO leaders' public participation in any process leading to compromise. Yet a growing number of NGOs are dipping their toes in this chilly water. They appear to have concluded that, because of the quality of their staff expertise and the size of their memberships, they are in positions of intellectual and political-clout parity with the other groups at the table and can afford to stick their necks out to make progress.

After 100 years of evolution, the American environmental NGO movement, as a whole, now boasts impressive technical and political expertise that can be applied in support of as well as in opposition to government and private-industry natural resources programs. The annual operating budgets of some of the major environmental NGOs are now in the tens of millions of dollars. These groups compete successfully with universities, industries, and government agencies to hire the best and brightest environmental scientists, economists, and technical writers. To a considerable extent the expertise gap between agency and NGO has been closed.

The differences of opinion on policies and priorities that persist between NGO and agency stem in part from the fact that the elected leaders of each NGO campaigned for the job of board member because they saw a need for changes in environmental policies. Every NGO board member wants to see those government policy changes happen during their tenure on the board. Persons who are satisfied with the government environmental *status quo* do not run for elective office in an NGO. NGOs are agents of change. They are never satisfied with the status quo.

Agencies, on the other hand, usually have a broader charter, are preoccupied with implementing existing policy direction, and must respond to many NGOs with varying and frequently conflicting goals.

Choose Your Modus Operandi

Because NGOs now have ready access to legislative bodies, courts, the news media, and a pool of experts, natural resource management professionals in the agencies, and in some private industries, are acknowledging this expertise by inviting NGO representatives to participate in their planning meetings. Whether the NGOs accept the invitation is another matter. The

NGOs' stock in trade, historically, has been protest and opposition to proposed agency and industry actions. They may see their hard-won image as advocates for the ideal environmental-protection outcome as being at risk if they go to the bargaining table and participate as full partners in binding negotiations. Based on recent history, some self-confident NGOs will be willing to bargain. Some will not, preferring to represent the ideologically pure position that attracted followers to them in the first place and has served them well.

Environmental organizations willing to participate in face-to-face negotiations with government and industry to achieve incremental, real-world progress may be rewarded. The Environmental Defense Fund's (EDF) efforts along these lines have resulted in a strong upward membership growth curve for that innovative group. Increasingly, EDF has turned to the financial carrot rather than the legal stick. For example, it crafted an acid rain control proposal built around market incentives that was adopted by President Bush, persuaded the Pacific Gas and Electric Company to adopt new energy options—cogeneration, wind, solar, conservation—to reduce the need for new coal and nuclear plants, and persuaded the McDonald's hamburger chain to stop using plastic "clamshell" sandwich containers (5).

Nonnegotiating NGOs will claim with some justification that their intransigence opens doors for other NGOs willing to "settle for less." Every environmental NGO that agrees to send representatives into agency and corporate conference rooms ready to deal risks being accused by their sibling NGOs of selling out. Each NGO must weigh the benefits and costs and determine the operational style with which it is most comfortable.

Organizational Diversity for Biological Diversity

In the United States, there is at least one NGO paired with every level of government for every natural resource issue. The ranges of issues and of NGOs dedicated to monitoring those issues are vast, and the NGOs' track record of accomplishment is impressive.

American conservationists come in many guises. One must include, in a big-tent definition of environmental conservationist, academic researchers uneasy with the very term "fact," public and private land managers interested in producing a steady flow of raw materials to be manufactured into products to sustain the national economy, conservation group magazine publishers and television show producers seeking to educate the general public, environmental law firms that use the judicial system to enforce antipollution statutes, and "deep ecologists" intent on merging environmental issues with issues of social justice ("environmental justice") and ready to perform acts of civil disobedience to save the Earth. The organizations they create and support reflect this diversity. They range from scientific and professional societies to industrial trade associations to direct-action activist coalitions seeking political and economic empowerment for minorities. All perform useful roles in American society.

Individuals new to the field of natural resources management and protection typically identify with the behavior and goals of some NGOs and feel uneasy about—or are appalled by—the actions (or inaction) of others. There is an environmental NGO to suit every mindset. Anyone interested in natural resources management and the protection of the environment should be able to find a comfortable NGO home that reflects his or her views if he or she looks hard enough at the NGO universe.

The 430-page *1993 Conservation Directory* published by the National Wildlife Federation identified nearly 550 private organizations in the United States at the national level, and additional thousands of private organizations at regional, state, and local levels who consider themselves qualified for inclusion. A number of would-be charismatic leaders conclude each year that their diagnosis and solution are unique and require the formation of a new organization. The result is the constant expansion of the NGO universe. According to Snow (5), these private groups can be lumped in the three categories: conservationist, preservationist, and environmentalist. Explains Snow (6):

> Any group whose principal mission is to foster the wise, sustained use of natural resources for human need, enjoyment, and betterment ought to be understood as a conservation group. Preservationist groups stand for the maintenance of natural living systems intact and as whole as possible, usually under the aegis of special protective designations, whether public or private. Environmentalist groups fight the pollution of land, air, water and sometimes workplace. Some environmentalists suggest that technology itself lies at the root of most environmental problems, which they view as deriving from a flawed set of ethics. The environmentalist camp must also claim some of the animal rights organizations. That these groups find themselves at odds with many of their conservationist cousins bears testimony to the richness of the overall movement.

Dunlap (7) quotes de Tocqueville to help explain the diversity of natural resources-related NGOs in the United States:

"In no country in the world has the principle of association been more successfully used or applied to a greater multitude of objects than in America." Thus Alexis de Tocqueville described the tendency of Americans in the early 19th century to use voluntary societies to express their will. Their descendants continued the tradition, and interest in nature has spawned a bewildering assortment of organizations.

Noonan (8) observes that "the real strength of the conservation and environmental community in the United States is its diversity. Each organization has its own unique mission, its own resources, its own constituency, and, in a real sense, its own agenda." And Roush (9) notes that, of the thousands of conservation groups in the United States, there are only about 50 with budgets in the tens of millions of dollars and with relatively large staffs. These groups, says Roush, wield influence "far greater than their number." The identity and membership size of these major players is as follows:

In a class by itself is the National Wildlife Federation, with 5.3 million supporters—members of its 51 state affiliates, subscribers to its magazines (associate members), purchasers of wildlife stamps, and other contributors. The National Wildlife Federation's actual expenses in 1993 totaled $97 million. The only other U.S. environmental conservation groups claiming millions of supporters are Greenpeace (2.5 million members) and the Humane Society of the United States, which has a wildlife conservation-related program (1.6 million members).

In the second tier of the majors (with number of members and/or contributors as of 1992 in parentheses), are Clean Water Action (700,000), Sierra Club (650,000), National Audubon Society (600,000), The Nature Conservancy (588,000), Ducks Unlimited (500,000), The Wilderness Society (300,000), National Parks and Conservation Association (285,000), Environmental Defense Fund (200,000), Cousteau Society (200,000), Natural Resources Defense Council (170,000), and Center for Marine Conservation (110,000). Several animal welfare groups are of this size as well.

In the 50,000-to-100,000-member tier are American Forests, Appalachian Mountain Club, Chesapeake Bay Foundation, Defenders of Wildlife, Earthwatch, Izaak Walton League of America, Rails-to-Trails Conservancy, Rocky Mountain Elk Foundation, and Trout Unlimited.

A fourth category of influential national organizations with memberships of between 20,000 and 50,000 includes American Farmland Trust, American Rivers, Appalachian Trail Conference, Earth Island Institute, Friends of the Earth, Save-the-Redwoods League, and Zero Population Growth.

Add several strong nonmembership groups such as The Conservation Fund, the Trust for Public Land, the Sierra Club Legal Defense Fund, Resources for the Future, Sport Fishing Institute, and Wildlife Management Institute, plus the diverse array of professional and scientific societies that serve this community such as the American Fisheries Society, American Society of Landscape Architects, Society for Conservation Biology, Society for Ecological Restoration, Society for Range Management, Society of American Foresters, Soil Conservation Society of America, and the Wildlife Society and you have Roush's 50 major nongovernmental, national players.

The extreme diversity of the NGO movement and its "causes" can be seen with even greater clarity in the list below, a posting of natural resource management issues together with the names of only some of the NGOs working on those particular issues (the larger groups defy pigeonholing and appear more than once):

Issue	NGO
Agriculture and farmlands	American Farmland Trust, Land Trust Alliance, Wildlife Management Institute
Air quality and acid rain	Environmental Defense Fund, Natural Resources Defense Council
Animal welfare	American Humane Association, Animal Protection Institute, Friends of Animals, Fund for Animals, Humane Society of the United States
Bats and caves	American Cave Conservation Society, Bat Conservation International
Birds and birding	American Birding Association, National Audubon Society
Conservation leadership	Conservation Fund, Institute for Conservation Leadership
Ecological restoration	Earth Island Institute, Trout Unlimited
Endangered species	Defenders of Wildlife, National Audubon Society, National Wildlife Federation, The Nature Conservancy, Sierra Club, Sport Fishing Institute, Trout Unlimited, The Wilderness Society, Wildlife Management Institute
Energy conservation and facility regulation	Environmental Action, Friends of the Earth, Greenpeace, National Audubon Society, Sierra Club

continued

Issue	NGO
Environmental and outdoor education	Alliance for Environmental Education, Earthwatch, National Audubon Society, National Wildlife Federation, Sierra Club, Worldwatch Institute
Environmental ethics	Association of Forest Service Employees for Environmental Ethics, Izaak Walton League of America, Public Employees for Environmental Responsibility
Environmental law	Environmental Defense Fund, Environmental Law Institute, National Wildlife Federation, Natural Resources Defense Council, Sierra Club Legal Defense Fund, Southern Environmental Legal Foundation
Fish and wildlife management and protection	Boone and Crockett Club, Defenders of Wildlife, Ducks Unlimited, Izaak Walton League of America, National Audubon Society, National Wildlife Federation, Rocky Mountain Elk Foundation, Sport Fishing Institute, Trout Unlimited, Wildlife Management Institute
Forests and rangelands	American Forests, Izaak Walton League of America, National Audubon Society, National Wildlife Federation, Natural Resources Defense Council
Hazardous toxic, and solid waste	Environmental Action, Environmental Defense Fund, Natural Resources Defense Council
Land use planning	American Planning Association, Chesapeake Bay Foundation, Greater Yellowstone Coalition, The Wilderness Society
Marine mammals, coasts, and oceans	Center for Marine Conservation, Cousteau Society, Defenders of Wildlife, Friends of the Earth, Greenpeace, Sea Shepherd Conservation Society
Minerals and mining	Mineral Policy Center
Outdoor recreation and trails	Appalachian Mountain Club, Appalachian Trail Council, National Recreation and Park Association, Rails-to-Trails Conservancy

continued

Issue	NGO
National forests, parks, public land management	Friends of the Earth, National Audubon Society, National Parks and Conservation Association, Grand Canyon Trust, National Wildlife Federation, Natural Resources Defense Council, Sierra Club, The Wilderness Society, Wildlife Management Institute
Pesticide misuse	Defenders of Wildlife, Environmental Defense Fund, National Audubon Society, National Wildlife Federation, Rachel Carson Council
Population growth	National Audubon Society, Planned Parenthood Federation of America, Population Action International , Population–Environment Balance, Population Institute, Population Reference Bureau, Sierra Club, Zero Population Growth
Predators	Defenders of Wildlife
Private land preservation and stewardship	Conservation Fund, Land Trust Alliance, National Audubon Society, The Nature Conservancy
Raptors	National Audubon Society, National Wildlife Federation, Peregrine Fund, Raptor Center
Redwoods	Save-the-Redwoods League, Sierra Club
Research natural areas	Natural Areas Association
River protection, dams	American Rivers, National Wildlife Federation, Sierra Club, Trout Unlimited
Scenic beauty	Grand Canyon Trust, Keep American Beautiful, Scenic America, Grand Canyon Trust
Soil conservation	National Association of Conservation Districts
Water quality	Clean Water Action, Izaak Walton League of America, Natural Resources Defense Council
Wetlands	Defenders of Wildlife, Ducks Unlimited, Izaak Walton League of America, National Audubon Society, National Wildlife Federation
Wilderness	American Wildlands, Cenozoic Society, Earth First!, Friends of the Earth, Sierra Club, The Wilderness Society, Wilderness Watch

Any organization that aggressively pursues a clearly defined special-interest goal over a period of time by employing a staff of experts to represent its position before legislative committees and with the media can carve itself a niche and develop a comparative advantage vis-à-vis other groups on that particular issue. A good example is the Mineral Policy Center, formed in 1988 to work for reform of the 1872 Mining Law. It filled a vacuum on the national scene and quickly became a source of special expertise for legislative committees and the news media as well as an identifiable "public" that agencies whose work involves that subject area must keep in touch with.

In addition to specialization by particular resource-management concern, NGOs can be grouped in other ways such as by the geographical scope of their concerns (i.e., local/watershed/state/bioregion/national/international) or by that segment of the policy process in which they specialize; for example:

- Research (example: Center for Field Research, a program of Earthwatch)
- Public education (National Wildlife Federation)
- Professional training (Environmental Law Institute)
- Land acquisition (Trust for Public Land)
- Land management (National Audubon Society)
- Legislation (Defenders of Wildlife)
- Litigation (Natural Resources Defense Council)
- Direct action (Greenpeace)

Using other criteria, Snow (10) has broken the NGO community into the following 11 categories, which I have illustrated with names of example organizations.

- Small, all-volunteer, issue groups (Gopher Tortoise Council)
- Small, quasi-volunteer naturalist groups (American Nature Study Society)
- Recreation and sporting clubs (Federation of Western Outdoor Clubs)
- State-based or regional advocacy groups (Greater Yellowstone Council)
- Education, research, and policy-development centers (Worldwatch Institute)
- Law and science groups (Environmental Law Institute)
- Small national and international membership groups (Earth Island Institute)
- Large national and international membership groups (Sierra Club)

- Real estate conservation groups (The Conservation Fund)
- Professional societies (The Wildlife Society)
- Support and service organizations (Keystone Center)

Of what accomplishments are the major environmental groups the most proud? Do these past accomplishments suggest the likely future directions of the U.S. environmental NGO community, or are new solutions needed for the problems of the 21st century? As the competition for limited resources and open space becomes more evident, how will the NGOs contribute to the well-being of human society, dependent as it is on the stability of the Earth's ecosystems? Here are some of the ways in which environmental NGOs will contribute to the amelioration of the Nation's—and the Earth's—environmental ills in the 21st century:

On the habitat diversity and open space conservation front it will be the NGOs who take the lead in converting the work product from the wildlife researchers' habitat gap analyses—maps identifying threatened but unprotected plant and animal communities and essential wildlife travel corridors between them—into timely action. This NGO action will result in a more complete de facto national network of species-rich biodiversity reserves and necessary landscape linkages. The Wilderness Society (in the wild backcountry), the National Trust for Historic Preservation (specializing in historic sites), and the Trust for Public Land (in and near urban areas) will be among the leaders of this campaign to protect open space and habitat, using a variety of tools including development easements and local land trusts as well as fee-simple acquisition. After their acquisition many of these tracts will be resold to public agencies for long-term administration.

On the policy analysis front, the environmental NGOs will devise and lobby for the adoption of thoughtful new approaches to the solution of sticky old problems. Examples: (1) the Natural Resources Defense Council's Western Water Project, an economics-based initiative to encourage conservation and to reduce federal water subsidies to large irrigators, thus leaving water for fish and wildlife; and (2) the work of the Society of American Forests Task Force on Sustaining Long-Term Forest Health and Productivity (11) and American Forests' Forest Policy Center (12). The work products of both address the need for practical ways to sustain long-term forest productivity by maintaining functional ecosystems and ensuring forest health.

Applications of the principles of landscape ecology will be formulated and advanced by environmental NGOs with a bioregional scope such as the Greater Yellowstone Coalition in Bozeman, Montana; the Grand Canyon Trust in Arizona and Utah; Friends of the Boundary Waters Wilderness in

Minneapolis, Minnesota; the West Virginia Highlands Conservancy in Charleston, West Virginia; and the Southern Appalachian Man and the Biosphere Foundation in Atlanta, Georgia. Central to all of their proposals will be joint land use planning among owners and managers of adjacent lands and the coordination of land uses throughout an ecosystem, to minimize the effects of fragmented ownership and political and property-ownership boundaries.

Because of the broad appeal of the species they work to protect (mainly the "charismatic megafauna") there will be continued growth of those environmental NGOs that specialize in the recovery of popular fish and wildlife such as ducks, trout, elk, and marine mammals. Following the successful pattern of Ducks Unlimited, organized in 1938 to save wetlands throughout North America, the Rocky Mountain Elk Foundation, organized in 1984, has become one of the country's fastest growing groups. Trout Unlimited and the Izaak Walton League both help local members "save our streams," while the Center for Marine Conservation helps organize local beach cleanups to assist sea turtle reproduction. Defenders of Wildlife (long an advocate for predators) has become closely associated with campaigns to restore gray wolves to the Rocky Mountains and red wolves to the southeastern states. Despite ecologists' preference that more attention be given to the welfare of ecosystems than to that of individual species, these species-specific campaigns will prosper.

In the future, NGOs will take a broader view of the opportunities they have to address the needs of society. There will be new programs to address ethical questions. The frustration of the professional employees of the USDA Forest Service blew up in 1989, into a full-fledged protest organization called the Association of Forest Service Employees for Environmental Ethics, to which hundreds of Forest Service employees belong. It seeks reforms within an agency that many of its employees believe had become blind to the ecological havoc being wreaked on the National Forests by excessive commercial timber harvests encouraged by official agency policy overly responsive to political pressures. The frustration of the ethical sportsman (members of the Izaak Walton League of America) with the poor behavior of a minority of hunters and anglers who leave litter behind, leave farm gates open, and otherwise misbehave has led the "Ikes" to create a grassroots, outdoor ethics program designed to teach sportsmen and youth how to behave in the out-of-doors and thus help perpetuate their sport. More such outdoor education programs will be needed if youngsters brought up in cities and their suburbs are to replenish the ranks of sportsmen who traditionally have been among the most staunch supporters of conservation programs.

A broader view of their responsibilities on the global stage has led an increasing number of environmental NGOs to add a population control plank to their environmental action platforms. The NGO specialists in formulating and publicizing the connection between human population growth and a decline in the quality of the environment have been Zero Population Growth and Population–Environment Balance, but strong population education programs also are in place at the National Audubon Society and the Sierra Club.

Public education and grassroots activist training constitute vital programs if there is to be an informed electorate and a savvy corps of environmental lobbyists to counter the forces of greed and thoughtless environmental despoliation. Millions of Americans have been awakened to the environmental crisis by the television series produced by the National Geographic Society, the National Wildlife Federation, the National Audubon Society, and the Cousteau Society, while thousands of grassroots activists have honed their lobbying skills by attendance at week-long activist training sessions in Washington, D.C., conducted by seasoned Capitol Hill veterans on the government relations staffs of The Wilderness Society, the National Wildlife Federation, and National Audubon Society.

Just as various industries have hired professional public relations firms to tout their causes and stuff the White House mailbox with favorable comments, some environmental NGOs have decided they too can play that game. For example, to shore up support for President Clinton's proposed energy-consumption tax, the Natural Resources Defense Council hired a public relations firm in February of 1993 to phone 10,000 of its members, urging them to call the White House in support of the energy tax (13). In the future an even greater use by environmental NGOs of top-rank public relations firms to advance their agendas, much of it provided on a pro bono basis, can be anticipated.

And lawsuits, to obtain injunctions to slow potentially irreversible environmental changes while the plaintiff NGO uses this time to seek a more permanent solution through the passage of new legislation, will continue to be a trump card in the NGOs' hands.

Future Options

Two themes dominate recent analyses of the American environmental movement. One is that environmental group leaders should collaborate more than they have in the recent past—that they must "form strategic alliances for the common good" (14). The other is that they should take human needs—particularly, the economic well-being of people—into account; that they should seek to "accommodate human needs in ecologically acceptable ways" (15).

On the former score environmental leaders can point with pride to the success of the broad-based Alaska Coalition in the 1970s that provided the grassroots kick behind the passage of the Alaska National Interest Lands Act signed by President Jimmy Carter in 1980. Regular intergroup communication is aided by the existence in Washington, D.C., of the Natural Resources Council of America, a clearinghouse group to which practically all national NGOs belong and which publishes a newsletter and arranges special events for the conservation community. The chief executive officers of the larger membership organizations, originally known as the Group of Ten, hold informal meetings on a quarterly basis to effect a limited amount of program coordination. Temporary coalitions comprised of Washington, D.C.-based staff specialists concerned with such well-defined goals as reauthorization of the Endangered Species Act, amendment of the Clean Air Act, and improvements in laws protecting marine mammals come and go depending on the Congressional calendar.

True communitywide strategic planning is lacking, however. The NGOs potentially involved apparently foresee true sharing of responsibility for adopting and advancing a joint action agenda as threatening their independence and hobbling their innate drive to out-compete the other organizations in the endless race for more media attention and membership and income growth. This traditional, every-group-for-itself mindset gives independent expert analysts heartburn; examples of their comments:

Patrick F. Noonan: "For many years, a guiding principle behind conservation and environmental activities was summed up in a simple phrase, Think globally, act locally. While that advice is valid today, it does not go far enough. We must add a third element: Work together. Collaboration is vital if we are effectively to manage our limited resources. Today, environmental concerns are too important to be left to environmentalists alone. We must actively engage all sectors of our society. Collaboration means building partnerships" (16).

Jon Roush: "It will not be enough to build successful organizations; leaders need to plan and form strategic alliances for the common good. . . . Ironically, as popular concern about conservation issues has grown and as the number of organizations working on those issues has increased, the conservation movement as a whole has not mobilized that growing, potential support into an effective national force" (17).

Donald Snow: "The environmental challenges that lie ahead . . . will require extraordinary new leadership of a kind rarely seen in the American conservation community. The new mandate for leadership demands that virtually every institutional sector of American life—education, government, business, public communications, and the not-for-profit sector—become deeply engaged in solving environmental problems. The NGO conservationists must and will lead in this endeavor. To do this, they must learn to dissolve the self-imposed boundaries that isolate them from other sectors of economic and educational enterprise. . . . [X]enophobia and internecine strife . . . are [the conservation–environmental movement's] most debilitating features" (18).

On the second recommendation—to take human needs into account—there have been uttered these words of caution for the NGO community:

Sierra Club Roundtable on Race, Justice, and the Environment: "The era of an American environmental movement dominated by the interests of white people is over. . . .Armed with proof of what has become known as 'environmental racism,' a loose alliance of church, labor, civil rights, and community groups led by people of color arose to demand environmental justice. Part of doing so meant confronting the so-called Group of Ten, the nation's largest—and largely white—environmental groups, and bluntly accusing them of racism" (19).

Bryan G. Norton: "The emerging consensus offers an alternative to simple reductionistic economics on the one side and onerous restrictions on the other. This alternative can be called 'restorationism.' A positive definition of ecosystem health, one that incorporates human activities as long as they do not threaten thresholds inherent in ecological systems, open the possibility of a truly positive ideal of humans living, creatively and freely, but harmoniously, within a larger, ecological context" (20).

Philip Shabecoff: "The new conventional wisdom that economic development and environmental protection are mutually dependent placed on environmentalists the responsibility of supporting appropriate economic growth. If long-term economic prosperity could not be sustained without protecting the land, air, and water and making wise use of other resources, then it followed that those resources could not be preserved without a healthy economy and a population whose economic needs were satisfied. . . . [M]odern environmentalism does not seek to halt economic growth; on the contrary, one of its overriding goals is to be sure that economic growth can be sustained over the long run" (21).

Edward O. Wilson: "Proponents of the New Environmentalism . . . recognize that only new ways of drawing income from land already cleared, or from intact wildlands themselves, will save biodiversity from the mill of human poverty. The race is on to develop methods, to draw more income from the wildlands without killing them, and so to give the invisible hand of free-market economics a green thumb" (22).

The following observations of two distinguished veterans of many decades of personal involvement in the conservation struggle, Nat Reed of Florida and Vic Scheffer of Washington State, constitute expert crystal ball-gazing to predict the future of the environmental movement in the United States. Observes Reed: "If there ever was a golden age when conservationists were brilliant amateurs who could outfox the government because God was on their side, it is gone, irretrievably. We cannot do without the professionalism that so many environmental groups have worked so long to acquire. On the other hand, we should be loath to drive out all the good generalists from our midst and even more careful not to cut ourselves off from the notions submitted by people with no claim to environmental expertise other than their concern for that special spot they know and love and want to save. All the professionalism in the world is no match for that kind of informed commitment" (23). Concludes Scheffer: "The goal of the environmental movement, then, is to somehow strike a balance between idealism and realism; to preserve the diversity and wondrous beauty of our world while recognizing that billions must steadily draw upon its substance for survival" (24).

I have seen no more complete recommended agenda for the U.S. environmental NGO community in the 21st century than that proposed by Scheffer:

"Assuming the goal of the environmentalists to be an integrated, harmonious, steady-state Earth, what steps would they take toward that goal? Eight steps seem absolutely necessary: (1) Placing more emphasis on reducing human overpopulation; (2) Measuring the carrying capacity of local ecosystems and managing them accordingly; (3) Restoring insofar as possible and protecting the agricultural base, the ancient and forever nursery of mankind; (4) Carefully rationing the use of irreplaceable minerals and fuels; (5) Stop disposing of wastes by dumping them somewhere else; (6) Measuring the health effects of the myriad anthropogenic poisons which, unrecognized, enter our bodies every day; (7) Placing more emphasis on protecting the purity of shared world environments such as tropical forests, the ocean, the atmosphere, and the stratosphere; (8) Preserving biological diversity, the Earth's greatest treasure" (25).

With 100 years of experience, the financial and moral support of millions of members, expert staffs, and an array of educational techniques and legal tools at their disposal, and with a latent consensus on an action agenda, the challenge to the environmental nongovernment organization community in the United States is clear. Based on the community's impressive record of accomplishment in the 20th century, there is good reason for optimism that the community will rise to the occasion in the 21st. But there are new challenges, created in large part by population growth and the concomitant need for more jobs, that demand new responses.

Clearly, business as usual will not suffice. New solutions and new approaches, involving the creation of a more broad-based constituency and the conduct of a focused, coordinated, prioritized, multiorganizational educational/political/legal national action campaign, must be developed and implemented if the American environment is to survive relatively intact to support human civilization for another century and longer. And this campaign must provide a large role for thousands of local "grassroots" volunteer activists. Just as all politics is local, all natural resource conservation, in the final analysis, is local, too.

Notes

1. John Grisham. 1992. The Pelican Brief. New York: Island Books.
2. Several U.S. federal agencies and their core programs came into being and have been saved from dismantling through the influence of NGOs. Examples are
   (1) National Forests. According to H.K. Steen (1976. U.S. Forest Service: a history, 26. Seattle, Washington: University of Washington Press), it was the American Forestry Association's law committee that persuaded Secretary of the Interior John W. Noble to intervene with a congressional conference committee to add language to the Forest Reserve Act of 1891 authorizing the president, for the first time, to reserve forest lands from the public domain.
   (2) National Parks. Attacks on the integrity of national parks began soon after they were created and continue to this day. L.M. Wolf (1978. Son of the Wilderness: the life of John Muir, 254–255. Madison, Wisconsin: University of Wisconsin Press) describes the founding of the Sierra Club in 1892 by John Muir and others as occurring "none too soon. For already the lumbermen and stockmen were organizing . . . a powerful opposition. In 1892, they had a bill introduced . . . to cut away nearly half the area of Yosemite National Park. The bill was rushed through the House by a large vote. But before it reached the Senate, John Muir and the Sierra Club swung into action. . . . As a result the bill was tabled." F. Tilden (1968. The National Parks, 27. New York: Knopf) notes that during World Wars I and II legislation introduced in Congress would have permitted the

grazing of livestock in all national parks and monuments, and that "throughout such dangerous periods the Park Service was sustained and fortified by public sentiment, expressed . . . through the many conservation societies that are alert to the needs of the national parks and to the potential dangers."

(3) National Wildlife Refuges. Some refuges were created by executive order. I.N. Gabrielson (1943. Wildlife Refuges, 9 New York: Macmillan) describes "the natal day of [the] federal wildlife refuge system"—March 14, 1903, when President Theodore Roosevelt created the first federal wildlife refuge, Pelican Island in Florida—as the result of years of work by the committee on bird protection of the American Ornithologists' Union. Other federal refuges were created by purchasing private wetlands. D.L. Lendt (1979. Ding. the life of Jay Norwood Darling, 68, Ames, Iowa: Iowa State University) documents the critical role of NGOs—Boone and Crockett Club, American Game Protective Association, More Game Birds in America Foundation—in convincing Congress in 1932 to authorize a federal hunting stamp. Since that time proceeds from the sale of the "duck stamp" have been used for waterfowl habitat acquisition and restoration.

(4) National Wilderness Preservation System. D.M. Roth (1984. The wilderness movement and the national forests: 1964. 180, 20. Washington, D.C.: USDA Forest Service) describes how, in 1954, a leader of the Wilderness Society, Howard Zahniser, left a meeting with the Forest Service dejected after learning that the agency would not support "his" first wilderness bill. The Wilderness Society and its allies prevailed in Congress a decade later.

3. The Keystone Center. 1991. Biological diversity on federal lands: report of a keystone policy dialogue, 1991.

4. See, e.g., 1993. Ancient forests in the balance. Forest Watch 13, no. 9.

5. Taylor, R.E. 1989. Ahead of the curve: shaping new solutions to environmental problems, 4, 13, 16–17. New York: Environmental Defense Fund; Gutfeld, R. 1992. Environmental group doesn't always lick 'em; It can join 'em and succeed. The Wall Street Journal, Aug. 20, B1, B3.

6. Snow, D. 1992. Inside the environmental movement: meeting the leadership challenge, 12–13. Washington, D.C.: Island Press.

7. Dunlap, T.R., 1988. Saving America's wildlife, 108. Princeton, New Jersey: Princeton University Press.

8. Noonan, P.F. 1992. Forward. In Voices from the environmental movement: perspectives for a new era. D. Snow, ed. Washington, D.C.: Island Press.

9. Snow, D., ed. 1992. Voices from the environmental movement: perspectives for a new era, 34. Washington, D.C.: Island Press.

10. Snow, D. 1992. Inside the environmental movement: meeting the leadership challenge, 15–20. Washington, D.C.: Island Press.

11. Society of American Foresters. 1993. Task Force Report on Sustaining Long-term Forest Health and Productivity.

12. Sample, V.A., director of American Forests' policy center, wrote Land Stewardship in the Next Era of Conservation (Milford, PA: Pinchot Institute for Conservation, 1991).

13. "For lobbyists, this is the big one," The Washington Post National Weekly Edition, Feb. 22–28, 14.

14. Snow, D., 5 (9).

15. Zentner, J. 1992. Zentner on Katz: The issue of restorability. Restoration and Management Notes 10, no. 2:115.

16. Noonan 1991 (8).

17. Snow, D., 5 (9).

18. Snow, D., xxx (10).

19. "A Sierra Roundtable on Race, Justice, and the Environment: A Place at the Table," Sierra 78, no. 3 (1993), 51.

20. Norton, B.G. 1991. Toward unity among environmentalists, 191. New York: Oxford University Press.

21. Shabecoff, P. 1993. A fierce green fire, 260. New York: Hill and Wang.

22. Wilson, E.O. 1993. The new environmentalism. Excerpted from 1992. The diversity of life. Cambridge: Harvard University Press. In Nature Conservancy 43, no. 2:38.

23. Snow, D., 50–51 (9).

24. Scheffer, V.B. 1991. The shaping of environmentalism in America, 197. Seattle: University of Washington Press.

25. Scheffer, 167 (24).

Chapter 12

Natural Resources Management by Litigation

Vawter Parker

> These public lands belong to the entire nation. In enacting [the National Forest Management Act] Congress viewed them from the perspective not of a day but of generations. Many observers have noted the Forest Service's habit of maximizing timber production at the cost of the other statutory values. . . . But such a practice, no matter how long it may have gone on, cannot change what the statute requires.
> —Judge William L. Dwyer
> U.S. District Court for the Western District of Washington
> *Seattle Audubon Society* v. *Moseley* (1)

Hardly a week goes by in the West without some senator or representative's complaining that the courts are managing our public lands. It is an exceptionally inviting charge for a politician to make. The courts are the least understood branch of government, and judges generally do not ask for equal time to defend themselves before local chambers of commerce, editors, and the general public. Thus, the politician has gotten his (or her) name in the paper and identified himself as against something that sounds bad, and there is little risk that anyone will ask informed and embarrassing questions.

Although the courts are not managing our federal lands, there is a grain of truth underlying this complaint that lends credibility to the broader charge. In the last two decades, some of the most significant decisions affecting the management of public lands have been made by federal judges. Always as a last resort, and in response to an agency's apparent lack of responsiveness and mismanagement of resources, public interest lawyers have brought suits to break the hold of the logging, mining, and grazing interests on such agencies as the United States Forest Service and the Bureau of Land Management. Court-imposed injunctions have barred agencies from carrying out their favored commodity production programs until they have also complied with those provisions of federal statutes intended to ensure sustainable use and to preserve water quality, wildlife, and recreation.

Courts are not managing our public lands. Increasingly, however, they are requiring federal agencies to comply with the law, and in doing that they are changing forever the way the agencies manage our lands.

Histories of public lands litigation usually begin with *Sierra Club* v. *Morton* (2), the 1972 case in which the United States Supreme Court back-handedly recognized the right of membership organizations to bring suits on behalf of their members to protect environmental values. The significance of *Sierra Club* v. *Morton* for environmental litigation, and for public lands management, is hard to overstate, for it gave private citizens and organizations access to the courts, called "standing," to enforce environmentally protective provisions in federal statutes. The case was not, however, the first in which the Supreme Court had dealt with the tendency of a government agency to convert natural, working ecosystems to a single use.

Five years prior to *Sierra Club* v. *Morton* the Supreme Court—or, more correctly, Justice William O. Douglas—had delivered an eloquent plea for federal agencies to consider the noncommodity impacts of their decisions. What was at stake was the fate of a river, and the issue before administrative agencies and the courts was whether private utilities, municipal utilities, or the federal government should have the right to dam it. Before the case was over, the question was whether a dam should be built at all, the Federal Power Act had been transformed into a multiple-use statute, and Justice Douglas had sketched the broad outlines of what would become one of the most important statutes in public land management, the National Environmental Policy Act (NEPA).

A perennial issue in the Pacific Northwest throughout the first two-thirds of this century was the conflict between public and private power. Following World War II, the debate focused on whether private utilities, municipal utilities, or possibly the federal government would build, own, and operate dams at various sites in Hells Canyon, the deep gash between northeastern Oregon and Idaho through which the Snake River flows north toward its eventual confluence with the Columbia.

Through the 1950s, the war between the private power companies and municipal utilities was fought dam by dam; the overall debate remained unresolved due to the combination of a Republican administration that favored private utilities, a block of senators and representatives within the region who favored municipal utilities, and the machinations of both private and municipal utilities as they pursued mutually exclusive licenses. In the meantime, an increasing number of people were raising questions about the impact of dams on salmon and steelhead and asking whether the Snake River should have any more dams at all.

The advent of the Kennedy administration, in 1961, changed the game. The federal government, which had been taken out of the dam-building competition under the Eisenhower administration, was suddenly back in again.

The two dams then under consideration were competing proposals. Washington Public Power Supply System (WPPSS), a consortium of Northwest municipal utilities, sought a license to build a dam, Nez Perce, on the Snake River at a site approximately three miles downstream from the point where the Salmon River enters the Snake from the Idaho side. A consortium of four private utilities led by the Pacific Northwest Power Company (later Pacific Power & Light) and Idaho Power Company sought a license to build a dam about four miles upstream at a site known as High Mountain Sheep. Clearly both could not be built, and in the early 1960s, the two power conglomerates were pitted against each other in hearings before the Federal Power Commission on the private utilities' application for the High Mountain Sheep site. Secretary of the Interior Stewart Udall had called for a moratorium on any new dams on the Snake pending a study of impacts on fisheries, but to no avail. In 1962, after the hearings had closed, but before the hearings officer had rendered a decision, Udall requested that the Commission reopen the hearings to consider yet a third proposal—that the federal government itself build the dam at the High Mountain Sheep site.

Despite the Secretary's move, the Commission eventually granted Pacific Northwest Power the High Mountain Sheep license. When the Court of Appeals for the District of Columbia Circuit upheld the Commission's action, Washington Public Power Supply System sought Supreme Court review, and the Court agreed to hear the case.

WPPSS argued before the Court that the preference for municipal utilities expressed in the Federal Power Act required that the Commission deny Pacific Northwest Power's license application and instead allow WPPSS to build at either the High Mountain Sheep or the Nez Perce site. In *Udall* v. *Federal Power Commission* (3), however, the Court, in 1967, did not even address that issue. Instead, Justice Douglas, writing for a majority of seven, ordered the Commission to reopen the hearings to consider the near-revolutionary proposition that the public interest might be best served by denying a permit to anyone for either dam:

> Section 10(a) of the [Federal Power] Act provides that "the project adopted" shall be such "as in the judgment of the Commission will be best adapted to a comprehensive plan for improving or developing a waterway [for commercial uses] and for other beneficial public uses, including *recreational* purposes. . . ."
>
> The objective of protecting "recreational purposes" means more than that the reservoir created by the dam will be the best

one possible or practical from a recreational viewpoint. There are already eight lower dams on this Columbia River system and a ninth one authorized; and if the Secretary is right in fearing that this additional dam would destroy the waterway as spawning grounds for anadromous fish (salmon and steelhead) or seriously impair that function, the project is put in an entirely different light. The importance of salmon and steelhead in our outdoor life as well as in commerce is so great that there certainly comes a time when their destruction might necessitate a halt in so-called "improvement" or "development" of waterways. The destruction of anadromous fish in our western waters is so notorious that we cannot believe that Congress through the present Act authorized their ultimate demise.

· · ·

. . . A license under the Act empowers the licensee to construct, for its own use and benefit, hydroelectric projects utilizing the flow of navigable waters and thus, in effect, to appropriate water resources from the public domain. The grant of authority to the Commission to alienate federal water resources does not, of course, turn simply on whether the project will be beneficial to the licensee. Nor is the test solely whether the region will be able to use the additional power. The test is whether the project will be in the public interest. And that determination can be made only after an exploration of all the issues relevant to the "public interest," including future power demand and supply, alternate sources of power, the public interest in preserving reaches of wild rivers and wilderness areas, the preservation of anadromous fish for commercial and recreational purposes, and the protection of wildlife (4).

In *Udall* v. *Federal Power Commission*, Justice Douglas laid the foundation for the increasing role of litigation and the judiciary in the management of public lands. In effect, he took a provision of the Federal Power Act referring to public uses and recreation and interpreted it to broaden the Commission's previously single-use mandate—to promote commercial development—into something approaching a multiple-use mandate. Indeed, his *Udall* opinion presaged two of the most important principles found in the National Environmental Policy Act, which Congress enacted two years later: the obligation of a federal agency to explore *all* the issues relevant to the public interest in making irreversible commitments of natural resources, and its duty to give serious consideration to what would later be called in NEPA parlance the "no action" alternative—leaving the resource in its existing state.

But *Udall* v. *Federal Power Commission* involved a government agency and potential developers with a financial interest in the agency's decision. If a resource agency chose to ignore a statutory directive that it act in the public interest, or failed to abide by some more specific legal requirement, there seemed to be little that anyone without a demonstrable economic interest could do about it. It was five years before the other shoe dropped. Drop it did, however, in *Sierra Club* v. *Morton*.

Sierra Club v. *Morton* is the title of the famous "Mineral King" case. The litigation arose out of the plans of the Forest Service and Walt Disney Productions to build a destination ski resort in the Mineral King valley of the southern Sierra, an area conservationists wanted to include in Sequoia National Park. In 1969, the Sierra Club filed a suit seeking an injunction prohibiting the Forest Service from issuing permits for the development and prohibiting the Department of the Interior from issuing permits for a power line and road to serve it. The Sierra Club alleged that issuance of the permits would violate a variety of federal statutes and regulations relating to the management of national forests, refuges, and parks. (Mineral King was part of Sequoia National Forest and also a congressionally designated game refuge, and the power line and road would cross Sequoia National Park.)

Not just anyone can bring a lawsuit for the violation of a statute. To be allowed to maintain its suit, the Sierra Club had to show that it had a special interest in Mineral King that set it apart from the general public and that this interest would be adversely affected if the development were built. Only if it could make that showing could the Sierra Club appear in court as a plaintiff to enforce the various federal statutes and regulations it claimed the federal agencies were ignoring. In legal terminology this is the test of the "standing" of a plaintiff to sue.

The Sierra Club attempted to meet the standing test by stating in its complaint that it was a membership corporation "with a special interest in the conservation and the sound maintenance of the national parks, game refuges and forests of the country." The federal district court in California held that this allegation, if true, was sufficient to allow the Club to sue to enforce the public lands statutes and regulations; the judge issued a preliminary, or temporary, injunction against issuance of the permits. When the government's lawyers appealed, the Ninth Circuit Court of Appeals held that the alleged interest was not sufficiently "direct" to allow the Sierra Club to sue. The Club then sought review by the United States Supreme Court. As in *Udall*, the Supreme Court agreed to hear the case.

Decided in April 1972, *Sierra Club* v. *Morton* is generally regarded as the case that established the right of conservation organizations to sue to enforce federal statutes and regulations against public lands agencies. From a very technical, legalistic point of view, it did no such thing. The Supreme Court actually held in the case that the Sierra Club had *not* alleged an interest in Mineral King and an injury to that interest so special that it should be permitted to bring suit.

In a footnote to its opinion, however, the Court pointed out that the Sierra Club apparently conducted outings of its members in Mineral King and that Club members used the area for recreational purposes. Further, the Court noted that the district court might allow the Sierra Club to amend its complaint to allege such usage by its members. The implication, of course, was that injury to members' recreational interest, established by a history of their recreational use, would be sufficient to allow an organization to maintain a suit as its members' representative.

Almost all environmental litigation involving the management of our public lands rests on this footnote. When the case was returned to the lower court, that court did indeed allow the Club to amend its complaint to allege use of the Mineral King area by its members, as well as to allege violations of a statute that had been enacted after the filing of the original complaint: the National Environmental Policy Act, with its requirement that federal agencies consider alternatives, including maintaining the status quo, when acting on proposals with potentially significant environmental impacts.

Odd as it may seem for a case that has achieved such historic importance, there was never a decision on the merits of *Sierra Club* v. *Morton*, and no court ever actually ruled on the question whether the Club's new allegations were sufficient to establish standing. The tide of public opinion had changed with regard to the best use of Mineral King, and it became clear over the years that no one, including the Disney corporation, had much interest in seeing Mineral King developed. *Sierra Club* v. *Morton* was simply dismissed for lack of prosecution in 1977, and in 1978, Congress passed legislation making Mineral King a part of Sequoia National Park (5, 6).

Although the Mineral King litigation is remembered primarily for the issue of standing, it exemplifies the use of litigation in a broader political context. Litigation saved the Mineral King valley. The injunction barring issuance of the permits prevented the destruction of the resources in question and allowed time for the public to learn about the competing proposals and values at risk and to affect the political process. With time, more people, agencies, and eventually Congress concluded that the public interest was best served by preserving Mineral King in its natural state than by developing it as a ski resort.

Thus, from its very inception, an important function of much public lands litigation has been to buy time for the public to work its will through the political process. The clearest examples of this use of public lands litigation all involve the protection of areas proposed by conservation organizations for inclusion in the National Wilderness Preservation System:

- In passing the Federal Land Policy and Management Act in 1976, Congress directed the Bureau of Land Management (BLM) to study for potential addition to the National Wilderness Preservation System all BLM roadless areas of 5000 acres or more and to preserve the wilderness characteristics of those areas pending a report and recommendations to Congress. In 1982, Secretary of the Interior James Watt attempted to evade this statutory directive by "releasing" from wilderness review and opening for development over 170 roadless areas totaling nearly 1.5 million acres; these included areas where the mineral rights beneath the BLM lands were privately owned or where the roadless areas were contiguous to existing wilderness areas. In 1983, environmental organizations took the Secretary to court and enjoined the "release," by then known more popularly as the "Watt drop." Congress has subsequently added many of these areas to the National Wilderness Preservation System.

- In 1981, BLM issued permits to an oil company to drill for gas and oil in the Little Granite Creek drainage in Wyoming's Bridger-Teton National Forest. Litigation before the Interior Board of Land Appeals and in the courts established that BLM had failed to comply with the National Environmental Policy Act in issuing the permits and that the oil company had no legal right to drill. Litigation protected the integrity of the Little Granite Creek drainage until Congress, in 1984, included it in the Gros Ventre Wilderness Area.

- In the 1960s, the Forest Service began constructing a major logging access road through northern California's Six Rivers National Forest; the road would link the towns of Gasquet and Orleans (hence the name "G-O Road") and would have opened to logging several hundred thousand acres of steep, wet, unstable forest and detracted from the religious significance of the area to the native Yukok, Karok, and Tolowa peoples. In 1983, a federal district court judge enjoined completion of the G-O Road on the grounds that the Forest Service had not adequately considered impacts on water quality and that the road would cause sedimentation and turbidity in excess of California water quality standards. While the injunction was in place, Congress, in 1990, gave the area permanent protection by adding it to the Siskiyou Wilderness.

Litigation is not limited to preserving potential wilderness areas. Almost from its inception, environmental litigation has been used to bring about changes in the way nonwilderness lands are managed. This use of litigation may entail focusing public attention on a problem and forcing Congress to address it.

Although the debate over the merits and drawbacks of clearcutting continues to this day, it reached its highest pitch in the late 1960s and early 1970s. In 1973, a number of conservation organizations challenged the practice of clearcutting on West Virginia's Monongahela National Forest. They alleged that clearcutting violated provisions of the Forest Service Organic Act of 1897, which limited the cutting of trees on national forests to those that were dead or mature and that the Forest Service had individually marked for cutting. The Forest Service and the timber industry argued that not all of the trees to be cut needed to be dead or mature and that the marking of individual trees was not necessary so long as the Forest Service designated the boundaries of the area to be logged. The district court concluded that the Organic Act of 1897 did indeed limit sales to dead and mature trees and that such trees must be individually marked, and the Court of Appeals affirmed that interpretation (7).

The Monongahela litigation was designed to put the issue of clearcutting before Congress. Clearcutting had been the standard practice on national forests in the far western United States for some time, but by the early 1960s the Forest Service was beginning to use it as the preferred method of logging in the East as well. Although criticism of the practice was often triggered by its aesthetic impacts, its effects on soils, water quality, wildlife, and tourism were increasingly of concern, and conservationists were pressuring Congress to address the problem. It was not, however, a problem that Congress wanted to deal with. Timber companies have always been major contributors to the campaign funds of officeholders from the big timber-producing states; given the deference of both houses of Congress to state delegations in matters affecting public lands, Congress repeatedly ducked the issue.

The plaintiffs in the Monongahela litigation knew that Congress would not be able to ignore a decision in their favor; the district court and the Court of Appeals were also aware of this. Despite the fact that the district court expressly limited its ruling to the Monongahela National Forest, pressure grew more intense when plaintiffs in a pending case in Alaska, involving logging on Admiralty Island in the Tongass National Forest, included in their complaint allegations of the same violations of the Organic Act. The Pacific Northwest, the other great timber producing region, could not be far behind. Now the timber industry wanted congressional intervention as much as the conservationists did. The action moved to Congress, and the result was the much fought over (both before and after passage) National Forest Management Act of 1976.

The National Forest Management Act (NFMA) is only one of several statutes enacted during the decade of the 1970s affecting the management of our public lands—a decade that might be termed the "golden age" of public lands legislation. The decade opened with passage of the National Environmental Policy Act (NEPA) of 1969, signed into law on January 1, 1970, and closed with the Alaska National Interest Lands Conservation Act of 1980. Between these two statutes came not only the NFMA (1976) but also the Endangered Species Act (ESA) in essentially its present form (1973), the Forest and Rangelands Renewable Resources Act (1974), the Federal Land Policy and Management Act (BLM lands)(1976), the Federal Coal Leasing Amendments Act (1976), the Surface Mining Control and Reclamation Act (1977), and the Clean Water Act (1977). All of these bear directly on public lands management.

Conservationists have brought litigation to enforce the environmentally protective provisions of these and other new statutes as they have been enacted. Many of the statutes attempt to address the concerns voiced by Justice Douglas in his opinion in *Udall* v. *Federal Power Commission* and require federal agencies to examine and protect a broad range of resources, including soils, water quality, wildlife, and recreational opportunities. Common among them are requirements that agencies engage in open planning processes involving public review and comment.

Of all these statutes, the ESA has to date spawned the most controversial litigation and has arguably had the greatest influence. The attraction of the statute is twofold. First, the language of the ESA admits of little bureaucratic maneuvering. Federal agencies, among others, are prohibited from "taking" a listed species without a permit, and the exceptions are narrow. Second, through its requirement that all federal agencies protect designated "critical habitat" for listed species, the ESA is the closest statute we have to an "Endangered Ecosystems Act."

Two of the best-known examples of the use of the ESA to change the way our public lands are managed involve the red-cockaded woodpecker of the Southeast and the northern spotted owl of the Pacific Northwest.

The primary red-cockaded woodpecker case is *Sierra Club* v. *Lyng* (8). Initially a case challenging the Forest Service's logging of trees in wilderness areas within Texas national forests as a pine beetle control measure, this case, in 1988, evolved into a challenge to clearcutting and even-age management within the habitat of the endangered red-cockaded woodpecker, an old-growth dependent species, and the first case to question the legal sufficiency of a forest plan adopted under the NFMA. After a four-day trial, the court concluded that the clearcutting of woodpecker habitat constituted a "taking" of the woodpecker within the meaning of section 9 of the ESA, even though the Fish and Wildlife Service had not designated "critical habitat" for the woodpecker's protection. The court also found that clearcutting jeopardized the continued existence of the woodpecker within the meaning of section 7, despite a Fish and Wildlife Service opinion that implementation of the Forest Service's management plans would not further endanger the species.

As a result, the court enjoined clearcutting and even-age management on approximately 200,000 acres of national forests in Texas, one-third their total acreage. The Fifth Circuit Court of Appeals affirmed the injunction in 1991. Through the filing of notices of intent to sue on other forests of the Southeast and through administrative appeals, the Forest Service was eventually forced to forgo clearcutting and even-age management on over one million acres of national forest lands throughout the Southeast.

The other well-known ESA litigation involves the northern spotted owl in the Pacific Northwest. The spotted owl was not a listed species when the litigation began—the initial injunctions were issued under the NEPA for failure of the Forest Service and BLM to consider the impacts of their land use plans on a species that was in fact endangered, regardless of its legal status. Eventually, however, a separate case brought under the ESA forced the Fish and Wildlife Service to list the owl throughout its range in Washington, Oregon, and northern California. Although the courts in those cases have continued to act primarily under the authority of the NEPA and the biodiversity mandates of the NFMA, the clear ability of the organizations that brought the suits to enjoin the logging of old-growth forests under the ESA has provided additional leverage in what has become a national political, as well as legal, issue. As a result of the litigation, not only the courts (9), but also the President of the United States, have called for an "ecosystem approach" to the management of the federal forests of the Pacific Northwest.

Cases involving public lands will continue to be brought before the courts and promise to influence further the management of our lands. They are necessary, because agencies such as the Forest Service and BLM all too often refuse, quite knowingly, to comply with the law. As a result of public interest litigation, however, the NEPA, the NFMA, and the ESA will increasingly guide the management of our public lands in the way Congress intended; the Clean Water Act is also likely to play an ever more prominent role.

Although injunctions put a halt to illegal practices, they often have a more positive effect. They allow—indeed, force—agencies to find new ways of doing things, and they provide room for people with a different vision of land management to come to the fore.

John Berry is the district ranger for the Clackamas Ranger District on the Mount Hood National Forest in Oregon. His district, subjected to heavy clearcutting for 40 years, contains three-fourths of the national forest acreage that gained notoriety in June 1992, when *The New York Times* published NASA satellite photographs comparing its destruction—unfavorably—to that taking place in Brazil's rainforest.

John Berry has different ideas about how a forest should be managed. In 1990, he divided his district into five sections, including four watersheds, and for each he appointed a Forest Service "steward" who made a commitment to stay in that position at least five years and to manage the forest for a variety of purposes, not just timber production. Berry also banned clearcutting—and still has sold more timber to local mills than any other district on the forest.

It is probably too early to tell whether John Berry and others like him are on the right track. What is clear is that there are agency personnel who are ready to try new ideas, including managing our public lands with a lighter hand to preserve a variety of values. Litigation is giving these people one of their big opportunities. Berry publicly credits the injunctions in the spotted owl controversy, as well as a windstorm that left him with salvage timber to sell, for providing the opportunity to try a more "holistic" approach to forestry.

"The chaos, controversy, injunctions and blowdown—these four factors have allowed us to seize the moment," he told a reporter. "We have a short window here for shifting gears and changing direction" (10).

Notes

1. *Seattle Audubon Society* v. *Moseley*, 798 F. Supp. 1484, 1490 (W.D. Wash. 1992).
2. *Sierra Club* v. *Morton*, 405 U.S. 727 (1972).
3. *Udall* v. *Federal Power Commission*, 387 U.S. 428 (1967).
4. *Udall* v. *Federal Power Commission*, 387 U.S. 438 (1967), 436–437, 450.
5. For a more complete and colorful telling of the Mineral King controversy, see Turner, T. 1990. Wild by law: the Sierra Club Legal Defense Fund and the places it has saved, 3–23. San Francisco, California: Sierra Club Legal Defense Fund.
6. Interestingly, Justice Douglas wrote a lengthy dissenting opinion to the Court's decision in *Sierra Club* v. *Morton*, and although he discoursed

at some length on the value of preserving natural areas from "the destructive pressures of modern technology and modern life," he did not mention his own majority opinion in *Udall*. Justice Douglas's dissent argued for expanding the doctrine of standing to permit litigation on behalf of environmental values regardless of human use.

7. *West Virginia Division of Izaak Walton League, Inc.* v. *Butz*, 367 F. Supp. 422 (N.D.W.V. 1973), aff'd, 522 F.2d 945 (4th Cir. 1975).

8. *Sierra Club* v. *Lyng*, 694 F.Supp. 1260 (E.D. Tex. 1988), modified, 926 F.2d 429 (5th Cir. 1991).

9. *Seattle Audubon Society* v. *Moseley*, (W.D. Wa., No. C92-479WD, May 14, 1993).

10. Durbin, K. 1992. Peace in the forest. The Oregonian. June 21.

Chapter 13

Shifting and Broadening the Economic Paradigm toward Natural Resources

John B. Loomis

> If environmental dollars and cents were part of every bill's fiscal impact, perhaps it would not take a world crisis to get the attention of policy makers.
>
> —Martha Ezzard, former Colorado State Senator

Scarcity of resources is what makes the science of economics relevant to many of the decisions made by individual consumers, producers, and government officials. However, the objects of scarcity change with time. In the 1600s, food and fuel were scarce while wetlands, forests, fish, and wildlife were abundant. The development of North America has seen this scarcity reversed. Today it is natural resources, particularly those not allocated through the market, that are quite scarce.

I will trace the evolution of the principles and concerns of natural resource economics from one that was primarily concerned about scarcity of commodity natural resources to a discipline that accords preservation of natural environments equal importance to development. While the same broad principles that guide efficient use of marketed natural resources apply to natural environments—fish, wildlife, water quality, and so on—there has also been much innovation in the conceptual and empirical foundation of modern natural resource economics. Unfortunately, federal natural resource agencies have been slow to adopt many of these conceptual and empirical advances that accord equal importance to nonmarketed natural resources. Nonetheless three case studies illustrate some recent application of modern natural resource economics to resource decision making.

The Early Years of Natural Resource Economics

In many respects, the majority of early concerns of economics dealt with natural resources. After all, prior to and even during the early years of the industrial revolution, most economies were essentially resource based.

Forests provided game, building materials, and fuel. A majority of employment was related to food production. It was against this background that
Thomas Malthus, in 1798, first expressed concern about scarcity of arable
land relative to rising population. His was the first of many "doomsday"
forecasts associated with running out of natural resources. Many early economic theories concerned themselves with optimal harvest of forests over
time (1) and the time path of exploitation of nonrenewable natural
resources (2).

Much of the mainstream economic theory of the time demonstrated that,
when certain assumptions were met (which will receive scrutiny below), the
competitive market yielded an efficient use of resources. By efficient, economists mean one of two things: (a) an allocation of resources such that no
one can be made better off without making someone else worse off; or (b)
the sum of total benefits to producers and consumers is maximized (although some specific individuals may be worse off, others gain sufficiently
that the gainers could, in principle, more than compensate those that have
been made worse off).

To bring these principles of economic efficiency to government decision
making in water resource investments, the federal government required a
comparison of benefits and costs in the Flood Control Act of 1936. Reflecting both the relative scarcity of marketed outputs and the state of economic science, these early benefit-cost analyses (BCA) simply attempted to
mimic the allocation of water resources that might result if a competitive
market was in place. In addition, since free-flowing rivers and wetlands
were abundant, relative to commodities, during the Great Depression, little
account was taken of the benefits of preserving unique natural environments from dams.

Broadening of Resource Economics

While technological innovation may have temporarily alleviated the
Malthusian doom for marketed commodities, that has not been the case for
many natural resources such as fisheries, groundwater, migratory wildlife,
and so on. These resources share another early theme of natural resource
economics: common pool resources. The rapid disappearance of many
wildlife species and certain fisheries was due to lack of enforceable property
rights over the resource. Ownership was only obtained upon taking of an animal, not from conserving the population of animals. Economic theory was
developed to show that overharvest would result unless a single owner
could control current and future use of the resource. With a well-defined
owner who can (at little cost) enforce their property rights, there is normally

sufficient incentive to make decisions today to conserve the resource for a continued harvest over time. The airshed is now a commons as well, one that affects scenic visibility at many national parks.

The notion of inefficient use (i.e., overuse) of a common resource also brings to the forefront one of the contributions of economic theory, one that is widely used in natural and environmental economics: the distinction between private profit and social benefits. Contrary to popular belief, economic theory clearly distinguishes between what is often privately profitable and what maximizes the benefit to society. The earliest examples of this in economics stem from analysis of monopolies. Any student who can pass a principles of economics class can demonstrate that while monopolies maximize profit for their owners, they do so at the cost of reducing social well-being (due to restricting output and charging prices in excess of the marginal cost of producing the last unit).

In common pool resources, individuals pursuing their own self-interest often impose costs upon other users of the commons. The logger who cuts trees in a forested watershed imposes two types costs on downstream users of water: (a) higher production costs to fishery managers, irrigators, dam operators, and municipal water treatment facilities; and (b) loss of enjoyment for river users, due to more turbid water. As (b) illustrates, an economic cost arises from a forgone benefit, and this forgone benefit need not involve any direct cash flow. The reduction in enjoyment of downstream swimmers is a loss in their well-being that can be measured using the swimmers visitation behavior. In most situations involving the commons, the cost imposed on others by the logger is not a cost paid by the logger. Therefore, that cost is external to his or her decision. Economists have termed this spillover cost from the decision maker to a third party an "externality." One solution to this externality is to place the entire watershed under control of a single owner. Now, the sedimentation costs of timber harvests are imposed on the same people affected by the sediment. Hence the sediment costs will now be explicitly balanced against the benefit of harvesting the trees. The result is to reduce the timber harvest. Several alternative solutions that emerge from economic theory include taxing the timber harvest an amount equal to the costs that sediment impose on downstream users. Forcing this cost back onto the loggers makes that cost internal to them. Faced with significantly higher costs, loggers reduce timber harvest.

Market Failures, Externalities, and Public Goods

While another popular myth is that economics worships the market, natural resource economists make much use of the economic concept of market failure (3). Externalities are one type of market failure. While much of the

concern over externalities has focused on external costs, the concept applies
equally well to external benefits or what is sometimes called public goods
(4). That is, an individual's decision to preserve property as a wetland be-
stows a benefit to many other people who will see the birds fly across the sky.
The market failure arises because there is no cost-effective way to charge
the beneficiaries for their viewing enjoyment. They can enjoy seeing the
birds (and simply knowing they occur there) without paying. Hence, when
the landowner decides whether to drain the wetland to produce an agricultural commodity for which people must pay to consume or to preserve the
wetland (where beneficiaries do not pay), more often than not, it is privately
profitable to drain the wetland. By ignoring the external benefit or public
good, too little preservation of natural environments results. Economic
theory suggests there can be net benefits to government intervention of
some form: public ownership of the wetland paid for by mandatory tax payments from all the beneficiaries or a subsidy to the landowner to maintain
the land as a wetland.

Incorporation of Externalities and
Public Goods into Federal Benefit-Cost Analysis

The recognition of externalities and public goods called for a broadening of
the federal government's benefit-cost analysis (BCA) of water projects. No
longer was the intent of BCA to simply emulate the market. Rather, the
BCA had to go beyond this and calculate maximum social value including
external costs and benefits. In some ways this naturally fit federal flood control projects. Building a dam created downstream flood control benefits to
everyone living below the dam. Flood control is a localized public good, the
benefits of which cannot be directly observed in a market like the price of
commodities, but nonetheless are real. Economic theory provided a concept for measuring benefits even in the absence of price: what would a fully
informed household pay to avoid flood damages? In principle, they would
pay up to the expected dollar flood damages avoided by the dam. This would
include the costs of cleaning out mud from their home, replacing belong-
ings, and so on. Since there were markets to determine the cleaning costs
and replacement costs, a maximum willingness-to-pay value could be inferred or calculated.

The first formal recognition in federal benefit-cost analysis of the need to
calculate benefits beyond those of marketed goods came in what became
known as the "Green Book" produced by the Federal Inter-Agency River
Basin Commission in 1950. Categories of nonmarketed benefits arising

from water resource projects that were specifically mentioned included recreation and the value of saving human life.

Emergence of Techniques to Value Nonmarketed Uses of Natural Resources

The early 1960s saw four major developments regarding economic valuation of natural resources. First was the implementation of Hotelling's idea, first suggested in 1949 (5), that recreationists' willingness to pay over and above their expenditures could be measured in dollar terms using a travel demand approach. Clawson (6) implemented a statistical technique to estimate a demand curve for recreation visitation to a particular site. Visits per capita from visitor-origin zones around a recreation site was the quantity variable and the visitor's travel cost to that site was the price variable. Since some visitors live closer than others but consume the same type of recreation experience in a visit to the same site, the additional willingness to pay of the closer visitors could be inferred by how much the more distant visitors had paid. While the technique (called the travel cost method) has become far more sophisticated in defining and measuring price and quantity, and augmenting the demand curve with measures of skill, tastes, site quality, and so on, the technique allowed commensurate valuation of recreation from actual visitor behavior (7).

The second major development was the formal inclusion of recreation as a project purpose into the federal water project in 1962, and the concomitant need for economic valuation of recreation. While this was initially done using a set of administratively approved unit day values, the rapid improvement in the travel cost method soon made it the method of choice by economists and, by the mid-1970s, by the Army Corps of Engineers (8).

A third major development was a survey-based method for valuation of nonmarketed natural resources (9). As originally developed, this technique created a hypothetical or simulated market in which visitors could reveal their willingness to pay by bidding. The essence of the survey is a statement of the resource to be valued, the consequences of paying (i.e., access will be provided, water quality improved by X percent, etc.), and the means of payment specified (i.e., higher entrance fees, annual pass, etc.). The individual is asked to either state the maximum they would pay or indicate if they would pay some preset increment (that varies across people). The technique is now referred to as the contingent valuation method (CVM). The method has been shown to be reliable (10) and valid (11). Of course, reliable and valid measurement requires carefully designed and pretested survey instruments with check questions (12). While initially applied to valuing recreation, the technique eventually saw application for valuing public goods, including what the fourth major development of the 1960s called option and existence values. For valuing public goods, CVM has been framed as a voter referendum. That is, would you vote in favor of natural resource action A (i.e., acquisition of new habitat or improvement in water quality financed via a bond act) if it cost you $X each year in higher taxes? Since the $X asked varies across households, it is possible to estimate maximum willingness to pay using a logistic regression (13).

The major conceptual contribution of the 1960s was the recognition that many people who were not direct users of natural environments nonetheless might have a value for preserving them. The first step along this continuum was the notion that nonvisitors might be willing to pay some form of an insurance premium to maintain the opportunity to visit some natural environment in the future (14). Specifically, if the area was faced with irreversible destruction and had some unique features not found elsewhere, then some people might be willing to pay more than their expected recreation benefits to preserve the natural environment from destruction, so they could visit in the future. This value became known as option value and has stimulated a large debate about its magnitude (15).

The other major conceptual breakthrough of the 1960s was Krutilla's suggestion that people never intending to visit might have a willingness to pay (WTP) to preserve natural environments simply to know they exist or so that future generations might have them (16). The WTP for simply knowing a particular natural environment or wildlife species exists is usually called existence value, although it is also known as a non-use value, which is somewhat of a misnomer since existence demand is more like an off-site use value. Bequest value is the value to the current generation from knowing that future generations will have the natural environment or wildlife species available.

Option, existence, and bequest values are pure public goods: preserving habitat for the spotted owl for one person provides option, existence, and bequest value to all others. Everyone can enjoy the knowledge that the spotted owl exists, without diminishing the amount of enjoyment available to others. In addition, it is impossible to exclude someone from enjoying the preservation of the spotted owl, even if they do not pay in some way. Even though the sum of option, existence, and bequest value per household might be quite small (e.g., $10 to $30), since they are available to everyone in the population, the aggregate social values may be quite high (17).

Application of New Concepts of Value and Techniques in Natural Resources Management

Valuation of natural resources for recreation using the travel cost method (TCM) was a major endeavor of academic economists during the 1960s and 1970s. Water-based recreation (18), stream fishing (19), river rafting (20), and wilderness recreation (21) were just a few of the examples. During the same time, CVM was applied to value waterfowl (22), scenic visibility (23), and water quality (24). Collectively these studies demonstrated the robustness of these techniques for a wide variety of natural resources.

In 1979, the federal interagency council that set BCA rules for the United States Army Corps of Engineers, Bureau of Reclamation, Soil Conservation Service, and Fish and Wildlife Service, issued regulations that recommended both TCM and CVM be the methods of choice for large projects involving recreational use of water resources (25). The strong endorsement of TCM and CVM also made them the techniques of choice of several other federal agencies. For example, the United States Environmental Protection Agency funded numerous studies on the value of water quality (26).

One of the clearest examples of the use of CVM in natural resource management can be seen in the research of Bishop et al. and Boyle et al. (27), regarding the effect of artificially peaking power flows on rafting benefits in Grand Canyon National Park. The Bureau of Reclamation, which operates Glen Canyon Dam upstream from the Grand Canyon, wanted to go to an extreme peaking power release schedule. This would have involved changing water releases from as little as 1500 cubic feet per second (cfs) during nonpeak power times to as much as 31,000 cfs during peak power times. Such fluctuations would significantly affect the quality of the much sought after rafting downstream in the Grand Canyon National Park. The Bureau of Reclamation and the National Park Service hired a consulting firm that employed economists Richard Bishop, Kevin Boyle, and Michael Welsh to design a CVM survey. The intent of the survey was to quantify in dollars the loss in rafting benefits associated with different water release patterns. These dollar values, along with ecological effects being measured by other agencies, would then be used in an Environmental Impact Statement (EIS) to select the most desirable water release pattern for all resources, not just hydropower.

Mail CVM surveys of the visitors were performed to quantify the value of rafting with different flow levels and degrees of fluctuations. The annual value of rafting under optimum flow conditions (found at stable flows of about 28,000 cfs) was $10 million (28). Lower and fluctuating flows dropped this annual value to around $4 million.

These results appear to have had a significant effect on the Bureau of Reclamation's operating plans. Since the CVM showed a significant and sizable change in value, the Bureau went to interim high, steady flows during the preparation of the EIS. In 1992, Congress passed the Grand Canyon Protection Act to formalize the steady interim flows while the EIS was being prepared. While one cannot claim the recreation values were the critical element (as beach erosion and potential impacts to endangered fish were also at risk from fluctuating flows), the results of the CVM survey certainly changed the perceptions and the nature of the debate. No longer was the recreation experience treated as merely a "nice to have" aesthetic experience that could be easily traded-off to more tangible power revenues. Having demonstrated the utility of CVM for measuring recreation use values, the Bureau has requested the same economists to measure the existence values to the general public from resource impacts associated with changes from steady flows to moderate peaking power flows.

Incorporating Existence Values in Federal Economic Analyses

The broadening of federal economic analyses to include valuation of option, existence, and bequest values has had a much more tortured path. Walsh et al. and Brookshire et al. (29) demonstrated the empirical significance of these off-site preservation values compared to on-site recreation use values. In the case of preserving roadless areas as Wilderness, about 50 percent of the total benefits were related to the off-site preservation values (30). Schulze et al. (31) found that an even larger relative share of total benefits for preserving visibility over the Grand Canyon was related to off-site values. Slightly more than 90 percent of the total benefits were attributable to households that did not plan to visit the Grand Canyon. Thus, in many situations, failure to include the public good benefits of preservation of natural environments would significantly undervalue protection.

It was not until 1986 that the federal government, in its procedures for valuing natural resource damages, included option, existence, and bequest values (32). These values were to be measured using CVM. However, this attempt at broadening resource valuation did not go unchallenged by United States industries. The American Chemical Manufacturers (representing numerous petrochemical companies among others) appealed the Department of Interior regulations. In 1988, the District Court of Appeals rejected industry's challenge. The court found that the intent of Congress when it passed the Comprehensive Environmental Response, Compensa-

tion and Liability Act (CERCLA) was to include the value of natural resources that were not necessarily directly used, but may be "passively used"
off-site in the form of existence values. CVM was also upheld as an adequate
technique for measuring such values.

With the *Exxon Valdez* oil spill in the remote Prince William Sound of
Alaska in 1989, the importance of existence values took on greater serious-
ness. Both the federal government and the state of Alaska planned to measure existence values of the environmental components and wildlife
harmed by the spill. Since these potential values could be in the billions,
Exxon hired numerous economists to demonstrate that CVM could be unreliable. Since nearly all of these economists had no experience with applying CVM, and given their task, it was not surprising they were able to
produce CVM studies that gave unreliable results.

Any technique, when badly applied, will yield less than desirable results.
By sufficiently publicizing these studies before they could be peer reviewed, Exxon was able to persuade the National Oceanic and Atmospheric
Administration (NOAA) to establish a blue ribbon panel to review the use
of CVM for measuring existence values. The panel included two Nobel
Prize-winning economists, a policy economist, and a survey research expert.
The panel's task was to recommend to NOAA whether CVM was reliable for
measuring passive use values in the context of the Oil Pollution Act of 1990
(passed partly in response to the *Exxon Valdez* spill).

In January of 1993, the Panel concluded that carefully designed and implemented CVM studies convey useful information for judicial and administrative decisions involving non-use or existence values. They further determined that such information is as reliable as marketing analyses of new
products and damage assessments normally allowed in court proceedings.
The Panel presented several guidelines on the design of CVM studies for
valuing non-use damages to natural resources. For example, to make CVM
as reliable as possible the referendum approach should be used rather than
open-ended WTP questions, and in-person (or telephone) interviews
should be used rather than mail surveys (33).

With this acceptance of CVM for measuring non-use values and the suggested procedures, we will no doubt see the continuation of CVM applications to natural resources with both use and non-use/existence values. The
procedures of Arrow et al. raise the standards that CVMs undertaken for
damage assessment must meet (33). As such, fewer but more carefully designed and conducted studies will likely be performed. At the same time,
the suggestions of Arrow et al. provide many testable hypotheses and require much refinement before routine implementation. In this sense the
research agenda for CVM has now been spelled out in more detail than at

perhaps any other time. Due to the higher cost to attain the standards, the rate of progress will depend very heavily on whether agencies upgrade their funding to match the standards required by Arrow et al.

Future Directions: Ecosystem Valuation

The next big step before CVM researchers relates to moving toward holistic valuation of ecosystems (see Chapter 19, by Costanza). By holistic, I mean valuing not just recreational, existence, and bequest values of individual species, but measuring these values for an entire ecological community. That is, valuing not just the pieces, but also species' interactions and interconnectedness. This would be a departure for many public land management agencies that now decompose an ecosystem into water flows, recreation services, wildlife, and so on and then apply standardized values to those components.

An ecosystem approach was taken with the valuation of the Mono Lake ecosystem and the San Joaquin Valley wetlands complex, respectively (34). Here CVM was used to arrive at one comprehensive value of changes in major features of the ecosystem such as water quality, bird's food supply, nesting habitat, reproductive success, air quality, and scenery associated with alternative management strategies.

However we should move on two fronts to improve this valuation effort. Given Arrow et al.'s recommendation to use in-person or telephone interviews, progress in valuation can be made at the micro and macro levels. At the micro level, contingent valuation surveys should present a schematic of the complete ecosystem including the soil microorganisms, nutrient cycling, predator–prey relationships, and so on, under different management regimes. In this way loss of biodiversity or particular components of the ecosystem are valued not only as separate entities, but also for how they affect other parts/species in these ecosystems. At the macro level, we should adopt more of a landscape ecology view. That is, we should focus not just on a particular piece of ground, but on how that area fits into the grand scheme of life requirements for particular indicator species. For example, how does a particular management alternative for an area influence the linkage of that species' habitat to other species? A larger, regional view of the role played by an area in providing a buffer for other areas, or as an additional habitat reserve that reduces risk of extinction due to environmental events such as catastrophic fires, is needed.

When the integrated micro and macro views are combined with a broadening of the sample frame to include the residents of the state where the land is located as well as adjacent states (or even nations if the natural environment is sufficiently unique), a human-centered economic valuation technique will have progressed considerably. The limits to more complete economic valuation will then be related to scientific understanding of ecosystems, the public's interest in understanding what is known about ecosystems, their appreciation of these ecosystems, and their sense of duty toward future generations. Human values toward nature have evolved over time from being very consumptive oriented to being more appreciative oriented. Economic valuation techniques and resulting dollar values have (with some lag) reflected this evolution in people's view of nature. Economics, being a system that reports on the values generated by people, will continue to provide updated values if people become more ecologically or biocentrically oriented. The last challenge is to integrate such values into agency and political decision making.

Notes

1. Faustmann, M. [1849] 1968. On the determination of the value which forest land and immature stands possess for forestry. In Martin Faustmann and the evolution discounted cash flow. M. Gane, ed. Institute Paper no. 42. Commonwealth Forestry Institute. London: University of Oxford.
2. Hotelling, H. 1931. The economics of exhaustible resources. Journal of Political Economy 39:137–175.
3. Bator, F. 1958. The anatomy of market failure. Quarterly Journal of Economics 72(2):351–379.
4. Samuelson, P. 1954. The pure theory of public expenditure. Review of Economics and Statistics 36(4):387–389.
5. Hotelling, H. 1949. The economics of public recreation. In The Prewitt report. Land and Recreation Planning Division. Washington, D.C.: National Park Service.
6. Clawson, M. 1959. Methods of measuring the demand for and the value of outdoor recreation. reprint no. 10. Washington, D.C.: Resources for the Future.
7. Clawson, M., and J. Knetsch. 1966. Economics of outdoor recreation. Baltimore, Maryland: The Johns Hopkins University Press. Ward, F., and J. Loomis. 1986. The travel cost method as an environmental policy assessment tool; a review of the literature. Western Journal of Agricultural Economics 11(2):164–178.
8. Brown, R., and W. Hansen. 1974. A generalized recreation day use planning model. In Plan formulation and evaluation studies—recreation., vol. v. Institute for Water Resources. Fort Belvoir, Virginia: U.S. Army Corps of Engineers.

9. Davis, R.K. 1963. The value of outdoor recreation: an economic analysis of the Maine woods. Ph.D. dissertation. Harvard University.

10. Kealy, M.J., J. Dovidio, and M. Rockel. 1988. Accuracy in valuation is a matter of degree. Land Economics 64(2):158–171.

    Loomis, J. 1989. Test-retest reliability of the contingent valuation method: a comparison of general population and visitor responses. American Journal of Agricultural Economics 71(1):76–84.

    Loomis, J. 1990. Comparative reliability of the dichotomous choice and open-ended contingent valuation techniques. Journal of Environmental Economics and Management 71(1):76–84.

11. Brookshire, D., W. Schulze, M. Thayer, and R. d'Arge. 1982. Valuing public goods: a comparison survey and hedonic approaches. American Economic Review 72(1):165–177.

    Welsh, M. 1986. Exploring the accuracy of the contingent valuation method: comparisons with simulated markets. Unpublished Ph.D. dissertation. Department of Agricultural Economics, University of Wisconsin.

12. Mitchell, R., and R. Carson. 1989. Using surveys to value public goods: the contingent valuation method. Washington, D.C.: Resources for the Future.

13. Loomis, J.B. 1988. Contingent valuation using dichotomous choice models. Journal of Leisure Research 20(1):46–56.

14. Weisbrod, B. 1964. Collective consumption services of individual consumption goods. Quarterly Journal of Economics 78(3):471–477.

15. Bishop, R. 1982. Option value: an exposition and extension. Land Economics 58(1):1–15.

16. Krutilla, J. 1967. Conservation reconsidered. American Economic Review 57:787–796.

17. Rubin, J., G. Helfhand, and J. Loomis. 1991. A benefit-cost analysis of the northern spotted owl. Journal of Forestry 89(12):25–30.

18. Burt, O., and D. Brewer. 1971. Evaluation of net social benefits from outdoor recreation. Econometrica 39:813–827.

19. Brown, W., A. Singh, and E. Castle. 1964. An economic evaluation of the Oregon salmon and steelhead sport fisheries. Technical Bulletin 78. Corvallis, Oregon: Oregon Agricultural Experiment Station.

20. Michaelson, E. 1977. An attempt to quantify the esthetics of wild and scenic rivers in Idaho. In Proceedings of a symposium on river recreation management and research. General Technical Report NC-28. St. Paul, Minnesota: U.S. Forest Service, North Central Station.

21. Smith, K., and R. Kopp. 1978. Toward a definition of the spatial limits of the travel cost recreational demand model. Discussion paper D-27. Washington, D.C.: Resources for the Future.

22. Brown, G., and J. Hammack. 1972. A preliminary investigation of the economics of migratory waterfowl. In Natural environments: studies in theoretical and applied analysis. J. Krutilla, ed. Baltimore, Maryland: The Johns Hopkins University Press.
23. Randall, A., B. Ives, and C. Eastman. 1974. Bidding games for valuation of aesthetic environmental improvements. Journal of Environmental Economics and Management 1:132–149.
24. Walsh, R., D. Greenley, R. Young, J. McKean, and A. Prato. 1978. Option values, preservation values and recreation benefits of improved water quality. Socioeconomic Environmental Studies Series #660/5-78-001. Washington, D.C.: U.S. Environmental Protection Agency.
25. U.S. Water Resources Council. 1979. Procedures for evaluation of national economic development (NED) benefits and costs in water resources planning (level C). Federal Register, 44(243):72892–72976.
26. Mitchell, R., and R. Carson. 1984. A contingent valuation estimate of national freshwater benefits. Washington, D.C.: Technical report to the United States Environmental Protection Agency.
    Vaughan, W., and C. Russell. 1982. Valuing a fishing day: an application of a systematic varying parameter model. Land Economics 58:450–463.
27. Bishop, R., K. Boyle, M. Welsh, R. Baumgartner, and P. Rathburn. 1987. Glen Canyon dam releases and downstream recreation. Madison, Wisconsin: HBRS. Boyle, K., M. Welsh, R. Bishop, and R. Baumgartner. 1987. Analyzing the effects of Glen Canyon Dam releases on Colorado River recreation using scenarios of unexperienced flow conditions. In Western regional research publication W-133, first interim report, comp. J. Loomis. Division of Environmental Studies. Davis, California: University of California at Davis.
28. Boyle et al. 1987 (27).
29. Brookshire, D., L. Eubanks, and A. Randall. 1983. Estimating option prices and existence values for wildlife resources. Land Economics 59(1):1–15.
    Walsh, R., J. Loomis, and R. Gillman. 1984. Valuing option, existence, and bequest demands for wilderness. Land Economics 60(1):14–29.
    Walsh et al. 1978 (24).
30. Walsh et al. 1984 (29).
31. Schulze, W., D. Brookshire, E. Walther, K. MacFarland, M. Thayer, R. Whitworth, S. Ben-David, W. Malm, and J. Molenar. 1983. The economic benefits of preserving visibility in the national parklands of the Southwest. Natural Resources Journal 23:149–173.
32. U.S. Department of the Interior. 1986. Natural resource damage

assessments; final rule. Federal Register 43 CFR Part 11; Vol 51(148): 27674–27753, 1 August.

33. Arrow, K., R. Solow, P. Portney, E. Leamer, R. Radner, and H. Schuman. 1993. Report of the NOAA panel on contingent valuation. Washington, D.C.: National Oceanic and Atmospheric Administration.

34. Loomis, J.B. 1988. Quantifying the economic values of public trust resources using the contingent valuation method: a case study of the Mono Lake decision. Transactions of the 54th North American Wildlife and Natural Resources Conference. Washington, D.C.: Wildlife Management Institute.

Loomis, J.B., T. Wegge, M. Hanemann, and B. Kanninen. 1990. The economic value of water to wildlife and fisheries in the San Joaquin Valley. Transactions of the 55th North American Wildlife and Natural Resources Conference. Washington, D.C.: Wildlife Management Institute.

Chapter 14

Thinking about Natural Resource-Dependent Economies: Moving beyond the Folk Economics of the Rear-View Mirror

Thomas Michael Power

> Practical men, who believe themselves to be quite exempt from any
> intellectual influences, are usually the slaves of some defunct economist.
> Madmen in authority, who hear voices in the air, are distilling their frenzy
> from some academic scribbler of a few years back.
> —John Maynard Keynes
> *The General Theory of Employment, Interest and Money*

The "Official" Economic Model of Natural Resource Economies

Natural resource managers, like most residents in "natural resource-dependent" communities, have a particular way of looking at the local economy and the role played by resource extraction in that economy. The extraction and processing in our timber, mining, and agricultural industries are seen as the dominant source of income flowing into the local economy and, therefore, as the primary economic engine. Because these industries are seen as dominating the local economy, public land managers tend to take as one of their primary responsibilities the "stabilization" of the local economy through the provision of "necessary" raw material supplies.

The extractive activities usually have a long history in these communities, often being associated with the original European settlement of the area. People commonly perceive their local economy as tied to such past patterns of economic activity rather than current economic reality. This is not surprising. Individuals, businesses, and the community tend to adjust their behavior and organization to accommodate important economic activities. In many ways they form themselves around those "means of livelihood." This creates a shared community vision of what the population "does for a living." When the pattern of economic activity begins to change, there is a considerable lag in intellectual and cultural adjustment. One of the last things to change is that collective understanding of what drives the local economy. In that sense, the conventional wisdom about the local economy is a "view through the rear-view mirror," a view tied to a past reality rather than the present pattern of economic activity. This conviction asserts that what was economically important in the past continues to be of central importance now and into the foreseeable future. From that past perspective, no other set of economic activities appears attractive or viable. Everything else appears unreliable and/or inferior. What could replace mining or ranching or timber in the old West, or farming in the "farm belt," or commercial fishing in our coastal ports?

A rear-view mirror, of course, is a very important safety device, especially if one is traveling in congested traffic or changing lanes. A safe driver would not want to be without one. At the same time, it would be terribly unsafe to try to negotiate through congested traffic while staring only into the rear-view mirror. To safely get where one wishes to go, one has to primarily be focused on the traffic and terrain ahead.

It is in that sense that a historically rooted view of the local economy can be dangerous to the economic health of the community. It tends to focus on the past at the expense of the present and the future. If our perspective is limited in this way, the economic well-being of the community cannot be protected or enhanced.

My chapter seeks to divert our vision of the local economy away from that rear-view mirror and onto the current and emerging economic reality that often is dramatically different.

The Extractive Economic Model

One of our most widely shared pieces of economic "knowledge" has been taught and retaught to us since our first introduction to economic geography in elementary school. Most of us remember the maps in our social science books that sought to associate regions with particular types of economic activity. On a map of the United States, there would be an icon of a blast furnace in Pittsburgh; an automobile in Detroit; corn in Iowa; Paul Bunyan and his blue ox in the Pacific Northwest; beer in Milwaukee; cotton in the deep South; and so on.

The economic lesson of such maps was that one could explain the geographic pattern of settlement by looking at the economic activities that drew people to certain areas and supported them there. It was the geographically specialized economic activities that explained why people lived where they did.

The economic theory behind this view has come to be labeled the economic base model. It argues that in order for people to inhabit any area, they need to have the money that allows them to purchase from the larger, external economy those things that they cannot easily produce themselves. To earn that income, they in turn must successfully market some exportable product. It is the income from their exports that allows them to pay for the imports that make life in that particular location viable.

In that sense, all economic activity is not of equal importance. Spending on locally oriented economic activities (child care, restaurant services, grocery stores, etc.) depends on income that is earned in the export sectors. That export-oriented economic activity is the basic driving force in the local economy. It is primary economic activity while the locally oriented activity is derivative or secondary. Export activity drives the rest of the economy in this model.

This causal relationship is often described in terms of an income or employment multiplier: export activity has an amplified effect on the rest of the economy, triggering cycle after cycle of local spending that puts people to work in locally oriented economic activities.

This familiar view of the local economy also contains a rather overt political message: All economic activities are not equal in importance. Some economic actors are significantly more important than others. A particular minority subset of all economic activities, either directly or indirectly, "butters all of our bread." Those "primary," usually export-oriented and extractive, economic activities need to be nurtured and supported, for without them our communities would cease to be viable and would begin the downward drift toward ghost town status. This view leads to a primitive version of the economic base model depicted in Figure 14.1 as the "Extractive Model" of the local economy. From this perspective, ghost towns are dramatic confirmations of the economic reality embodied in the model: Communities exist only as long as their extractive natural resource base remains viable.

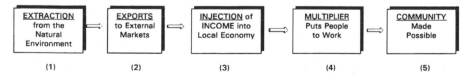

Figure 14.1   The extractive view of the local economy. (1) Natural environment as a warehouse of commercial resources waiting to be extracted. (2) Extractive exports are what drive the whole economy. (3) Extractive exports are the only reliable source of income for the community. (4) Locally oriented businesses are derivative or secondary. (5) Without extractive industry we wouldn't be living here.

Anything that threatens the viability of that extractive natural resource base, threatens the continued existence of the entire community.

Economic Anomalies or Economic Trends?

The last decade has been a hard one for communities that rely on natural resource extraction. Natural resource industries have fluctuated widely but mostly moved downward in terms of both income and employment. As disruptive as this has been for various communities and their families, it also provides us with an opportunity to test the dominant folk economics. It asserts that as extractive economic activity declined, the rest of the economy should have declined in a similar but amplified way. But, in general, this is not what has happened. The threatened modern-day ghost towns have not been developing despite the virtual elimination of many communities' extractive economic bases. Consider the following examples.

Figure 14.2 depicts the decline, largely because of environmental constraints, in the harvest of timber off of public lands in the Bitterroot Valley in "timber-dependent" western Montana. Over the last two decades, almost 80 percent of the harvest has been lost and all but one of its half-dozen lumber mills have shut down. Yet the local economy expanded briskly in terms of real personal income during the periods of sharpest decline in timber supply. Similar patterns can be observed throughout "timber-dependent" Montana and Idaho: the Flathead Valley in Montana leads the state in economic growth despite plummeting timber harvests; the towns of Dubois, Wyoming, and McCall, Idaho, lost their lumber mills, but instead of going into an economic death spiral, they have shown considerable economic vitality (1).

During the 1980s, many copper and silver mining and smelting operations throughout the West largely shut down, some permanently. For instance, in 1974, almost two-thirds of the basic industry earnings in the Butte-Anaconda area of Montana were associated with the Anaconda Copper Company. By 1982, those operations were permanently shut down and the company ceased to exist. The extractive economic model would have suggested that a modern-day ghost town would quickly emerge. Given the harsh climate and ravaged environment of the area, this might have seemed all the more likely. Although the area did see its population shrink by 25 percent, the rest of the economy, as indicated by real income received outside of the copper industry (but excluding unemployment compensation and income maintenance programs), actually modestly expanded and then

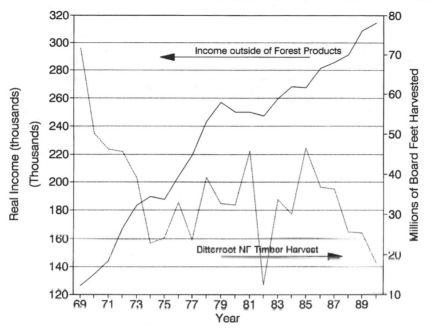

Figure 14.2   Real income versus timber harvest in Bitterroot Valley (Ravalli County), Montana. (From Regional Economic Information System CD ROM, Bureau of Economic Analysis, U.S. Department of Commerce; Region One, U.S. Forest Service, U.S. Department of Agriculture.)

held steady (see Figure 14.3). The rest of the economy, previously considered heavily dependent on the copper industry, proved to have a resiliency and life of its own.

If one looks at other mining towns in the northern Rocky Mountains, one sees a similar pattern. The parts of the local economies not directly tied to mining and ore processing do not simply passively follow changes in mining sector income. The nonmining part of the economy shows considerably more stability than mining itself. Figures 14.4, 14.5, and 14.6 depict the Silver Valley in the Panhandle of Idaho, the Salmon area in central Idaho, and the Stillwater region of Montana, respectively.

In the Silver Valley of Idaho, mining and smelting employment boomed in the late 1970s and then collapsed in the early 1980s. Neither the boom nor the bust had a significant impact on personal income being received from the nonmetal parts of the economy, despite the fact that the metals sector was the source of over half of all personal income (2) (see Figure 14.4).

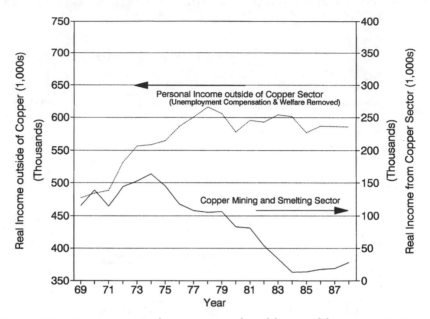

Figure 14.3 Copper sector real income versus that of the rest of the economy in Butte-Anaconda, Montana. (From Regional Economic Information System CD ROM, Bureau of Economic Analysis, U.S. Department of Commerce.)

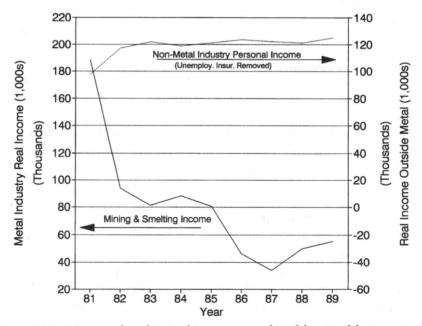

Figure 14.4 Mining and smelting real income versus that of the rest of the economy in Silver Valley (Shoshone County), Idaho. (From Regional Economic Information System CD ROM, Bureau of Economic Analysis, U.S. Department of Commerce.)

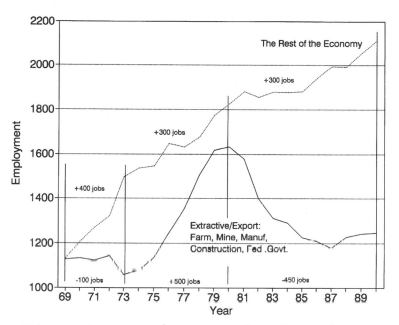

Figure 14.5 Extractive/export employment versus that of the rest of the economy in Salmon (Lemhi County), Idaho. (From Regional Economic Information System CD ROM, Bureau of Economic Analysis, U.S. Department of Commerce.)

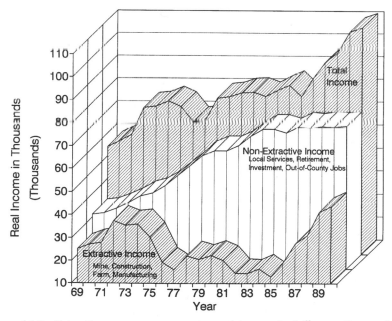

Figure 14.6 Extractive versus nonextractive real income in Stillwater County, Montana. (From Regional Economic Information System CD ROM, Bureau of Economic Analysis, U.S. Department of Commerce.)

In the remote Salmon area (Lemhi County) in the Upper Salmon region of central Idaho, mining operations have come and gone, and the timber industry has declined. The impact of these wide fluctuations in extractive economic activity on employment in what is usually assumed to be the dependent "derivative" sectors (retail trade, finance, services, and local government) appears to have been almost nonexistent. During periods of contracting extractive employment, the nonextractive economy expanded rapidly. During periods of rapid expansion in the extractive sectors, there was no acceleration in the growth in employment in the nonextractive sectors (see Figure 14.5).

In southwestern Montana, northeast of Yellowstone Park, the nation's only platinum mine opened in 1985. This and other fluctuations in basic income over the last two decades had a significant impact on total income, but its impact on the nonbasic sectors is much less clear. During the collapse in basic income in the early 1970s, the rest of the economy grew significantly. During the mining boom in the late 1980s, there was almost no change in the nonbasic sources of income (see Figure 14.6).

When even mining towns demonstrate an economic stability in the non-mining sectors in the face of very large fluctuations in mining employment and income, it suggests that there are stabilizing forces operating that are not adequately dealt with by the extractive economic model. That model does an inadequate job of identifying all of the important economic forces operating within our natural resource-dependent communities. That is true on a larger regional basis as well. If one looks at the economic performance of the aggregate of extractive industries in entire states such as Montana, Idaho, Wyoming, Utah, and Oregon, or multistate regions such as the Greater Yellowstone region or the Northern Rockies, one sees instability and decline since the late 1970s. This is in sharp contrast with the expansion that has taken place in those broad regions' nonextractive sectors that the extractive model predicts should passively follow their extractive bases (see Figure 14.7).

Reinterpreting the Economic Base Model to Save It

One reason these natural resource economies do not seem to behave the way the economic base model predicts is that the model is misinterpreted. A standard interpretation of the economic base model is that exports and the income they inject into the local economy are the only matters of concern. Those income injections enable all other economic activities. It is the

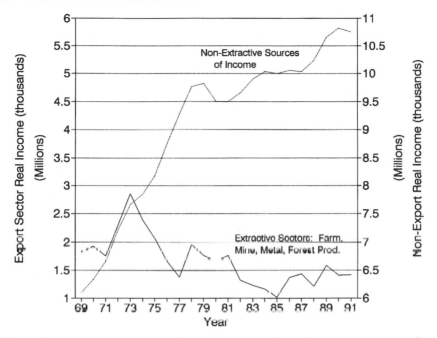

Figure 14.7   Extractive/export real income versus other real income sources in the Montana economy. (From Regional Economic Information System CD ROM, Bureau of Economic Analysis, U.S. Department of Commerce.)

income earned in export-oriented activities that circulates through the local economy, putting people to work in the locally oriented economic activities that provide the vast majority of local jobs. Fluctuations or growth in export income cause fluctuations or growth in the nonexport sectors. The relationship between them is summarized by a more or less constant multiplier.

But this is not the only, or most appropriate, interpretation of the economic base model. In fact, it is this misinterpretation that has led to the false "ghost town" predictions. This interpretation ignores what it is that determines the "multiplier." The "multiplier" is determined by the character and structure of the local economy. The more quickly the injected income leaks out of the local economy, the smaller the multiplier. The multiplier is related to the reciprocal of the fraction of local spending that goes to importing goods. The more self-sufficient a local economy is, the longer the injected income circulates within the local economy and the larger is the overall "multiplier" impact.

In that sense, the impact of any particular level of export earnings on the local economy is determined by the structure of the local economy and the range of locally produced goods and services available. It is not just export earnings that matter. The character of the local economy is crucially important, too. The standard interpretation of the economic base model would dismiss a restaurant or recreational facility as "derivative" or "secondary," passively relying on export earnings to survive. An alternative interpretation is that such local economic activities absorb and hold dollars longer in the local economy, increasing the jobs and income that result. That is, locally oriented economic activity also directly generates jobs. In fact, it is the richness and diversity of those locally oriented sectors that determine the size of the multiplier.

Consider, for example, an Arctic outpost where minerals are being extracted. Despite huge amounts of export activity and high volumes of income being generated by that export activity, it is unlikely that any economic development will take place at the cite of the extraction. Because the area is not an attractive residential location, workers will be temporarily imported along with all of the goods and services needed to support them. Those workers will travel away from the extractive site every opportunity they get, will send their income elsewhere to support their families, and will leave as soon as that particular extractive activity is finished. No local community or economy will develop despite the high volume of export activity. Clearly, more than just the volume of exports matters in determining local economic impacts.

The economic base model should not be interpreted as asserting that only exports really matter. Rather, that model asserts that export earnings interact with the structure of the local economy to determine the character of the overall level of local economic activity. Both export earnings and local economic structure matter.

Economic Dependence versus Economic Development

An even stronger statement can be made about the role of export earnings in local economic development. "More of the same," in the sense of an expansion in an already specialized export industry, rarely can be labeled economic development. Economic development consists of spinning a complex web of locally oriented economic activities that make an area increasingly less dependent on imports and, as a result, not as dependent on export earnings. In addition, successful import substitution activities often lead to new exports and the diversification of the economy.

Economic development does not consist of increased specialization in a few exports. That is a prescription for dependence and instability. It must be kept in mind that it is through the export industries that fluctuations in the national and international markets are imported into the local economy. Commodity price cycles, general business cycles, and long-term declines tied to technological change all threaten an economy that specializes in the export of a few products. It is the instability that goes with such specialization that explains the lack of prosperity that characterizes most of our mining, mill, or agricultural towns. Most of these specialized export centers have a run-down, decaying look to them. Because of the instability and uncertainty associated with the export markets, both individuals and business are hesitant to reinvest in these towns. As a result, despite high wage levels, these towns look anything but prosperous.

Including All of the Outside Sources of Income

The economic base model, because it tends to emphasize exports, often ignores sources of income to the community that are substantial but not tied directly to the export of a product. Consider, for instance, the income brought to an area when a person who has retired decides to settle there. The retirement income those people bring with them gets spent within the local economy in exactly the same way as the income of a mill worker. But nothing has been exported. Such "footloose" sources of income are not small in volume. As much as 40 to 50 percent of a local area's personal income may be associated with retirement income, investment earnings (dividends, rent, and interest), government income support payments, and so on (3). Whatever features of the local area attract or hold income of this sort are a major part of the local economic base even though they involve the export of no goods or services.

Retirement income is just one type that may be drawn to a community because of an area's attractive qualities. There are others. Small businesses that are relatively flexible in terms of location can follow the locational preferences of their owners. Individuals and families relocating to a preferred area are likely to spend money from savings to get established in an area. Finally, purposely mentioned last, are the expenditures of recreationists and tourists who come to a particular location because of special features of its natural or cultural environment. In thinking about the local economy from an economic base point of view, these nonexport sources of income also have to be taken into account. In almost all cases, these nonlabor income flows are several times larger than the sum of all incomes being earned in extractive industries (see Figure 14.8).

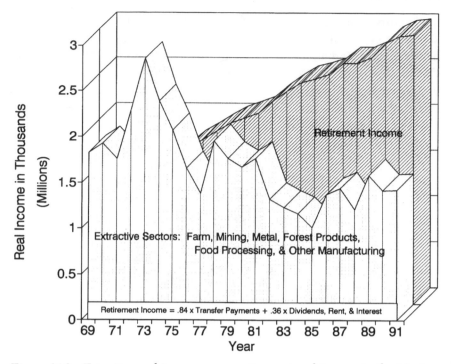

Figure 14.8   Extractive real income versus retirement real income in the Montana economy. (From Regional Economic Information System CD ROM, Bureau of Economic Analysis, U.S. Department of Commerce.)

Counter-Factual Assumptions and the Economic Base Model

The economic base model is built on a foundation of assumptions that are familiar enough to seem quite plausible and unremarkable. Unfortunately, those familiar assumptions often are contradicted by economic reality. The primary assumptions are that people have to move to where jobs are located, and that job location is dictated by fundamental facts of economic geography such as the location of a natural resource, transportation costs, and the location of markets. People must adapt their residential location to a predetermined geographic pattern of economic activity.

This view, that people go looking for work and, as a result, get distributed in a particular way across the landscape, matches many of our personal experiences with the economy. It also matches the focus of those local economic development policies that seek to recruit new businesses or retain existing ones through tax breaks and subsidies.

But these are not simple, "intuitively obvious," assumptions. Stated differently these assumptions are: (1) people do not care where they live; (2) firms do not care about labor supply. There is nothing in economic theory or economic fact to support such assumptions. Quite the contrary, we know that both of these assumptions, in general, are wrong.

Consider the second assumption, that firms do not care about the adequacy, cost, or quality of the available labor supply. This view assumes that workers will quickly relocate to wherever there are employment opportunities, and for that reason, there will always be an adequate labor supply wherever a firm chooses to locate. Clearly, historical as well as contemporary experience contradicts this view. Industry often relocates in pursuit of a cheaper labor force. The movement of the textile industry from New England to the rural South earlier in this century; the more recent shift of the meat packing industry from the Chicago area to the rural midwest; and the current concern with the migration of businesses from the northeast and north-central "frost belt" to the "sun belt" and across the border into Mexico are all dramatic examples of industries relocating in pursuit of a relatively inexpensive labor supply. In general, labor supply will operate as a powerful force in determining the geographic distribution of economic activity. Some economists have gone so far as to argue that it is primarily labor supply that determines the location of economic activity in an economy where resources are mobile (4). At the very least, the adequacy, quality, and cost of the local labor supply has a significant impact on an area's economic development.

The other assumption, that people do not care where they live and passively shift their residence to where economic activity is located, is equally unsupportable. The economic geography of the United States has been transformed during the second half of the 20th century as a result of the population acting on their preferences for particular types of living environments. How else is one to explain the suburbanization of our metropolitan areas after World War II? For the first several decades of this residential relocation, it represented a move away from both employment and commercial centers. Certainly the negative aspects of living in the central city—congestion, pollution, crime, ethnic conflict—played a role in these location decisions. So did the positive aspects of suburban and exurban living: lower density settlement; more open, parklike settings; lower levels of social conflict (5). People had definite preferences for the qualities they desired in their living environments and proceeded to act in the pursuit of those preferences.

Similar things can be said about the settlement of the desert Southwest and the "sun belt" in general. In fact, the term "amenity" was coined by a geographer in southern California to explain the postwar population boom in that area (6). The ongoing growth in the economies of many rural counties with particular landscape features, while most of nonmetropolitan America suffered through a serious depression during the 1980s, testifies to the on-going, broad-ranging impact of the pursuit of preferred living environments on the distribution of economic activity (7).

Environmental economists have spent the last several decades empirically documenting the real economic importance individuals attach to non-marketed environmental goods and services (see Chapter 13, by John Loomis) (8). These noncommercial economic environmental values are real and substantial. Because of that, one would expect pursuit of them to significantly influence the location of economic activity. And that is exactly what we observe (9).

Recognition of the elemental economic facts that people care where they live and that businesses care about labor supply can change dramatically how we look at local economic health and local economic development. Attractive qualities associated with the social and natural environments become both important determinants of local economic well-being and important sources of local economic vitality.

An Environmental View of the Local Economy

Figure 14.9 sketches out the view of the economy that emerges if one abandons the counterfactual economic assumptions built into the economic base model. It has been labeled an *environmental* view because of the importance of peoples' and businesses' preferences for living environments in determining the location of economic activity.

This alternative view recognizes that people have preferences for living environments and act to satisfy those preferences by moving to preferred social and natural environments. This creates an available supply of labor at relatively low cost because of the relative excess supply of people trying to live in those particular areas. That labor supply, in turn, attracts economic activity. In addition, those residential location decisions are also likely to inject income into the local economy as individuals expend savings and make investments as they seek to "make a living" in those particular areas. Retirement incomes also follow the residential location decisions made by retirees. The net effect on the local economy is expansionary.

Entrepreneurs seeking to remain in these areas will explore every opportunity to replace imported goods or to capture dollars that would otherwise flow out of the area by developing a more sophisticated array of locally avail-

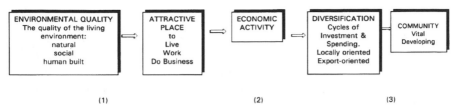

Figure 14.9   An environmental view of the economy: (1) Natural environment, recreation opportunities, cultural richness, cost of living, community/neighborhood, security, quality of public services. (2) Seeking to live and work; enhanced labor force attracts business with high quality, lower cost; retirement income. (3) Ongoing economic development.

able goods and services. Those businesses that are most successful at displacing imports and serving local needs may build on that success and begin exporting to the larger economy.

All of this allows the number of residents that the local economy can support to expand. This increases the "critical mass" of the economy and expands the range of goods and services that can be produced and marketed locally. The more sophisticated local economy reduces the isolation and the cost of inputs that might otherwise be barriers to the relocation of economic activity to the area. This allows ongoing cycles of expansion as long as the area remains a relatively attractive place to live, work, and do business. This view of the local economy is labeled the environmental view in Figure 14.9 to underline the important economic role being played by environmental quality both in determining local economic well-being and in providing vitality to the local economy (10).

Reinterpreting the Natural Resource-Dependent Community

Because the environmental model of community economic development shifts the emphasis away from exclusive focus on extractive industry, it might be interpreted as suggesting that natural resources do not matter as much to these communities any longer. But its message is quite different. It is that the role of natural resources in the local economy is not diminishing but changing from extraction and export to nonconsumptive and environmental. Economic health of communities continues to depend on the surrounding natural resources, but in a different way.

In evaluating this shift, several long-run trends have to be kept in mind (11).

· · ·

Extractive industries will be a declining source of jobs and income. Our extractive industries are mature industries in which there are ongoing opportunities to substitute technology, capital, and energy for human labor. Even if the resource base is not being depleted, the employment that can be supported by any given level of extraction will continue to decline significantly over time. In addition, most extractive industries do not operate on a sustained yield basis. They tend to "mine" their raw material on a rapid basis and then move to other areas for additional supplies. Finally, their products are traded in world markets where they compete with much poorer, more desperate nations who often can undercut American operations. For all of these reasons, the employment and income trajectory of our extractive industries is likely to be volatile but downward.

· · ·

Economic activity is shifting away from goods production toward service production. Because services tend to be produced locally, this allows a decentralization of economic activity that increases the relative self-sufficiency of local economies. This allows local economic expansion when the export base is not expanding or even when it is contracting. Employment and income growth will largely be located in these local services sectors. These are not necessarily low-wage, unskilled, "dead end" jobs. They include many of the skilled professions, such as medical, educational, and business services.

· · ·

Small-scale entrepreneurial activity is the primary source of local economic vitality. Local economic vitality is not tied to recruiting new factories to replace closed mines and mills. Local economic vitality is associated with citizens "making a living" for themselves by starting new businesses and expanding existing ones. Self-employment, small-scale enterprise, and entrepreneurial energy in general are the sources of local economic vitality. Community support for these much smaller scale local economic development efforts is far more important than business recruiting or subsidization of failing, historically important industries.

· · ·

More than exports matter. Local economic development consists of creating a web of local economic interdependencies that allow neighbors to economically "scratch each other's backs" and "take in each other's wash." These activities help trap and hold dollars in the local economy in ways that have multiple benefits. It is the *structure* of the local economy that matters, not the volume of exports of raw materials.

· · ·

Foot-loose incomes play an important role in the local economy. Incomes not derived from current local economic activity, such as retirement incomes and savings, are playing an increasingly important role in determining total local income. Attention needs to be paid as to what determines the communities into which these dollars flow.

. . .

The quality of the living environment is a primary source of local economic vitality. It is not just commercial economic activities that determine local economic vitality. Communities have to be able to attract and hold residents. Such attachment to place is closely tied to the quality of the natural and social environments. These in turn depend on a community's ability to act collectively to develop and protect the qualities associated with its educational, cultural, social, and political environments. In addition, it depends on protecting the qualities of its natural environment and the recreational opportunities that it provides. People care where they live, and because of that, a ravaged environment, no matter what the income it generates in the short run, cannot lay the basis for economic development and community survival. Extractive industry by itself does generate ghost towns. High-quality living environments prevent ghost towns.

All of these changes in the economic landscape, of course, have profound implications for the natural resource manager. A narrow focus on natural resource extraction while mitigating environmental impacts is usually considered absolutely necessary for the economic health of the community. Managers must get the timber cut out. They must permit the mine expansion. They must keep grazing at historical levels. If they fail to do these things, the traditional folk economics tells them, they will fail the communities that depend on them, and community decline will be the result.

Something almost the reverse may have already developed. The natural resource of primary economic importance to the long-run economic well-being of the community may be environmental quality, not extractive resources. If that is the case, as I think the economic data increasingly indicates, then the managers should not focus on simply trying to mitigate the worst of the environmental damage caused by extractive activities. Rather, the primary economic resource should be seen as the high-quality natural environment, and extractive activities that threaten to degrade the environment should be assumed to be incompatible with local economic stability. This of course is the reverse of what is usually said about extractive activity and resource-dependent communities, but is much closer to the truth in virtually all of the communities that I have studied. Given the local economies that have already emerged or are emerging, the traditional extractive view is dangerous to the economic health of our communities, especially if it is guiding the decisions of the resource manager. It is vitally important for resource managers to check just where it is they have their eyes focused and shift their view away from the rear-view mirror.

Notes

1. For a review of the declining role of timber harvests in the economies of the Northern Rockies, see T.M. Power. 1992. The timber employment impact of the Northern Rockies ecosystem protection act, four volumes on Montana, Idaho, Eastern Washington and Oregon, and Northwestern Wyoming. Missoula, Montana: Alliance for the Wild Rockies.
2. As with the income data for the Butte-Anaconda, Montana, area unemployment compensation and other emergency income maintenance payments have been removed from the personal income data.
3. The most convenient data source on these nonlabor income flows into local economies (county basis) is the Regional Economic Information Service (CD ROM) of the Bureau of Economic Analysis, U.S. Department of Commerce. This provides annual information on transfer payments including various types of federally supervised retirement income. It also provides data on the sum of rents, interests, and dividend income by county.
4. Borts, G.H., and J.L. Stein. 1962. Economic growth in a free market. New York: Columbia University Press.
5. See D.F. Bradford and H.H. Kelejian. 1973. An economic model of the flight to the suburbs. Journal of political economy 81(3):566–589.
6. E. Ullman. 1954. Amenities as a factor in regional growth. Geographic Review 44:119–132.
7. K. Deavers. 1989. The reversal of the rural renaissance: a recent historical perspective. Entrepreneurial Economy Review September/October, 3–5.
8. For a summary discussion of the economic value of environmental amenities also see chapters 4, 5 and the references in my earlier book: T.M. Power. 1988. The economic pursuit of quality. New York: M.E. Sharpe Publishers.
9. For an earlier theoretical development of this point, see T.M. Power. 1980. The economic values of the quality of life. Boulder, Colorado: Westview Press. For a discussion of the inadequate development of the connection between environmental economics and local economic development see U.S. Forest Service. 1992. The economic value of wilderness: the view from the local economy. In The economic value of wilderness. Southeast Forest Experiment Station, General Technical Report SE-78. Asheville, North Carolina.
10. For a more complete discussion of this way of viewing the determinants of the economic distribution of economic activity, see T.M. Power. 1992. Sense of place and local economic vitality: the view from the rural West.

1992 Regional Science Association International 39th North American Meetings. Also see G. Rudzitis and H.E. Johansen. 1989. Amenities, migration, and nonmetropolitan regional development, a report to the National Science Foundation, Department of Geography, University of Idaho. For more technical theoretical development of this perspective, see J. Roeback. 1982. Wages, rents, and the quality of life. Journal of Political Economy December, 1257–1278.

11. Empirical support for these general trends as they have been manifested in particular regions can be found in, for instance, my earlier work: T.M. Power. 1992. Ecosystem preservation and the economy of the greater Yellowstone area. Conservation Biology 5:3; T.M. Power. 1992. The timber employment impact of the Northern Rockies ecosystem protection act in Montana, Idaho, Eastern Washington and Oregon, and Northwestern Wyoming, four volumes and an executive summary. Missoula, Montana: Alliance for the Wild Rockies; T.M. Power. 1991. Wildland preservation and the economy of Utah. Utah 2000 Project, State of Utah: reprinted in Southern Utah Wilderness Alliance Newsletter; T.M. Power. 1991. An alternative view of the Idaho economy. Idaho's Economy. Boise: Boise State University; T.M. Power. 1992. Extractive industry and economic performance in the Northern Rockies. In Proceedings of the Pacific Northwest regional economic conference. Seattle, Washington: Northwest Policy Center.

PART III

The Future

THE FINAL PART LOOKS TO THE FUTURE of natural resources management. Here, we traverse "new ecology," "new education," "new ethics," "new economics," and other new approaches to managing our environment. Whereas the activities and phenomena described in earlier parts have already happened and are happening, this part offers approaches and ideas that may be critical ingredients in the upheaval of the status quo that dominated the latter half of the 20th century.

To an ecologist, perhaps the single most important requirement for effective natural resources management is the scientific viewpoint, or paradigm, that one holds. In this part's introductory chapter, Pickett and Ostfeld describe an ecological world view quite different from the one that prevailed earlier and, they explain, one that was largely responsible for a variety of the resource management failures already discussed in this book. The classical model of ecology is captured in the phrase "the balance of nature," while the emerging theme is expressed as "the flux of nature." The traditional belief was that nature was primarily closed, self-regulating, subject to a single stable endpoint, and that disturbances and humans were largely excluded from the list of normal ecological factors. The new paradigm counters that ecosystems are open, largely subject to the effects of disturbance, equilibrium end points are rare, and humans play pivotal roles in how ecosystems are shaped. The historical reliance on the "balance of nature" led many resource agencies to believe in a similar concept, "nature knows best." Indeed, for some resource agencies, such as the National Park Service, confidence in this view fed the illusion that within park boundaries the best policy was just to let nature take its course. Today, we realize the danger of this assumption. Boundaries are not closed, external factors can play significant roles in shaping what occurs within a park, and humans, intentionally or otherwise, are one of the most significant elements in ecosystems. Pickett and Ostfeld conclude with the recognition that the new model has much to offer resource management in the next century. Indeed, the elements inherent in the phrase "the flux of nature" are the critical factors in "ecosystem management," the concept that federal land management agencies have embraced.

If the overarching ecological paradigm is changing, then it is not surprising that the approaches and tools to natural resource management should be going through a metamorphosis as well. Chapter 16, by Knight and George, offers stark contrast to the traditional methods of natural resource management spelled out by Anderson in the book's first part (Chapter 3). While resource managers traditionally focused on single species, in the future they will be working with ecological processes and landscape features to impact many species simultaneously. The scientific discipline that best captures the new approaches and tools to natural resource management is the field of conservation biology. Conservation biology is concerned with both understanding and preserving biological diversity, and embraces elements from such diverse fields as landscape ecology, ecosystem science, restoration ecology, population biology, community ecology, and population genetics. Knight and George suggest three general approaches to managing for biological diversity, each focusing on a different element: species, ecological processes, and landscape features. Strengths and weaknesses of each approach are discussed and the authors suggest that any effective management program will incorporate elements of each. After examining these new approaches to natural resource management, Knight and George then briefly introduce a number of new tools, ranging from genetic analyses to computer modeling. Whether the scale of interest be genes, species, communities, or landscapes, a rapidly growing arsenal of resources is available to managers that wish to face the increased complexities of resource management.

Perhaps the most obvious response to the information presented in Chapter 16 is that the natural resource manager of the 21st century will require a different sort of education. Historically, resource managers were educated within a specialized discipline that did not prepare them to deal with the realities of resource issues. In response to this need, Susan Jacobson (Chapter 17) develops a new approach to educate our future natural resources managers. She describes an educational curriculum that falls within the breadth offered by the discipline of conservation biology. Buttressing her belief that conservation biology is the correct educational approach to natural resource management, Jacobson criticizes the commodity-orientations of traditional resource educations that revolved around game species, timber, and grass production. Because conservation biology is a blend of theory and application, Jacobson believes a curriculum with this discipline as its core will better prepare students to manage for whole ecosystems and landscapes. In addition to disciplinary depth and cross-disciplinary breadth, the new natural resource curriculum needs to emphasize exposure to the social sciences and human dimensions. Increasingly, solutions to resource challenges go beyond the ecological expertise necessary to understand them. Today and in the future, the resource manager must have been educated in using social science information to design education programs to affect people's beliefs and motivations toward the environment. This exposure to information not present in most natural resource curricula needs to be supplemented with courses in political science, economics, and education in order to work effectively within the context of human institutions. Jacobson asserts that "Understanding resource policies and how they are formed is a prerequisite for improving how natural resources will be managed, who will manage them, and who or what will benefit when the policies are implemented." She concludes with the assertion that only integrative, cross-disciplinary programs within our universities can provide these educational opportunities.

Emphasizing the importance of social values raised in Chapter 17, James Kennedy and Jack Ward Thomas, in Chapter 18, offer a model that emphasizes that natural resource management is largely one of managing social values. In criticizing university curricula, they observe that "Many young natural resources graduates are disappointed and frustrated to discover that being an effective professional and public servant is ultimately a social endeavor." Kennedy and Thomas argue "that a professional orientation of managing natural resources as social value is not inconsistent with a biocentric perspective and is a more valid, comprehensive, and evolutionary management paradigm than focusing primarily on the physical or biological resources—much as we cherish them." Their model consists of four interrelated parts: the natural environmental system, the social system, the economic system, and the political system. Natural resource values originate in the social system and are expressed through the economic, social, and political systems. The environmental system itself does not originate or express natural resource social values. Kennedy and Thomas are not denigrating the importance of resource managers to be technically competent; instead they are advocating that "resource managers should be better able to understand and cope with the multitude of environmental social values by viewing their role as accommodating and participating in evolving American value systems."

Perhaps it is not surprising, given that the traditional economics of natural resources has been largely synonymous with commodity uses, that a new form of economics would arise. Robert Costanza (Chapter 19) introduces "ecological economics," a type of economics that integrates ecosystems and economic systems. Ecological economics differs from both

conventional economics and ecology in that it attaches greater importance
to the interactions between the two. It differs from traditional economics in
that it places greater importance on sustainability than on growth and substitutability; it differs from conventional ecology in that humans are perceived as being much more important, particularly in terms of their cultural
evolutionary capacity. Cultural evolution is a unique and critical component
in that "The price human cultures pay for their ability to adapt rapidly is that
of becoming too dependent on quick solutions and, therefore, ignoring
long-term answers and issues of sustainability." Because ecological economics places such importance on sustainability, it differs radically from
economics-as-usual with its emphasis on short-term growth and private interests. Ecological systems support life on earth and form the basis for all
economic activity. To the degree that ecological systems are functioning,
they provide excellent models of sustainable systems. Because of this, ecological economics derives much of its inspiration from nature. For example,
"there is no 'pollution' in climax ecosystems—all waste and by-products are
recycled or harmlessly dissipated. This implies that a characteristic of sustainable economic systems should be a similar 'closing the cycle' by finding
economic uses and recycling 'pollution,' rather than simply storing it, exporting it, diluting it, or changing its state." The concept of sustainability is
central to ecological economics because economic growth is not sustainable. Because sustainability is "the amount of consumption that can be continued indefinitely without degrading capital stocks" it forces humans to
consider the condition of natural capital (soil, forests). Today we inhabit a
world where the limiting factors are no longer human-made capital, but instead are natural capital. In Costanza's words, "Timber is limited by remaining forests, not sawmill capacity; fish catch is limited by fish populations, not by the number of fishing boats; crude oil is limited by remaining
petroleum deposits, not by pumping and drilling capacity." A potentially
grave error can occur when we believe that natural capital is substitutable
for human-made capital. If ecosystems are not sustainable, we may soon
discover that by damaging our life-support systems, we have constrained future options for our species and that of others.

In the book's penultimate chapter, Holmes Rolston sketches an environmental ethic that goes beyond duties to endangered species to include ethical responsibilities of humans to the earth. Historically, we have held certain feelings for species, either for what they do for us, or for what we feel
toward them. Rolston presents a comprehensive ethic, enveloping species
within ecosystems and discussing our relationship with these broader entities. "Species increase their kinds; but ecosystems increase kinds." Rolston
believes we are in a post-evolutionary era where cultural selection, not nat-

ural selection, drives our species. Because human culture, coupled with its accompanying technologies, is so pervasive today we live on a managed planet. Therefore, humans have to accept the responsibilities of environmental steward, and discard their more traditional role as subjugator. Rolston observes that in most human-nature encounters, humans win and have come to think they should always win. But, he thinks "humans ought not invariably be the winners. They should constrain their behavior for the good of plants and animals." Rolston thinks that human-nature encounters need not always be adversarial. There can also be win–win encounters where humans and nature nourish each other in a sustainable relationship. In developing an environmental ethic that is truly global, natural resources must be viewed on a spatial scale that transcends national boundaries. Resources are unevenly distributed around the globe and economies that depend on these resources are also highly disparate. "On global scales, if the controlling interest is national sovereignty, gross national product, and welfare alone, we may be prevented from the ethics we need by the fallacy of misplaced community." Rolston asks, if humans are indeed global managers, then is this the end to nature? Rolston notes the genius of humans but places more credence in the unappreciated "genius" in nature. After all, he notes, humans came out of nature. In the end, he believes that only by entering into a mutual relationship with planet Earth will we be able to have a sustainable relationship with the one entity capable of truly nourishing us, both spiritually and physically.

Our book ends with a personal essay by Edward Grumbine, titled "Three Bear Stories: Toward a Sustainable Resource Management Future." By relating his encounters with bears on three separate occasions, Grumbine develops insights on resource management that leave the traditional way of doing things far behind. Bears are a useful metaphor, as they symbolize the sometimes heavy hand of human-the-manager as well as emerging perspectives of citizens who view bears as symbols of how best to manage ecosystems. Grumbine sees these as diverging viewpoints in our relationship with the natural world. In one, the view is of humans above and controlling nature, while in the other, humans are responsible stewards showing respect and accepting responsibility for unthinking nature. Grumbine presents five conservation goals he believes are necessary to accommodate this latter approach to the natural world: concern for diversity of native species; concern for ecosystem types; the ecological processes that sustain this diversity; the ability for the evolutionary potential of this diversity to be expressed; and the opportunities for humans to use resources in a sustainable way. Yet Grumbine believes there is more required of wise stewardship. "Conservation biology may not be much different from multiple-use sustained yield if

we forget that, though science can census grizzly bears, dusky seaside sparrows, and Siskiyou cypresses, and recommend appropriate habitat protection plans, it cannot make final decisions. That is the job for humans who
value one set of goals and outcomes over another." So, in concluding
Chapter 21 and completing our book, Grumbine leaves us with a broad
theme that runs through the center of these 21 essays. Humans must assume their responsibilities of earth steward, and this can only be done by developing values which, while keeping us at the center of things, make us feel
duties to the health and welfare of this planet, which has sustained us
through our evolutionary history and is today burdened by the weight of our
cultural growth.

Chapter 15

The Shifting Paradigm in Ecology

S. T. A. Pickett and Richard S. Ostfeld

> To the ecological mind, balance of nature has merits and also defects. Its
> merits are that it conceives of a collective total, that it imputes some
> utility to all species, and that it implies oscillations when balance is dis-
> turbed. Its defects are that there is only one point at which balance occurs
> and that balance is normally static.
> —Aldo Leopold
> *The River of the Mother of God and Other Essays*

This chapter summarizes how the science of ecology has changed over the
last few decades, and explores the implications of those changes for natural resource managers. The changes we describe are the most general
ones a science can exhibit: changes in its paradigm. A paradigm is the
viewpoint a science takes of the world, which consists of the often unspoken
background assumptions of the science, and the way the science approaches
and answers questions. These two components are often summarized as a
world view or belief system, and the exemplars for problem solving.
Because a paradigm is so broad in scope, it is an excellent way to encapsu-
late the more detailed changes in data, techniques, and theories that a science might experience.

We use the synthetic tool of the paradigm to suggest the management
implications of some of the vast changes that ecology has undergone. Many
of these changes reinforce changes in management strategy already being
practiced, while others invite continued evaluation of management goals
and techniques.

We first present elements of the classical paradigm in ecology. We then
indicate the implications of the classical paradigm for resource management. The failings of the classical strategy are indicated in general terms.
The relationship of the classical paradigm and management to the everyday
metaphor of "the balance of nature" will be explored. Because the classical
paradigm has failed, we outline the new paradigm in ecology, and point out
its significance for management. Along the way, we describe a metaphor,
the "flux of nature," which is consistent with the new paradigm, and discuss
important cautions that managers must practice when employing the new

paradigm and its common sense label. The new paradigm calls for new kinds of management, such as process management, ecosystem management, or adaptive management. But it also calls for a firm ecological foundation, and a broad and careful vision in its application.

The Classical Paradigm in Ecology

The classical ecological paradigm comprises six key points that form a network of closely related background assumptions (1). Historically, ecological systems were considered to be primarily closed, self-regulating, and subject to a single stable equilibrium. Furthermore, any changes in communities or ecosystems through time were thought to occur by successions that must always pass through the same phases. Any disturbances that might affect natural systems were considered to be exceptional events, and humans were excluded from the roster of normal ecological factors. What does each of these points mean in real ecological systems? Before giving examples, we must emphasize that the points refer to a whole array of ecological units and entities, including individuals, populations, communities, landscapes, and ecosystems. Throughout this chapter, the term *system* is used to mean any of these units of ecological interest.

Considering ecological systems to be closed means that the important structures and interactions occur within the boundaries set for studying them. Even under this assumption, of course, thermodynamics calls for energetic openness of ecological systems, and ecologists have uniformly recognized external physical constraints or inputs imposed on ecological systems by climate. Thus, assuming ecological systems to be closed is paradigmatic only when applied to the local factors that ecologists invoke to explain the mechanistic workings of their objects of study. For example, the nutrient capital of an ecosystem would be derived from weathering of the local bedrock or parent material; and the organisms involved in important mutualisms would be local residents only.

The paradigmatic assumption that ecological systems are self-regulating follows, in part, from the assumption that systems are closed. If systems are indeed self-contained, then they must be internally regulated if they are to persist. For example, the local cycling of nutrients would govern productivity; within-community interactions would account for species coexistence; internal interactions within populations would regulate the density of the population.

Classically, ecologists focused on single, stable equilibria as the defining points of reference for their systems. But such end points were taken as much more than useful abstract points of reference. They were for a long time considered concrete states that must exist in nature. Such a focus on equilibrium points limits the explanatory mechanisms that can be applied to answer ecological questions. Examples of equilibrium points include the single "climax" state for a community on a coarse scale, the fixed carrying capacity of a population and the saturation number of species fixed by resource partitioning in a community.

When the classical paradigm allowed change in ecological systems, it was by fixed pathways. For example, successions were deterministic in that they required that invading plants appear before later stages; overshoot of a population from its carrying capacity would necessarily decline again to that level, perhaps with orderly fluctuation around that constant; community membership would be reproduced after a perturbation.

Disturbance was thought to be an exceptional occurrence under the classical ecological paradigm. This meant that the primary goal of ecological studies could be the understanding of undisturbed systems. As a result, ecologists emphasized pristine and apparently "natural" systems. Alternatively, they could focus on the return of systems from a disturbed state to the single point of equilibrium. Ecologists largely ignored such systems that were burned or blown down, populations apparently not regulated internally, managed landscapes, and organisms living beyond their usual ranges.

Humans were not considered by ecologists to be part of the classical paradigm because humans violated, either accidentally or intentionally, many of the other assumptions of that paradigm. Humans were often purposely left out of ecology because they introduced multiple states to systems, acted as disturbance agents, transported materials and organisms beyond their usual distributions, acted as external regulators of ecological systems, and prevented orderly, deterministic successions.

Relationship to Resource Management

The classical paradigm has clear parallels in classical management. Not all resource managers have accepted all of these assumptions, however, as there have always been independent and visionary practitioners (2). Indeed, rejection of these assumptions is increasingly seen in the management of natural areas. Laying out the assumptions in their bald form, as we do here, almost immediately illuminates their barrenness.

SYSTEMS AS CLOSED

If managers accept this assumption, they would consider any unit of the natural world to be manageable as a separate entity. National parks would be cordoned off, toxic waste sites would be mitigated as isolates, an endangered species could be saved as an entity.

Systems as self-regulating

The internal dynamics of natural resource systems would adjust to environmental changes. Such systems could simply be left alone if they were self-regulating. For example, a mammal population would be regulated by internal behavioral and reproductive feedbacks to maintain a relatively stable density through time. Likewise, a species distributed patchily throughout a landscape would maintain its density and distribution by adjusting rates of immigration and emigration among patches. Therefore, the dominant ingredient in management of many systems would be benign neglect.

Equilibrium as a point

Systems possess a single point at which their composition or function is in equilibrium with the environment. The implication is that ecological systems are at or close to equilibrium. For example, there is a single stable state for vegetation set by a particular climate, soil, elevation, and exposure. Likewise, the "carrying capacity" for a population is a fixed constant. If a single stable point equilibrium is the dominant kind of stability in nature, then managers can simply observe how nature is at any one time, and do whatever is necessary to maintain that state. A second bias about equilibria found in the classical paradigm is that they were the most desirable state of nature (3). These assumptions about equilibria as fixed points link with the previous one to underwrite management by benign neglect.

Succession as fixed

This assumption suggests that systems subjected to a disturbance will recover their previous state through an obligatory succession. Managers may usefully help the rate of succession along, but the pattern of states through time is fixed, and it inexorably leads to the expected end point, which was often assumed to be the most desirable state of the system. For example, although the post-agricultural succession in tallgrass prairie was long considered to be the necessary sequence of annual weeds, annual grasses, bunch grasses, and climax prairie, that sequence is not often found (4).

Disturbance as exceptional

If disturbance, the disruption by a sudden event of the structure, resource availability, or environmental controls of a system, is seen as very uncommon or restricted in space, then managers could make and execute their plans without taking it into account. This assumption would lead managers to be unprepared for disturbance when it finally did occur. The assumption could even lead them to attempt to prevent or to compensate inappropriately for the effects of disturbance that should in fact be a part of the system. For example, the assumption that fire did not belong in presumably equilibrium systems led to its exclusion from management strategies in many systems. A related error is made by those who believe that a large patch of windthrown trees in a moist, broadleaved forest is an unfortunate scar rather than an event that is part of the dynamics of such forests.

HUMANS EXCLUDED

The assumption that humans are not a component of systems to be managed could lead to management plans that neglected historic or contemporary human influences on a particular system. If such influences were actually important structuring variables in the system, the management strategy would be flawed (5). For example, forgetting the effect of Native Americans on vegetation and animal communities could result in neglecting important ecological controls on systems. Neglecting human effects is unfortunately easy, because many such effects are subtle, or originate at a distance from the site of interest.

In pointing out the general ways in which the assumptions of the classical paradigm could translate into management decisions, we have suggested how they can fail. In idealizing and simplifying the ecological world, the tenets of the classical paradigm have blinded ecologists and managers to critical factors and events that can govern systems. The assumptions have also caused scientists and managers to neglect important dynamical pathways and states, and to disregard important connections among different systems (6).

Balance of Nature and the Classical Paradigm

While it would be unwise to either blame or credit ecology for too much of the practice of natural resource management, at the very least, it is clear that the two areas have shared many of the same assumptions in the past. This situation may reflect the cultural origins of some of the largest assumptions any science makes. Ecology and resource management may both have adopted certain key components of their classical outlooks from the larger society (7). Such a situation is suggested by the pervasiveness and apparently comfortable acceptance of the idea of the "balance of nature."

The balance of nature is a poorly articulated idea that is a cultural metaphor rather than an exact scientific concept. The metaphor implies that natural systems exhibit tight control and adjustment to an equilibrium state. It has extremely deep historical roots (8), is held in high esteem, and often is misused as an apparently unassailable bastion in discussion. Because the idea is not scientific, it is unclear just what its assumptions are, where and when it might apply, what mechanisms might lead to it, and how one might test it.

Yet the balance-of-nature metaphor can stand for some valid scientific ideas. The fundamental truth about the natural world that the idea may relate to is the fact that natural systems persist, and they do so by differential response of various components. The idea also points toward the ecological principle that there are limitations in natural systems. No component of a natural ecological system, at whatever level of organization, grows without limit. Furthermore, the idea also indicates the frequently observed trends of ecological systems toward equilibrium states, given a specified environment and a sufficiently long time. Examples are density-dependent processes (i.e., the tendency of populations to grow when small and shrink when large) and the existence of successional trajectories by which communities tend to approach a stable "climax" state. All these principles are powerful ecological generalizations. But, ecologists themselves have sometimes relied on the venerable, yet vague, metaphor of the balance of nature to represent these principles in a public dialogue about conservation and management. This is inappropriate for two reasons.

First, the balance-of-nature metaphor has serious limitations even as a vessel for valid ecological generalizations. It can lull people into accepting equilibrium points as persistent, and into assuming that trajectories toward presumed equilibrium will necessarily succeed. Second, the metaphor has been closely associated with the classical paradigm in ecology, with its emphasis on equilibrium, containment, regulation, and so on. This is a serious liability now that the basic assumptions of the classical paradigm in ecology have failed. The failure of the classical paradigm is most cogently indicated by how rarely a stable equilibrium point is actually achieved (9). Constraints on equilibrium-seeking tendencies are common and effective, as illustrated by the burgeoning study of natural disturbance (10). The examples of the six assumptions of the classical paradigm we gave earlier in the chapter indicate the pervasive problems with them. We elaborate the failings and replacement paradigm below.

The Flux of Nature and a New Paradigm

The pitfalls of the classical paradigm calls for a new paradigm in ecology. The nonequilibrium paradigm can be connoted in the metaphor, the "flux of nature" (11). The term *flux* highlights variation, fluidity, and change in natural systems, rather than stasis, which is implied by the term *balance*. Although this metaphor does not deny the existence of stable points in nature, it focuses our attention on the fact that natural systems, which certainly do persist, do so as a result of a variety of fluxes. These include not only the obvious exchanges of energy and matter that are the currencies for trophic relationships of species, but also fluxes that range from the relative migration of various phenotypes and genotypes, through the shifts of dominance within communities, to the movements of patch types in landscapes. Many other kinds of fluxes could be cited. Some may exhibit equilibrium distributions while others may exhibit erratic or steady trajectories.

The new paradigm also must accommodate the contradiction of the six background assumptions of the classical paradigm. Ecological systems are never closed, but rather experience inputs such as light, water, nutrients, pollution, migrating genotypes, and migrating species. Note that the novel emphasis of the modern paradigm is not that ecological systems are self-regulating, but rather experience important limits from external sources. For example, successional rates can be controlled by herbivores from adjacent communities, and populations can rely on mutualists that reside elsewhere. Stable point equilibria are rare, although some systems of sufficient size and duration may exhibit stable frequency distributions of states. For example, a landscape may be a shifting mosaic of patches or community types, and in some cases, the number of young and old communities can remain constant, even though specific spots change as a result of disturbance and succession. Successions are rarely deterministic, but are affected by specific histories, local seed-sources, herbivores, predators, and diseases. Disturbance is a common component of ecological systems, even though some sorts of disturbance are not frequent on the scale of human lifetimes. Indeed, many biotic interactions have the same sort of impacts as physical disturbances, like wind and fire, in altering species composition, interaction between species, and availability of resources in systems. And finally, landscapes that have not experienced important human influences have been the exception for hundreds if not thousands of years (12).

These points together constitute the contemporary paradigm in ecology. In a sense, this contradicts the classical paradigm, since it shows that the classical background assumptions are not necessarily true. But although the classical assumptions are not universally true, on certain temporal or spatial scales and under certain conditions, those assumptions may apply. For example, equilibrium states can be a special case under the new paradigm. The new paradigm does not deny the empirical existence or theoretical utility of equilibrium states as special cases or points of reference, but it does not assume that equilibria are the dominant or controlling states in the real world.

So far, we have treated the new paradigm as both a contradiction of the old and an expansion containing the good points of the classical paradigm. To completely appreciate the new paradigm, we must examine several other modern tools for understanding the natural world.

The entities that ecologists study are parts of networks. This, of course, emphasizes the openness of systems, and the potential that regulation resides outside the system of interest. For example, changes in populations other than the one an ecologist is trying to understand may change or constrain its density (13). Interacting populations may be inconspicuous, such as parasitic lung worms relative to their elk hosts. Or the interacting populations can live separately from the focal population for a time. For instance, the butterflies whose larvae attack passion flower vines rely as adults on the flowers of cucumber vines that live in entirely different habitats (14). Changes in number of a prey population may result from asynchronous changes in the dynamics of a predator population that indirectly affects its numbers (15). Similarly, there may be lags between the time a population receives a signal from other populations, and the time when it responds reproductively or behaviorally (16). Finally, internal changes in the population of interest, whether genetic or phenotypic, may affect how that population responds to other populations and physical signals (17). In a sense, for the population level of organization, the general message is that population ecology must in fact be community ecology (18).

In studying networks or communities in ecology, relating change and stability become important tasks. Pimm (19) has defined four kinds of change in networks. Resilience is the rate of recovery to a specified former state. Persistence is the period over which a state exists before a new state is reached. Resistance is the change in a variable following change in interacting variables. For example, an ecological community is resistant if its species composition changes little after the invasion of an exotic species. Finally, variability is the degree of change over time. Variability indicates that fluctuations are accounted for in Pimm's (20) conceptual system.

The new paradigm recognizes that understanding and working with ecological systems depends on their spatial and temporal extent relative to the extent and duration of processes and structures in those systems. *Scale* is the term used to describe the relationships between two measurements such as extent over which a process occurs and spatial extent of a system. Scaling determines what is internal or external to the system. Whether some event is considered a disturbance or not, what is considered normal variation, what is considered self-regulation, and in fact whether the system is in equilibrium, all depend on the scale the system takes. At some scales, events that are considered external disturbances become incorporated into the system. For example, observing biomass of a prairie over a few years detects a fire as a disturbance to the biomass value. In contrast, observing species composition of that same prairie over decades accommodates a regime of fires as a regular part of the system (21). The contemporary paradigm equips us to deal with the structure and function of systems regardless of what scale they are observed on, and whether that scale incorporates all disturbances or regulatory factors within the system. Of course, the lives of both scientists and managers become simpler if we are assigned complete systems that internalize all important factors and exist at scales over which equilibrium can be attained. But neither the natural world nor administrators are usually so kind.

A final spur to adopt the new paradigm is the growing awareness of chaos (22). Chaos technically refers to system behavior that seems totally unpredictable and random, but is driven by strictly necessary (deterministic) relationships without any random elements. Although exactly how chaos might be expressed in ecological systems, and whether our data sets are long or detailed enough to allow that detection are open questions (23), the possibility of chaos in ecology casts further doubt on the utility of the equilibrium paradigm with its focus on linear, deterministic relationships (24).

Opportunities for New Management Strategies

We have already outlined some of the ways traditional management approaches have been limited by the classical ecological paradigm. Assuming systems to be closed and self-regulating, and to possess a stable point equilibrium reached by deterministic successions after rare disturbance events unaffected by humans, has reinforced a particular philosophy of management. Additional kinds of limitations have grown out of this classical paradigm. Management has been limited by its focus on individual components versus management of systems (25).

Here we want to emphasize the organizational implications of the term *system*. A system is any collection of entities linked by functional relationships. Managing an individual entity may neglect important relationships or contexts that are in fact critical to the persistence of the focal entity. Management of commodities, for example, may neglect the remainder of the system, especially inconspicuous or infrequent interactions, on which the commodity depends. Managing an individual population, such as a fishery, is also an example. Modeling specific fisheries as isolated populations has often failed to predict the collapse of the stock. While obvious requirements such as habitat and food may be provided for, the structuring of the population by historical events, or its periodic control by fluctuations in mutualists or consumers may be harder to detect without an explicit system approach. For example, the decline in the black-footed ferret resulted from both a decline in availability of its main prey (prairie dogs) and the introduction of canine distemper resulting from close proximity to humans and their pets. An additional danger of focusing on isolates of systems is that desirable attributes of the entire system may be damaged in the effort to optimize a single entity (26). This has been the case with isolated guilds, such as edge-requiring wildlife, which have been managed to the detriment of more sensitive forest-interior species (27). The increase in white-tailed deer and the brown-headed cowbird are examples of untoward results of management of a single guild or species. Deer inhibit forest regeneration, while the parasitic cowbirds reduce the nesting success of forest interior birds.

The contemporary paradigm suggests that the fluctuations in the natural world are not simply oddities and dismissable excursions from nature's "real" state. Rather, fluctuations in the form of physical disturbances, climate shifts, population cycles, range shifts and the like are significant normal parts of the real world. Management cannot proceed as though such fluctuations did not occur or were not important. Managers must proceed as though fluctuations mattered.

Fortunately, just as we are now in a scientific window of opportunity for developing and applying new management strategies, we may well be in a social window as well. There are enough well-publicized and debated cases of the failure of classical management, or of the failure of policy that did not account for the flux of nature, that the time may be ripe for establishing a new foundation for management. Management within a world of open systems that are subject to internal and externally driven fluxes can be labeled "ecosystem management" or "process management." Whatever it is called, and whether its focus is on some spatial unit or on some dynamic process, management must be able to adapt to natural change.

Fortunately, there is an emerging framework for the accommodation of natural flux, that of adaptive management (28). Under this strategy, the goals of the management plan are articulated using an explicit model of the system that should encompass the components, interactions, and likely fluctuations. Then, appropriate techniques are applied to the system, the results are monitored, and the tactics or even the goals are modified according to what is learned from the response of the system. In other words, management can, like science, be used to test hypotheses. The difference is that in testing management hypotheses, the purpose of the management can be changed if it is found to be unrealistic, ineffective, or counter to the persistence of the system (29).

For example, the management by neglect practiced in many old-growth oak forests has been found to permit those forests to change composition and structure in undesirable ways. Many are shifting to a predominance of maples with a concomitant decline in understory diversity. One major way in which adaptive management can be useful is in refining the basic model of the system. The failure of a management strategy may indicate that the model of the system is incomplete, perhaps because it does not incorporate some important flux or connection that actually functions in the system. Because conceptual models of systems, whether they be production landscapes or nature reserves, are always tentative, such a strategy is important to adopt widely.

Process Management and Its Constraints

We have said that management for maintaining processes that structure the system of interest is especially appropriate to the new paradigm in ecology. The processes include the relationships to environmental resources and regulators, interactions among populations, and system dynamics or succession over time. However, the concept of "process" should not be taken too narrowly. A narrow meaning might focus solely on biogeochemical flows without concern for the diversity of biological entities that interact with biogeochemical transformations. Ecosystem models are often reduced to such a form, consisting of boxes for the pools of chemicals and arrows showing the chemical transformations within the ecosystem. However, ecosystem scientists recognize the community and population context of the biogeochemical pools and transformations encapsulated in such an abstract model (30).

But we must recognize additional kinds of processes in management. A complete framework for processes of concern in management would include the following: (1) disturbance regimes; (2) movement of materials, energy, and organisms; (3) succession; and (4) species interactions. It may be necessary to prioritize processes and manage to optimize certain ones, depending on the goals. However, even if only one or a few processes are to be optimized, their relationships to other processes must be known in order to avoid management surprises.

A disturbance regime is the spatial and temporal pattern of disturbance in some area. It consists of the agents, intensities, sizes, distributions, and frequencies of disturbances that affect a system. The term *disturbance regime* does not mean that the identity, temporal, or spatial patterns of disturbance are fixed and regular, only that such distributions can be characterized and understood as system attributes. They can be modified and compensated for by management.

Movement of materials and entities is a second focus of process management. The things moving can be either abiotic or biotic. Abiotic fluxes include the familiar ecosystem fluxes of energy and nutrients. In human-modified landscapes, which is beginning to mean most of the Earth, the materials would also include pollutants and plumes of thermally altered air and water, which can interact with natural ecosystems, communities, and populations.

Biotic fluxes include the movement of organisms. The specific processes include natural dispersal, migration, and the transport of exotics. But biotic fluxes also involve larger scales. Shifting mosaics of communities in landscapes is an example of a coarse-scale biotic flux (31).

One of the most universal of ecological processes is succession, the change in community composition or structure through time. Succession must therefore be a concept in the toolkits of all managers (32). It is driven by characteristics of sites determined by natural or human disturbances, by the differential availability of organisms, and by the differential performance of organisms at those sites. Managing a system without information on its successional status or rate is risky, and is likely to produce unexpected results (33).

Species interactions are among the most well-known interactions that must be managed. Although interactions are often labeled by their "net effect" on the populations involved, such that competition is a joint negative effect and mutualism is a joint positive effect, it is important to know just how such interactions proceed. This is because there can be hidden, indirect chains of effects, or interactions mediated by third parties. Thus, competition between two species may be only "apparent" (34), and the outcome driven instead by the stimulatory effects of one of the species in the "competitive pair" on an enemy of the second. Voles and shrews are affected by the same predators, and change in one of the prey species may cause the predator to change its impact on the other prey (35). If just the small mammals are studied, the dynamic would appear as competition. Indirect effects such as apparent competition appear to be legion in natural communities.

How does a process approach to management relate to "ecosystem management"? In reality they can be considered the same thing, because a good management plan will be based on a comprehensive model of an ecosystem. The model will indicate the spatial extent of interest, the inputs and outputs of resources and populations, and the direct and indirect interactions of populations, as well as the interactions between the populations and the physical substrate and fluids in the ecosystem. So ecosystem management must include the processes that occur within that ecosystem and which connect it with others. The phrase *ecosystem management* is valuable because of the spatial implications of the term *ecosystem*. Ecosystem management reminds us to consider the landscape or regional connections of the situation to be managed (36). And the metaphor, flux of nature, is a reminder that the nature of the system and its context can both change through time, sometimes episodically.

Caveats for Using the Flux of Nature

The metaphor, the flux of nature, is a powerful tool for communicating the new ecological paradigm. It reminds us that the basic substance of nature, the networks of species interacting with one another and exchanging matter and energy with their surroundings, do persist over long periods. But the persistence is the result of dynamism and flux on different scales (37). The assemblages of species change in identity with evolution on the long term, and with natural disturbance and succession on the short term. The assemblages shift in local composition and architecture on the local scale, while the arrangement of patterns in landscapes shift under disturbance regimes and climate change. The richness that evolution has produced is a response to the opportunities produced by disturbance, natural extinction, climate shifts, and the arrival of new immigrants. On a more local scale, even though the time frame may be long for an individual human life, the fall of a mature tree in an old-growth forest generates opportunities for establishment, growth, or reproduction of species that had been excluded from or suppressed on the forest floor. Various animals, microbes, and plants may use the new site, while others avoid it. But over the long term and large areas, the variety of opportunities, resources, and environmental signals is answered by a richness of organisms. That is the beauty of the flux of nature. Most spasms of nature become opportunities, and if the accidents of evolution and history have made organisms available, then they will appear to fill the stage. Subsequent changes in the environment, the species pool, or the nature of interactions may occur. They are all part of the flux of nature, none more intrinsically desirable than another. This is the shifting stage and shifting play that ecologists must understand and managers must deal with.

For all its scientific intrigue and poetic beauty, the flux of nature is a dangerous metaphor. The metaphor and the underlying ecological paradigm may suggest to the thoughtless or the greedy that since flux is a fundamental part of the natural world, any human-caused flux is justifiable. Such an inference is wrong because the flux in the natural world has severe limits.

Knowing what these limits of natural flux are is a critical step in management. In general terms, these limits are functional, historical, and evolutionary. Functional limits are the physiological constraints that organisms operate under. For example, certain molecules cannot be detoxified, leaves must remain open to pollutants if they are to take up CO_2 for photosynthesis, and high temperatures denature proteins. Such limits cannot be overcome due to the mechanics and chemistry of cells and organs. An anthropogenic flux outside those limits is an insult to natural flux.

Historical limits are those that result from the suites of species that have become established through time at a site, the accumulation of resources and organic matter, and the kinds and patterns of disturbances that have operated there over time. For example, if the disturbance regime of a site has not included massive stand-opening events that leave the roots and soil intact, then there are not likely to be species present that can respond rapidly to a novel anthropogenic disturbance of that type.

Evolutionary limits are imposed by the amount of genetic variation available for selection to act on, the intensity of selection, and the time over which selection may have acted. Evolution is also constrained by the physical structures elaborated in the past. If human-induced changes reduce the capacity of lineages to evolve by reducing genetic variation, elevating levels of gene flow, or altering population mating structures, then their effect on the flux of nature will be damaging, perhaps permanently.

Problematic human changes or fluxes are those that are beyond the limits of physiology to tolerate, history to be prepared for, or evolution to react to. Two characteristics of a human-induced flux would suggest that it would be excessive: fast rate and large spatial extent. Natural systems respond to, even exploit flux, if the rates of flux are within the capacity of physiology to adjust, new assemblages to accumulate, and evolution to generate new diversity. Where rates of human-generated flux exceed the natural rates of response, policy makers and managers should be alerted that undesired changes may result. Managers may be in a position to compensate for inappropriate rates of human-caused changes.

The second problem of current human-generated flux is its great spatial extent. Natural flux takes space for the shifting mosaics of landscapes, the sources of genetic novelty, and the refuges from disturbance, predation, and disease. Human-generated flux that subtracts from the area available for natural flux must be carefully evaluated and compensated for.

Conclusion

We have examined the paradigm shift that has been taking place in ecology over the past several decades. The classical paradigm, the equilibrium world view of the discipline, assumed that ecological systems were closed, self-regulating, possessed of single equilibrium points reached by deterministic dynamics, rarely disturbed naturally, and separate from humans. Classical management strategies were cast as though they followed these same assumptions. However, the failures of management reflecting this paradigm became apparent, and along with the accumulation of new data and scales of observation in ecology, contributed to the demise of the classical, or equilibrium, paradigm. With the demise of the equilibrium paradigm, the inappropriateness of the formerly comfortable metaphor of the balance of nature became apparent.

A new ecological paradigm has emerged that recognizes ecological systems to be open, regulated by events arising outside of their boundaries, lacking or prevented from attaining a stable point equilibrium, affected by natural disturbance, and incorporating humans and their effects. A new metaphor of the flux of nature symbolizes the new, or nonequilibrium, paradigm effectively. The new paradigm suggests that the management approaches being developed are much more appropriate to the variability, contingency, and openness of ecological systems. The intimate linkage of opportunity and response that is embedded within the flux of nature takes long times and large spaces to work. Ecosystem management, carried out in an adaptive way in which management plans are viewed as hypotheses based on inclusive models of the systems to be managed, is likely to exploit the contemporary understanding of ecological systems.

Neither process nor ecosystem management should be considered to mean that nutrient or energy flows should be managed without attention to the biodiversity with which they interact. In addition, management for the flux of nature must respect the physiological, historical, and evolutionary limits inherent in natural systems if management is to be successful and sustainable.

Acknowledgments

We thank Dan Binkley and Rick Knight for reviews that improved the structure and clarity of our presentation. This is a contribution to the program of the Institute of Ecosystem Studies with partial support from the Mary Flagler Cary Charitable Trust.

Notes

1. Pickett, S.T.A., and P.S. White. 1985. The ecology of natural disturbance and patch dynamics. Orlando, Florida: Academic Press.

2. Holt, S.J., and L.M. Talbot. 1978. New principles for the conservation of wild living resources. Louisville, Kentucky: Wildlife Society.

3. Jefferson, R.G., and M.B. Usher. 1986. Ecological succession and the evaluation of non-climax communities. In Wildlife conservation evaluation. M.B. Usher, ed. 69–91. London, England: Chapman and Hall.

4. Collins, S.L., and D.E. Adams. 1983. Succession in grasslands: thirty-two years of change in a central Oklahoma tallgrass prairie. Vegetation 51:181–190.

5. Wagner, F.H., and C.E. Kay. 1993. "Natural" or "healthy" ecosystems: are U.S. national parks providing them? In Humans as components of ecosystems: the ecology of subtle human effects and populated areas. M.J. McDonnell and S.T.A. Pickett, eds. 257–270. New York: Springer-Verlag.

6. Botkin, D.B. 1990. Discordant harmonies: a new ecology for the twenty-first century. New York: Oxford University Press.

7. Oelschlaeger, M. 1991. The idea of wilderness from prehistory to the age of ecology. New Haven, Connecticut: Yale University Press.

8. Egerton, F.N. 1973. Changing concepts of the balance of nature. Quarterly Review of Biology 48:322–350.

9. Botkin 1990 (6).

10. Pickett and White 1985 (1).

11. Pickett, S.T.A., V.T. Parker, and P. Fiedler. 1992. The new paradigm in ecology: Implications for conservation biology above the species level. In Conservation biology: the theory and practice of nature conservation, preservation, and management. P. Fiedler and S. Jain, eds. 65–88. New York: Chapman and Hall.

12. McDonnell, M.J., and S.T.A. Pickett, eds. 1993. Humans as components of ecosystems: the ecology of subtle human effects and populated areas. New York: Springer-Verlag.

13. Pimm, S.L. 1991. The balance of nature? Ecological issues in the conservation of species and communities. Chicago, Illinois: University of Chicago Press.

14. Gilbert, L.E. 1980. Food web organization and the conservation of neotropical diversity. In Conservation biology: an evolutionary-ecological perspective. M.E. Soule and B.A. Wilcox, eds. 11–33. Sunderland, Massachusetts: Sinauer Associates.

15. Hansson L., and H. Henttonen. 1988. Rodent dynamics as community processes. Trends in Ecology and Evolution 3:195–200.

16. Hanski, I., P. Turchin, E. Korpimäki, and H. Henttonen. 1993. Population oscillations of boreal rodents: regulation by mustelid predators leads to chaos. Nature 364:232–235.

17. Ostfeld, R.S., C.D. Canham, and S.R. Pugh. 1993. Intrinsic density dependent regulation of vole populations, Nature 366:259–261.
18. Pimm 1991 (13).
19. Pimm 1991 (13).
20. Pimm 1991 (13).
21. Allen, T.F.H., and E.P. Wyleto. 1983. A hierarchical model for the complexity of plant communities. Journal of Theoretical Biology 101:529–540.
22. Schaffer, W.M., and M. Kot. 1985. Nearly one-dimensional dynamics in a simple epidemic. Journal of Theoretical Biology 112:403–427.
23. Sugihara, G., and R.M. May. 1990. Nonlinear forecasting as a way of distinguishing chaos from measurement error in time series. Nature 344:734–741.
24. Allen, J.C., W.M. Schaffer, and D. Rosko. 1993. Chaos reduces species extinction by amplifying local population noise. Nature 364:229–232.
25. Franklin, J.F. 1993 Preserving biodiversity: species ecosystems, or landscapes Ecological Applications 3:202–205.
26. Committee on Scientific and Technical Criteria for Federal Acquisition of Lands for Conservation. 1993. Setting priorities for land conservation. Washington, D.C.: National Research Council.
27. Harris, L.D. 1988. Edge effects and conservation of biotic diversity. Conservation Biology 2:330–332.
28. Barrett, G.W. 1985. A problem-solving approach to resource management. BioScience 35:423–427; Schroeder, R.L., and M.E. Keller. 1990. Setting objectives: a prerequisite of ecosystem management. In Ecosystem management: rare species and significant habitats. R.S. Mitchell, C.J. Sheviak, and D.J. Leopold, eds. 1–4. Albany, New York: New York State Museum.
29. Irwin, L.L., and T.B. Wigley. 1993. Toward an experimental basis for protecting forest wildlife. Ecological Applications 3:213–217.
30. Jones, C.G., and J.H. Lawton. 1995. Linking species and ecosystems. New York: Chapman and Hall.
31. Pickett and White 1985 (1)
32. Niering, W.A. 1987. Vegetation dynamics (succession and climax) in relation to plant community management. Conservation Biology 1:287–295.
33. Luken, J.O. 1990. Directing ecological succession. New York: Chapman and Hall.
34. Holt, R.D. 1977. Predation, apparent competition and the structure of prey communities, Theoretical Population Biology 12:197–229.
35. Hansson and Henttonen 1988 (15)

36. Risser, P.G. 1985. Toward a holistic management perspective. Bio-
    Science 35:414–418.
37. Allen, T.F.H., and T.W. Hoekstra. 1992. Toward a unified ecology. New
    York: Columbia University Press.

Chapter 16

New Approaches, New Tools: Conservation Biology

Richard L. Knight and T. Luke George

A thing is right when it tends to preserve the integrity, stability, and beauty of the biotic community. It is not when it tends otherwise.
—Aldo Leopold
A Sand County Almanac

Aldo Leopold, who is credited with developing the discipline of wildlife management and who articulated the concept of the land ethic, most certainly had sustainable ecosystems in mind when he penned these words. Landscapes that would allow people and wildlife to coexist in harmony were among Leopold's principal motivations for studying and attempting to understand the complexities of the "land organism" (1). A half-century after he penned these words, land managers are revisiting this arena and confronting the difficulties with managing ecosystems sustainably (2). Indeed, one reason for the disarray natural resource disciplines find themselves in today is the widespread public belief that the disciplines do not champion good land stewardship.

Chapters in the first part of this book clearly indicate the traditional approaches and motivations that drove the development of natural resource disciplines. Resources were viewed as inexhaustible and useful only to the degree they could be exploited (3). When resources declined locally, commodity users either moved on or began to develop management approaches that would result in species recovery. Eventually, all of these extractive users and uses of natural resources developed into sciences with accompanying professional organizations and university curricula. Even though university departments and scientific organizations grew and prospered, they still largely focused on teaching and conducting research on wildlife for game, trees for lumber, and grass for cattle.

New Approaches

Grumbine, in his widely acclaimed book *Ghost Bears: Exploring the Biodiversity Crisis* (4), argued that two things were necessary for managing sustainable ecosystems, a new set of ethics and a new set of scientific standards. Environmental ethics for the new century are being addressed by Holmes Rolston (5) and his colleagues, and the new scientific standards have been the focus of an innovative discipline, conservation biology (6). It is our goal here to present some new approaches and new tools that are available for managing natural resources into the next century. The underlying themes for these emerging approaches are the concepts of sustainability and the maintenance of biological diversity. These approaches are the antithesis of single-species, commodity utilization that characterized the early years of natural resource disciplines.

There are three categories into which most species fall. First, some species are specifically managed for sport or commercial harvest (e.g., big game, Douglas-fir). Second, some species are experiencing population declines. By their very designation, these species are presently unsustainable. The list of species with declining populations is growing far faster than any organized effort to deal with it (7). The third category includes organisms that fall within neither the commercial species nor endangered species designations. Concern for these species has generated interest in the maintenance of biological diversity and its resulting metadiscipline of conservation biology (8).

The goal of managing exploited species is to produce a sustainable surplus that can be cropped indefinitely, whereas the goal of managing imperiled species is to recover the population's viability. A goal of managing species communities is to "maintain or preserve the status of these species as members of the community of an area. Status is usually evaluated by the relative abundance of the species within the community" (9).

Natural resource management had its origins in the overexploitation of economically valuable populations. The resultant declines of many temperate bird and mammal species from indiscriminate slaughter necessitated the creation of state and federal agencies with specific mandates of recovering game species and producing sustainable harvests for sportsmen. The successes of these agencies are among the great conservation accomplishments of the 20th century and were based on the theory of sustained-yield harvest (10).

During the past several decades increasing attention has focused on species experiencing population declines. A general approach used to recover declining populations was to manipulate the species in such a way that the population increased and approached carrying capacity. A species threatened with extinction is best managed close to carrying capacity so as to minimize the harmful effects of low population size (e.g., loss of genetic diversity, skewed sex ratios).

The final category, maintenance of biological diversity, comprises the vast majority of organisms, yet has received the least attention. This may be due to the absence of any economic importance attributed to this category, although nature viewers and pharmaceutical firms would be among those quick to dispute that assertion. It may also be due to the seemingly impossible task of managing simultaneously for so many species. Managers are comfortable with the idea of manipulating single species; however, until recently, they have been largely unfamiliar with approaches to managing species assemblages (11). Indeed, the attempt of land managers to identify "indicator species," "keystone species," "umbrella species," or "guild-indicator species" demonstrates their reluctance to abandon the single-species paradigm. Ecological hierarchy theory (12) predicts that higher levels of organization (e.g., communities) constrain and control lower levels (e.g., species). Thus, to understand and manage species, it is necessary to understand factors occurring at higher levels.

When managing for species communities, three principal approaches may be employed: (1) a species approach, (2) an ecosystem approach, and (3) a landscape approach. The species approach concentrates on demographic variables such as birth and death rates, and ecological concepts such as predation and parasitism. For example, this approach might attempt to increase productivity of a community of songbirds by controlling brown-headed cowbird populations in order to reduce nest parasitism. Other examples would be to maintain viable populations of keystone species, such as prairie dogs or Pacific salmon, on which a large array of other species either directly or indirectly depend.

A problem with the single species approach is that it focuses on one or a few species and, unless it is firmly embedded in management at the landscape level, will exhaust the resources of management organizations.

The second approach takes an ecosystem perspective and draws on ecosystem science for its inspiration. Natural resource managers taking this approach focus on ecosystem processes (e.g., tree gap formation, insect diseases, fire). This approach assumes that if ecosystems are properly functioning, then the naturally occurring biological diversity will be intact.

A drawback to the ecosystem approach is that ecosystem function can become more important than species composition. Accordingly, the actual identity of a species is not as important as its functional role in the community (e.g., decomposer, consumer). An exotic species, if it performs the same function as a native species (e.g., pollinator), is no worse than the equivalent native species (13).

A third way to manage for biological diversity is a landscape approach and relies on the principles generated from the discipline of landscape ecology. This strategy manipulates habitat and landscapes in such a way as to collectively influence groups of species in the desired direction. For example, to maintain songbird communities of late successional stage forests, agencies would want to manage forest stands for large size and decreasing edge and isolation.

Landscape and stand characteristics that will influence species communities include: stand size, stand shape, connectivity of stands, amounts and distribution of vegetative successional stages, the distribution and densities of various habitat patches, and surrounding land types and uses. These landscapes will have to be viewed at different spatial scales, which will necessitate management with two basic components (14). First, the patches themselves will have to be managed so as to maintain or simulate internal dynamics of natural systems. These internal dynamics include such diverse natural disturbances as fire, insect/plant disease epidemics, energy flow, and nutrient cycling. Second, there will have to be management focusing on factors external to the patches but that influence internal patch dynamics. These include such things as logging, road building, pollution, urbanization, spread of exotics, and alterations of water regimes.

For larger fragments, emphasis should be placed on the internal dynamics; for smaller fragments, emphasis should concentrate on the external influences. External factors (e.g., acid rain, climate change), however, can be important regardless of the remnant size.

Since most impacts on habitat fragments originate from the surrounding landscape, there is clearly a need to depart from traditional notions of management and look instead toward integrated landscape management (15). Traditional natural resource management stopped at the reserve boundary; fluxes of water, pollutants, and organisms do not. Placing the conservation reserves firmly within the context of the surrounding landscape and attempting to develop complementary management strategies seems to be the only way to ensure the long-term viability of native biological diversity.

Problems associated with a landscape approach include the difficulty in acquiring enough protected areas to be effective in managing at spatial and temporal scales that ensure the maintenance of species communities. In addition, parks and reserves are traditionally protected for their recreational or aesthetic purposes; not because of their productivity or unique vegetation types. Also, there are fundamental difficulties for integrating management that crosses artificial administrative boundaries.

A sequence of steps that could be modified by land managers faced with the dilemma of managing landscapes for biological diversity is presented in Table 16.1. This strategy incorporates aspects of the ecosystem and landscape approaches.

A Conflict in Single-Species and Species Community Management

A dilemma of considerable import when managing species one at a time is that this strategy will inevitably result in management that contradicts other management. For example, wildlife management has tended to simplify communities by managing for a handful of harvested species. If managing for sustained yield harvest of ungulates, what happens if the process of getting there entails altering populations of predators, competitors, diseases, or

Table 16.1

Steps for Managing for Species Communities

Step 1	Set clear objectives (e.g., ;maximizing diversity of native species, minimizing the number of species that fall below minimum populations).
Step 2	Associate species communities with specific habitat configurations. This approach uses environmental suitability (vegetation structure, geomorphology, primary productivity, climate) as a surrogate for species demography.
Step 3	Determine the minimum subsets of habitat fragments that are required to represent the diversity of a given area. Need to know the distribution of species and ecosystem types.
Step 4	Assess the potential sensitivity of groups of species to landscape change. This may be based on the life-history strategies of the species, or on the amount and distribution of suitable habitats.
Step 5	Formulate specific questions based on overall objectives and integration of existing information.
Step 6	Choose "ecological indicators" at appropriate scales.
Step 7	Design and implement a monitoring scheme with appropriate statistical protocol.
Step 8	Manage system to meet the predetermined objectives. Management will have to be ongoing and a monitoring system should be devised to measure responses of habitats and species.

Sources: Modified from Hansen et al. 1991 (32), Saunders et al. 1991 (14).

parasites; or landscape patterns that might alter the amount of edge or connectivity? Following this, if the management practices are successful, what happens after the population increases and we begin to see alterations in ecological communities. For example, browsing by white-tailed deer can profoundly affect the abundance and population structure of several woody and herbaceous plant species (16).

Instead of accentuating the differences between single-species and multiple-species management, agreement and harmony should be sought. What is needed is a synthetic approach rather than the existing dualism. For example, the Hawaiian Islands have an inordinate number of endangered species. We need to focus on particular aspects of each of these species' life histories in order to recover them while at the same time taking an ecosystem and landscape approach to ensure the integrity of the life-support systems. It is useful to remember that one way of describing an ecosystem is to measure its productivity; another is by counting the number of species it supports.

New Tools

The change in emphasis in natural resource management from single species and commodity extraction to the maintenance of biological diversity has necessitated the use of a variety of new techniques and tools. Most of these "new tools" have been borrowed from other disciplines as resource managers find themselves facing questions that cannot be addressed using traditional tactics. Here we summarize some of these tools and discuss how they may be applied to current problems facing resource managers.

To provide a framework for discussing these new techniques, it is necessary to define the levels and attributes of biological diversity. Biological diversity is commonly measured at four levels: genetic, population, community, and landscape. Within each of these levels of diversity, three attributes may be measured: composition, structure, and function (17). Composition is the simple enumeration of the number of elements at a particular level. For example, the number of different alleles at a particular chromosomal locus, the number of species in a community, or the number of vegetation types in a landscape are examples of composition measures at different levels. Structure refers to the physical or spatial arrangement of elements within a particular level. At the landscape scale this includes attributes such as patch size and connectivity, while at the genetic level this would include measures of genetic diversity and changes in allelic frequencies from one location to another. Measures of structural diversity can generally be computed from composition data if spatial information is collected at the same time. Functional aspects of diversity refer to the ecological and evolutionary processes such as gene flow, demographic parameters, and large-scale disturbances that influence the dynamics of biological diversity over space and time. Measuring all of these attributes of diversity at each level necessitates using a variety of methods. Noss (18) provides an excellent overview of current techniques that are available for measuring diversity at various scales. These approaches are discussed in brief below.

Genetics

A variety of methods have been developed to assess genetic diversity. Gel electrophoresis and karyotyping are commonly used to assess genetic variation within populations. In addition, a number of techniques are now available to measure variation in the nucleotide sequences of nuclear and mitochondrial DNA. The appropriate technique depends on the question being addressed and the amount of variation that is present in the species or taxon being considered. Lande and Barrowclough (19) provide an excellent review of appropriate techniques.

Structural measures of genetic diversity can generally be computed from compositional data along with information on the physical location and identity of the individuals from which the genetic data were collected. Functional measures such as inbreeding depression, gene flow, and selection intensity are much more difficult to measure and require studies of allelic frequencies and associated fitness parameters.

Populations

Despite the emphasis on multispecies management as a new approach to resource management, population biology will remain a major focus of many conservation projects. The tools for estimating population parameters such as population size, age structure, age-specific fecundity and survival, and sex ratio have a rich history in the wildlife profession. Krebs (20) provides an excellent overview of the methods that have been developed to estimate these variables. Although the tools for estimating population parameters are well known, it is only recently that structural features of populations such as metapopulation (a collection of subpopulations connected through dispersal) dynamics and dispersal have been examined. Telemetry studies using radio and now satellite transmitters have made it feasible to gather data on the distribution and movement of individuals over large areas. These studies combined with population models that incorporate spatial effects suggest that the physical arrangement of populations and habitat across the landscape can have profound consequences on the persistence and dynamics of populations (21).

Functional considerations of diversity at the population level have focused on the factors that influence the persistence of populations. The study of these factors has spawned a new subdiscipline within conservation biology called Population Viability Analysis (PVA) (22). The objective of PVA is to estimate the probability that a population will go extinct in a particular period given a set of initial conditions and predicted future conditions.

Island biogeography theory provided the catalyst for the first theoretical treatments of extinction of small populations. The first models focused on random birth–death processes and predicted long persistence times for small populations (above approximately 20 individuals) (23). Subsequent models demonstrated that environmental variation may greatly reduce population persistence (24). Catastrophe theory applied to population viability analysis emphasized the vulnerability of populations to large environmental variations and the need to "spread the risk" among different subpopulations (25). Many of the current theoretical treatments have focused on the effects of the spatial arrangement of suitable habitat on the persistence of populations. These spatial models suggest that the size and arrangement of suitable habitat patches in the landscape can have profound consequences on population persistence (26).

Making predictions about the viability of natural populations is a challenging problem. To help managers make decisions about the potential effects of different management approaches on population persistence, a number of computer programs have been developed that estimate population trajectories. RAMAS SPACE® (27) and VORTEX® (28) are two such packages that allow the user to simulate population persistence while varying different parameters. Although both of these programs allow the user to manipulate a variety of variables, they cannot mimic the complexity of real populations. In addition, like all models these are based on assumptions that can greatly affect the results. For instance, neither of these programs includes a negative feedback between genetic factors and demographic parameters that can potentially cause a population to spiral to extinction (29). The application of these models is also limited by the lack of demographic data for most species. Thus, while these tools may increase our general understanding of the factors that affect extinction, they must be used with caution.

Communities

Biodiversity is most commonly measured at the community level and is generally computed from field surveys of particular taxonomic groups. Richness (number of species) can be computed from simple presence–absence surveys while measures of evenness (relative abundance) and diversity (both richness and evenness) require some measure of the number of individuals of each species in a community. Krebs (30) provides a good overview of the various diversity measures and how to compute them.

One problem with using diversity indices as a goal in resource management is that the identity of the species is not considered in the equations. For instance, in conservation terms, an area with a large number of "weedy" species may be less desirable than an area with a few local or rare species. However, naive measures of diversity may rank the former site higher than the latter. Because of these kinds of problems, some ecologists have cautioned against using local species diversity as a goal of conservation efforts (31). More useful indices may be obtained by focusing on a particular group of interest. For example, the richness or diversity of old growth-dependent species in an area has been suggested as a management index for forest landscapes in the Pacific Northwest (32).

Structural and functional diversity can be more difficult to estimate directly. Noss (33) suggests that habitat patterns can be used to infer the distribution of species across an area. The adequacy of this approach of course depends on the accuracy of the wildlife habitat models that are used. Even though there is considerable debate about the accuracy of many wildlife habitat models (34) this approach at least provides hypotheses that can be refined as more accurate models are developed. The functional aspects of communities include factors such as predation, competition, and abiotic factors that may influence the species composition of communities. Although difficult to estimate, these factors provide insight into community dynamics.

Landscapes

The landscape is the largest spatial unit that is usually inventoried. Most approaches focus on mapping the distribution of vegetation communities over a large area such as a watershed or an administratively defined management unit. The large area involved in landscape studies often necessitates the use of aerial photography or satellite imagery to inventory at this scale. Aerial photography is the traditional approach that has been used to map vegetation over large scales. The drawback to this approach is that it is time consuming and somewhat subjective. Satellite imagery holds promise for mapping vegetation over large areas relatively inexpensively. However, it is often impossible to distinguish vegetation types in sufficient detail to produce maps that are useful to ecologists. In addition, without ground verification, misclassification may diminish the usefulness of the results.

Geographic Information Systems (GIS) hold great promise for studying structural aspects of communities. Landscape patterns such as patch size, edge/area ratios, connectivity, and contiguity may have profound effects on the persistence of populations within landscapes (35). Once a spatial inventory of habitats and physical features has been compiled, these attributes can be quantified using a GIS. Managers can also use GIS to examine the impact of alternative management options on landscape patterns. Thus, inventorying and mapping the vegetation and placing this information on a GIS should be considered a high priority for resource managers.

Functional aspects of landscapes include large-scale disturbances such as fire, landslides, climate variation, and human-induced changes as well as more predictable responses such as succession and nutrient flow. Natural disturbances are often unpredictable, making it difficult to determine where and when they will occur. However, once a disturbance has occurred, the subsequent successional changes in the vegetation are often very predictable. There already have been a number of attempts to combine succession models with wildlife-habitat models to predict long-term changes in wildlife communities across a landscape (36). Although this approach holds great promise, a number of difficulties must be overcome before these models can provide reliable predictions for wildlife managers (37).

Use of Models

Natural resource policy decisions involve very complex living systems for which managers frequently do not have the data necessary to make decisions. Thus models permit problem solving that would be too large and too expensive for experimental approaches. Although models can reduce the uncertainty of the consequences of management decisions, decision makers seem all too eager to embrace poorly tested, poorly analyzed models.

Modeling has been used for a variety of purposes by managers; however, the chief function has been to examine how populations change in size. This is a reflection back to the life table approach in population estimation (38). By using natality, mortality, and population age structure, wildlife biologists looked at population growth rates and made determinations about how environmental variables affected population size. Initially, models for endangered species were very much like those for exploited species in that they were deterministic and yielded useful insights on the relative importance of birth and death rates (39).

In the ensuing years alternative approaches were developed. For example, the U.S. Fish and Wildlife Service produced Habitat Suitability Index models that assessed the sensitivity of wildlife to habitat perturbations (40). Population viability analysis and metapopulation models are now being used for species experiencing population declines (41). Population viability analysis is useful when managing small populations sensitive to stochastic phenomena such as loss of genetic diversity and catastrophic events (42). The metapopulation concept is equally applicable to harvested species and is the first attempt to formally integrate landscape ecology into the dynamics of a species' population (43).

Most recently, in attempts to understand the effects of landscape-level changes on populations, spatially explicit models are being developed and implemented. As with most models, parameter estimation and reliability present substantial challenges, and the danger of natural resource managers viewing model output as reality can lead to disastrous results.

The final frontier for modelers will focus on community models that capture the interrelatedness among species. Although there have been only a few attempts at community modeling, the ones available have provided useful insights into how landscape configurations can influence species assemblages (44).

Measures of Success

Indicators of sustainable populations and communities are necessary to evaluate progress toward meeting management goals. For single-species populations, measurements that are necessary include changes in population sizes or densities, birth and death rates, and dispersal patterns. Specifically, for harvested species, managers need to monitor changes in harvest rates, as well as changes in age and sex ratios. For endangered species, indicators of sustainability include such things as species reaching the minimum viable population estimates or a species being delisted.

Measurements of sustainable species communities may fall within either a species approach or an ecosystem/landscape approach. The use of particular species as surrogates to monitor the health of communities found early popularity (45); however, it has recently received considerable criticism

(46). There are two inherent assumptions when using indicator species as representative of biological diversity. First is the assumption that the indicator species is an appropriate agent for a larger suite of species of interest, and that a change in the indicator species' population is reflective of widespread habitat-environmental changes. Second is the supposition that a change in the population of the indicator species can be used to predict environmental variables that are responsible for these changes (47). These assumptions fail on both conceptual and empirical grounds (48).

Alternatives do exist, however, for taking a species approach to monitor communities. For instance, a useful index might be ratios that reflect the number of species going extinct over the number of species extant, the number of species being listed or delisted as endangered over the number of species extant, or an index comprising the total number of native species divided by the total number of species (both native and exotic) found in an area of concern (49).

A landscape approach might include monitoring changes in land-use patterns (e.g., percent of forest being converted to farmland); changes in patch characteristics and landscape mosaics (distributions of patch sizes, connectivity, shape, etc.), or ratios reflecting the amount of an area of interest that is in a natural or disturbed condition. Ecosystem approaches could be measurements of human resources necessary to maintain functioning ecosystems, or incidences of ecosystem processes such as tree-gap formation, fire, or disease outbreaks. Regardless of the approaches used, it is essential to monitor biological diversity at all levels (50).

The Challenge

How does a society shift from a resource management paradigm that focuses on single species, to a paradigm where land stewards strive to ". . . preserve the integrity, stability, and beauty of the *"biotic community"*? This is clearly more than just a scientific dilemma, although natural resource managers are experimenting with new approaches and technologies. This challenge embraces the diverse and complex fabrics and colors of our society as a whole. Diverse publics find it easy to support efforts to save a whooping crane or grizzly bear, for here one can easily see the results of concerted efforts. The publics are not near as facile, however, with ecosystem and landscape approaches. Size, shape, and connectivity of habitat patches, or natural fire regimes or forest gap formation are neither easily understood nor easily appreciated by a largely ecologically semiliterate citizenry. Other than the overwhelmingly important goal of increasing citizen ecological literacy, we would suggest a possible answer to this impasse. Scientists need to increasingly stress the values of ecosystem functions to society as a whole. When discussing the wealth of benefits we accrue from watershed management, flood control, soil formation and the decrease in soil erosion, the proper balance of atmospheric gases, or the full spectrum of biological diversity, land stewards need to emphasize that these values are only fully realized when ecosystems are healthy. Once a society understands that ecosystem processes are more basic to an ecosystem than elements (read "species"), that the processes create and ensure the maintenance of the elements, then perhaps we will truly begin to manage for sustainable biological diversity.

Notes

1. Meine, C. 1988. Aldo Leopold. His life and work. Madison, Wisconsin: University of Wisconsin Press.
2. Kessler and Salwasser, this volume.
3. Anderson, this volume.
4. Grumbine, R.E. 1992. Ghost bears: exploring the biodiversity crisis. Washington, D.C.: Island Press.
5. Rolston, this volume.
6. Soulé, M.E., and B.A. Wilcox, eds. 1980. Conservation biology: an evolutionary-ecological perspective. Sunderland, Massachusetts: Sinauer Associates.
7. Gibbons, A. 1992. Mission impossible: saving all endangered species. Science 256:1386.
8. Temple, S.A., E.G. Bolen, M.E. Soulé, P.F. Brussard, H. Salwasser, and J.G. Teer. 1988. What's so new about conservation biology? Transactions North American Natural Resources Conference 53:609–612.
9. Temple, S.A. 1986. Ecological principles of wildlife management. In Management of nongame wildlife in the Midwest: a developing art. J.B. Hale, L.B. Best, and R.L. Clawson, eds. 11–21. 47th Midwest Fish and Wildlife Conference. Grand Rapids, Michigan.
10. United States Department of the Interior. 1987. Restoring America's wildlife: 1937–1987. USFWS. 394 pp.
11. Noss R.F. and L.D. Harris 1986. Nodes, networks, and MUMs: preserving diversity at all scales. Environmental Management 10:299–309.
12. Allen, T.F.H., and T.B. Starr. 1982. Hierarchy: perspectives for ecological complexity. Chicago, Illinois: University of Chicago Press.

13. Lugo, A.E. 1992. More on exotic species. Conservation Biology 6:6.

14. Saunders, D.A., R.J. Hobbs, and C.R. Margules. 1991. Biological consequences of ecosystem fragmentation: a review. Conservation Biology 5:18–32.

15. Pickett and Ostfeld, this volume.

16. Anderson, R.C., and O.L. Loucks. 1979. White-tail deer (*Odocoileus virginianus*) influence on the structure and composition of *Tsuga canadensis* forests. Journal of Applied Ecology 16:855–861.

    Alverson, W.S., D.M. Waller, and S.I. Solheim. 1988. Forests too deer: edge effects in northern Wisconsin. Conservation Biology 2:348–358.

17. Franklin, J.F., K. Cromack, W. Denison, et al. 1981. Ecological characteristics of old-growth Douglas-fir forests. USDA Forest Service General Technical Report PNW-118. Portland, Oregon: Pacific Northwest Forest Range Experiment Station.

18. Noss, R.F. 1990. Indicators for monitoring biodiversity: a hierarchical approach. Conservation Biology 4:355–364.

19. Lande, R., and G.P. Barrowclough. 1987. Effective population size, genetic variation and their use in population management. In Viable populations for conservation. M.E. Soulé, ed. 87–123. Cambridge, England: Cambridge University Press.

20. Krebs, C.J. 1989. Ecological methodology. New York: Harper Collins.

21. McKelvery, K., B.R. Noon, and R.H. Lamberson. 1992. Conservation planning for species occupying fragmented landscapes: the case of the northern spotted owl. In Interaction and global change. P.M. Kareiva, J.G. Kingsolver, and R.B. Huey, eds. 424–450. Sunderland, Massachusetts: Sinauer Associates.

22. Soulé, M.E., ed. 1987. Viable populations for conservation. Cambridge, England: Cambridge University Press.

23. MacArthur, R.H. 1972. Geographical ecology. Princeton, New Jersey: Princeton University Press; Goodman, D. 1987. The demography of chance extinction. In Viable populations for conservation. M.E. Soulé, ed. 11–34. Cambridge, England: Cambridge University Press.

24. Goodman 1987 (23)

25. Ewens, W.J., P.J. Brockwell, J.M. Gani, and S.I. Resnick. 1987. Minimum viable population size in the presence of catastrophes. In Viable populations for conservation. M.E. Soulé, ed. 59–68. Cambridge, England: Cambridge University Press.

26. Lande, R. 1988. Demographic models of the northern spotted owl (*Strix occidentalis caurina*). Oecologia 75:601–607.

Doak, D. 1989. Spotted owls and old-growth logging in the Pacific Northwest. Conservation Biology 3:389–396.

Ginzberg, L.R., S. Ferson, and H.R. Akcakaya. 1990. Reconstructibility of density dependence and the conservative assessment of extinction risks. Conservation Biology 4:63–70.

27. Ginzberg, et al. 1990 (26)

28. Lacy, R.C., and T. Kreeger. 1992. VORTEX users manual: a stochastic simulation of the extinction process. Chicago, Illinois: Chicago Zoological Society. 31 pp.

29. Gilpin, M.E., and M.E. Soulé. 1986. Minimum viable populations: processes of species extinction. In Conservation biology: the science of scarcity and diversity. M.E. Soulé, ed. 19–34. Sunderland, Massachusetts: Sinauer Associates.

30. Krebs 1989 (20).

31. Noss, R.F. 1987. Do we really want diversity? Whole Earth Review (summer):126–128.

32. Hansen, A.J., S.L. Garman, B. Marks, and D.L. Urban. 1993. An approach for managing vertebrate diversity across multiple-use landscapes. Ecological Applications 3:481–496.

33. Noss 1990 (18).

34. Laymon, S.A., and R.H. Barrett. 1986. Developing and testing habitat-capability models: pitfalls and recommendations. In Wildlife 2000: modeling habitat relationships of terrestrial vertebrates. J. Verner, M.L. Morrison, and C.J. Ralph, eds. 87–92. Madison, Wisconsin: University of Wisconsin Press.

35. Harris, L.D. 1984. The fragmented forest: island biogeography theory and the preservation of biotic diversity. Chicago, Illinois: University of Chicago Press.

36. Christensen, N.L., and L.S. Davis. 1986. Introduction: linking wildlife models with models of vegetation succession. In Wildlife 2000: modeling habitat relationships of terrestrial vertebrates. J. Verner, M.L. Morrison, and C.J. Ralph, eds. 337. Madison, Wisconsin: University of Wisconsin Press.

37. Mayer, K.E. 1986. Summary: linking wildlife models with models of vegetation succession—the manager's viewpoint. In Wildlife 2000: modeling habitat relationships of terrestrial vertebrates. J. Verner, M.L. Morrison, and C.J. Ralph, eds. 411–413. Madison, Wisconsin: University of Wisconsin Press.

Sweeney, J.M. 1986. Summary: linking wildlife models with models of vegetation succession—the researcher's viewpoint. In Wildlife 2000:

modeling habitat relationships of terrestrial vertebrates. J. Verner, M.L. Morrison, and C.J. Ralph, eds. 415–416. Madison, Wisconsin: University of Wisconsin Press.

38. Caughley, G. 1977. Analysis of vertebrate populations. New York: John Wiley and Sons.

39. Grier, J.W. 1980. Modeling approaches to bald eagle population dynamics. Wildlife Society Bulletin 8:316–322.

40. Schroeder, R. 1986. Habitat suitability index models: wildlife species richness in shelterbelts. U.S. Fish Wildlife Service FWS/OBS-82/10.28. 17 pp.

    Van Horne, B., and J.A. Wiens. 1991. Forest bird habitat suitability models and the development of general habitat models. U.S. Fish Wildlife Service, Fish Wildlife Research 8, 31 pp.

41. Soulé. 1987 (22); Gilpin, M., and I. Hanski, eds. 1991. Metapopulation dynamics: empirical and theoretical investigations. Biology Journal Linnean Society 42:1–336.

42. Hedrick, R.W., and P.S. Miller 1992. Conservation genetics: techniques and fundamentals. Ecological Applications 2:30–46.

43. Murphy, D.D., and B.R. Noon. 1992. Integrating scientific methods with habitat conservation planning: reserve design for northern spotted owls. Ecological Applications 2:3–17.

44. Temple, S.A., and J.R. Cary. 1988. Modeling dynamics of habitat-interior bird populations in a fragmented landscapes. Conservation Biology 2:340–347.

45. United States Department of the Interior. 1980a. Habitat Evaluation Procedures (HEP). Ecological Services Manual Number 102. Division of Ecological Services, U.S.D.I. Fish and Wildlife Service, Washington, D.C.

    United States Department of the Interior. 1980b. Standards for the development of Habitat Suitability Index Models. Ecological Services Manual Number 103. Division of Ecological Services, U.S.D.I. Fish and Wildlife Service, Washington, D.C. Code of Federal Regulations. 1985. 36 CFR Chapter II 219:19–64.

46. Verner, J. 1984. The guild concept applied to management of bird populations. Environmental Management 8:1–14.

    Landres, P.B., J. Verner, and J.W. Thomas. 1988. Ecological uses of vertebrate indicator species: a critique. Conservation Biology 2:316–328.

    Temple, S.A., and J.A. Wiens. 1989. Bird populations and environmental changes: can birds be bio–indicators? American Birds 43:260–270.

47. Van Horne and Wiens 1991 (40).
48. Landres et. al 1988 (46).
49. Anderson, J.E. 1991. A conceptual framework for evaluating and quantifying naturalness. Conservation Biology 5:347–352.
50. Noss 1990 (18).

Chapter 17

New Directions in Education for Natural Resources Management

Susan K. Jacobson

> Human needs and aspirations the world over can only be satisfied as environmental awareness leads to appropriate action at all levels of society, from the smallest local communties to the whole community of nations. Appropriate action requires a solid base of sound information and technical skills. But action also depends upon motivation, which depends upon widespread understanding, and that, in turn, depends upon education.
>
> Mostafa K. Tolba (former Director)
> United Nations Environment Program

The need for an integrated approach to natural resource management has become widely recognized as environmental and social problems become increasingly acute. Extinction of species, destruction of forests and wetlands, contamination of water and air, and modification of global hydrological and carbon cycles, have underscored the need to better manage natural resources.

Critics of the existing pattern of resource management often blame our past failure on an overly narrow, technical focus that has failed to address the underlying sociopolitical causes of ecological deterioration and natural resources depletion. An understanding of the interrelationships among biological, social, and economic constraints is rarely evident because few people have training outside their own disciplines. Academic institutions, traditionally the source of new ideas and innovative approaches, have not effectively responded to this intellectual challenge, resulting in a concomitant lack of professionals who are able to integrate ecological conservation with natural resource development. This dearth has been repeatedly emphasized in studies such as those by the Office of Technology Assessment, U.S. Congress (1), and the World Wildlife Fund (2). The inability of academic institutions to effectively address complex natural resource issues often stems from their traditional, disciplinary approach that emphasizes specialization. Ecologists are not trained in the economic and social implications of environmental conservation, nor do economists study the biological or resource management aspects of these same efforts. Yet problems in the real world seldom fall into discrete disciplines. This is particularly true of the major conservation and natural resource development problems facing us today.

New Directions

New directions in training are demanded (3), most vociferously by the students themselves. While a number of programs addressing natural resource themes have been operating for decades, more comprehensive approaches are just emerging. In the past two decades, public interest has increased in a natural resource management philosophy that includes values associated with complex, diverse, and healthy ecosystems. At the same time, theoretical and applied developments in science have increasingly offered insights and new directions, particularly in related areas of landscape ecology, ecosystem management and restoration, and sustainable development (4). Conservation biology, when broadly defined to include these new approaches, is an integrative new field that offers the hope for appropriate environmental management in the future.

Only a decade has passed since conservation biology became an identifiable and proliferating element at a number of universities. The birth of conservation biology commonly is attributed to the First International Conference on Conservation Biology held at the University of San Diego in 1978, and the ensuing publication of the *Conservation Biology* volume by Soulé and Wilcox in 1980. The initial fabric of conservation biology was woven from basic biology. This was reflected in the 1980 volume's invitation to students and scientists with a "concern for the preservation of biological diversity and its evolutionary potential" to embrace this "mission-oriented discipline" that covers topics from "molecular biology to population biology" (5). The inclusion of other disciplines that are relevant to the mission has been an increasingly more vocal and visible development.

Controversy has accompanied the growth of conservation biology. Its basic biological roots have been criticized for being too pure and impractical, while the elements of conservation biology stemming from traditional resource management disciplines have been denigrated as well. For example, the traditional management orientation such as represented by the Wildlife Society, has been chastised for being a deer-and-duck club, lacking in theory (6). Although in 1937, Bennitt et al. wrote in the first issue of the *Journal of Wildlife Management* that "wildlife management along sound biological lines is also part of the greater movement for conservation of our entire native flora and fauna" (7), traditional commodity biases remain. This criticism is substantiated by perusal of publications in the field. Tallying up articles in the *Journal of Wildlife Management*, Capen found that 85 percent of the papers in 1969 concerned game species (8). He found that this decreased to 73 percent in 1979, with the remaining papers focusing on such topics as endangered species, community ecology, and threats to wildlife by contemporary land-use practices—topics embraced by conservation biologists. A decade later, however, the traditional emphasis on game species and the consumption aspects of wildlife had not changed; 73 percent of the papers in 1988 concerned game species (9). During the same year, only 13 percent of the papers published in the journal *Conservation Biology* were contributed by people from traditional wildlife departments in universities or wildlife agencies (10).

The increased integration of the traditional management fields with basic biological sciences provides needed breadth to the field of conservation biology. The further incorporation of knowledge from a number of disciplines is required to provide the underpinnings to develop new and innovative approaches to managing wildlife and forests, as well as whole ecosystems and landscapes. Some natural resource management professionals recognize the need for greater breadth and recommend that in order to put students of conservation biology "in closer touch with the real world" (11), they should be required to take courses in policy, resource economics, range management, forestry, agriculture, and other subjects. This need for cross-disciplinary (12) breadth has also become more widely recognized among leading conservation biologists, as evidenced by Lovejoy's comment in the foreword to *Conservation Biology* that "biology is inextricably interwoven with sociology and economics" (13). With the publication of the second *Conservation Biology* volume in 1986, Soulé stated that the discipline of conservation biology should "attract and penetrate every field that could possibly benefit and protect the diversity of life. . . ." (14).

Although many agree that natural resource management should integrate the protection, maintenance, and restoration of the planet's biodiversity with sustainable natural resource development, educators debate the scope of appropriate educational experiences needed to train scientists and managers in a holistic, integrative manner. There is a growing consensus that in order to address problems in biological conservation, academia must incorporate cross-disciplinary perspectives. This is echoed by agencies and organizations involved in conservation work. For example, at the 1989 conference, "Conservation and Sustainable Development," held at the World Bank, speakers from conservation organizations, such as the World Wildlife Fund, World Resources Institute, and Wildlife Conservation Society, as well as the World Bank, defined the training needs they envisioned for future employees. They identified characteristics that focused more on real-world problem-solving skills and less on narrow, disciplinary technical skills. These included (1) cross-disciplinary breadth as well as disciplinary depth; (2) field experience; (3) language and communication skills; and (4) leadership skills, identified as including a mix of diplomacy and humility (15).

The broad range of skills needed to be effective in the real world also has become increasingly acknowledged by traditional resource practitioners. Hunter (16) surveyed the needs of administrators in state fish and wildlife agencies throughout the United States. Almost all of the respondents reported that additional training in social science and interpersonal skills would improve their job performance. Few respondents believed that additional natural science (technical) training would enhance their performance.

The need for a diversity of knowledge, skills, and abilities was further reflected in a survey of state and provincial fish and wildlife agencies by their responses regarding the qualities listed on typical "biologist" job announcements. These included: "knowledge of biological, ecological, and conservation principles and practices; knowledge of fauna and flora and their habitat requirements; knowledge of laws, regulations, and functions of state and federal agencies and private organizations involved in conservation and management; skills in the operation and maintenance of motorized equipment, scientific instruments, and gear for various sampling techniques and methodologies in both field and laboratory; ability to plan and conduct surveys of habitat and organisms to define problems and recognize opportunities; ability to develop and implement effective and efficient management plans and operations; ability to apply scientific methods and approaches in the planning and conducting of research projects and resource investigations; ability to apply statistical procedures, to analyze and evaluate data, and apply sound judgment in arriving at conclusions and recommendations; ability to write clear and concise reports, technical publications, and informative popular articles; ability to effectively communicate orally with subordinates, peers, supervisors, other scientists, and the public; ability to plan, assign, supervise, and evaluate the work of subordinates and maintain effective working relations; and ability and motivation to perform as a professional for the benefit of the public served, the resources, and the agency" (17).

Traditional resource managers are recognizing that much of their work requires an understanding of the public's concerns, needs, and desires. In a survey of 171 New York State Bureau of Wildlife staff conducted in 1990, 84 percent reported frequent contact with the public, 74 percent were involved in implementation of programs that required contact with the public; 46 percent reported conducting public meetings; and 29 percent were involved in establishing public policy. Most (82 percent) of the staff suggested that their agency should do more to provide human dimensions training for their staff (18).

Traditional Constraints (19)

In the past few decades, many universities have developed programs in conservation science that attempt to provide students with new approaches necessary to deal successfully with diverse local, regional, and global environmental problems. These programs often lacked departmental status, however, and were therefore disadvantaged compared to traditional disciplines. This was often exacerbated by an inadequate understanding of the field by other faculty and students at the institution. In fact, the development of natural resource management programs that encompass conservation biology and sustainable development as a cross-disciplinary field faces obstacles in every major aspect of academia, including communication, reward systems, research, curriculum, and evaluation. The root of these problems lies in the contemporary structure of academic institutions. Many commentators have noted that society's environmental and social problems are not compartmentalized into the discrete disciplines found in universities. Although academic institutions have been described as a community of scholars, whether this community should or can work together to address real-world problems remains controversial. Some maintain that Kerr's dry description of a modern university as "a series of individual faculty entrepreneurs held together by a common grievance over parking" (20) has changed little.

Communication among departments is difficult due to differences among disciplines in philosophical outlook, paradigm development, research approaches, and terminology (21). The reward structure—assistantships, recognition, jobs, promotion and tenure—is departmentally based, and multidisciplinary or interdisciplinary efforts often go unrewarded. Compounding this problem are external constraints such as the lack of funds to support cross-disciplinary efforts that are frequently misunderstood, considered outside of mainstream science, and consequently underfinanced (22).

Peer review, the traditional means of quality control in academia, is difficult to implement in cross-disciplinary research. Concepts and research methodology may be required from a number of disciplines, but not necessarily from the frontier of each discipline involved. This also affects curriculum development. Some academics protest that problems do not provide an inherent structure or key philosophic concept around which to build an education (23). Partially because of this, cross-disciplinary training is often given the academic onus of proving that it is not "mish-mash" (24). In spite of the fact that many scientists have identified the lack of cross-disciplinary training as one of the three most important issues facing the scientific community today (25), the conflict between disciplinary depth and cross-disciplinary breadth remains unresolved. A cross-disciplinary synthesis may be the optimal model for the curriculum, but the methods for making such integration and synthesis effective have not yet been adequately identified or tested. Training approaches incorporating field courses, internships, case studies, and cross-disciplinary research projects have served as effective mechanisms (26).

New Educational Approaches

Many professionals in the field support an eclectic approach for training in conservation biology and sustainable resource development. Governmental, research, teaching, and private organization positions all require different expertise; thus, academic programs must offer diverse educational alternatives. In addressing some of these training needs, many universities are starting to introduce biological conservation and development issues into the university structure at a variety of levels. These include: (1) synthesis of topics from many disciplines to create an interdisciplinary unit in biological conservation; (2) addition of biological conservation materials to disciplinary courses; (3) multidisciplinary overview courses; (4) broader training of specialists in existing disciplines to facilitate communication with other fields; and (5) training of generalists.

A major academic challenge is to define the core of study of conservation biology and sustainable resource development and to determine how conservation problems can serve as a focus or orientation in the same way as a traditional discipline. It is necessary for researchers to delineate the field of biological conservation, as well as to define those disciplines that are integral to it. The real task, then, lies in synthesizing the knowledge of these disciplines to solve conservation problems.

It may become most appropriate to view conservation biology and sustainable resource development as a metadiscipline—a level of knowledge beyond the individual disciplines and differing from them in important ways (sensu Caldwell) (27). Although its substance draws heavily from biology, applied management, and a variety of other disciplines, this derivative knowledge is synthesized to form new information and insights not directly deducible from any one of the individual disciplines. The way knowledge is perceived and organized is an artifact of the mind: "There is logic in the way disciplines are defined and categorized, but the logic is mutable" (28). The majority of sciences and academic disciplines are less than a century old, and their divisions and recombinations are continuing phenomena. Ehrenfeld already finds the area of conservation biology to be a discipline, with a "coherent body of facts, theories, and technologies" (29). For now, the paradigm of the field may simply be that the work follows from the problem, that of stemming the biological impoverishment we now face.

Natural resource management in the 21st century will embody not only an understanding of basic biology and traditional resources such as game, timber, or range, but the structure and function of ecosystems and the integral relationship with human beings and human institutions. The argument that natural resource education should prepare students to manage the environment in whole ecological or landscape units based on integrative biological, physical, and social assessments is not a new one (30). However, the vast majority of current resource professionals come from single-disciplined, specialized backgrounds; thus, it is not surprising that problems in the past have tended to be viewed through the narrow lens of a single academic specialty. In Figure 17.1, a broad array of elements involved in natural resource management training and education that encompasses biological conservation and sustainable resource development is depicted. This array reflects the real world problem-solving skills that are increasingly needed as management problems become more complex.

Debate will continue about the optimal mix of disciplinary depth versus interdisciplinary breadth in higher education. While all components must be included in the education of natural resource managers and scientists, the mix and emphasis will depend on academic levels, institutional strengths, and individual goals. It is the synthesis and integration of areas of knowledge through new teaching materials and new approaches combined with a problem-solving orientation that will result in a concise and useful natural resource curriculum.

Three areas of knowledge and skills critical for producing effective resource managers and scientists in the future are outlined below.

· · ·

1. Natural and Physical Sciences

To comprehend the structure and processes of natural systems, students must learn the basic principles of zoology, ecology, botany, chemistry, and

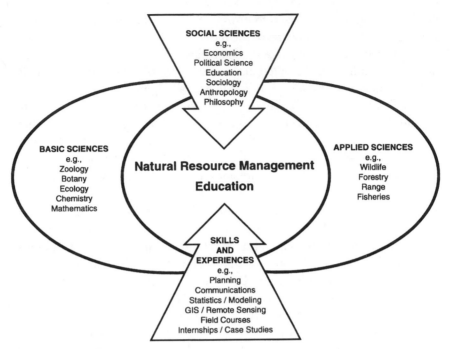

Figure 17.1   Diagram of natural resource management education.

physics. Mechanisms for applying these principles to real-world needs and problems must be understood. A better integration of these fields of inquiry with courses such as wildlife, fisheries, and forestry is needed to enable students to approach the management of natural resources with a holistic, ecosystem-based orientation. Better synthesis of ecological theory and practice can lead to new knowledge. For example, the current understanding of ecological relationships and disturbance regimes has provided restoration ecologists with new techniques for restoring degraded ecosystems and communities.

. . .

2. Social Sciences and Implementational Skills

In the past two decades, recognition that resource managers must deal more effectively with the human aspects of natural resource management has spawned a subdiscipline in this field called Human Dimensions (31). Solutions for many resource management problems may have little to do with wildlife population manipulation or habitat improvement, but rather the solution may lie in using social science information to design communication or education programs to affect people's beliefs, knowledge, attitudes, behaviors, and motivations toward natural resources or their management. New information is needed for making management decisions. As human demands on natural resources increase, the number of stakeholders grows and people's values will continue to dictate decisions about the management of ecosystems and wildlife populations and the use of these resources.

Students must complement their understanding of scientific tools for addressing natural resource problems with knowledge of equally useful concepts and tools from sociology, political science, economics, and education to address these same problems and to work effectively within the context of human institutions. Understanding resource policies and how they are formed is a prerequisite for improving how natural resources will be managed, who will manage them, and who or what will benefit when the policies are implemented (32).

. . .

3. Technical Skills and Real-World Experience

Managing natural resources involves monitoring and often manipulating the environment. Students must acquire knowledge for monitoring ecosystem structure and function (including humans) to provide the feedback required for the regulatory process and for reassessing management goals to conserve biodiversity and to sustainably develop resources. Knowledge of quantitative techniques of statistics and integrative modeling, Geographic Information Systems (GIS), remote sensing, and other new technologies is needed for solving many resource management problems. Students also must develop better thinking skills. They must be able to analyze problems quantitatively and qualitatively; "probabilistically and deterministically; deductively, inductively, analogically, and algorithmically; and imaginatively" (33).

Additional educational activities essential for resource managers and scientists include real-world problem-solving experiences. Practical training in the field is important. This can be obtained through case studies, integrative models, team projects, field courses, laboratory sessions, and interdisciplinary research activities. It is enhanced through summer employment or internships with state and federal agencies, nongovernmental organizations, and industry all dealing with the complexities of managing natural resources.

. . .

Reaching beyond the Academy

The resource management profession exists because the results of management are valued by people—the general public, special interest groups, and policymakers, among others. It is imperative that the maintenance of the Earth's biodiversity is viewed as necessary and beneficial to humankind, and thus a worthwhile goal of management. For this reason, conservation education cannot be relegated to the ivory tower. Conservation education should start with the small child and, using both formal, school-based programs and nonformal programs promulgated through museums, nature centers, government agencies, conservation organizations and the media, should extend throughout life, to all sectors of society. Programs also must reach beyond today's youth to target policymakers, professional, business, and religious organizations, and other groups, for the resource issues are critical and time is short.

In the United States, resource management professionals and their agencies and conservation organizations are often more interested in and supportive of conservation education than is the professional education establishment. In California, for example, pressure from the state's Secretary for Resources and a number of conservation associations precipitated legislative hearings resulting in the establishment of curriculum requirements for conservation and environmental education, as well as an office of environmental education in the state's Department of Education (34). In a number of states, financial support for conservation education professionals and curricula materials is provided by the state's natural resource agencies, not by the education departments. At the federal level, leadership also is primarily supplied by conservation organizations and resources agencies, such as new environmental education initiatives within the Environmental Protection Agency. The Department of Education has shown minimal interest or involvement in this area. Resource management professionals must recognize this situation and support effective conservation education programming to be implemented both through the education establishment and through nonformal means to create an informed and responsible environmental ethic among students and the public.

In addition to formal and public education, the new developments in natural resource management demand the expansion of educational opportunities for practicing managers and scientists. Continuing education can enhance individual knowledge, attitudes, and skills, and by so doing, concomitantly improve the profession. Today's subject matter in relatively traditional courses such as botany, economics, and sociology certainly differs from that offered a decade or more ago; new subject areas such as human dimensions, restoration ecology, and GIS were in an embryonic stage when many resource managers, now in decision-making positions, received their training. A variety of approaches are used in continuing education, including shortcourses, workshops, mass media, tutorial classes, seminars, self-study, and professional meetings. Cross-disciplinary orientations and problem-solving approaches are well suited to managers seeking knowledge to solve complex problems. Although the professional resource management societies set standards for initial certification or accreditation, none mandate professional development through continuing education. Efforts to provide updated educational opportunities in biological conservation and sustainable resource development must be expanded for practicing professionals to ensure that state-of-the-art management is occurring on the ground.

Conclusion

New educational approaches are needed to provide the cognitive foundation for the next generation of natural resource managers and scientists. A number of reasons underscore this need: the biodiversity crisis continues unabated; traditional policy solutions have been ineffective at slowing environmental degradation; theoretical and empirical developments in science offer new insight and direction; environmental laws are stretched to their limits by industrial expansion, human population growth, and resource consumption; traditional management practices have largely ignored biological conservation concerns and failed the public's desire for meaningful participation; and finally, societal views of appropriate human relationships with nature appear to be in flux (35). The complex relationship and inevitable conflicts among resource management programs and the variety of benefits that can result highlight the need to integrate across the natural and social sciences and to incorporate real-world skills and experiences into the education and training of the resource professionals of the future.

Academia is starting to overcome traditional constraints to address this need. In a 1993 survey of universities participating in an initiative, "Integrated Approaches to Training in Conservation and Sustainable Development," 30 universities reported that a total of 475 new educational activities, including courses, seminars, internships, and cross-disciplinary research projects addressing conservation and sustainable development, had been developed during the past five years (36). There is growing evidence that cross-disciplinary synthesis will contribute to confronting the enormous problems found in the natural resources conservation and development arena. The new resource professionals who are equipped to address real-world problems using integrative approaches should have a profound impact on government, industry, and academia, and ultimately, the biosphere on which we all depend.

Acknowledgments

I am grateful to C. Gentry and J. Hardesty for thoughtful review of this manuscript. I thank C. Gentry for graphic assistance and E. Vaughan and S. Miller for library and secretarial assistance.

Notes

1. Office of Technology Assessment, U.S. Congress. 1987. Technologies to Maintain Biological Diversity (OTA-F-330) Washington, D.C.: U.S. Government Printing Office. 54 pp.
2. World Wildlife Fund. 1980. Strategy for training in natural resources and environment: a proposal for development of personnel and institutions in Latin America and the Caribbean. Washington, D.C.: World Wildlife Fund Publ. 416 pp.
3. Lusigi, W.J. 1988. The new resources manager. In World Wilderness Congress, 1987, Denver, Colorado, For the Conservation of Earth. M. Vance, ed. 42–45. Golden, Colorado: Fulcrum Inc.
4. Lubchenco, J., et al. 1991. The sustainable biosphere initiative: an ecological research agenda. Ecology 72:371–412.
5. Soulé, M.E., and B.K. Wilcox, eds. 1986. Conservation biology: an evolutionary-ecological perspective. Sunderland, Massachusetts: Sinauer Associates.
6. Anonymous. 1989. The future of wildlife resources cannot afford strange or unwilling bedfellows. Wildlife Society Bulletin 17:343–344.
7. Bennitt, R., J.S. Dixon, V.H. Cahalane, W.W. Chase, and W.C. McAtee. 1937. Statement of policy. Journal of Wildlife Management 1 (July, 1–2):1–2.
8. Capen, D.E. 1989. Political unrest, progressive research, and professional education. Wildlife Society Bulletin 17:340–343.
9. Edwards, T.C. 1989. The Wildlife Society and the Society for Conservation Biology: strange but unwilling bedfellows. Wildlife Society Bulletin 17:340–343.
10. Wagner, F.H. 1989. American wildlife management at the crossroads. Wildlife Society Bulletin 17:354–360.

11. For example, see Bolen, E.G. 1989. Conservation biology, wildlife management and Spaceship Earth. Wildlife Society Bulletin 17:351–354.
12. The term *cross-disciplinary* includes: (1) multidisciplinary programs in which conservation biology is infused into existing disciplines, and (2) interdisciplinary programs in which a number of disciplines are synthesized in a common program.
13. Soulé and Wilcox 1986 (5).
14. Soulé, M.E., ed. 1986. Conservation biology: the science of scarcity and diversity. Sunderland, Massachusetts: Sinauer Associates.
15. Jacobson, S.K., and J.G. Robinson. 1990. Training the new conservationist: cross-disciplinary education in the 1990s. Environmental Conservation 17(4):319–327.
16. Hunter, R.G. 1984. Managerial professionalism in state fish and wildlife agencies. a survey of duties, attitudes, and needs. Fisheries 9(5).2–7.
17. Anderson, R.O. 1982. Expectations for entry-level biologists: what are state and provincial agencies looking for? Transactions of the 47th North American Wildlife and Natural Resources Conference 47:209–218.
18. Gigliotti, L.M., and D.J. Decker. 1992. Human dimensions in wildlife management education: pre-service opportunities and in-service needs. Wildlife Society Bulletin 20:8–14.
19. This discussion about constraints summarizes Jacobson, S.K. 1990. Graduate training in conservation biology. Conservation Biology 4(4):431–440.
20. Kerr, C. 1963. The uses of the university. Cambridge, Massachusetts. Cited in Hill, B. 1976. Multi-disciplinary courses—mush or muscle? The Australian University (May):48–57.
21. For example, see Mar, B.W., W.T. Newell, and B.O. Saxberg. 1976. Interdisciplinary research in the university setting. Environmental Science and Technology 10:650–653.
22. 1988. Removing the Boundaries: Perspectives on Cross-Disciplinary Research; Final Report on an Inquiry into Cross-disciplinary Science. New Haven, Connecticut: May. 81 pp.
23. For example, see Wolman, M.G. 1977. Interdisciplinary education: a continuing experiment. Science 198 Nov. 25:800–804.
24. Caldwell, L.K. 1984. Environmental studies: discipline or metadiscipline? The Environmental Professional 5:247–259.
25. Sigma Xi, The Scientific Research Society.
26. Jacobson, S.K., J.G. Robinson, T.C. Moermond, K. Hansen, J.G. Schmitt, J.D. Allan, and K.H. Redford. 1992. Building graduate

programs: integrating conservation and sustainable development. The Environmental Professional 14:284–292.

27. Caldwell, L.K. op. cit.

28. Caldwell, L.K. ibid.

29. Ehrenfeld, D. 1987. Editorial. Conservation Biology 1:6.

30. For review, see Slocombe, D.S. 1993. Implementing ecosystem-based management: development of theory, practice and research for planning and managing a region. BioScience 43(9):612–622.

31. For discussion, see Doig, G.E. 1987. Applying wildlife values information in management planning and policy making. In Valuing wildlife: economic and social perspectives. D.J. Decker and G.R. Goff, eds. 305–308. Boulder, Colorado: Westview Press; and Decker, D.J., T.L. Brown, and G.F. Mattfeld. 1989. The future of human dimensions of wildlife management: can we fulfill the promise? Transactions of the 54th North American Wildlife and Natural Resources Conference 54:415–425.

32. For discussion, see Clark, T.J. 1988. The identity and images of wildlife professionals. Renewable Resources Journal 6(3):12–16; and Lyons, J.R. and T.M. Franklin. 1987. Practical aspects of training in natural resource policy: filling an educational void. Transactions of the 52nd North American Wildlife and Natural Resources Conference 52:729–737.

33. Romesburg, H.C. 1991. On improving the natural resources and environmental sciences. Journal of Wildlife Management 55(4):744–756.

34. Schafer, R.J.H. 1987. Educators and resource managers: a partnership with a future. Transactions of the 52nd North American Wildlife and Natural Resources Conference 52:422–430.

35. Grumbine, R.E. 1994. What is ecosystem management? Conservation Biology 8(1):27–38.

36. Jacobson, S.K.. Evaluating impacts on graduate education: The Conservation and Sustainable Development Initiative. The Environmental Professional. In press.

Chapter 18

Managing Natural Resources as Social Value

James J. Kennedy and Jack Ward Thomas

> "Everything is" is one extreme.
> "Nothing is" is the other.
> Between these two I teach the truth
> of interdependent origination.
>
> —The Buddha

Young natural resources or environmental managers are usually attracted to their professions to be outdoors, away from the maddening crowd and its sociopolitical problems, working with physical and biological resources (1). Yet these new foresters, wildlife biologists, or ecologists often find themselves immersed in less tangible, more ambiguous *social value* issues as much as the natural resources they love and want to manage (e.g., owls vs. jobs vs. biological diversity values). This is especially true of those professionals employed by public agencies. Many young natural resource graduates are disappointed and frustrated to discover that being an effective professional and public servant is ultimately a social endeavor (2).

Our essay presents natural resource or environmental professionals' primary role as managing for social value. If natural resource managers were role-modeled and taught this social value perspective in college, they might not be so shocked and frustrated with their entry into the "real world" of being state or federal public servants. Although not a detailed operational model, our social value perspective addresses how and where natural resource values *originate* and how they are *expressed* to natural resource managers and the rest of society. We argue also that a professional orientation of managing natural resources or the environment as social value is not inconsistent with a biocentric perspective and is a more valid, comprehensive, and evolutionary management paradigm than focusing primarily on the physical or biological resources—as much as we cherish them.

Origin and Expression of Social Values in Natural Resources Management

Our conceptual model (Figure 18.1) places natural resource values in an interrelated set of four systems: (1) the *natural environmental system* of biosphere elements, such as human and wildlife populations, natural resources, or ecosystems; (2) the *social system* of human attitudes, values, behavior, institutions, and technology; (3) the *economic system* that focuses on human attitudes, institutions, and behavior related to the allocation of land, labor, and capital; and (4) the *political system* of policy, laws, courts, and public agencies. Note that system interrelationship and interdependency is the norm in this conceptual model, with the natural environment and resources (in the environmental system) providing and receiving impacts from the other three systems.

Natural resource (or environmental) social values *originate* or are *endorsed* in one system only: the social system. They are *expressed* to natural resource managers (and the rest of society) through three systems: the economic, social, and political. In this model, the environmental system *itself* neither originates nor expresses natural resource or environmental social

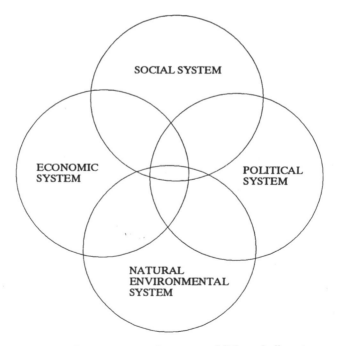

Figure 18.1   Systems that originate and express wildlife and all environmental social values.

value. Only human interaction with the natural environment *originates* social values (be they utilitarian or biocentric), which are *expressed* in various ways—by laws, bounties, sociopolitical action, TV nature programs, governmental budgets, or wildlife pictures and messages on T-shirts. Below, we explore these concepts in more detail.

The Origin or Endorsement of Natural Resource Social Values

Our conceptual model is anthropocentric and holds that (1) all human value orientations toward nature are ultimately devices of the mind, (2) shaped by interactions among self–culture–environment, and (3) originate in the social system (3). But this perspective accommodates both ends of the anthropocentric natural resources or environmental value spectrum, from (what we will call) "human-dominant" to "human-mutual" nature values.

The Judeo-Christian and Greek heritage of Western culture tends to view few things (such as human life or soul) as having intrinsic value that is independent of human endorsement. From such a *human-dominant* anthropocentric perspective, nature and its natural resources are valued only as they fulfill human needs—be these needs material, recreational, or spiritual (4). Verbs used to describe relationships between humans and nature at this pole of the spectrum would be humans "create," "establish," or "endow" nature with value by use, ownership, or institutions. Utilitarian values and human-dominant relationships usually prevail here; where humans often must devour and digest all stuff (the "source") to give it value (i.e., to transform nature "sources" of value into natural "resources"). There usually is little tolerance for intrinsic, spiritual, non-use, or nonownership nature values at this human-dominant pole of the nature value spectrum (5).

During European settlement in North America, natural resources had utilitarian value primarily for subsistence, economic development, and sport. A more biocentric world view (6) accepts intrinsic values in the natural world, independent of utilitarian or direct human value endowment. Such beliefs are increasingly embraced by post-industrial, urbanizing Western society. Our model accommodates this *human-mutual* pole of nature values and relationships. But the model remains anthropocentric in holding that human minds and society are still involved with this more humble and sophisticated recognition of the mutuality and interdependence of humans with other species and our shared, complex, diverse global environment. Spiritual, aesthetic, and nonconsumptive nature values are important at this (more biocentric) end of the value spectrum. This can evolve to a recognition and celebration that other species and our shared habitats have intrinsic worth or value similar to humans (7). Our model still maintains that biocentric value frameworks still require human recognition and endorsement—as indicated by often associating such biocentric values with Buddhist or Native American cultures and social value systems. At this human-mutual pole of the nature value spectrum, the social system merely *endorses* (vs. creates or endows) complex, diverse, and inherent nature values that could exist independent of our human use and appreciation— even if humans no longer existed.

Our conceptual model suggests that, from a professional perspective, there are no universal laws or principles of ecology that mystically establish natural resource values or guide their management on some obvious, pre-ordained path. Natural resource management is a very human and social endeavor that has changed greatly in the minds and lifetimes of professional pioneers such as Aldo Leopold (8). With the environmental movement, conservation biology, animal rights, biological diversity concerns, and other current social awareness and movements, natural resource or environ-mental social values have changed greatly in the last part of this century. Yet a wide spectrum of utilitarian to biocentric nature social values have existed and functioned on this planet thousands of years before the development of any natural resource management professions. The disciplines of forestry, wildlife, or watershed management primarily offer (1) concepts and infor-mation to change social awareness or behavior, (2) ability to predict and monitor the consequences of management options, and (3) ability to imple-ment management processes in pursuit of natural resource social values— values that originate in the social system.

Of course, natural resource values are not formed in isolation within the social system, but as that system interacts with the environmental and other systems. Natural resource values also evolve, as do most social values. For example, agricultural societies tend to have different interactions with na-ture than do urban societies, often resulting in different natural resource perceptions, values, and uses (9). Many modern controversies over natural resource or environmental issues are conflicts of agricultural (human-dom-inant) and urban (more human-mutual) values about human relationships with and the use of nature (e.g., 1080 poisoning of predators; managing wild horses; harvesting old-growth forests). None of these nature value perspec-tives fall from heaven, nor do they have different origins. They are part of a continuum of nature values that originate in the minds of individuals and groups as their changing perceptions and human needs interact with the en-vironmental and the other three systems.

America became an industrial society in the last part of the 19th century, with increasing sociopolitical concern for predictable, long-term flows of natural resource goods and services. The American conservation movement

(1880–1969), with its sustained-yield philosophies of timber and forage flows or harvestable game surpluses, accommodated this sociopolitical need. Natural resource agencies and forest or game management professions were created (10). Recreational, aesthetic, and biocentric values were an important component of some early conservation visionaries, centered largely in urban areas and championed by people such as John Muir. Yet these values did not become a dominant force in natural resource management until the 1960s—with the advent of the environmental movement. America was then beginning its urban post-industrial stage of socioeconomic development. Many of its citizens offered a formidable challenge to the view that utilitarian and economic values were the most legitimate indicator of forest or wildlife worth. Legislation was passed to express these values (e.g., National Environmental Policy Act of 1969, or Wild Horse and Burros Protection Act of 1971). Recently there has even been a basic management paradigm shift in such powerful and traditional agencies as the USDA Forest Service, where an industrial era, output-focused, sustained-yield orientation has evolved to the sustainable system focus of "ecosystem management" (11). But this expression of social value is the subject of the next section.

The Expression of Natural Resource Social Value

Historically, public natural resource managers have been conditioned to respond to values expressed by political and social systems that were very sensitive to the economic values derived from resource use and development. Laws or budgets are *political* system expressions of natural resource values. Wildland use, license sales, effectiveness of nongame wildlife contributions on state tax forms, or newspaper editorials are primarily *social* system expressions of natural resource values. Of course, these values are rarely expressed solely through one system. For example, an Audubon chapter (in the social system) may lobby a state legislature (political system), obtain financial endorsement of corporations (economic system), and encourage its members to write legislators (social and political systems) to increase a state's nongame management budget. We continue this explanation of expressions of natural resource social values with a focus on wildlife.

In the first half of this century, game managers and their legislative supporters were major forces in communicating new wildlife and natural resource social values (of an emerging American industrial society) by debating, passing, and enforcing game related laws. Aldo Leopold's campaign for Wisconsin antlerless deer hunting is a good example of a professional participating in sociopolitical changes of wildlife attitudes and public policy

(12). In the last few years, antihunting and animal rights groups are involved in similar social and political systems to express their values by restricting use of steel traps or attempting to ban hunting of moose in Maine (13). An indication of the amount, intensity, and marketability of substantive or symbolic wildlife social values is the frequency that wildlife issues are featured in newspaper headlines, in news broadcasts, on T-shirts or TV shows.

Wildlife managers seem to have a curious, often antagonistic, attitude toward understanding and responding to social values expressed by the *economic* system. With the prodding of Leopold and others, the *1930 American Game Policy* had a section on "Inducements for Landowners" (14). It supported economic subsidies to rural landowners to provide wildlife habitat and hunting access. Midwestern farmers, for example, allocate land, labor, and capital to the production of corn and pork because people express their social value for these commodities through the economic system. Leopold and others wanted similar economic expressions of game values (via payments, damage insurance, or tax incentives) to better compete with agricultural commodities.

The American heritage of relatively abundant, cheap, and state-owned wildlife populations, the mobility of some wildlife species, and the Great Depression operated against wildlife values being adequately expressed by hunter payments or government subsidies as the *1930 American Game Policy* proposed. Yet today, the economic system is of increasing importance in expressing wildlife values. This is reflected in the rental of goose hunting blinds on the Atlantic flyway, wildlife viewing tours or safaris, or interstate hunting rights franchises (e.g., the American Sportsman Assoc.). A half-century after Leopold and others proposed economic inducements for landowners, their profession and state agencies increasingly are supporting this policy.

As in the past, most American wildlife values are still expressed socially and politically (e.g., in state and federal laws guiding game and nongame management, in stream channelization or wetland drainage projects that diminish wildlife values to enhance others). Although passage of wildlife legislation or changes in government policy are usually the focus of much public attention, it is often in budget allocation that the relative political values of wildlife (vs. other programs) are most clearly expressed. For example, Alston (15) studied the relative values Congress placed on national forest wildlife management versus timber sale or range programs. Between 1955 and 1972, Congress gave the USDA Forest Service 97 percent (mean) of its budget requests for timber sales and 90 percent for range management. Yet it only approved 79 percent of its (much lower) wildlife habitat budget requests in that period. This has changed dramatically in the last decade, as wildlife and fisheries budgets and biologists have been the fastest growing segment of the agency. For example, there were 275 Forest Service wildlife and fisheries biologists in 1979; 10 years later there were about 850, a rise from 3 to 10 percent of their professional work force (16). Congress also provided the agency 20 percent more wildlife and fisheries dollars than requested in its FY 1991 budget.

In as many diverse and intricate ways as nitrogen is exchanged in complex ecosystems, our post-industrial American society is communicating increasing amounts and types of wildlife or other natural resource/environmental social values to us managers and to the rest of society.

Closing Comment

If one accepts that natural resource professionals manage to accommodate immediate and long-term social values in the environmental system, then natural resource management can be viewed as *social value management*— just as validly as forest, fisheries, or recreation management. This new management paradigm encourages natural resource professionals to focus beyond the important physical and biological resource strata of their traditional forest, water, or wildlife management models, and to define our central role and social responsibility anew. Namely, that natural resource or environmental management professions strive to accommodate a mix of social values for current society, while maintaining viable, sustainable, natural resource values and options for future generations. If one acknowledges that many natural resource social values conflict with one another or with other social or political systems, then natural resource management also can be viewed as *social conflict management*. In what we natural resource professionals do (and do not do), we can intensify or dampen such value conflicts.

How many natural resource managers were attracted to their professions or educated in college to understand and manage social value conflict? College students with the desire and temperament to deal with social conflict usually major in social work, labor management, or law. These students accept few values as intrinsic and are educated and role-modeled by their professors to identify, engage in, and resolve social value conflicts. In contrast, natural resources students are usually drawn to their profession by love of nature, a desire to manage or protect intrinsically valuable wildland or environmental resources, and an attraction to work away from the problems of a complex urban society. Their education generally focuses on manipulation of physical and biological variables. Few economics, sociology, or political science courses are required or elected (17), and many natural resource professors may not project a respect or tolerance for these social science disciplines.

Upon graduation, natural resource professionals are often confronted with managing moose in Maine, wild horses in Nevada, winter sports or wilderness areas on the Colorado urban fringe. Such management is often the focus of social conflict—where some clients value moose for hunting while others focus on moose symbolic value (18), ranchers battling wild horse advocates, snowmobilers versus cross-country skiers versus vacation home owners. New professionals expecting to manage natural resource *things*, in tranquil rural settings, often experience considerable "reality shock" after college (19). They find themselves managing natural resources in the courthouse, the newspaper, or legislative conference rooms as much as in the field. Some USDA Forest Service wildlife professionals have identified themselves as "combat biologists" in what they perceive as an abnormal sociopolitical environment—a management environment that is merely the modern, post-industrial world. It is in these sociopolitical arenas that wildlife or other natural resource social values are often debated and "resolved" today, as much as in lecture halls or the field.

This is not to argue that natural resource managers be primarily educated and competent in the social sciences versus ecology. It's a plea that traditional natural resource education and management be placed in a broader and evolving social value context. Like fresh engineers or science graduates (20), natural resource managers are expected to be, first and foremost, technically competent. However even at the entry level or technical stage of their professional careers, natural resource managers should be better able to understand and cope with the multitude of environmental social values by viewing their role as accommodating and participating in an evolving American value system. As natural resource managers move up career ladders, away from the field and into administrative and political arenas, viewing themselves as social value and conflict managers may have even greater survival and effectiveness advantages (21).

Finally, our social value perspective does not suggest that natural resource managers completely become instrumental public servants and endorse a consumer-is-always-right code. The most valid role of natural resource and environmental professionals is to inform society of the complex, interrelated functions of ecosystems and the sustainability consequences of pursuing certain social value options. In addition, *current* society are not the major stockholders of natural resource social values—especially on public lands and waters. For all of us living who seek fulfillment of our social values, there are many, many more humans yet to live whose social values must be accommodated by the ecosystems they will inherit from us. They, too, are an important public for us professionals and public servants to serve.

Acknowledgments

This project was funded by the Utah State Agricultural Experiment Station, MacIntire–Stennis Project 712 (Journal Pap. 3095) and a cooperative grant from the USDA Forest Service.

Notes

1. Kennedy, J.J., and J.A. Mincolla. 1985. Early career development of fisheries and wildlife biologists in two Forest Service Regions. Transactions of the North American Wildlife and Natural Resources Conference 50:425–435.
2. Magill, A.W. 1983. The reluctant public servant. Journal of Forestry. 81:82.

    Kennedy, J.J. 1986. Early career development of Forest Service fisheries managers. Fisheries 11:8–12.

    Thomas, J.W. 1986. Effectiveness: the hallmark of the natural resource management professional. Transactions of the North American Wildlife and Natural Resources Conference 51.27–33.
3. Kennedy, J.J. 1985. Conceiving forest management as providing for current and future social value. Forest Ecology and Management 13:121–132.

    Wagner, F.H. 1989. American wildlife management at the crossroads. Wildlife Society Bulletin 17:354–360.
4. Passmore, J. 1974. Man's responsibility for nature. New York: C. Scribner's Sons. 213 pp.

    Foley, M.W. 1977. Who cut down the sacred tree? The Co-Evol. Q. Fall: 60–67.
5. Rolston, H., III. 1988. Environmental ethics. Philadelphia, Pennsylvania: Temple University Press. 391 pp.
6. Devall, B., and G. Sessions. 1984. The development of natural resources and the integrity of nature. Environmental Ethics 6:293–322.
7. Rolston 1988 (5).
8. Leopold, A. 1940. The state of the profession. Journal of Wildlife Management 4:343–346.

Flader, S. 1974. Thinking like a mountain—Aldo Leopold and the evaluation of an ecological attitude toward deer, wolves, and forests. Columbia, Missouri: University of Missouri Press. 284 pp.

Kennedy, J.J. 1984. Understanding professional career evolution—an example of Aldo Leopold. Wildlife Society Bulletin 12:215–226.

9. Kennedy, J.J. 1973. Some effects of urbanization on big and small game management. Transactions of the 38th North American Wildlife and Natural Resources Conference 38:248–55.

Kellert, S.R. 1980. Contemporary values of wildlife in American society. In Wildlife values. W.S. Shaw and E.H. Zube, eds. 55–62. Centennial for Assessment of Noncommodity Natural Resource Values. Tucson, Arizona: University of Arizona.

10. Hays, S.P. 1959. Conservation and the gospel of efficiency. Cambridge, Massachusetts: Harvard University Press. 197 pp.

11. Kessler, W.B., H. Salwasser, C.W. Cartwright Jr., and J.A. Caplan. 1992. New perspectives for sustainable natural resources management. Ecological Applications 2:221–225.

Overbay, J.C. 1992. Ecosystem management. Paper at national workshop on taking an ecological approach to management. (Reprint available from USDA Forest Service, Washington, D.C.) 8 pp.

12. Flader 1974 (8); Meine, C. 1988. Aldo Leopold—his life and work. Madison, Wisconsin: University of Wisconsin Press. 638 pp.

13. Lautenschlager, R.A., and R.T. Bowyer. 1985. Wildlife management by referendum: when professionals fail to communicate. Wildlife Society Bulletin 13:564–570.

14. Wildlife Management Institute. 1973. The North American wildlife policy—1973. Washington, D.C. 57 pp.

15. Alston, R.M. 1972. F.O.R.E.S.T.: goals and decision-making in the Forest Service (INT-128) USDA Forest Service, Intermountain Forest and Range Experiment Station, Ogden, Utah. 114 pp.

16. USDA Forest Service. 1990. Workforce data book 1989. Personnel and Civil Rights, Washington, D.C. 62 pp.

17. Cutler, M.R. 1982. What kind of wildlifers will be needed in the 1980s? Wildlife Society Bulletin 10:75–79.

Kennedy, J.J. 1985. Viewing wildlife managers as a unique professional subculture. Wildlife Society Bulletin 13:571–579.

18. Shaw, K. 1984. On moose in Maine. B.A. Thesis, Department of Environmental Studies. Providence, Rhode Island: Brown University 112 pp.

Kennedy, J.J. 1988. The symbolic infrastructure of natural resource management: an example of the U.S. Forest Service. Society and Natural Resources 1:241–251.

19. Hughes, E.C. 1958. Men and their work. Glencoe, Illinois: Free Press. 245 pp.
20. Dalton, G.W., P.H. Thompson, and R.L. Price. 1977. The four stages of professional careers. Organ. Dynamics 6:19–42.

Chapter 19

Ecological Economics: Toward a New Transdisciplinary Science

Robert Costanza

> We need to make no apology
> For thinking about world ecology.
> For mere economics
> Is stuff for the comics
> Unless we can live with biology.

—Kenneth E. Boulding
*Ecological Economics: The Science and
Management of Sustainability*

An Ecological Economic World View

There is increasing awareness that our global ecological life support system is endangered, and that decisions made on the basis of local, narrow, short-term criteria can produce disastrous results globally. Societies are beginning to realize as well that traditional economic and ecological models and concepts fall short in their ability to deal with these problems.

Ecological economics is a new transdisciplinary field of study that addresses the relationships between ecosystems and economic systems in the broadest sense. These relationships are central to many of humanity's current problems, and to building a sustainable future, but are not well covered by any existing field.

By *transdisciplinary*, I mean that ecological economics goes beyond our normal conceptions of scientific disciplines and tries to integrate and synthesize many different perspectives. It focuses more directly on the problems, rather than the particular academic tools and models used to solve them, and it ignores arbitrary intellectual turf boundaries. No field has intellectual precedence in an endeavor as important as achieving sustainability. While the academic tools used in this quest are important, they are secondary to the goal of solving the critical problems of managing the human role on the planet. The focus on instruments and techniques must be transcended so that we avoid the image of "a person with a hammer to whom everything looks like a nail." Rather, people should consider the task, evaluate the ability of existing mechanisms to handle the job, and design new ones when they are ineffective. Ecological economics uses agents of conventional economics and ecology as appropriate. The need for new intellectual strategies will emerge where the coupling of economics and ecology is not currently possible.

How Is Ecological Economics Different from Conventional Approaches?

Ecological economics differs from both conventional economics and conventional ecology in terms of the breadth of its perception of the problem and the importance it attaches to environment–economy interactions. It takes this wider, longer view in terms of space, time, and the parts of the system to be studied.

Figure 19.1 illustrates one aspect of the relationship—the domains of the different subdisciplines. The upper-left box represents "conventional" economics, that is, the interactions of economic sectors (for example, mining,

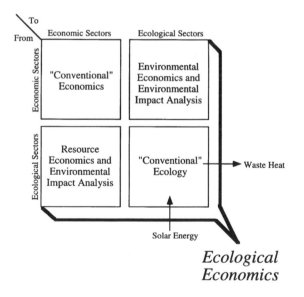

Figure 19.1   The domains of conventional economics, conventional ecology, environmental and resource economics, and ecological economics.

manufacturing, or households) with each other. "Conventional" ecology, the interactions of ecosystems and their components with each other, is in the lower-right box. The lower-left box represents the inputs from ecological sectors to economic sectors. This is the usual domain of resource economics and environmental impact analysis—the use of renewable and nonrenewable natural resources by the economy. The upper-right box represents the "use" by ecological sectors of economic "products," which are usually unwanted by-products of production and the ultimate wastes from consumption. This is the usual domain of environmental economics and environmental impact analysis—pollution and its mitigation, prevention, and mediation. Ecological economics encompasses and transcends these disciplinary boundaries and sees the human economy as part of a larger whole. Its domain is the entire web of interactions between economic and ecological sectors.

Some of the other major differences among ecological economics and conventional economics and conventional ecology are listed in Table 19.1. The basic world view of conventional economics is one in which individual human consumers are the central figures. Their tastes and preferences are taken as given and are the dominant, determining force. The resource base is viewed as essentially limitless due to technical progress and infinite substitutability. Ecological economics takes a more holistic view with humans as one component (albeit a very important one) in the overall system. Human preferences, understanding, technology, and cultural organization coevolve to reflect broad ecological opportunities and constraints. Humans have a special place in the system because they are responsible for understanding their own role in the larger system and for managing it sustainably.

This basic world view is similar to that of conventional ecology, in which the resource base is limited and humans are merely another (albeit seldom studied) species. But ecological economics differs from conventional ecology in the importance it gives to humans as a species, and its emphasis on the mutual importance of cultural and biological evolution.

The concept of evolution is a guiding notion for both ecology and ecological economics (1). Evolution is the process of change in complex systems through selection of transmittable traits. Whether these traits are the shapes and programmed behavioral characteristics of organisms transmitted genetically, or the institutions and behaviors of cultures passed on through cultural artifacts, books, and tales around the campfire, they are both evolutionary processes. Evolution implies a dynamic and adapting nonequilibrium system rather than the static equilibrium system often assumed in conventional economics. Evolution does not imply change in a particular direction (i.e., progress).

Table 19.1

Comparison of "Conventional" Economics and Ecology with Ecological Economics

	"Conventional" economics	"Conventional" ecology	Ecological economics
Basic world view	**Mechanistic, static, atomistic** Individual tastes and preferences taken as given and the dominant force. The resource base viewed as essentially limitless due to technical progress and infinite substitutability.	**Evolutionary, atomistic** Evolution acting at the genetic level viewed as the dominant force. The resource base is limited. Humans are just another species but are rarely studied.	**Dynamic, systems, evolutionary** Human preferences, understanding, technology, and organization co-evolve to reflect broad ecological opportunities and constraints. Humans are responsible for understanding their role in the larger system and managing it sustainably.
Time frame	**Short** 50 years max, 1–4 years usual	**Multiscale** Days to eons, but time scales often define noncommunicating subdisciplines.	**Multiscale** Days to eons, multiscale synthesis
Space frame	**Local to international** Framework invariant at increasing spatial scale, basic units change from individuals to firms to countries.	**Local to regional** Most research has focused on smaller research sites in one ecosystem, but larger scales have become more important.	**Local to global** Hierarchy of scales
Species frame	**Humans only** Plants and animals only rarely included for contributary value.	**Nonhumans only** Attempts to find "pristine" ecosystems untouched by humans.	**Whole ecosystem including humans** Acknowledges interconnections between humans and rest of nature.

	Growth of national economy	Survival of species	Ecological economic system sustainability
Primary macro goal			
Primary micro goal	**Max profits** (firms) **Max utility** (individuals) All agents following micro goals leads to macro goal being fulfilled. External costs and benefits given lip service but usually ignored.	**Max reproductive success** All agents following micro goals leads to macro goal being fulfilled.	**Must be adjusted to reflect system goals** Social organization and cultural institutions at higher levels of the space/time hierarchy ameliorate conflicts produced by myopic pursuit of micro goals at lower levels, and vice versa.
Assumptions about technical progress	*Very optimistic*	*Pessimistic or no opinion*	*Prudently skeptical*
Academic stance	*Disciplinary* Monistic, focus on mathematical tools.	*Disciplinary* More pluralistic than economics, but still focused on tools and techniques Few rewards for integrative work.	*Transdisciplinary* Pluralistic, focus on problems.

Ecological economics uses an expanded definition of the term *evolution* to encompass both biological and cultural change. Biological evolution is slow relative to cultural evolution. The price human cultures pay for their ability to adapt rapidly is that of becoming too dependent on quick solutions and, therefore, ignoring long-term answers and issues of sustainability. Biological evolution imposes a built-in, long-run constraint that cultural evolution does not have. To ensure sustainability, societies may have to reinstate long-run constraints by developing institutions (or effectively using existing ones) to bring the global, long-term, multispecies, multiscale, whole systems perspective to bear on short-term cultural evolution.

The issue of the human role in shaping the combined biological and cultural evolution of the planet is of critical importance. Humans are conscious of these processes and cannot avoid being anthropocentric. If people are to manage the whole planet effectively, however, they must develop the capacity for a broader, biocentric perspective that treats all species with respect and fairness. People need to further recognize that most natural systems are self-regulating, and that the best "managerial strategy" is often to leave them alone.

The time frame, space frame, and species frame of ecological economics all tend to be broader than conventional economics and are more similar to the "frames" of conventional ecology. There is explicit recognition, though, of the need for integrated, multiscale analysis. This view is beginning to take hold in conventional ecology, but it is virtually absent from traditional economics. In practice, conventional ecology ignores humans; conventional economics ignores everything but humans; and ecological economics tries to manage the whole system while acknowledging the interconnections between humans and nature. The human system is a subunit within the larger ecological system. This implies not only a relationship of interdependence, but ultimately a relation of dependence of the part on the whole. The first questions to ask about a subsystem are: how big is it relative to the total system; how big can it be; and how big should it be? These questions of scale are only now beginning to be asked (2).

The macro goal of ecological economics is sustainability of the combined ecological economic system. Traditional ecology's macro goal of species survival is similar to sustainability but is generally confined to single species and not the whole system. Conventional economics emphasizes growth over sustainability at the macro level. At the micro level, ecological economics is unique in acknowledging the two-way linkage between scales, rather than the one-way view of the orthodox sciences in which all macro behavior is the simple aggregation of micro behavior. In ecological economics, social organization and cultural institutions at higher levels of the space/time hierarchy ameliorate conflicts produced by myopic pursuit of micro goals at lower levels, and vice versa.

Perhaps the key distinctions between ecological economics and the conventional sciences lie in their academic stances and their assumptions about technical progress. As already noted, ecological economics is transdisciplinary, pluralistic, integrative, and more focused on problems than on tools.

Traditional economics is very optimistic about the ability of technology to ultimately remove all resource constraints to continued economic growth. Ecology really has very little to say directly about technology since it tends to operate outside the human context. To the extent that it has an opinion, conventional ecology would be pessimistic about technology's ability to remove resource constraints, because all other existing natural ecosystems that do not include humans are observed to be resource limited. Ecological economics is prudently skeptical in this regard. Given our high level of uncertainty about this issue, it is irrational to bank on technology's ability to remove resource constraints. If people guess wrong about technology, the result will be disastrous, irreversible destruction of our resource base and civilization itself. Societies should, at least for the time being, assume that technology will not be able to remove resource constraints. If it does, we can all be pleasantly surprised. If it does not, we are still left with a sustainable system.

A Hierarchy of Goals and Incentives

No complex system can be managed effectively without clear goals and appropriate mechanisms for achieving them. In managing the Earth, people are faced with a nested hierarchy of goals that span a wide range of time and space scales. In any rational system of management, global, ecological, and economic health and sustainability should be "higher" goals than local, short-term, national economic growth or private interests. Economic growth can only be supported as a policy goal in this context to the extent that it is consistent with long-term global sustainability.

Unfortunately, most of our current institutions and incentive structures deal only with relatively short-term, local goals and incentives (3). This would not be a problem if these immediate agendas reflected appropriate behavior globally, as many assume they do. Unfortunately, this often is very far from being the case. Individuals, firms, or countries pursuing their own private self-interests, in the absence of mechanisms to account for community and global interests, frequently run afoul of these larger goals and can often drive themselves to their own demise.

These goal and incentive inconsistencies have been characterized and generalized in many ways, beginning with Hardin's classic paper (4) on the tragedy of the commons and continuing through more recent work on "social traps" (5). Social traps occur when local incentives that guide behavior are inconsistent with the overall goals of the system. Examples are cigarette and drug addiction, overuse of pesticides, economic boom and bust cycles, and a host of others. Social traps are also amenable to experimental research to see how people behave in trap-like situations and how to best avoid and escape from social traps (6). The bottom line emerging from this research is that in cases where social traps exist, the system is not inherently sustainable, and special steps must be taken to harmonize goals and incentives over the hierarchy of time and space involved. Explicit, special steps must be taken to make the global and long-term goals incumbent on and consistent with the local and short-term goals.

This is in contrast to natural systems which are forced to adopt a long-term perspective by the constraints of genetic evolution. In natural systems, "survival" generally equates to continual viability of the species as part of a larger ecosystem, and natural selection eventually yields sustainable systems. Humans have broken the bonds of genetic evolution by the expanded use of learned behavior our large brains allow, and by extending our physical capabilities with tools. The price paid for this rapid adaptation is a partial isolation from long-term constraints and a susceptibility to social traps.

Another general result of social trap research is that the relative effectiveness of alternative corrective steps is not easy to predict from simple "rational" models of human behavior prevalent in conventional economic thinking. The experimental facts indicate the need to develop more realistic models of human behavior under uncertainty that acknowledge the complexity of most real-world decisions and our limited information-processing capabilities (7).

Perhaps the most glaring and important lack of global harmony exists today at the interface between ecological and economic systems. A primary purpose of ecological economics is to harmonize these pursuits through a better understanding of the linkages between ecological and economic systems, especially long-term global ones.

The Interface between Ecological and Economic Systems

Ecological systems play a fundamental role in supporting life on earth at all hierarchical scales. They form the life-support system without which economic activity would not be possible. They are essential in global material cycles like the carbon and water cycles. They provide raw materials, food, water, recreational opportunities, and microclimate control for the entire human population. In the long run, a healthy economy can exist only in symbiosis with a healthy ecology; isolating them for academic purposes has led to distortions and poor management.

Ecological systems are our best current models of sustainable systems. Better understanding of ecological systems and how they function and maintain themselves can yield insights into designing and managing sustainable economic systems. For example, there is no "pollution" in climax ecosystems—all waste and by-products are recycled or harmlessly dissipated. This implies that a characteristic of sustainable economic systems should be a similar "closing the cycle" by finding economic uses and recycling "pollution," rather than simply storing it, exporting it, diluting it, or changing its state, and allowing it to disrupt ecosystems.

A Research Agenda for Ecological Economics

To achieve sustainability several steps are necessary, including innovative research. This research should not be divorced from the policy and management process, but rather integrated into it. The research agenda for ecological economics suggested below is a snapshot, a first guess, intended to begin the process of defining topics for future ecological economic research, rather than a final word. The list of topics can be divided into five major parts: (1) sustainability, or maintaining our life support system; (2) valuation of natural resources and natural capital; (3) ecological economic system accounting; (4) ecological economic modeling at local, regional, and global scales; and (5) innovative instruments for environmental management. Some brief background on each of these topics is given below.

Sustainability: Maintaining Our Life Support System

"Sustainability" does not imply a static, much less a stagnant, economy, but we must be careful to distinguish between "growth" and "development." Economic growth, which is an increase in quantity, cannot be sustainable indefinitely on a finite planet. Economic development, which is an improvement in the quality of life without necessarily causing an increase in quantity of resources consumed, may be sustainable. Sustainable growth is an impossibility. Sustainable development must become our primary long-term policy goal (8).

Nature is the economy's life support system, and by ignoring it we may inadvertently inflict damage beyond nature's ability to repair itself. Indeed, there is much evidence that we have already done so. Several authors have stressed the fact that current economic systems do not incorporate concern about the sustainability of our natural life support system and the economies that depend on it (9). Pearce (10) discusses the reasons for the inability of existing forms of economic organization (free market, mixed, planned) to guarantee sustainability. In an important sense sustainability is merely justice with respect to future generations. This includes future generations of other species even though the main focus may be ourselves.

Sustainability has been variously construed (11), but a useful definition is the amount of consumption that can be continued indefinitely without degrading capital stocks, including "natural capital" stocks (12). In a business, capital stock includes long-term assets such as buildings and machinery that serve as the means of production. Natural capital is the soil and atmospheric structure, plant and animal biomass, and the like, forming the basis of all ecosystems. This natural capital stock uses primary inputs (sunlight) to produce the range of ecosystem services and physical natural resource flows. Examples of natural capital include forests, fish populations, and petroleum deposits. The natural resource flows yielded by these natural capital stocks are, respectively, cut timber, caught fish, and pumped crude oil. We have now entered a new era in which the limiting factor in development is no longer human-made capital, but remaining natural capital. Timber is limited by remaining forests, not sawmill capacity; fish catch is limited by fish population, not by the number of fishing boats; crude oil is limited by remaining petroleum deposits, not by pumping and drilling capacity. Most economists view natural and human-made capital as substitutes rather than complements. Consequently, neither factor can be limiting; only if factors are complementary can one be limiting. Ecological economists see human-made and natural capital as fundamentally complementary, and therefore emphasize the importance of limiting factors and changes in the pattern of scarcity. This is a fundamental difference between ecological economics and prevailing economic theory that needs to be reconciled through debate and research.

Definitions of sustainability are obviously dependent on the time and space scale we are using. We need to concentrate on how different scales interact and how we might construct multiscale operational definitions of sustainability.

While acknowledging that the sustainability concept requires much additional research, the following working definition of sustainability has been developed (13):

> Sustainability is a relationship between dynamic human economic systems and larger dynamic but, normally, slower-changing eco-

logical systems in which (a) human life can continue indefinitely; (b) human individuals can flourish; (c) human cultures can develop; but in which (d) effects of human activities remain within bounds, so as not to destroy the diversity, complexity, and function of the ecological life support system.

Valuation of Ecosystem Services and Natural Capital

To achieve sustainability, we must incorporate ecosystem goods and services into our economic accounting. The first step is to determine values for them comparable to those of economic goods and services. In determining values we must also consider how much of our ecological life support system we can afford to lose. To what extent can we substitute manufactured for natural capital, and how much of our natural capital is irreplaceable (14)? For example, could we replace the radiation screening services of the ozone layer that is currently being destroyed?

Some argue that we cannot place economic value on such "intangibles" as human life, environmental aesthetics, or long-term ecological benefits (15). In fact, we do so every day. When we set construction standards for highways, bridges, and the like, we value human life—acknowledged or not—because spending more money on construction will save lives. To preserve our natural capital we must confront these often difficult choices and valuations directly rather than denying their existence.

Because of the inherent difficulties and uncertainties in determining values, ecological economics acknowledges several independent approaches. There is no consensus on which approach is right or wrong—they all tell us something—but there is agreement that better valuation of ecosystem services is an important goal for ecological economics.

The conventional economic view defines value as the expression of individual human preferences, with the preferences taken as given and with no attempt to analyze their origins or patterns of long-term change. For goods and services with few long-term impacts (like tomatoes or bread) that are traded in well-functioning markets with adequate information, market ("revealed preference") valuations work well.

Ecological goods and services (wetland sewage treatment or global climate control), however, are long term by nature, are generally not traded in markets (no one owns the air), and information about their contribution to an individual's well-being is poor. To determine their value economists try to persuade people to reveal what they would be willing to pay for ecological goods and services in hypothetical markets (16). For example, we can ask people the maximum they would pay to use national parks even if they do not have to actually pay it. The quality of results using this method depends on how well-informed people are, and it is difficult to induce individuals to reveal their true willingness to pay for natural resources when the question is put directly. Contingent referenda (willingness to be taxed as a citizen along with other citizens as opposed to inclination to pay as an individual) are superior to straightforward studies in this regard. This method, though, does not adequately incorporate long-term goals since it excludes future generations from bidding in (even hypothetical) markets.

In practice, valuation, or shadow pricing, of environmental functions may require some collectively set quantitative standard. Then shadow prices can be calculated subject to the constraint represented by that standard (17).

An alternative method for estimating ecological values assumes a biophysical link with value (18). This theory suggests that in the long run humans come to value things according to how costly they are to produce, and that this cost is ultimately a function of how organized they are relative to their environment. To organize a complex structure takes energy, both directly in the form of fuel and indirectly in the form of other organized structures like factories. For example, a car is a much more organized structure than a lump of iron ore, and therefore it takes a lot of energy (directly and indirectly) to organize iron ore into a car. Thus, the amount of solar energy required to grow forests can serve as a measure of their energy cost, their organization, and according to this theory, their value.

The results of applying these two radically different approaches, one based on human perceptions (willingness to pay or WTP) and one based on biophysical production (energy analysis or EA) to the valuation of wetlands in Louisiana is shown in Table 19.2 (19). The striking feature is just how close the results are to each other. They can, in fact, be interpreted as setting the range within which the true value probably falls. The WTP method sets the low end of the range since it must enumerate all the individual non-marketed services of the ecosystem and develop pseudomarkets (via questionnaires or observations of behavior) to evaluate each one. This process will almost certainly miss some important services. The EA method, on the other hand, assumes that all the production of the ecosystem is valuable, directly or indirectly, and to the extent that some ecosystem services are not ultimately valuable to humans, it overestimates.

The point that must be stressed, however, is that the economic value of ecosystems is connected to their physical, chemical, and biological role in both the short-term and the long-term global system—whether the present generation of humans fully recognizes that role or not. If it is accepted that each species, no matter how seemingly uninteresting or lacking in immediate utility, has a role in natural ecosystems (which do provide many direct

Table 19.2

Summary of Wetland Value Estimates (1983 Dollars)		
Method	Per acre present value at specified discount rate	
	8%	3%
WTP-based		
Commercial fishery	$317	$846
Trapping	151	401
Recreation	46	181
Storm protection	1915	7549
TOTAL	$2429	$8977
Option and existence values	?	?
EA-based		
GPP conversion	6,400–10,600	17,000–28,200
"Best estimate"	$2429–6400	$8977–17,000

Source: Costanza et al. (1980), see note 19.

benefits to humans), it is possible to shift the focus away from our imperfect short-term perceptions and derive more accurate values for long-term ecosystem services. Using this perspective, we may be able to better estimate the values contributed by, say, maintenance of water and atmospheric quality to long-term human well-being

Ecological Economic System Accounting

Gross national product (GNP), as well as other related measures of national economic performance, have come to be extremely important as policy objectives, political issues, and benchmarks of the general welfare. Yet GNP, as presently defined, ignores the contribution of nature to production, often leading to peculiar results.

For example, a standing forest provides real economic services for people by conserving soil, cleaning air and water, providing habitat for wildlife, and supporting recreational activities. As GNP is currently figured, though, only the value of harvested timber is calculated in the total. On the other hand, the billions of dollars that Exxon spent on the Valdez cleanup—and the billions spent by Exxon and others on the more than 100 other oil spills following it—all actually *improved* our apparent economic performance. Why? Because cleaning up oil spills creates jobs and consumes resources, all of which add to GNP. Of course, these expenses would not have been necessary if the oil had not been spilled, so they shouldn't be considered "benefits." But GNP adds up all production without differentiating between costs and benefits, and is therefore not a very good measure of economic health.

In fact, when resource depletion and degradation are factored into economic trends, what emerges is a radically different picture from that depicted by conventional methods. For example, Herman Daly and John Cobb (21) have attempted to adjust GNP to account mainly for depletion of natural capital, pollution effects, and income distribution effects by producing an "index of sustainable economic welfare (ISEW)." They conclude that while GNP in the United States rose over the 1956–1986 interval, ISEW has remained relatively unchanged since about 1970. When factors such as loss of farms and wetlands, costs of mitigating acid rain effects, and health costs caused by increased pollution are accounted for, the United States economy has not improved at all. If we continue to ignore natural ecosystems, we may drive the economy down while we think we are building it up. By consuming our natural capital, we endanger our ability to sustain income. Daly and Cobb acknowledge that many arbitrary judgments go into their ISEW, but claim nevertheless that it is less arbitrary than GNP as a measure of welfare.

A number of additional promising approaches are being developed to account for ecosystem services and natural capital (22), and this area promises to be a major focus of research in ecological economics. The approaches are based on differing assumptions but share the goal of attempting to quantify ecological economic interdependencies and arriving at overall system measures of health and performance. The economist Wassily Leontief (23) was the first to attempt detailed quantitative descriptions of complex systems to allow a complete accounting of system interdependencies. Leontief's input–output (I–O) analysis has become a standard conceptual and applied tool in economic accounting. Isard (24) was the first to attempt combined ecological economic system I–O analysis. The same type of model has been proposed by several other authors as well (25). Ecologists have also applied I–O analysis to the accounting of material transfers in ecosystems (26). We refer to the total of all variations of the analysis of ecological and/or economic networks as "network analysis."

Network analysis holds the promise of allowing an integrated quantitative treatment of combined ecological economic systems. One promising route is the use of "ascendancy" (27) and related variables (28) to measure the degree of organization in ecological, economic, or any other networks. Measures like ascendancy go several steps beyond the traditional diversity indices used in ecology. They estimate not only how many different species (or sectors) there are in a system but, more important, how those species are organized. This kind of measure may provide the basis for a quantitative and general index of system health applicable to both ecological and economic systems.

Another promising avenue for research in network analysis has to do with its use for "pricing" commodities in ecological or economic systems (29). The "mixed units" problem arises in any field that tries to analyze interdependence and limiting factors in complex systems that have many different types and qualities of interacting processes and commodities. Ecology and economics are two such fields. Network analysis in ecology has avoided this problem in the past by arbitrarily choosing one commodity flowing through the system as an index of interdependence (i.e., carbon, enthalpy, nitrogen, etc.). This selection ignores the complex interdependencies among commodities and assumes that the chosen commodity is a valid "tracer" for relative value or importance in the system. This assumption is unrealistic and severely limits the scope of an analysis whose major objective is to deal comprehensively with whole systems.

There are evolving methods for dealing with the mixed units problem based on analogies to the calculation of prices in economic input–output models. Starting with a more realistic "commodity by process" description of ecosystem networks that allows for joint products, one can ultimately convert the multiple commodity description into a pair of matrices that can serve as the input for standard (single commodity) network analysis. The new single-commodity description incorporates commodity and process interdependencies and limiting-factor relationships in a manner analogous to the way economic value incorporates production interdependencies in economic systems (30). This analysis allows a biophysical valuation of components of combined ecological and economic systems as a complement to subjective evaluations.

This approach, like all others, is limited by its underlying assumptions and the precision of the data that go into it. There is no single modeling approach that can give us all the information we need about something as large and complex as the biosphere. Even with the best conceivable modeling capabilities, we will always be confronted with large amounts of uncertainty about the response of the environment to human actions. Learning how to effectively manage the environment in the face of this uncertainty is critical.

Ecological Economic Modeling at Local, Regional, and Global Scales

Since ecosystems are threatened by a host of human activities, protecting and preserving them requires the ability to understand the direct and indirect effects of human activities over long periods of time and over large areas. Computer simulations are now important tools to investigate these interactions. Without the sophisticated global atmospheric simulations now being done, our understanding of the potential impacts of increasing carbon dioxide concentrations in the atmosphere due to fossil fuel burning would be much more primitive. Computer simulations can now be used to understand not only human impacts on ecosystems, but also our economic dependence on natural ecosystem services and capital, and the interdependence between ecological and economic components of the system (31).

Several recent developments make such computer simulation modeling feasible, including the accessibility of extensive spatial and temporal databases and advances in computer power and convenience. Computer simulation models are potentially one of our best tools to help understand the complex, nonlinear, and often chaotic dynamics of integrated ecological economic systems.

Even with the best conceivable modeling capabilities, though, we will always be confronted with large amounts of uncertainty about the response of the environment to human actions (32). Learning how to effectively manage the environment in the face of this uncertainty is critical (33). The research program of ecological economics should pursue an integrated, multiscale, transdisciplinary, and pluralistic approach to quantitative ecological economic modeling while acknowledging the remaining uncertainty inherent in modeling these systems. The program should then develop new ways to effectively deal with this uncertainty (34).

Innovative Instruments for Environmental Management

Current systems of regulation are not very efficient at managing environmental resources for sustainability, particularly in the face of uncertainty about long-term values and impacts (35). These regulations are inherently reactive rather than proactive. They induce legal confrontation, obfuscation, and government intrusion into business. Rather than encouraging long-range technical and social innovation, they tend to suppress it. They do not mesh well with the market signals that firms and individuals use to make decisions, and do not effectively translate long-term global goals into short-term local incentives.

We need to explore promising alternatives to our current command and control environmental management systems and to modify existing government agencies and other institutions accordingly. The enormous uncertainty about local and transnational environmental impacts needs to be incorporated into decision making. We also need to better understand the sociological, cultural, and political criteria for acceptance or rejection of policy instruments.

One example of an innovative policy instrument is a flexible environmental assurance bonding system designed to incorporate environmental criteria and uncertainty into the market system, and to induce positive environmental technological innovation (36).

In addition to direct charges for known environmental damages, a company would be required to post an assurance bond equal to the current best estimate of the largest potential future environmental damages; the money would be kept in interest-bearing escrow accounts. The bond (plus a portion of the interest) would be returned if the firm could show that the suspected damages had not occurred or would not occur. If damage does occur, the bond would be used to rehabilitate or repair the environment and to compensate injured parties. Thus, the burden of proof would be shifted from the public to the resource user, and a strong economic incentive would be provided to research the true costs of environmentally damaging activities and to develop cost-effective pollution control technologies. This is an extension of the "polluter pays" principle to "the polluter pays for uncertainty as well" or the "precautionary polluter pays principle" (37). Other innovative policy instruments include tradable pollution and depletion quotas at both national and international levels. Also worthy of mention is the newly emerging global environmental facility of the World Bank, which will provide concessionary funds for investments that reduce global externalities.

Policy Recommendations

Sustainability as the Goal

We should institute a consistent goal of sustainability in all institutions at all levels from local to global. We should strive to address prevailing values and decision-making processes by increasing the awareness of institutions and persons about ecological sustainability. We should promote long-term thinking, the use of a systems approach in decision making, and use of "ecological auditors" (i.e., trained environmental professionals) by public and private institutions whose activities affect the environment.

For example, the World Bank is an important global institution that directly affects economic policy which, in turn, has severe environmental secondary effects, especially on the environmental conditions of developing nations. We recommend that the Bank and similar institutions require that all projects meet the following criteria: for renewable resources, the rate of harvest should not exceed the rate of regeneration (sustainable yield), and the rates of waste generation from projects should not exceed the assimilative capacity of the environment (sustainable waste disposal);

for nonrenewable resources, the rates of waste generation from projects should not exceed the assimilative capacity of the environment, and the depletion of the nonrenewable resources should require comparable development of renewable substitutes for that resource. These are safe, minimum sustainability standards; and once met, the Bank should then select projects for funding that have the highest rates of return based on other, more traditional economic criteria.

We recognize that this policy will be very difficult at first, and that the policies will likely shift as more information is developed about managing for sustainability. However, there is a need for major institutions to not only affirm, but to operationalize the goal of sustainability because of the global scope of their programs and of the impact their example will provide for smaller institutions worldwide. We also recognize that goal setting is an ethical issue, and that it is absurd to ignore the normative preconditions of policy, however necessary it may be to avoid mixing normative and positive statements in analysis. Both economists and ecologists (if they want to talk about policy) must offer much more explicit ethical support for their goals whether they be sustainability or growth.

Maintaining Natural Capital to Assure Sustainability

A minimum necessary condition for sustainability is the maintenance of the total natural capital stock at or above the current level. While a lower stock of natural capital may be sustainable, given our uncertainty and the dire consequences of guessing wrong, it is best to at least provisionally assume that we are at or below the range of sustainable stock levels and allow no further decline in natural capital. This "constancy of total natural capital" rule can thus be seen as a prudent minimum condition for assuring sustainability, to be abandoned only when solid evidence to the contrary can be offered (38). There is disagreement between technological optimists (who see technical progress eliminating all resource constraints to growth and development) and technological skeptics (who do not see as much hope for this approach and fear irreversible use of resources and damage to natural capital). By limiting total system natural capital at current levels (preferably by using higher severance and consumption taxes), we can satisfy both the skeptics (since resources will be conserved for future generations) and the optimists (since this will raise the price of natural capital resources and more rapidly induce the technical change they predict). By limiting physical growth only, development is allowed, and this may proceed without endangering sustainability.

Improving Our Use of Policy Instruments

We need to use a wide variety of policy instruments including regulation, property rights, permits, marketable permits, fees, subsidies, and bonds to assure sustainability. Criteria for the use of policy instruments are equity, efficiency, scientific validity, consensus, frugality, and environmental effectiveness. We should institute regulatory reforms to promote the appropriate use of financial, legal, and social incentives. We may use market incentives where appropriate in allocation decisions. In decisions of scale, individual freedom of choice must give way to democratic collective decision making by the relevant community.

Economic Incentives: Linking Revenues and Uses

We should implement fees on the destructive use of natural capital to promote more efficient use and ease up on income taxes, especially on low incomes, in the interest of equity. Fees, taxes, and subsidies should be used to change the price of activities that interfere with sustainability versus those that are compatible with it. This result can be accomplished by using the funds generated to support an alternative to undesirable activities that are being taxed. For example, a tax on all greenhouse gases (with the size of the tax linked to the impact of each gas) could be tied to development of alternatives to fossil fuel. Gasoline tax revenues could be used to support mass transit and bike lanes. Current policies that subsidize environmentally harmful activities (for example, subsidies on virgin material extraction) should be stopped, allowing recycling options to effectively compete. Crop subsidies that dramatically increase pesticide and fertilizer use should be eliminated, and forms of positive incentives should also be used. For example, debt-for-nature swaps should be supported and receive much more funding. We should also offer prestigious prizes for work that increases awareness of or contributes to sustainability issues, such as changes in behavior that develop a culture of maintenance (i.e., cars that last for 50 years) or promotes capital and resource saving improvements (i.e., affordable, efficient housing and water supplies).

Ecological Economic Research

While economics has developed many useful tools of analysis, it has not directed these tools toward the thorny questions that arise when considering the concept and implementation of sustainability. In particular, we need to better understand preference formation, time preference formation in

particular. We also need to understand how individual and group time preferences may differ, and how the tendencies of institutions that will be critical to the success or failure of sustainability are established. We have
heretofore paid too little attention to ecological feedbacks. An understanding of these will be critical to the implementation of sustainability
goals, whatever they may be. We need to concentrate on the valuation of important nonmarket goods and services provided by ecosystems. We need to
better understand the effects of various regulatory instruments that can be
used to attain sustainability. This goal may require experimental testing of
behavior in a laboratory context. Most important, we need to study how positive sustainability incentives can be employed to induce reluctant participants to lengthen their time horizons and think globally about their resource
policies.

We also need to develop an ecological history of the planet (to complement the existing human economic history) that would contain trends of resource use, development and exhaustion, changes in science and technology, and so on. We should promote the use (as one of a bundle of
decision-making tools) of broad benefit-cost analyses that include the consideration of all market and nonmarket costs and benefits.

Ecological Economics Education

Our education system is currently characterized by overspecialization and
disciplinary isolation (see Chapter 17, by Jacobson). We need to develop
transdisciplinary curricula and job and academic support systems for both
specialists and generalists. These systems need to be combined with an emphasis on the value of general education and personal development, versus
the more narrow training of professional technical specialists.

An ecological economics core curriculum and degree-granting programs
that embody the skills of both economics and ecology are necessary. This
implies a curriculum with some blending of physical, chemical, and biological sciences, and economics. Within this curriculum, quantitative methods
are essential, but they should be problem-oriented rather than mathematical tools for their own sake. This kind of education will produce broadly
trained environmental scientists whose jobs will be to provide ongoing environmental assessment as an input to the decision-making processes of various institutions.

There should be development of a capacity for experimentation that provides ecological economics with a solid empirical base that is built on creative and comprehensive theory. We need to develop extension programs
that can effectively transfer information among disciplines and nations.

We should promote at all levels education that weaves together fundamental understanding of the environment with human economic activities and social institutions, and promotes research that facilitates this inter-weaving process. In particular, awareness by the media of the shared bene-fits of sustainability should be promoted to ensure accuracy in reporting; the media should be encouraged to use opportunities to educate others through special reports and public service announcements.

Institutional Changes

Institutions with the flexibility necessary to deal with ecologically sustain-able development issues are lacking. Indeed, many financial institutions are built on the assumption of continuous exponential growth, and will face major restructuring in a sustainable economy. Many existing institutions have fragmented mandates and policies, and often have not optimally used market and nonmarket forces to resolve environmental problems. They have also conducted inadequate benefit-cost analyses by not incorporating ecological costs, use of short-term planning horizons, inappropriately as-signing property rights (public and private) to resources, and by not making appropriate use of incentives.

There is a lack of awareness and education in institutions about sustain-ability, the environment, and causes of environmental degradation. In addi-tion, much environmental knowledge held by indigenous peoples is being lost, as is knowledge of species, particularly in the tropics. Institutions have been slow to respond to new information and shifts in values (concerns about threats to biodiversity or the effects of rapid changes in communica-tions technologies are examples). Finally, many institutions do not freely share or disseminate information, do not provide public access to decision making, and do not devote serious attention to determining and repre-senting the wishes of their constituencies.

Many of these problems are a result of the inflexible bureaucratic struc-ture of modern institutions. Experience (i.e., Japanese industry) has shown that less bureaucratic, more flexible, more peer-to-peer institutional structures can be much more efficient and effective. We need to de-bureaucratize institutions so that they can effectively respond to the coming challenges of achieving sustainability.

Notes

1. Boulding, K.E. 1991. What do we want to sustain?: environmentalism and human evaluations. In Ecological economics: the science and man-agement of sustainability. R. Costanza, ed. 22–31. New York: Columbia University Press.

2. Daly, H.E. 1991. Elements of environmental macroeconomics. In Ecological economics: the science and management of sustainability. R. Costanza, ed. 32–46. New York: Columbia University Press.
3. Clark, C.W. 1973. The economics of overexploitation. Science 181:630–634.
4. Hardin, G. 1968. The tragedy of the commons. Science 162:1243–1248.
5. Platt, J. 1973. Social traps. American Psychologist 28:642–651.

   Cross, J.G., and M.J. Guyer. 1980. Social traps. Ann Arbor, Michigan: University of Michigan Press.

   Teger, A.I. 1980. Too much invested to quit. New York: Pergamon.

   Costanza, R. 1987. Social traps and environmental policy. BioScience 37:407–412.

   Costanza, R., and W. Shrum. 1988. The effects of taxation on moderating the conflict escalation process: an experiment using the dollar auction game. Social Science Quarterly 69:416–432.

   Costanza, R., and C.A. Perrings. 1990. A flexible assurance bonding system for improved environmental management. Ecological Economics 2:57–76.
6. Edney, J.J., and C. Harper. 1978 (Teger, 1980) (5). The effects of information in a resource management problem: a social trap analog. Human Ecology 6:387–395.

   Brockner, J., and J.Z. Rubin. 1985. Entrapment in escalating conflicts: a social psychological analysis. New York: Springer-Verlag.

   Costanza and Shrum 1988 (5).
7. Heiner, R.A. 1983. The origin of predictable behavior. American Economic Review 75:565–601.
8. Ahmad, Y.J., S. El Serafy, and E. Lutz, eds. 1989. Environmental accounting for sustainable development. UNEP World Bank Symposium. Washington, D.C.: The World Bank.

   Daly, H.E., and J.B. Cobb, Jr. 1989. For the common good: redirecting the economy toward community, the environment, and a sustainable future. Boston, Massachusetts: Beacon.

   Boulding 1991 (1); Daly 1991 (2).
9. Clark, C.W. 1991. Economic biases against sustainable development. In Ecological economics: the science and management of sustainability. R. Costanza, ed. New York: Columbia University Press.

   Hardin, G. 1991. Paramount positions in ecological economics. In Ecological economics: the science and management of sustainability. R. Costanza, ed. New York: University of Columbia Press.
10. Pearce, D. 1987. Foundations of an ecological economics. Ecological Modeling 38:9–18.
11. Brown, B.J., M.E. Hanson, D.M. Liverman, and R.W. Merideth, Jr.

1987. Global sustainability: toward definition. Environmental Management 11:713–719.

World Commission on Environment and Development. 1987. Our common future. Oxford, England: Oxford University Press.

Pezzey, J. 1989. Economic analysis of sustainable growth and sustainable development. Environment Department Working Paper No. 15. Washington, D.C.: The World Bank.

12. El Serafy, S. 1991. The environment as capital. In Ecological economics: the science and management of sustainability. R. Costanza, ed. New York, Columbia University Press.

13. Costanza, R., H.E. Daly, and J.A. Bartholomew. 1991. Goals, agenda, and policy recommendations for ecological economics. In Ecological economics: the science and management of sustainability. R. Costanza, ed. New York. Columbia University Press.

14. El Serafy 1991 (12).

15. Norton, B.G. 1986. On the inherent danger of undervaluing species. In The preservation of species. B.G. Norton, ed. Princeton, New Jersey: Princeton University Press.

16. Conrad, J.M. 1980. Quasi-option value and the expected value of information. Quarterly Journal of Economics 94: 813–820.

Randall, A., and J. Stoll. 1980. Consumer's surplus in commodity space. American Economic Review 70:449–455.

Bishop, R. 1982. Option value: an exposition and extension. Land Economics 58:1–15.

Brookshire, D.S., L.S. Eubanks, and A. Randall. 1983. Estimating option prices and existence values for wildlife resources. Land Economics 59:1–15.

Bartlett, E.T. 1984. Estimating benefits of range for wildland management and planning. In Valuation of wildland benefits. G.L. Peterson and A. Randall, eds. Boulder, Colorado: Westview Press.

Randall, A. 1986. Human preferences, economics, and the preservation of species. In The preservation of species. B.G. Norton, ed. Princeton, New Jersey: Princeton University Press.

17. Hueting, R. 1991. Correcting national income for environmental losses: a practical solution for a theoretical dilemma. In Ecological economics: the science and management of sustainability. R. Costanza, ed. New York: Columbia University Press.

18. Costanza, R. 1980. Embodied energy and economic valuation. Science 210:1219–1224.

Cleveland, C.J., R. Costanza, C.A.S. Hall, and R. Kaufmann. 1984. Energy and the United States economy: a biophysical perspective. Science 255:890–897.

Cleveland, C.J. 1991. Natural resource scarcity and economic growth revisited: economic and biophysical perspectives. In Ecological economics: the science and management of sustainability. R. Costanza, ed. New York: Columbia University Press.

Costanza et al. 1991 (13).

19. Costanza, R., S.C. Farber, and J. Maxwell. 1989. The valuation and management of wetland ecosystems. Ecological Economics 1:335–361.

20. Costanza et al. 1989 (19).

21. Daly and Cobb 1989 (8).

22. Ahmad et al. 1989 (8); El Serafy 1991 (12).

Faber, M., and J.L.R. Proops. 1991. National accounting, time and environment: a neo-Austrian approach. In Ecological economics: the science and management of sustainability. R. Costanza, ed. New York: Columbia University Press.

Hannon, B. 1991. Accounting in ecological systems. In Ecological economics: the science and management of sustainability. R. Costanza, ed. New York: Columbia University Press.

Hueting 1991 (17).

Peskin, H. 1991. Alternative environmental and resource accounting approaches. In Ecological economics: the science and management of sustainability. R. Costanza, ed. New York: Columbia University Press.

Ulanowicz, R.E. 1991. Contributory values of ecosystem resources. In Ecological economics: the science and management of sustainability. R. Costanza, ed. New York: Columbia University Press.

23. Leontief, W. 1941. The structure of American economy, 1919–1939. New York: Oxford University Press.

24. Isard, W. 1972. Ecologic-economic analysis for regional development. New York: The Free Press.

25. Daly, H. 1968. On economics as a life science. Journal of Political Economy 76:392–406.

Victor, P.A. 1972. Pollution, economy, and environment. Toronto, Canada: University of Toronto Press.

Cumberland, J.H. 1987. Need economic development be hazardous to the health of Chesapeake Bay? Marine Resource Economics 4:81–93.

26. Funderlic, R., and M. Heath. 1971. Linear compartmental analysis of ecosystems. Oak Ridge National Lab, ORNL-IBP-71-4.

Hannon, B. 1973. The structure of ecosystems. Journal of Theoretical Biology 41:535–546.

Finn, J. 1976. The cycling index. Journal of Theoretical Biology 56:363–373.

Hannon, B. 1976. Marginal product pricing in the ecosystem. Journal of Theoretical Biology 56:256–267.

Barber, M., B. Patten, and J. Finn. 1979. Review and evaluation of I-O analysis for ecological applications. In Compartmental analysis of ecosystem models, vol. 10 of Statistical ecology. J. Matis, B. Patten, and G. White, eds. Burtonsville, Maryland: International Cooperative Publishing House.

Hannon, B. 1979. Total energy costs in ecosystems. Journal of Theoretical Biology 80:271–293.

Costanza, R., and C. Neill. 1984. Energy intensities, interdependence, and value in ecological systems: a linear programming approach. Journal of Theoretical Biology 106:41–57.

Costanza, R., and B.M. Hannon. 1989. Dealing with the "mixed units" problem in ecosystem network analysis. In Network analysis of marine ecosystems: methods and applications. F. Wulff, J.G. Field, and K.H. Mann, eds. 90–115. Coastal and Estuarine Studies Series. Heidelberg: Springer-Verlag.

Hannon 1991 (22).

27. Ulanowicz, R.E. 1980. An hypothesis on the development of natural communities. Journal of Theoretical Biology 85:223–245.

Ulanowicz, R.E. 1986. Growth and development: ecosystems phenomenology. New York: Springer-Verlag.

28. Wulff, F., J.G. Field, and K.H. Mann. 1989. Network analysis of marine ecosystems: methods and applications. Coastal and Estuarine Studies Series. Heidelberg: Springer-Verlag.

29. Costanza 1980 (18).

Costanza, R., and R.A. Herendeen. 1984. Embodied energy and economic value in the United States economy: 1963, 1967, and 1972. Resources and Energy 6:129–163.

Costanza and Hannon 1989 (26).

30. Costanza and Hannon 1989 (26).

31. Braat, L.C., and W.F.J. van Lierop. 1985. A survey of economic-ecological models. Laxenburg, Austria: International Institute for Applied Systems Analysis.

Costanza, R., F.H. Sklar, and M.L. White. 1990. Modeling coastal landscape dynamics. BioScience 40:91–107.

Braat, L.C., and I. Steetskamp. 1991. Ecological economic analysis for regional sustainable development. In Ecological economics: the science and management of sustainability. R. Costanza, ed. New York: Columbia University Press.

32. Funtowicz, S.O., and J.R. Ravetz. 1991. A new scientific methodology

for global environmental issues. In Ecological economics: the science and management of sustainability. R. Costanza, ed. New York: Columbia University Press.

33. Costanza 1987 (5).

Perrings, C. 1987. Economy and environment: a theoretical essay on the interdependence of economic and environmental systems. Cambridge, England: Cambridge University Press.

Perrings, C. 1989. Environmental bonds and the incentive to research in activities involving uncertain future effects. Ecological Economics 1:95–110.

Costanza and Perrings 1990 (5).

Perrings, C.A. 1991. Reserved rationality and the precautionary principle: technological change, time and uncertainty in the environmental decision-making. In Ecological economics: the science and management of sustainability. R. Costanza, ed. New York: Columbia University Press.

34. Norgaard, R.B. 1989. The case for methodological pluralism. Ecological Economics 1:37–58.

35. Perrings 1987 (33).

Costanza, R. 1989. What is ecological economics? Ecological Economics 1:1–7.

Cumberland, J.H. 1990. Public choice and the improvement of policy instruments for environmental management. Ecological Economics 2:149–162.

36. Perrings 1989 (33); Costanza and Perrings 1990 (5); Perrings 1991 (33).

37. Costanza, R., and L. Cornwell. 1992. The 4P approach to dealing with scientific uncertainty. Environment 34:12–20, 42.

38. Costanza, R., and H.E. Daly. 1987. Natural capital and sustainable development. Conservation Biology 6:37–46.

Chapter 20

Global Environmental Ethics: A Valuable Earth

Holmes Rolston III

> Suddenly from behind the rim of the moon, in long, slow-motion mo-
> ments of immense majesty, there emerges a sparkling blue and white
> jewel, a light, delicate sky-blue sphere laced with slowly swirling veils of
> white, rising gradually like a small pearl in a thick sea of black mystery. It
> takes more than a moment to fully realize this is Earth—home.
> —Edgar Mitchell, quoted by K.W. Kelley, 1988

Nature and Culture

The Earth is remarkable, and valuable, for both the nature and the culture
that occur on it. Evolutionary history has been going on for billions of years,
while cultural history is only about a hundred thousand years old. But certainly from here onward, culture increasingly determines what natural history shall continue. The next millennium is, some say, the epoch of the end
of nature. But another hope is that we can launch a millennium of culture in
harmony with nature.

Humans evolved out of nature; our biochemistries are natural and we
draw our life support from the hydrological cycles and photosynthesis;
we too have genes and inborn traits; we are subject to natural laws. But
human life is radically different from that in wild, spontaneous nature. Unlike coyotes or bats, humans are not just what they are by nature; we come
into the world by nature quite unfinished and become what we become by
culture. Humans deliberately rebuild the wild environment and make rural
and urban environments.

Information in nature travels intergenerationally on genes; information
in culture travels neurally as persons are educated into transmissible cultures. In nature, the coping skills are coded on chromosomes. In culture,
the skills are coded in craftsman's traditions, religious rituals, or technology
manuals. Information acquired during an organism's lifetime is not

349

transmitted genetically; the essence of culture is acquired information transmitted to the next generation. This information transfer is several orders of magnitude faster and overleaps genetic lines. Children are educated by taking classes from dozens of teachers, by reading hundreds of books, using libraries with tens of thousands of books, written by authors to whom they are genetically unrelated, who may have been dead for centuries.

Animals are without options in what they shall be, even if they make some limited choices. Humans have myriads of lifestyle options. Educated persons criticize their cultures. Natural selection pressures are relaxed; humans help each other out compassionately with charity, affirmative action, or headstart programs. They study medicine to cure their diseases. They worry about overpopulation in developing nations and overconsumption in developed nations. The determinants of animal and plant behavior, much less the determinants of climate or nutrient recycling, are never anthropological, political, economic, technological, scientific, philosophical, ethical, or religious.

Animals do not read or write books trying to recommend the future of natural resource management. They do not try to get clear about the differences between nature and culture. One critical difference is that humans are moral agents and their behavior is constrained by what they value, by values they recognize in other humans. Increasingly, we are here arguing, they *ought* also take into account the nonhuman values in the natural world.

The debate about ethics as applied to nature (often thought of as "natural resources") asks whether the primary values about which we should be concerned are cultural, that is, anthropocentric, or whether there is also intrinsic natural value, independent of humans, which humans ought to consider. Asking such a question is quite outside the capacity of plants and animals. Humans can and ought to see outside their own sector. Only humans have conscience enough to do this. Though humans evolved out of nature, they have significantly evolved *out of* it. We need to understand the difference in being human, and after we clarify that, we also want to see the senses in which, though evolved out of it, culture has and ought to remain in relative harmony with nature.

Although all deliberate human behaviors differ from the processes of spontaneous nature, some are healthy for humans because they agree with the natural systems with which their cultural decisions interact. In a relative sense, what humans do can be natural. Conservation values are not the only values; there are numerous values autonomous to cultures. Some of these can be gained by the sacrifice of natural values. So the environmental ethics of the next century will increasingly have to ask whether and why cultures should preserve any natural values at all, and what kind of balance ought to be reached. Here we may wonder how much of the time humans ought to win. They cannot lose all the time; but we may also hold that humans ought not invariably be the winners. They should constrain their behavior for the good of plants and animals.

Sometimes too, decisions can be win–win. There are nonrival, complementary goods. Properly to care for the natural world can combine with a strategy for sustainability. The idea here is that nature provides the life support system for culture, and therefore what is good for nature is often good for culture. Fauna, flora, and people all need clean air and water, good soil. It is hard to have a healthy culture on a sick environment. Nature and culture have entwined destinies.

It is true that Earth is now in a post-evolutionary phase. Culture is the principal determinant of Earth's future, more now than nature; we are passing into a century when this will be increasingly obvious. Indeed, some say, that will be the principal novelty of the new millennium—Earth will be a managed planet. Meanwhile, the technosphere remains in the biosphere; we are not in a post-ecological phase. The management of the planet must conserve environmental values. Hopefully, such policy can, in places, let nature take its course.

Intrinsic Natural Values

"Human beings are at the centre of concerns. . . ." So the *Rio Declaration* begins, the creed (once to be called the *Earth Charter*) formulated at the United Nations Conference on Environment and Development (UNCED), and signed by almost every nation on Earth. The claim is, in many respects, quite true. The humans species is causing all the concern. Environmental problems are people problems, not gorilla or sequoia problems. The problem is to get people into "a healthy and productive life in harmony with nature" (1). And yet those who put themselves at the center of concerns are liable to the fallacy of misplaced values.

Does this make nature peripheral or marginal? The center of a circle is circumscribed by, embedded in, the larger area. Being located at the center may highlight, rather than reduce, ties and responsibilities. We need to assess the human values that require natural values, asking also what human values may override, or ought to yield to, natural values. We need to ask whether there are many, or any, natural values independent of humans.

"Every form of life is unique, warranting respect regardless of its worth to man." That is how the UN *World Charter for Nature* begins. It is as nonanthropocentric as the *Rio Declaration*'s beginning is anthropocentric (2). One hundred and twelve nations endorsed this charter, though the United States vigorously opposed it. It is possible, we should notice, for humans to be at the center of concerns and also for every form of life to have its worth regardless of humans. Both can be true. The Society of American Foresters, while continuing to affirm that forestry is for the good of society, has recently adopted a land ethic canon that, they say, "demonstrates our respect for the land." This means, says Raymond S. Craig, chair of their Land Ethic Committee, that foresters also "value all components of ecosystems, without regard to their usefulness to humans, because all components have intrinsic value" (3).

When we think about it, biological conservation did not begin when the United Nations promulgated a *World Charter for Nature*, nor when Teddy Roosevelt withdrew forest reserves. Biological conservation in the deepest sense is not something that originates in the human mind. Organisms are self-maintaining systems; they resist dying. They reproduce. They keep recomposing themselves. Life is an energetic fight uphill in a world that overall moves thermodynamically downhill. The "genius" of life is coded into genetic sets. The DNA is really a set of *conservation molecules*.

Biology can refer to the science humans have produced—that which appears in textbooks and laboratories. This is a subjective affair in human heads. Take away humans, and biology, like the other sciences, disappears. Biology can also refer to the life metabolisms on Earth. Such biology is objective out there in the world. Take away humans, and this nonhuman biology remains. This biology is primary, and such biology without conservation is impossible, a contradiction in terms, a condition that can exist in the actual world only temporarily, since biology without conservation is death.

Broadly, two different philosophical perspectives are possible when a human valuer encounters an *x* in the world. (1) What is *x* good for? (2) What is *x*'s own good? The first is a question about instrumental value, the second about intrinsic value. What is Sally good for? She can serve as a cook or legislator. What is Sally's good? Her well-being of body and mind, the meaning she finds in life. This is also true, in comparative ways, confronting animals and plants. Beyond dispute, animals and plants defend a good of their own, and use resources to do so. Warblers preserve their own lives, and make more warblers; they consume (and regulate) insects and avoid raptors. They have connections in their ecosystems that go on "over their heads," but what is "in their heads" (and in their genes) is that being a warbler is a good thing. Every organism has a *good of its own*; it defends its kind as a *good kind*. In this sense, a genetic set is a *normative set*; it distinguishes between what *is* and what *ought to be*.

This does not mean that the organism is a moral system, or has lifestyle options among which it may choose. These levels of value are reached only much later, dramatically in humans. Nevertheless the organism grows, reproduces, repairs its wounds, and resists death. A life is defended for what it is in itself, without necessary further contributory reference—although such lives invariably do have further ecosystemic reference. There is intrinsic value when a life is so defended. That *ipso facto* is value in both biological and philosophical senses.

Intrinsic value in nature is always in a web that connects with others. The tiger, valued for what it is in itself, is at the top of a trophic food pyramid that moves downward through gazelles, grass, microbes, requires the rainfall, the geomorphic and erosional cycles that produce the soil, and so on. In this sense, the traditional concepts of instrumental and intrinsic value need to be set in a more comprehensive picture, that of ecosystems and, before we conclude, of the home planet Earth. In that sense an ecosystem is valuable, that is, value-able, able to produce and sustain values. Organisms value and defend only their selves, with species increasing their numbers. But the evolutionary ecosystem spins a bigger story, limiting each kind, locking it into the welfare of others, promoting new arrivals, increasing kinds and the integration of kinds. Species increase their kind; but ecosystems increase kinds. The individual is programmed to make more of its kind, but more is going on systemically than that; the system is making more kinds. Communal processes generate an ever-richer community. Hence the evolutionary toil, elaborating and diversifying the biota.

Ethical conservatives, in the humanist sense, will say that ecosystems are of value only because they contribute to human experiences. They will put humans at the center of concerns. But that mistakes the last chapter, perhaps the climax, for the whole story, as though there were no concerns except those in center focus. Humans count enough to have the right to flourish here on Earth, but not so much that we have the right to degrade or shut down ecosystems, not at least without a burden of proof that there is an overriding cultural gain. The ethical conservative in the ecological sense sees that the stability, integrity, and beauty of biotic communities is what is most fundamentally to be conserved. That is, in fact, where the real ability to produce value arises; it does not arise, as we in our anthropocentric arrogance might say, only when we humans arrive on the scene to assign and project our values there. Making the fallacy of misplaced values, this is like dipping water at a fountain of life, watering a lush land, then valuing the water and the fountain instrumentally, and commenting that nothing was of value until I came. It is like finding a goose that lays golden eggs and valuing the eggs but not the goose.

Spontaneously, natural history organizes itself. This is what we call its systemic value. In one sense nature is indifferent to mountains, rivers, fauna, flora, forests, and grasslands. But in another sense nature has bent toward making and remaking these projects, millions of kinds, for several billion years. These performances are worth noticing—remarkable, memorable—and not just because they produce this noticing in certain recent subjects—our human selves. The splendors of Earth do not simply lie in their roles as human resources, supports of culture, or stimulators of experience. The most plausible account will find some programmatic evolution toward value.

How do we humans come to be charged up with values, if there was and is nothing in nature charging us up so? A systematic environmental ethic does not wish to believe in the special creation of values, nor in their dumbfounding epigenesis at the moment that humans appear on the scene. It discovers that values have evolved out of a systemically valuable nature.

From this more objective viewpoint, there is something naive about living in a reference frame where one species takes itself as absolute and values everything else in nature relative to its utility.

Placing one's own species at the center, a biologist may insist, is just what goes on in the woods; warblers take a warblo-centric point of view; spruce push only to make more spruce. Other biologists will also insist, however, that the system takes no such particular points of view but generates myriads of such kinds. Humans are the only species who can see an ecosystem for what it objectively is, a tapestry of interwoven values. Conservation biologists, in addition to saving fauna and flora, can save humans by daily rescuing us from this beguiling anthropocentrism through a perennial contact with the primeval biological and geomorphic givens. Conservation biology should liberate us from a narrow humanism—from putting ourselves at the center—and help us gain fuller humanity by transcending merely human interests. It reforms human character in encounters with a value-laden world.

Natural and National Resources

There is one Earth; on it are 178 sovereign nations, a politically fragmented world. "The Earth is one but the world is not" (4). True, the one Earth is plural in its landmasses and supports myriads of diverse ecosystems, species, and peoples. Still, the really divisive troubles arise among the world states. The national sovereignties are not well adapted for harmonious relations with the Earth commons. The rights of nations, and rights as claimed by citizens of these political states, are not well aligned with the ecology and geography. In the 20th century, the commons problem became transnational; at the turn of the millennium it is becoming global. Our citizenship in nations is not well synchronized with our residence in geographic places, nor with our sense of global dwelling on our home planet.

Many of Earth's natural resources, unevenly distributed, have to flow across national lines. Few, if any, nations are self-sufficient in all of the natural resources they need or desire, and many are quite deficient. No one familiar with ecosystems will dislike interdependencies and networked communities, or be surprised by competition for resource allocation. Still, cultures differ radically from ecosystems. Animals do not live in nations and trade in markets. In ecosystems, there are no taxes and trade tariffs, no balance of payments to be protected, no GNP; there is no management and labor, no hiring and firing, no capital acquisition, no international loans to be repaid, no money exchange rates. So a new trouble appears. Nation states, and the relations between them, are often ill-adapted for the efficient use of natural resources. Divisiveness, struggle, even wars can result.

People are fighting for what is of value in nature, but they are also fighting as citizens of nations that have economic policies and political agendas, demanding loyalties in support. Their access to natural resources comes filtered through political and industrial units that are not formed, or continued, with these ecologies in mind. They want resources, but the political alignments can often mean suboptimal and unjust solutions to the problems of resource distribution. *Natural* resources have to become *national* resources, and "nationalizing" natural resources can be as much part of the problem as part of the answer, especially when the sovereign independence of nations is asserted without regard for the interdependencies of these nations—both those with each other and those of the global ecosystems. When biological resources are taken to be national possessions in dispute, rather than an Earth commons to be shared, it can become difficult to find a way to share them.

On Earth, there are two major blocs, the G-7 nations (the Group of 7, the big industrial nations of North America, Europe, and Japan), and the G-77 nations, once 77 but now including some 128 lesser developed nations, often south of the industrial North. The G-7 nations hold about one-fifth of the world's five billion persons, and they produce and consume about four-fifths of all goods and services. The G-77 nations, with four-fifths of the world's people, produce and consume one-fifth (5). If we draw a pie chart of the goods produced by consuming Earth's resources, four-fifths of the pie goes to one-fifth of the people. Can this be fair?

Answers are complex. Earth's natural resources are unevenly distributed by nature, and national boundaries were nearly all drawn before many of the modern essential resources were resources at all: coal, electric power, iron ore. One quarter of the known petroleum reserves are in Saudi Arabia, and more than half are in the Middle East. The need for petroleum is dispersed around the globe. The divisions of nation states, rather accidentally related to the location of this most valuable resource, often compound the problem. The biodiversity resources on Earth are likewise unevenly located, and here the problem is that, though these resources are important to all nations, they may be located in the less developed nations, who most need to develop, possibly using up these resources (such as cutting their forests), or who, if they wish to conserve these resources, may be least able to afford the costs of conservation.

A second cause is that the myriad diverse societies on Earth have taken different directions of development; they have different governments, ideologies, and religions, have made different social choices, valued material prosperity differently. Typically, where there is agricultural and industrial development, people think of this as an achievement. If we imagine a pie chart of production again, different nations have different powers to produce this pie. People ought to get what they earn. There is nothing evidently unfair in dividing a pie unequally, until we consider who produced the pie. Fairness nowhere commands rewarding all parties equally; justice is giving each his or her due. That can mean unequal treatment proportionate to earnings.

In America, we think that our forefathers got what they got by Yankee ingenuity, hard work, thrift; they built the nation, plowed the prairies, hoed the corn, split the rails, paved the roads, developed the natural resources, and on and on. There is a commendable genius in the American blend of democracy, industry, labor, and resource conservation and use; that is, in fact, what has made the United States the envy of much of the world. Similar things can be said for any prosperous nation. If so, the distribution pattern reflects achievement; and what the other nations need to do is to imitate this. Unproductive people need to learn how to make more pie.

But do we believe that some countries have more merit than others? We have all been cautioned of ethnocentrism. One is reluctant to be too proud about success. Perhaps by the time one reaches the scale of country, statistical averages take over, and every country has its mix of deserving and undeserving persons, success and failure. People are the same all over the globe, and excellence is no respecter of national boundaries. We do not want to be discriminatory; we want to be fair.

Exploitation can be a third cause of this asymmetrical distribution. Many in G-77 nations find themselves deprived rather than blessed by the capitalism that originated in Europe and spread abroad, enabling the G-7 nations to take advantage not only of their own resources but also of those in other nations. These poor are, as they see it, the victims of colonialism. It is difficult to consider the one-fifth-consuming-four-fifths distribution pattern and not think that something is unfair, even when we make allowances for differential earnings and merit. Is some of the richness on one side related to the poverty on the other? Regularly, the poor come off poorly when they bargain with the rich; and wealth that originates as impressive achievement can further accumulate when such wealth becomes a means of exploitation.

Those in the G-7 nations who emphasize the earnings model tend to recommend to the G-77 nations that they produce more, often offering to help them by investments that can also be productive for the G-7 nations. Those in the G-77 nations realize that the problem is sharing too. A continually growing production can be as much part of the problem as part of the solution. One way to think of a circular pie chart of Earth goods is that this is planet Earth, and we do not have any way of producing a bigger planet. Maybe too, Earth is not just a big pie to be eaten up. Earth is valuable on its own and has produced fauna and flora that are worth conserving for what they are in themselves.

On global scales, if the controlling interest is national sovereignty, gross national product, and welfare alone, we may be prevented from the ethics we need by the fallacy of misplaced community. This mistakes the nature and character of the communities to which one belongs, and it gives such disproportionate emphasis to some communities (one's nation, one's city, one's industrial company) that one becomes blind to others (the larger community of life, the biotic community in which one resides, the global village). The wrong conclusions and inappropriate actions follow. An effort by a developed country to aid a developing nation is typically interpreted, for example, as "foreign" aid, when such effort could better have been interpreted by the developed country as saving their "home" planet. On the global scale, none of us are aliens—we are all at home. "The common heritage of mankind" is the classical category for valuing this global commons.

Keeping each nation oriented to global perspectives by instruments of international law is a major role of the United Nations. Since the United Nations is not a sovereign state, its appeal must be largely persuasive, negotiatory, ethical—based on rights and responsibilities more than on military force or political power. Laws will be soft laws, but still they will be aspirational and can orient nations. The UNCED Conference, for instance, produced the *Convention on Biological Diversity* and the *Framework Convention on Climate Change*. The United Nations Environment Programme played an important role in negotiations leading to the 1987 Montreal ozone protocol. We have already noted the *Rio Declaration* and the *World Charter for Nature*. *Agenda 21*, one of the most complex international documents ever negotiated, is a comprehensive strategy for blending environmental conservation and national development. There are more than 150 international agreements registered with the United Nations that deal directly with environmental problems (6).

Nature, Natural Resources, and Rights to Development

There are problems of overpopulation, overconsumption, and the under-distribution of resources. But a moral humanist can plausibly object that, when it comes to individual persons caught up in these social forces, we should factor out all three, none of which are the fault of the persons who may wish to develop their lands. "I did not ask to be born; I am poor, not overconsuming; I am not the cause but rather the victim of the inequitable distribution of wealth." Surely there is a right to use whatever natural resources one has available, as best one can, under the exigencies of one's particular life, set though this is in these unfortunate circumstances. "I only want enough to eat, is that not my right?"

Certainly a human right to an environment with integrity will be one of the chief goals of biological conservation. Human rights must include the right to subsistence, to have basic needs of food, clothing, and shelter met. So even if particular persons are part of an undesirable pattern of population growth, even if there is some better social solution than the wrong one that is in fact happening, have they not a right that will override the conservation of natural value? Granted that culture is unhealthy, will it not just be a further wrong to them to deprive them of their right to what little they have? Can human rights ever be overridden by a society that wants to do better by conserving natural value? Should nature win, while such unlucky persons lose?

Answering such questions requires some weighing of values. Consider tropical forests. There is more richness there than in other regions of the planet—half of all known species. On the one continent of South America, there are one-fifth of the planet's species of terrestrial mammals (800 species); there are one-third of the planet's flowering plants (7). Given the ecology of the tropical forests, which does not respond well to fragmentation, these species can be preserved only if large Amazonian rainforests and other wetland regions of South America are left relatively undeveloped and at low population densities. The peak of global plant diversity is the combined flora of the three Andean countries of Colombia, Ecuador, and Peru.

There more than 40,000 species occur on just 2 percent of the world's land surface (8). But population growth in South America has been as high as anywhere in the world (9), and people are flowing into the forests, often crowded off other lands.

What about people? Consider people who are not now there but might move. This is not good agricultural soil, and such would-be settlers are likely to find only a short-term bargain, a long-term loss. Consider people who already live there. If they are indigenous peoples, and wish to continue to live as they have for hundreds and even thousands of years, there will be no threat to the forest. If they are cabaclos (of mixed European and native races), they can also continue the lifestyles known for hundreds of years, without serious destruction of the forests. Nothing is taken away from them.

Can these indigenous and cabaclos peoples modernize? Can they multiply? The two questions are connected, since it is modern medicine and technology that enables them to multiply. These are problematic questions for, in a sense, a modernized, much-multiplied indigenous people is not an indigenous people any more. The cabaclos' lifestyle modernized has really been transformed into something else. Have they the right to develop into modern peoples, if this requires an exploitation of their resources that destroys the rainforests? The first answer is that they do, but with the qualification that all rights are not absolute, some are weaker, some stronger, and the exercise of any right has to be balanced against values destroyed in the exercise of that right.

The qualification brings a second answer. If one concludes that the natural values at stake are quite high (perhaps higher than anywhere else in the world), and that the opportunities for development are low, because the envisioned development is inadvisable, then a possible answer is: No, there will be no development of these reserved areas. There will be development elsewhere, to which such persons will be facilitated to move, if they wish. If they stay, they must stay under the traditional lifestyle of their present and past circumstances. So they must pay, if you like, an opportunity cost, if they remain. They do have the right to develop, but not here.

Anywhere there is legal zoning, persons are told what they may not do on the lands on which they reside, in order to protect various social and natural values. Land ownership is limited, "imperfect," as lawyers term it. One's rights are always constrained by the harm one does to others. Environmental policy regulates the harms that people do on the lands on which they live, and it is perfectly appropriate to set aside conservation reserves to protect natural values, because of the ecological, scientific, economic, historical, aesthetic, religious, and other values people have at stake, as well as for intrinsic values in fauna and flora. Indeed, unless there is such reserving counterbalancing the pressures for development, there will be almost no conservation at all. Every person on Earth is told that there are some areas that he or she cannot develop.

If one is residing in a location where development is constrained, this may seem unfair, to force relocation. Does that not violate human rights? Consider relocation in general, and start on the development side. Every large dam ever built has forced people to move. Kariba Dam, on the Zambezi River between Zambia and Zimbabwe, supplies water, electricity, fish, and benefits wildlife, but forced 50,000 Tonga people to move from their ancestral homelands. Typically we think this a justifiable overriding of their rights; we may also think that compensation is required. General Motors is closing 21 plants, affecting 76,000 jobs between 1990 and 1995, choosing subcontracting for parts, production overseas, and getting better efficiency in other plants. During 1920–1960, most textile mills in Lowell, Massachusetts, moved south, in search of cheaper, nonunion labor, lower taxes, to get closer to the cotton, to modernize plants, and, no longer needing water power, to take advantage of cheaper electricity provided by TVA, and other government incentives to develop the South. The United States closes military bases and tens of thousands have to move.

We may not think these decisions are always right, but they sometimes are. We require people to relocate in the interests of various social goods. On a parity with this, but on the conservation side, we may also ask people to relocate—as when national parks have been established. What is so amiss about asking people to relocate in the interest of protecting nature, where the stakes are especially high? No more human rights are being "violated" for the conservation of nature than have regularly been "violated" (as is alleged) in the name of development. Rights, at least some of them, are constrained by larger goods, which we may not have any right to block or destroy.

This will be especially permissible where we ask persons to relocate only if they are revising their lifestyles in ways that put new threats on the environment. They are proposing to introduce changes, and the burden of proof should be on them to say why they should jeopardize nature there, rather than move to less sensitive areas. One way of putting this is that the people have options; the forests do not. People can move; forests cannot, nor can the animals they contain. Saving the natural values present, optimizing the mix of values in nature and culture can require limiting the options of people in order to save the nonoptional forest values.

Human rights to development, even by those who are poor, though they are to be taken quite seriously, are not always and everywhere absolute, but have to be weighed against all the other values at stake. A person may be doing what would be, taken individually, a perfectly good thing, a thing he has a right to do, were he alone. But taken in collection with thousands of others doing the same thing, it becomes a harmful thing, which he has no right to do because it destroys the commons and irreversibly destroys natural values. These poor may not have so much a right to develop in any way they please, as a right to a more equitable distribution of the goods of the Earth that we, the wealthy, think we absolutely own.

A Managed Earth and the End of Nature?

William Clark writes, in a *Scientific American* issue devoted to "Managing Planet Earth," "We have entered an era characterized by syndromes of global change. . . . As we attempt to move from merely causing these syndromes to managing them consciously, two central questions must be asked? What kind of planet do we want? What kind of planet can we get?" (10). Those questions do not preclude nonanthropocentric answers; but they strongly suggest that humans are being asked what they want out of the planet, and the planetary managers will figure out how to get it for them. That puts humans at the center of concerns. The root of "manage" is the Latin "manus," hand. Humans will handle the place. This can even mean that *Homo sapiens* is the professional manager of an otherwise valueless world. Nature is to be harnessed to human needs.

Now an opposite worry strikes us. This managing the planet begins to sound like the end of nature, the replacement of spontaneous nature with a new epoch of deliberate control, humanizing the Earth. Is that what we have or what we want? Let's face the facts, the technocrat will insist. Humans now control 40 percent of the planet's land-based primary net photosynthetic productivity (11). A study for the World Bank found that 35 percent of the Earth's land has now become degraded (12). Surely, our only option is to intervene more intelligently—to manage the planet.

Now no one wishes to oppose more intelligent intervention. We want a sustainable society with its health and integrity, superposed on a natural world with its health and integrity. But we are not so sure that managing the valueless planet is the apt paradigm, besides which all other conservation ideologies are backward romanticisms. Why not, for instance, think of ourselves as residents who are learning the logic of our home community, or as moral overseers trying to optimize both the cultural and the natural values on the planet? Is our only relationship to nature one of engineering it for the better? Perhaps what is as much to be managed is this earth-eating, managerial mentality that has caused the environmental crisis in the first place.

Penultimately, management is a good thing; but, ultimately management is no more appropriate for Earth than for people, because it only sees means not ends. The scientific managers still have the value questions on their hands. On planetary scales, and even on continental and regional scales, it is not so clear that we really do want to manage the environment; rather we want to manage human uses of the environment so that they are congenial to letting the planet go on managing itself. Managers do not really dwell in an environment; they only have resources, something like the way in which bosses, as such, do not have friends, only subordinates. Even the most enlightened exploiters, *qua* exploiters, do not live as persons in a community; they are not citizens of a world, only consumers of materials. They reduce their environment to resource and sink. The environment must be this much, but it can be much more. For consummate managers, proportionately as the development ethic increases, the environment is reduced to little more than exploited resource.

We cannot simply take nature ready to hand, but we must remake it for the supporting of agriculture, industry, culture. After that, perhaps, on the larger planetary scales, it is better to build our cultures in intelligent harmony with the way the world is already built, rather than take control and rebuild the planet by ourselves and for ourselves. An overweening trust in science, technology, and industry may result in too little trust in Mother Earth.

The planetary manager wants human genius to manage the system, but there is already a considerable "genius" in the system. Is man the engineer in an unengineered world? The word *engineer* comes from the root *ingenium*, an innate genius, an inventive power, and hence our word *ingenious*, "characterized by original construction." Etymologically, "nature" and "genius" (and hence "engineer") come from the same root, *gene (g)nasci, natus*, to give clever birth. In that sense there is ample inventive and engineering power in nature, which has built Earth and about perhaps a billion species, keeping the whole machinery running, with these species coming and going, for several billion years.

Who built the engineers, with their clever brains and hands, with which they propose now to manage the planet? Isn't building people out of protozoans, and protozoans out of protons a rather ingenious achievement? Maybe we should reconsider our models. Nature is not the antithesis of engineering; it is the prototype of ingenuity. Engineers and managers cannot know what they are doing, until they know what they are undoing. We ought to spend adequate effort making sure we know what a place is, especially if it is the only home planet, before we decide to remake it into something else. Hands are for managing and also for holding in loving care.

Perhaps there looms before us what some call, rather dramatically, "the end of nature." In the 21st century, there will only be nature that has been tampered with, not spontaneous nature. Indeed, laments Bill McKibben, already "we live in a postnatural world," in "a world that is of our own making." "There's no such thing as nature any more" (13). Earlier, wild nature could remain alongside culture; the natural givens stayed in place. There could not be wilderness everywhere, but there could be wilderness somewhere, lots of it, all over the world. Wild creatures could coexist on their own in the reserves, the woodlots, the fencerows, the nooks, the crannies of civilization. But with acid rain, with pollutants everywhere, with carcinogens in the food chains, such coexistence is impossible. With global warming accelerating climate change a hundred times over, "changing nature means changing everything" and this "seems infinitely sad." Everything, everywhere "bears the permanent stamp of man." "We live at the end of nature, the moment when the essential character of the world . . . is suddenly changing." There is no more nature *"for its own sake"* (14).

Has or might nature come to an end? The answers are both matters of fact and of philosophical analysis. Is it the case that, owing to human disturbances in the Yellowstone Park ecosystem, we have lost any possibility of letting the park be natural? There will be an absolute sense in which this is true, since there is no square foot of the park in which humans have not disturbed the predation pressures, no square foot on which rain falls without detectable pollutants. But it does not follow that nature is absolutely ended because it is not absolutely present. Answers come in degrees. Events in Yellowstone can remain 99.44 percent natural on many a square foot, indeed on hundreds of square miles, in the sense that we can designate there "an area where the earth and its community of life are untrammeled by man, where man himself is a visitor who does not remain" (15). We can put the predators back and clean up the air. Even where the system was once disturbed and subsequently restored or left to recover on its own, wildness can return.

On other lands, past certain thresholds, so far as land is managed for agriculture or industry, so far as it is fenced for pasture or mowed as lawns, wild nature has ended. This ending may be always, in its own way, a sad thing; but it is sometimes an inevitable thing, and the culture that replaces nature can have compensating values. It would be a sadder thing still, if culture had never appeared to grace the Earth, or if cultures had remained so modest that they had never substantially modified the landscape. We do not always lament our presence, even though we want some untrammeled lands. Where the human presence permanently alters the land, wilderness is impossible, but some portions of the Adirondacks of New York can be rural and still relatively natural.

Still, the more drastic the intervention, the more nature has ended. If, for instance, global warming introduces climatic changes so dramatic that natural environments cannot track these changes, then there will be no more nature. Again, this is not absolute, for some natural processes will remain, but the system will be unrecognizably natural. The epoch of spontaneously self-organizing systems, of wild nature with integrity, will be effectively over, and that will be a tragedy. Similarly if other toxics choke up the system, or if the extinction rate reaches the projected disastrous levels, or if deforestation or soil loss reach levels that cause the system to crash. So the end of nature is not absolutely here, it is not absolutely possible, but it is relatively to be feared. Some end of nature is a good thing; but too much of any good thing is a bad thing. Beyond, beneath, and around our culture, we do not want the *end of nature*. We value nature as an *end in itself*.

Earth Ethics

The astronaut Michael Collins recalled being earthstruck: "I remember so vividly . . . what I saw when I looked back at my fragile home—a glistening, inviting beacon, delicate blue and white, a tiny outpost suspended in the black infinity. Earth is to be treasured and nurtured, something precious that *must* endure" (16). The UN Secretary-General, Boutros Boutros-Ghali, closed the Earth Summit: "The Spirit of Rio must create a new mode of civic conduct. It is not enough for man to love his neighbour; he must also learn to love his world" (17).

Neither is thinking merely anthropocentrically of Earth as a big resource to be exploited for human needs, a pie to be divided up for human consumption. Rather, Earth is a precious thing in itself because it is home for us all; Earth is to be loved, as we do a neighbor, for an intrinsic integrity. The center of focus is not people, but the biosphere. But valuing the whole Earth and responsibilities to it are unfamiliar and need philosophical analysis.

Dealing with an acre or two of real estate, perhaps even with hundreds or thousands of acres, we can think that the earth belongs to us, as private property holders. Dealing with a landscape, we can think that the earth belongs to us, as citizens of the country geographically located there. But on the global scale, Earth is not something we own. Earth does not belong to us; rather we belong to it. We belong on it. The question is not of property, but of community. The valuing of nature and natural resources is not over until we have risen to the planetary level, and valued this system we inhabit. Earth is really the relevant survival unit.

Earth is, some will insist, a big rockpile like the moon, only one on which the rocks are watered and illuminated in such a way that they support life. So it is really the life we value and not the Earth, except as instrumental to life. We have duties to people, perhaps to living things. We must not confuse duties to the home with duties to the inhabitants. We do not praise the earth so much as what is on Earth. But this is not a systemic view of what is going on. We need some systematic account of the valuable Earth we now behold, before we beheld it, not just some value that is generated in the eye of the beholder. Finding that value will generate a global sense of obligation.

The evolution of rocks into dirt into fauna and flora is one of the great surprises of natural history, one of the rarest events in the astronomical universe. We humans too rise up from the humus, and we find revealed what earth can do when it is self-organizing under suitable conditions. This is pretty spectacular dirt. On an everyday scale earth seems to be passive, inert, an unsuitable object of moral concern. But on a global scale? The scale changes nothing, a critic may protest, the changes are only quantitative. Earth is no doubt precious as life support, but it is not precious in itself. There is nobody there in a planet. There is not even the objective vitality of an organism, or the genetic transmission of a species line. Earth is not even an ecosystem, strictly speaking; it is a loose collection of myriads of ecosystems. So we must be talking loosely, perhaps poetically, or romantically of valuing Earth. Earth is a mere thing, a big thing, a special thing for those who happen to live on it, but still a thing, and not appropriate as an object of intrinsic or systemic valuation. We can, if we insist on being anthropocentrists, say that it is all valueless except as our human resource.

But we will not be valuing Earth objectively until we appreciate this marvelous natural history. This really is a superb planet, the most valuable entity of all, because it is the entity able to produce all the Earthbound values. At this scale of vision, if we ask what is principally to be valued, the value of life arising as a creative process on Earth seems a better description and a more comprehensive category than to speak of a careful management of planetary natural resources.

Do not humans sometimes value Earth's life-supporting systems because they are valuable, and not always the other way round? It seems parochial to say that our part alone in the drama establishes all its worth. The production of value over the millennia of natural history is not something subjective that goes on in the human mind. The creativity within the natural system we inherit, and the values this generates, are the ground of our being, not just the ground under our feet. Earth could be the ultimate object of duty, short of God, if God exists.

Notes

Quotation: Kelley, K.W., ed. 1988. The home planet, photo 42. Reading, Massachusetts: Addison-Wesley.

1. UN Conference on Environment and Development. 1992. The Rio declaration. UNCED Document A/CONF.151/5/Rev. 1, 13 June.
2. World Charter for Nature. 1982. UN General Assembly Resolution No. 37/7 of 28 October.
3. Craig, R.S. 1992. Land ethic canon proposal: a report from the task force. Journal of Forestry 90, no. 8 (August):40–41.
4. UN World Commission on Environment and Development. 1987. Our common future, 27. The Brundtland Report. New York: Oxford University Press.
5. World Development Report 1991. New York: Oxford University Press.
6. United Nations Environment Programme. 1991. Register of international treaties and other agreements in the field of the environment. Nairobi, Kenya. Document No. UNEP/GC.16/Inf.4, May.
7. Mares, M.A. 1986. Conservation in South America: problems, consequences and solutions. Science 233:734–39.
8. Wilson, E.O. 1992. The diversity of life, 197. Cambridge, Massachusetts: Harvard University Press.
9. Coale, A.J. 1983. Recent trends in fertility in the less developed countries. Science 221:828–832.
10. Clark, W. 1989. Managing planet Earth. Scientific American 261, no. 3 (September):47–48.
11. Vitousek, P., P. Ehrlich, A. Ehrlich, and P. Matson. 1986. Human appropriation of the products of biosynthesis. BioScience 36:374.
12. Goodland, R. 1992. The case that the world has reached limits. In Population, technology, and lifestyle. R. Goodland, H.E. Daly, and S. El Serafy, eds., 3–22. Washington, D.C.: Island Press.
13. McKibben, B. 1989. The end of nature, 60,85,89. New York: Random House.
14. McKibben, 78–79, 174–175, 210 (13).
15. United States Congress. Wilderness Act of 1964, sec. 2(c). Public Law 88–577. 78 Stat 891.
16. Collins, M. 1980. Foreword. In Our universe. R.A. Gallant, ed., 6. Washington, D.C.: National Geographic Society.
17. Boutros-Ghali, B. 1992. Extracts from closing UNCED statement, in an UNCED summary, Final Meeting and Round-up of Conference, 1. UN Document ENV/DEV/RIO/29, 14 June.

Chapter 21

Three Bear Stories:
Toward a Sustainable Resource
Management Future

R. Edward Grumbine

> I have never been able to cure a patient who did not believe that he or
> she was part of something larger.
>
> —C. G. Jung

On a warm summer day in July, a few years ago, I caught a glimpse of the
future of resource management for North America. I was not attending a
conference or reading a book on the subject. There were no managers, policymakers, environmentalists, or industry groups present. The general
public was absent. Instead, I was in the company of three bears, one university student, and the never-logged Vista Creek watershed on the
northern flanks of the giant ice cone named Glacier Peak in the northern
Cascades of Washington State.

I had been traveling in the mountains for three weeks with 12 students
studying federal land management. Our coursework focused on how conservation biology was challenging traditional resource management practices. Along the way, the group had waded through required readings,
lectures and seminars, quizzes, and the rest of what passes for education in
a university. But we had also trekked to the United States–Canadian border,
miles from any road, and witnessed the 60-foot cleared gash that stamps
"political boundary" across the mountains. United States Forest Service sil-
viculturalists had shared their visions of new forestry, and National Park
Service rangers had discussed fire management in the post-Yellowstone
fires era. We had traversed the Cascade Crest from west to east and back
again, hiking in dry ponderosa pine forests and westside old-growth
Douglas-fir. Most important, the students were living in the field, wrapped
in the landscape, witnessing first-hand how humans could create miles of
clearcuts as well as protected parks and wilderness areas.

Our final hike was a 9-day backpack up the Suiattle River in the Glacier
Peak Wilderness. The Suiattle had raged out of its banks during the previous
winter and had eaten large chunks of road before receding. What was once

367

a busy thoroughfare for multiple use that led to a large trailhead parking lot, was now closed except to those who didn't mind walking 10 miles on asphalt. Few availed themselves of this opportunity. Most hikers, with the scenic high country as a goal, rejected an extra day's passage through clearcuts, managed second growth, remnant old-growth patches, and riparian alder forests.

But for students of the landscape of management, the route was a compelling classroom. Almost every resource conundrum we had studied was in evidence. And everyone experienced the ephemeral nature of all human efforts to control nature—one winter's worth of duff in some places had already hidden the blacktop. Tiny seedlings were rising up.

On the penultimate afternoon of our hike I gave a morning-long final exam. After discussion and lunch we agreed that our last afternoon in the backcountry would be open for packing, swimming, and personal time to say goodbye.

I elected to hike up Vista Creek to visit one of my favorite old-growth forests anywhere in the Cascades. As the group was splitting up, one of the students, Jesse, asked if he could accompany me. Though I had been wanting to walk alone, I welcomed his company. We set off up the trail.

Jesse had been a key member of the group. He was a journalism major in school, a graduating senior, an urban-funk disc jockey at the campus radio station, and, prior to the program, had never strapped on a backpack in his life. He had applied for the trip because he had no ecology classes on his transcript. With major requirements behind him, he wanted to catch a first-hand glimpse of the natural world. Jesse also wanted some adventure.

Over the course of the program three traits of Jesse became clear. First, he had the humor and timing of a stand-up comedian. Second, he possessed a wonderful generosity of spirit toward others. And third, he was deathly afraid of bears.

On the first day of the trip, after my backcountry safety lecture (which included camping behavior in grizzly and black bear country), Jesse had pulled me aside and queried me thoroughly about the likelihood of us encountering *Ursus*. I had not seen a black bear in the Cascades for years, and grizzlies were scarce indeed. But my soothing talk did little to assuage his fear. Yet no one in the group had seen any bears, and now we were soon to leave the backcountry.

Hiking up the trail, Jesse and I talked about the group and reviewed the past three weeks. Jesse remarked that he had grown both in his knowledge of resource management and in self-understanding. He also mentioned that, though he was comfortable now with backpacking in wildlands, he was happy that he had not seen any bears.

Our conversation died down as we came under the spell of a forest undisturbed for almost a millennium. Huge mountain hemlocks and western red cedars rose around us. A winter wren sang shimmering glissandos. We walked in silence; I was in front, Jesse some distance behind.

Up ahead and around a low rockface that jutted out of a steep sideslope on our right, I heard what I took to be a raven calling. But this call didn't quite match any of the vocalizations I had heard ravens utter previously. The sound was more a squeal than a call and seemed to be coming from well below the canopy. Perplexed, I rounded the buttress.

Thirty feet in front of me a bear cub shot up a silver fir sapling. I am always amazed at how agile bears can be. As it scrambled up the trunk, the cub squawked the guttural cry I had heard a moment ago. It sounded unlike any bear cub I had ever heard before.

Jesse drew up beside me, a quizzical look on his face.

"A bear cub's up that tree," I said.

Terror spread across Jesse's face and he immediately turned to flee.

"Wait a minute, it's only a cub," I remarked and grabbed him by the arm. He settled down just a bit as I cajoled him toward his first look at a wild bear.

"Ed, what's that over there?" Jesse pointed off to the right. A thicket of salmonberry shook and another cub burst out of the shrubs and headed up a neighboring snag.

I hadn't seen any bears for four years even during months of time in the backcountry. I urged Jesse closer and offered my binoculars to him for a better view. Jesse still wasn't sure whether to run away or stand and stare at the two dark balls of wildness howling from the trees. He began to let go and relax as he watched the cubs watching us. Then a shadow crept across his face and he turned to me.

"Where's the mother, Ed?" Jesse spoke insistently, his fear rising.

"I dunno, Jesse, she might be. . ." A sharp hiss came form our rear. We both wheeled around to see the sow a mere 25 feet behind us standing directly on the trail.

I don't remember clearly what happened next. I do remember that she was a black bear, that Jesse became extremely agitated, and that there was nowhere for us to retreat. Up trail would take us closer to the cubs. Backtracking would send us toward the sow, who was, like Jesse, feeling increasingly threatened as the seconds passed. The only choice was to go downslope into thorny devils club and huge deadfall.

I fought to calm Jesse, pacify the sow, and settle myself toward action. There wasn't much time. The sow took a step forward, hissed, opened and closed her jaws. She hesitated. We backed down and away into the brush, searching for footholds on a steep incline where we could not see the ground. I pulled Jesse with me into the thicket, trying to gain purchase, forcing him to look ahead instead of behind. We clambered onto a giant deadfall that lifted us up above the tangle. I glanced back. The sow remained in place, staring through us, black eyes hard.

We balanced above the forest floor on a highway of downed tree trunks. It was like crossing a wet footlog over a swollen creek—you couldn't slip and fall. Jesse was shaking; sweat stung my eyes. But we crab-crawled over the logs toward safety. Fifteen yards and we could not hear the cubs or see the sow. Fifty yards and our breathing came a little easier. One hundred yards and the quiet forest wrapped us in its arms.

We never saw the bears again.

Later we sat in a clearing under ancient firs and talked. We agreed that it had been a close call and that we had been inattentive, foolish. I apologized for my lack of caution. Jesse said he was sorry for being incapacitated and difficult to get to safety. He thanked me for calming him down, for being firm, for knowing what to do. We both acknowledged that we were fortunate to have encountered three bears at close range and lucky enough to have things come out right. Then we both were quiet, our thoughts full of black fur, the smell of bruised leaves, bear cub howls, and the sharp snap of huffing jaws.

Jesse glanced at me.

"I've got two questions for you, Ed. Number one, how did you know what to do? And, two, what if they had been grizzlies?"

•   •   •

As this chapter's epigraph suggests, over the course of his career the psychologist C.G. Jung gained the wisdom to understand that the well-being of his patients was somehow linked to broader patterns of health, to "something larger." There is an echo here that resource managers in the 1990s can attest to—actions focused only on a single species, stand, or scale are not likely to succeed. Managers today are learning to approach problems at a variety of ecological scales. They are also beginning to view issues within social, political, economic, and ethical contexts.

This has not always been so. As this book demonstrates, resource management has not remained static over time.

Where is management headed? More specifically, how does one story of an encounter with bears in the North Cascades illuminate the future of resource management?

Jesse's questions have remained with me ever since that Cascades afternoon. But not because my answers to him were particularly compelling. I knew what to do because of 20 years of encounters with wild bears throughout North America. As for the second question, if the bears had been *Ursus arctos* instead of *Ursus americanus*, we probably would not have survived. Yet I believe Jesse's questions reveal much about our response to nature and natural resources in the United States. Just as Jesse brought fear and lack of experience to our meeting with the bears, resource managers bring their own baggage to any action. I believe that bear management serves as a microcosm of the collective baggage that we, in the United States, bring to all resource management endeavors. But two additional bear stories need to be told before one can comprehend the full implications of our Cascades encounter for resource management on the cusp of the 21st century.

The following tales share a contemporary plot line that will be familiar to many. They also share the same set of historical facts and biological data that managers have used to track the plight of the grizzly bear in North America.

Ursus arctos first migrated to the New World across Beringia 250,000 years ago. By 1800, their population was estimated to be about 100,000 animals ranging from Alaska and Canada down into central Mexico. Grizzlies lived widely. Along the California coast they fed on beached gray whale carcasses. They dug roots on the lowland plains of Nebraska and Colorado.

Westward expansion of Euro-Americans precipitated a dramatic decline in grizzly bear populations that proceeded in several overlapping waves. In the early to mid-1800s, trappers killed many bears. Ranchers and homesteaders, appropriating habitat for cattle, sheep, and farming, next came into conflict with the species. By the late 19th century, loggers were cutting the prime lowland habitat of the grizzly. All these activities combined to force the bear out of the valleys and into the mountains.

Today, the grizzly bear population has declined to about one percent of its former size. About 1000 individuals survive. The geographic range of the bear in the Lower 48 States is restricted to six to seven completely isolated subpopulations found primarily on federal lands in the wildest parks of the western United States. (These subpopulations are located in the North Cascades, Selkirk Mountains, Cabinet-Yaak country, Northern Continental Divide, Bitterroot Mountains, Greater Yellowstone Ecosystem, and, possibly, the San Juan Mountains of Colorado.) Since 1975, the grizzly has been listed as threatened under the Endangered Species Act.

The two stories diverge here.

. . .

Since 1983, the Interagency Grizzly Bear Committee (IGBC) has coordinated federal, state, and private research and management of the grizzly bear. The IGBC is responsible for recovery efforts on the animals' behalf.

In 1990, the IGBC released a draft revision of its grizzly bear recovery plan as mandated under the Endangered Species Act (1). There was little conservation biology in the plan. Instead of linking the separate subpopulations back together, the draft advocated population augmentation where individual bears would be captured and moved by managers from one area to another to facilitate breeding. A separate recovery target was assigned to each subpopulation, but the numbers did not reflect the viable population requirements of the species. For example, the proposed target for the Northern Continental Divide Ecosystem around Glacier National Park was the same as the lowest estimate for the population in 1980, just a few years after the bear's initial listing. Facing criticism from biologists outside of the government, the IGBC withdrew the draft.

A second draft plan was released for review in 1992 (2). Though much improved, the new draft was still flawed. Viable population theory was discussed, but recovery targets still reflected a poor understanding of conservation science. A critique of the draft by Dr. Mark Shaffer, the biologist on whose original work with grizzly bear population viability the IGBC based its analysis, showed that the plan would likely result in extinction instead of recovery (3). Shaffer pointed out that the sum of all the targets for each subpopulation was far below what most biologists considered acceptable. He also showed that the government had no intention to boost recovery beyond those lands that the bear inhabited at the time it was listed in 1975. Though the new plan discussed establishing linkages between subpopulations and mandated a 5-year study of where biological corridors might be placed, it provided no interim management protection for any of the potential corridors.

At best, the new draft strategy is a prescription for short-term population stability, not population recovery as required by law. The last chapter of this story has yet to be written as managers and biologists await the release of the final plan.

.   .   .

The third bear story comes out of the work of the Great Ecosystem Alliance (GEA). GEA, a grassroots environmental group in Bellingham, Washington, is attempting to bring an ecosystem-based management to the Greater North Cascades Ecosystem in Washington and British Columbia. This vast wildland harbors one of the smallest grizzly subpopulations in the United States.

GEA biologists, using the same scientific facts as the IGBC, adopted a radically different management strategy. They noted that the most recently published computer simulation model of grizzly population dynamics estimated the size of a single viable subpopulation to be from 1600 to 2000 individuals (4). By combining this information with demographic data from Yellowstone, the GEA staff hypothesized that the Greater North Cascades might provide enough habitat to support about 350 bears. A population of 1600 animals might require an area of land equal to some 50 percent of the entire state of Washington.

Based on these theoretical calculations, GEA pursued three goals. In 1990, the group petitioned the United States Fish and Wildlife Service to formally list the North Cascades subpopulation as threatened under the Endangered Species Act. The petition was denied as "warranted but precluded" in 1991. In response, however, the IGBC declared the North Cascades an official grizzly bear recovery area. GEA also supported the Northern Rockies Ecosystem Protection Act, a bill introduced into the U.S. House of Representatives in 1992. The bill required regional-scale protection of ecosystems occupied by the bear with an emphasis on habitat linkages. GEA wanted the legislation extended westward to include the North Cascades subpopulation. The group also worked on new legislative proposals in concert with other environmental groups that would create an international reserve spanning Canada and the United States to protect bears on both sides of the border.

As with the IGBC version, there is as yet no end to the GEA story of how to manage grizzly bears. But a look beneath the surface of these two stories provides a profound lesson in resource management past and present. The striking fact is that both stories (1) are based on the same historical facts outlining the decline of the bear, (2) have access to the same scientific data, and (3) must uphold the same legal requirements of the Endangered Species Act and other United States laws. But the management prescriptions differ dramatically. Why?

The two stories diverge because they are rooted in different ethical conceptions of resource management.

The IGBC story implicitly draws a hard line between people and bears, humans and nature. Inside this story the world gains value only as people transform nature into goods and services for human use. *Resourcism* places people above grizzlies and the rest of nonhuman nature. This story unfolds wherever we see varmints for predators, lumber for forests, ore for rocks, real estate for landscapes, labor for people, well-having for well-being. We often employ economics to measure such transformations and call the results progress. Resourcism is based on three assumptions: human demands need only be met over the short term, Earth's abundance is inexhaustible, and technological savvy will continue to push back any limits to growth. Traditional resource management, as practiced by virtually all federal, state, and private agencies, is based on these fundamental assumptions. The IGBC version is but one of many stories that result from this approach to a working relationship between people and nature.

The GEA version of the grizzly bear management story represents an attempt to move away from producing resources toward protecting ecosystems. It differs from traditional resource management in at least three important ways. First, the GEA story uses the best scientific information in the service of conserving biodiversity at all scales. The IGBC story, in contrast, is a classic example of the selective use of biological data to serve the maintenance of the status quo. Second, ecosystem management as envisioned by GEA and conservation biologists, emphasizes sustaining species, communities, and landscapes as prerequisite to the production of goods and services for human use. Resource management, on the other hand, has traditionally focused on multiple-use production with science as a tool for efficiency rather than a gauge of sufficiency. The third factor distinguishing the GEA story from that of the IGBC is that in ecosystem management, humans are seen as part of nature, embedded in ecosystems just as much as grizzly bears. Regardless of the role of scientific knowledge, people play an explicit role in shaping ecosystem management goals. Furthermore, in the GEA story, people have no a priori right to reduce species and ecosystems to levels that may result in extinction.

For those who inhabit versions of the GEA-ecosystem management story, solutions to the biodiversity crisis are straightforward. To sustain ecological integrity, managers must endorse five goals (5):

1. Maintain viable populations of all native species *in situ*.

2. Represent, within protected areas, all native ecosystem types across their natural range of variation.

3. Maintain evolutionary and ecological process (i.e., disturbance regimes, hydrological processes, nutrient cycles, etc.).

4. Manage over periods of time long enough to maintain the evolutionary potential of species and ecosystems.

5. Accommodate human use and occupancy within the above constraints.

Some guidelines to accomplish these goals are: increase funding for applied conservation biology research; hire more conservation scientists for management agencies; establish monitoring of management actions; and pursue interagency cooperation. These goals and guidelines represent the short-term future of resource management in this country.

Yet for all the obvious attractions of ecosystem management, advocates have not yet come to grips with several issues. First, because it is still a developing science, conservation biology lacks empirical support for many of its hypotheses. There is a knowledge gap between what biologists predict to be true and what we have hard evidence for. This exacerbates ongoing problems of defining scientific certainty in a complex political arena. Second, the nonscientific aspects of implementing a new ecosystem approach are often discounted in an attempt to make management appear to be only a technical problem. But this isn't true. Issues of which goals to select, who makes decisions, how power flows in centralized bureaucracies, and the role of citizens in the management process are all critical elements that share the stage with science.

Third, though science still wears a "value-free" cloak in the eyes of the American public, this is becoming less accepted as debates over resource management (e.g., ancient forests/northern spotted owl) reveal conflicting values. In short, a scientifically derived ecosystem alternative to traditional resource management may be necessary but is not likely sufficient. Conservation biology may not be much different from multiple-use sustained yield if we forget that, though science can census grizzly bears, dusky seaside sparrows, and Siskiyou cypresses, and recommend appropriate habitat protection plans, it cannot make final decisions. That is a job for humans who value one set of goals and outcomes over another.

But when people come into conflict with protecting biodiversity, what management standards should prevail? Where do we take a stand? Which story is the truth?

There aren't really rights and wrongs in ecosystems, but there are certain biological and ecological truths that must guide the setting of new management standards. Our old standards have never been explicit. We have spoken of wise use, but our management practice has not reflected that.

Multiple use sustained yield has given us single-use resource depletion—forests cut down, rivers dammed, and grasslands grazed away. Amenity preservation has resulted in parks as ecological islands, crown jewels without a crown. The history of resource management should alert us to the fact that we have not accomplished what we set out to do even in the most limited sense—protect natural ecosystems so that future human generations can also be sustained by them.

It is time to untangle the scientific search for correct management practices from inherently value-laden questions about management goals. We must recognize that the choices we make not only reflect values but also limit the direction of our hands-on work with nature. Goals and practices must be based on the best scientific understanding we have of the limits that come with being only one more dependent species in a world of diversity. Conservation biology contributes to resource management by exploring the biological bottom line at various scales: extinction of species,

viable populations, endangered ecosystems, and landscape-level disturbance patterns. The biodiversity hierarchy may not literally exist, may be no
more than a temporary expedient for a particular analysis, but that is not the
point. The point is that ecology and biology are epistemological tools, our
best shot, for the moment, of describing, understanding, and fitting in with
the world. We know that the risk of extinctions increases under definable
conditions, that wildfires cannot be long suppressed without significant successional consequences, that certain species play more important roles in
ecosystems than others. We are also coming to realize that resourcism has
for so long prevented us from putting our ecological knowledge to work
that we are now hard up against the limits of life for many species.

What all this suggests to me is that, for the long run, we need to search
for an alternative to both the traditional IGBC resource management story
and the rapidly evolving GEA ecosystem story. While the new ecosystems
view may, over the next decades, help us to find better ways to cut timber,
protect water quality, and design a functional biodiversity protection network, over the long term we need a management story that allows us to
reinterpret our place on the planet as but one species dependent on many.
We need a new story that will teach us to celebrate diversity as well as
manage it. And this leads me back to Vista Creek, three black bears, and
Jesse in the woods.   .   .   .

"How did you know what to do?"
"What if they had been grizzly bears?"
Questions concerning values are fundamental. What is good? What is
bad? What duties and obligations do we have toward others? Jesse posed his
questions out of a fear based on a lack of experience with bears. Having
never seen one, all he had to go on was hearsay—my brief verbal description of diagnostic field marks, safety precautions, and our culture's general
aversion to large carnivores who occasionally attack and kill us. The people
who lived in the North Cascades prior to Euro-Americans also encountered
grizzlies, hunted them, and, at times, were killed by them. Yet the Methow
and Okanogan peoples and other native tribes created complex ceremonies
that honored *Ursus*. As far as anthropologists can determine, the original
human inhabitants of the North Cascades celebrated the grizzly as a powerful teacher (6).

Our modern management stories suggest that bears don't have much to
teach us at all. Resourcism, of course, underlies this belief, but to create a
new management story for the future, it is important to fathom how this
world view has played out in North America.

Several formative influences stand out. As many have observed, our forebears from the Old World brought with them the cultural baggage that I have labeled resourcism. These attitudes, in turn, when mixed with the incredible diversity and richness of the New World, ignited manifest destiny, westward expansion, and the flowering of industrial capitalism on a scale never seen before. These trends legitimized the wholesale destruction of North American species and ecosystems as well as the cultural genocide of native peoples. By the end of the 19th century, a minority movement against resource depletion became a new influence on resource management. Both Gifford Pinchot's Progressive wise use conservation and (to a lesser extent) John Muir's preservation were based on romantic notions of harmony and the balance of nature. But neither of these match well with what we now know about nature's stochastic processes. Finally, the great age of ecology in the 1960s to 1970s saw citizens gain legal standing in management decision making, a new host of government regulations, and the consolidation of federal and state management bureaucracies.

With each of these influences came key assumptions. When we crossed over from the Old World to the New, we assumed that where we lived had little direct bearing on how we lived. As we peopled the American West, we believed that there were no consequences to the oppression of "savages" or the destruction of nature. As we divided the world into commodities (multiple-use) and amenities (preservation), we were blind to the notion that this dichotomy had anything to do with our values. And as the National Environmental Policy Act, the Clean Air Act, the Wilderness Act and other laws went onto the books, we assumed that as the government passed laws it would also implement them. People believed the sprawling resource management bureaucracy would do its job effectively with minimal citizen input.

The management assumptions of the first human residents of North America were different. Though cross-cultural comparisons have obvious limits, let me suggest some elements of older traditions that I believe are critical for understanding all three bear stories.

Old ways cultures, without the raw power of environment-changing technology (aside from fire), had to assume that where one lived was inseparable from how one lived. With no fossil fuel subsidy there was little margin for error. Compared to modern societies, the consequences of living poorly in one's place were immediate. The fence between people and nature was not as high as it is today, and the world of bears and people was filled with mutual action, influence, dependence, and reciprocity. Life was a matter of manners, the exchange of privilege and responsibility. Somehow,

people believed that they shared a common fate with bears and all of nature, and that just as bear meat sustained humans at times, so did humans
sustain bears through their management actions.

It is here that Jung's sense of "something larger" rings clear. To resource
managers, Aldo Leopold's description of humans as "plain members and citizens" of the "land community" echoes the psychologist's dictum (7). It may
well be that the biodiversity crisis, fomenting the change from traditional
resource management to ecosystem management, is providing nonnego-
tiable evidence that we are part of and dependent on the entire web of life.
But no form of management will be sustainable if new practices do not also
transform how we experience our place in nature, how me manage ourselves. Management so reframed might give us the opportunity to understand that bear cubs, salmon fry, and wolf pups all have vital needs that bind
their future with ours.

Yet Leopold also warned that management "without a keen realization of
its vital conflicts . . . falls to the level of mere Utopian dream" (8). Manners
toward grizzly bears?

There is nothing utopian or final about living as if nature mattered. Our
encounter with the bears and Jesse's questions are instructive not because
they offer easy solutions or direct guidelines to a future resource management; they are insightful because they are full of the possibility of learning.
Jesse asked me two things that managers must also ask if they wish to go beyond both multiple-use and ecosystem management toward sustaining
landscapes and lifeways. Jesse first wanted to understand the behavior that
moved us from danger to safety: "How did you know what to do?" Though
at first I did not model my experience with cubs and sow well, I answered
that respect for bears is the beginning of wisdom. If one is attentive to what
bears communicate through their behavior, one will be on the right track.
Jesse may someday learn to reframe his question to "What do black bears
teach?" My hope is that as management evolves, managers will learn to recast their own questions similarly.

The more challenging question, of course, is the second of the two—if
the bears had been grizzlies, our story would have ended quickly. But Jesse
was really asking "How much control do we have over the world?" Resource
managers, in a similar vein, may ask "How can we defeat uncertainty?" or
"How can we be guaranteed the outcomes we desire?" I responded to Jesse
by saying that one doesn't visit grizzly bear country unless one is willing to
accept risk. Part of accepting uncertainty is knowing how to behave. But a
major share of one's preparation is knowing that there are limits to certainty
and control. The philosopher Holmes Rolston suggests that "an ecologically
informed society must love lions-in-jungles [or grizzly bears in plains and

mountains], organisms-in-ecosystems, or else fail in vision and courage" (9). It is admissible to reduce risk, but hubris results when we think that we can overcome uncertainty—one part, by definition, can never control any system successfully. As long as resource managers, traditional or otherwise, believe that we can escape uncertainty there will be no place for bears or sustainability for humans. Maybe the Methow and other native peoples of the North Cascades celebrated grizzlies as teachers because the bears embodied the limits at the heart of living in the world.

. . .

What can we really know about resource management a century hence? In 1894, debate was raging in Congress over the fate of the newly declared forest reserves. Americans were hard at work creating a high-speed economy geared toward profit, population growth, technological specialization, and resource consumption. There were no national forests, parks, or resource management agencies. As for 2094, I can provide no specific guidelines, only the three bear stories I have already shared. But stories, like bears, are creatures of time. For the present, grizzly bears are ghosts in the continental United States, off trail, beyond the campfire's light, living in the hills unseen, playing at the edge of dreams.

Just as the bear has suffered as a citizen of industrial society, so too have the lessons embedded in older conceptions of resource management been branded as meaningless. Be that as it may, these tales suggest several ethical standards that guide us toward the future, toward home. A resource management philosophy that is rooted in endless growth and social and political inequality will not stand indefinitely. Hope is being kindled everywhere as managers, scientists, and citizens move away from traditional resource management values toward sustaining ecosystems. This process of building an ecosystem management in the short term will help us create a more profound practice over time. Bears and the biodiversity crisis have given us a lucid definition of who "the people" are, and we are inextricably joined with all life on Earth. The connection is more than momentary. For even as difficult lessons provide the insight with which to create ecosystem management today, they point beyond the present toward what kind of people we may become tomorrow.

Notes

1. USDI Fish and Wildlife Service. 1990. Draft grizzly bear recovery plan. Interagency Grizzly Bear Committee, Missoula, Montana.
2. USDI Fish and Wildlife Service. 1992. Second draft grizzly bear recovery plan. Interagency Grizzly Bear Committee, Missoula, Montana.

3. Shaffer, M.L. 1992. Keeping the grizzly bear in the American West. Washington, D.C.: The Wilderness Society.

4. Allendorf, F.W., R.B. Harris, and L.H. Metzger. 1992. Estimation of effective population size of grizzly bears by computer simulation. Proceedings of the 4th International Congress of Systematic and Evolutionary Biology.

5. Grumbine, R.E. 1994. What is ecosystem management? Conservation Biology 8 (1):27–38.

6. Rockwell, D. 1991. Giving voice to bear: North American Indian rituals, myths, and images of the bear. Niwot, Colorado: Roberts Rinehart.

7. Leopold, A. 1949. A sand county almanac. New York: Oxford University Press.

8. Leopold, A. 1937. Review of A.E. Parkins and J.R. Whitaker, Our natural resources and their conservation. Bird Lore 39 (1):74.

9. Rolston, H. 1987. Duties to ecosystems. In Companion to A Sand County Almanac. J.B. Callicott, ed. 258. Madison, Wisconsin: University of Wisconsin Press.

Conclusion

While it is difficult to draw generalizations from a series of separately written pieces, we were struck by several overarching themes that emerged as we assembled this book. First, a number of the authors urged natural resources managers, educators, and policy makers to incorporate social values in resource decisions—to recognize and acknowledge that people are an important part of the landscape and that decisions are more than scientific determinations of what is "best." Second, many authors noted a change in natural resources management from an anthropocentric view to a broader, "biocentric" perspective. In other words, resources are increasingly viewed in a broad ecological context, not merely as potential goods for human use.

Are these themes in conflict? One argues for a greater recognition of human norms and the other for a less central role for human consumption. We believe the themes are consistent and, indeed, complementary. As one recognizes the larger context of one's existence—the community, the region, and the biosphere—one also must acknowledge the connections among all the components of that diverse and complex fabric. Natural resources management is moving away from simplistic, resource-specific approaches based on scientific, technical "fixes" (thus the theme of recognizing social values in balancing various priorities and making resource decisions) and toward a more integrated, holistic approach that attempts to preserve whole, sustainable living systems (thus the theme of broader, biocentric perspectives). As natural resources management advances, it must recognize the complexities of nature, the powerful and responsible role of human beings, and the moral imperative to seek long-term solutions.

So, whether the topic is education, economics, ethics, or approaches and tools, virtually every way we perceive natural resources and our environment has changed. What is the future of natural resource management in America? The late Wallace Stegner, in his book *The American West as Living Space*, proposed that public land managers have a duty to "maintain the health and beauty of the lands and waters they manage" rather than to offer "bargain-basement" use of public resources to commodity and amenity users. To the degree that this occurs, there will be a new era for natural resource management.

Index

About the Contributors

Stanley H. Anderson is the unit leader of the Wyoming Cooperative Fish and Wildlife Research Unit at the University of Wyoming.

Sarah F. Bates is past associate director of the Natural Resources Law Center at the University of Colorado School of Law. Presently, she is the director of the Utah office of The Grand Canyon Trust.

Peter Berck is a professor in the Department of Agricultural and Resource Economics at the University of California at Berkeley.

Mark W. Brunson is an assistant professor in the Department of Forest Resources at Utah State University.

Robert Costanza is director of the Maryland International Institute for Ecological Economics at the University of Maryland.

M. Rupert Cutler was formerly president of Defenders of Wildlife. Presently, he is the executive director of Virginia's Explore Park, a living history museum in Roanoke, Virginia.

Jeff DeBonis is the founder and publisher of *The Inner Voice*, and founder and director of the Association of Forest Service Employees for Environmental Ethics. Recently, he has organized and now directs the Public Employees for Environmental Responsibility, headquartered in Washington, D.C.

T. Luke George is an assistant professor in the Department of Wildlife Management at Humboldt State University.

R. Edward Grumbine is the director of The Sierra Institute at the University of California at Santa Cruz.

Dale Hein is a professor in the Department of Fishery and Wildlife Biology at Colorado State University.

Gloria E. Helfand is an assistant professor in the Department of Agricultural Economics at the University of California at Davis.

Susan K. Jacobson is an associate professor in the Department of Wildlife and Range Sciences, and the director of the Program for Studies in Tropical Conservation at the University of Florida.

Eric Katz is an associate professor of philosophy and director of the Science, Technology, and Society Program at the New Jersey Institute of Technology.

James J. Kennedy is a professor of forest resources and formerly assistant dean in the College of Natural Resources at Utah State University.

Winifred B. Kessler was formerly the assistant director of the USDA Forest Service's New Perspective Program. Currently, she is professor of Natural Resources and Environmental Studies, and Chair of Forestry, at the University of Northern British Columbia at Prince George.

Richard L. Knight teaches wildlife conservation at Colorado State University.

John Loomis is an associate professor in the Department of Agricultural and Resource Economics at Colorado State University.

Curt D. Meine is a conservation writer and consultant. He is presently affiliated with the International Crane Foundation in Baraboo, Wisconsin, and the Biodiversity Support Program in Washington, D.C.

Robert H. Nelson was formerly a member of the Office of Policy Analysis of the U.S. Department of the Interior. Presently, he is a professor in the School of Public Affairs at the University of Maryland-College Park.

David W. Orr is a professor in the Environmental Studies Program at Oberlin College.

Richard S. Ostfeld is an assistant scientist at the Institute of Ecosystem Studies at Millbrook, New York.

Vawter Parker is vice president for program at the Sierra Club Legal Defense Fund, Inc.

S.T.A. Pickett is a scientist at the Institute of Ecosystem Studies at Millbrook, New York.

Thomas Michael Power is a professor and chairman of the Department of Economics at the University of Montana.

Holmes Rolston, III is a University Distinguished Professor, and a professor in the Department of Philosophy at Colorado State University.

Hal Salwasser was formerly director of the USDA Forest Service's New Perspectives Program. Presently, he is the Boone and Crockett Professor of Wildlife Conservation at the University of Montana.

Jack Ward Thomas was formerly the senior research scientist of the USDA Forest Service Pacific Northwest Research Station at La Grande. Presently, he is the chief of the USDA Forest Service.